T0220738

3D Printing with Delta Printers

Charles Bell

Apress®

3D Printing with Delta Printers

Copyright © 2015 by Charles Bell

This work is subject to copyright. All rights are reserved by the Publisher, whether the whole or part of the material is concerned, specifically the rights of translation, reprinting, reuse of illustrations, recitation, broadcasting, reproduction on microfilms or in any other physical way, and transmission or information storage and retrieval, electronic adaptation, computer software, or by similar or dissimilar methodology now known or hereafter developed. Exempted from this legal reservation are brief excerpts in connection with reviews or scholarly analysis or material supplied specifically for the purpose of being entered and executed on a computer system, for exclusive use by the purchaser of the work. Duplication of this publication or parts thereof is permitted only under the provisions of the Copyright Law of the Publisher's location, in its current version, and permission for use must always be obtained from Springer. Permissions for use may be obtained through RightsLink at the Copyright Clearance Center. Violations are liable to prosecution under the respective Copyright Law.

ISBN-13 (pbk): 978-1-4842-1174-8

ISBN-13 (electronic): 978-1-4842-1173-1

Trademarked names, logos, and images may appear in this book. Rather than use a trademark symbol with every occurrence of a trademarked name, logo, or image we use the names, logos, and images only in an editorial fashion and to the benefit of the trademark owner, with no intention of infringement of the trademark.

The use in this publication of trade names, trademarks, service marks, and similar terms, even if they are not identified as such, is not to be taken as an expression of opinion as to whether or not they are subject to proprietary rights.

While the advice and information in this book are believed to be true and accurate at the date of publication, neither the authors nor the editors nor the publisher can accept any legal responsibility for any errors or omissions that may be made. The publisher makes no warranty, express or implied, with respect to the material contained herein.

Managing Director: Welmoed Spahr
Lead Editor: Michelle Lowman
Technical Reviewer: Johann Rocholl
Editorial Board: Steve Anglin, Gary Cornell, Louise Corrigan, James T. DeWolf, Jonathan Gennick, Robert Hutchinson, Michelle Lowman, James Markham, Matthew Moodie, Jeffrey Pepper, Douglas Pundick, Ben Renow-Clarke, Gwenan Spearing, Matt Wade, Steve Weiss
Coordinating Editor: Kevin Walter
Copy Editor: Kimberly Burton-Weisman
Compositor: SPi Global
Indexer: SPi Global
Artist: SPi Global

Distributed to the book trade worldwide by Springer Science+Business Media New York, 233 Spring Street, 6th Floor, New York, NY 10013. Phone 1-800-SPRINGER, fax (201) 348-4505, e-mail orders-ny@springer-sbm.com, or visit www.springeronline.com. Apress Media, LLC is a California LLC and the sole member (owner) is Springer Science + Business Media Finance Inc (SSBM Finance Inc). SSBM Finance Inc is a Delaware corporation.

For information on translations, please e-mail rights@apress.com, or visit www.apress.com.

Apress and friends of ED books may be purchased in bulk for academic, corporate, or promotional use. eBook versions and licenses are also available for most titles. For more information, reference our Special Bulk Sales–eBook Licensing web page at www.apress.com/bulk-sales.

Any source code or other supplementary materials referenced by the author in this text is available to readers at www.apress.com. For detailed information about how to locate your book's source code, go to www.apress.com/source-code/.

I dedicate this book to all of the educators using 3D printers in their curriculum. I believe 3D technology can be used to inspire youth to explore the engineering and design disciplines. My own love of engineering stemmed from teachers who took the time to explain how things worked. It is my hope that books like this will further enable those intrepid educators to inspire as many young minds as possible.

—Dr. Charles Bell

Contents at a Glance

Contents

About the Author

Dr. Charles Bell conducts research in emerging technologies. He is a development manager on the Oracle MySQL Development team, directing the development of MySQL High Availability solutions. He lives in a small town in rural Virginia with his loving wife. He received his Doctor of Philosophy in Engineering from Virginia Commonwealth University in 2005. His research interests include database systems, software engineering, sensor networks, and 3D printing. He spends his limited free time as a practicing Maker focusing on microcontrollers, 3D printers, and printing projects.

Dr. Bell's research and engineering projects make him uniquely qualified to author this book. He is an engineer by trade, hobby, and life choice, and has extensive knowledge and experience in building, maintaining, and using 3D printers.

About the Technical Reviewer

 **Johann Rocholl** was born in Rostock, Germany. He has a computer science degree from the University of Stuttgart and works for Google as a site reliability engineer. He designed the first successful open source linear delta 3D printer, called Rostock, in 2012, followed by the Mini Kossel in 2013. He lives in Seattle with his wife, four children, and five chickens.

Acknowledgments

I would like to thank all of the many talented and energetic professionals at Apress. I appreciate the understanding and patience of my editor, Michelle Lowman, and managing editor, Kevin Walter. They were instrumental in the success of this project. I would also like to thank the army of publishing professionals at Apress for making me look so good in print. Thank you all very much!

I'd like to especially thank the technical reviewer, Johann C. Rocholl, for his often profound insights, constructive criticism, and encouragement.

A special thank you is well deserved for the nice people at SeeMeCNC, OpenbeamUSA, and MatterHackers for their help with this book. I could not have completed my research without you. Thank you also for your considerations in products offered, permission to use images, and your helpful suggestions. It is my hope this book is a testament to your hard work in building and promoting delta printers.

Most importantly, I want to thank my wife, Annette, for her unending patience and understanding while I spent so much time with my 3D printers and laptop.

Introduction

Delta printers are not the arcane engineering marvels or cantankerous contraptions that are usable only by the most advanced enthusiasts. To use them, they neither require an engineering degree nor arcane knowledge.

Intended Audience

I wrote this book to share my passion for all manner of 3D printers. I especially wanted to show how anyone can use a delta printer and achieve the same level of enjoyment and success as the more popular Cartesian 3D printers.

This book therefore is for the novice and intermediate 3D enthusiast who wants to learn how delta printers work and how to become an expert using them. Even enthusiasts who have been using their Cartesian 3D printers for some time will find information in this book that will help further enhance their skills.

More importantly, I wrote this book to help those who have become frustrated trying to learn how to use a delta printer. I have read where some have given up on their printer, discarding it as hopeless, or selling it to anyone willing to buy it for scrap. It is my hope that the popularity of delta printers will grow and perhaps even compete with or even surpass that of Cartesian printers. Perhaps that is too much to wish for, but if I get one person to turn their lament to enjoyment, I'll be happy.

How This Book Is Structured

The book is written to guide the reader from a general knowledge of 3D printing to expertise in modifying delta printers. The first several chapters cover general topics, including a short introduction to 3D printing, the hardware of delta printers, and the software used. Additional chapters cover build tips, configuration, and calibration. The book concludes with chapters covering delta printer maintenance and improvements.

■ **Note** This book is a natural companion to my book, *Maintaining and Troubleshooting Your 3D Printer* (Apress, 2014). Readers who want a deeper understanding of maintenance and troubleshooting may want to read this book as well. It may also be helpful for those who want to use both Cartesian and delta printers.

The following is a brief overview of each chapter included in this book.

- *Chapter 1: Introduction to Delta 3D Printers.* This chapter presents an introduction to 3D printing, including the anatomy of a 3D delta printer and the types of filament available.

- *Chapter 2: Delta Printer Hardware.* This chapter presents a detailed look at the hardware used to construct delta printers, as well as a brief overview of the types of delta printer designs.

- *Chapter 3: Delta Printer Software.* This chapter presents an overview of the software used with 3D printing, with emphasis on the software supporting delta printers.

- *Chapter 4: Tips for Building a Delta Printer.* This chapter presents a set of best practices and advice for those wishing to build their own delta printer. It offers specific tips and covers the tools and skills required.

- *Chapter 5: Calibrating the Printer.* This chapter provides and in-depth look at how to calibrate a delta printer. A thorough description and an example of all delta printer calibration are included.

- *Chapter 6: Delta Printer Troubleshooting.* This chapter presents some of the most common things that can go wrong and how to solve them. Topics range from first layer issues, to curling and cracking, to hardware failures.

- *Chapter 7: Delta Printer Maintenance.* This printer presents best practices and practical examples of how to maintain your delta printer.

- *Chapter 8: Delta Printer Enhancements.* This chapter describes some of the most common enhancements available for delta printers, including those for the Mini Kossel, Kossel Pro, and Rostock Max v2.

Appendix

This book includes an appendix that contains diagnostic charts to help you zero-in on the cause of a print quality issues, failures, and other problems with hardware and software.

How to Use This Book

There are several ways that you can use this book, depending on your experience level, and, of course, the time that you have to devote to study. After all, you want to enjoy your new acquisition, yes? The following sections describe two likely levels of experience. You may find you fit both categories—that's OK. The sections are not intended as the only ways to read and apply the material presented. Indeed, you can read it cover-to-cover or a single chapter at a time in any order. Only you know your needs. However, if you want some guidance, I provide such in the following.

You Are New to 3D Printing and Delta Printers

This section is for those who are new to 3D printing and have either just bought a delta printer or plan to in the near future. It also covers topics of interest to those who want to learn to build their own delta printer. You will learn all about delta printers, including the hardware used to build them, as well as the software to run them.

If this fits your needs, I recommend you read through the first five chapters of this book carefully before trying to spend a lot of time with your printer. You may want to read Chapters 3, 4, and 5 twice before starting to build or calibrate your delta printer.

The time you spend reading about calibration and proper setup may make the difference between buyer's remorse and enthusiasm.

Once you have your printer going and have had success printing several things, you can move on to the remaining chapters, which will help you understand troubleshooting and the maintenance needs for your printer.

You Own a Cartesian 3D Printer but Are New to Delta Printers

This section covers those who have had some experience with a 3D printer but want to learn about how delta printers work, and more importantly, how to properly set up a delta printer to improve its print quality.

If this is you, I recommend skimming through the first three chapters of the book to ensure that you have learned all the key concepts of delta printers. Even if you have already set up your own delta printer and have installed the software, it is a good idea to read about these topics in a more general aspect. If nothing else, you will see some of the choices you could make concerning filament, hardware, and software solutions.

From there, I would recommend reading through the next four chapters, one chapter at a time, to apply the techniques you've learned. This includes proper calibration, setup, maintenance, and troubleshooting your prints.

The troubleshooting chapter alone is the one area where intermediate enthusiasts have a lot of frustration. As I mention in the chapter, there are a lot of opinions and solutions out there for common maladies; some are no more than voodoo or wishful thinking, some work for only a few people, and most are too specific to a model or situation to be a general cure. If you are having print issues, you will learn many solutions that can make almost all of your problems vanish.

Once you have your printer dialed in and your printing woes cured, take a look at the remaining chapter to ensure that you are following proper maintenance to keep your printer running in top shape.

Downloading the Code

The code for the examples shown in this book is available on the Apress web site, `www.apress.com`. A link can be found on the book's information page under the Source Code/Downloads tab. This tab is located underneath the Related Titles section of the page.

Contacting the Author

Should you have any questions or comments—or even spot a mistake you think I should know about—you can contact the author at `drcharlesbell@gmail.com`.

CHAPTER 1

■ ■ ■

Introduction to Delta 3D Printers

The most fascinating three-dimensional (3D) printer design to watch print is the delta printer. The delta design is quite different from most 3D printers and is best known for its vertical orientation and relatively small footprint (although larger units can be quite tall). This book will help you learn what you need to buy or build your own delta printer, as well as how to get the most out of your delta printer.

A delta 3D printer, hence delta printer, is a type of parallel robot that uses geometric algorithms to position each of three vertical axes simultaneously to move the nozzle to any position in a cylindrical build area. Thus, when the printer is printing, all three axes move in a mesmerizing ballet of mathematical magic.[1] If all this sounds too fantastic, don't worry; I will present the mechanics of the delta printer in detail throughout this book.

Before we jump into how the hardware mechanisms work, let's take a short tour on what 3D printing is all about. A firm understanding of the concepts of 3D printing is essential to getting the most out of your 3D printer investment. Even if you are already a 3D printing enthusiast (and especially if you have never used a delta printer), you may want to read the following sections because I present the material with delta printers in mind.

Getting Started

The world of 3D printing is growing in popularity as more people find creative ways to use 3D printers. People buy 3D printers for creating solutions for the home, gifts, artistic expression, and of course, for rapid prototyping of components for manufacture. I have even seen 3D printers used in architectural firms to replace the somewhat tedious art of 3D modeling[2]—from scale models of buildings to elaborate terrain maps.

The major contributor for this expansion is that 3D printers are getting easier to find and afford. While far from the point of finding a 3D printer in your local small retailer or as a bonus for buying a new mattress, you don't have to look very far to find a 3D printer manufacturer or reseller. Even printing supplies are getting easier to find.

In fact, some of the larger retailers such as Home Depot are starting to stock 3D printers and supplies. For some time now, MakerBot Industries has sold their products on the Microsoft online store, as well as at their own retail stores. Similarly, other 3D printer suppliers have opened retail stores.

Naturally, nearly all 3D printing retailers have an online store where you can order anything from parts to build or maintain your own, to printing supplies such as filament and other consumables. So the problem that you are most likely to encounter is not *finding* a 3D printer, but rather it is *choosing* the printer that is best for you.

---

[1]It's at this point you may be wishing you paid more attention in trigonometry class.
[2]My early passion was architecture. I was quite good at making scale models, but not so much with tedious lettering skills.

Indeed, the challenges today are less about where to buy and more about whether to buy or build your own from a kit (or from scratch), and if so, which kit to buy, which prebuilt printer to buy, what filament to use, and perhaps more importantly, what printing technology you want to use.

Unless you have spent some time working with 3D printers and have mastered how to use them, the myriad of choices may seem daunting and confusing. I have encountered a lot of people who, despite researching their chosen printer, have many questions about how the printer works, what filament to use, and even how to make the printer do what they want it to.

Too often I have discovered people selling their 3D printer because they cannot get decent print quality, or it doesn't print well, or they don't have the time or skills to complete the build, or they have had trouble getting the printer calibrated. Fortunately, most of these issues can be solved with a bit of knowledge and some known best practices.

This section will help you avoid these pitfalls by introducing you to the fundamentals of 3D printing with a specific emphasis on delta printers. You will learn that there are several forms of 3D printing and be provided with an overview of the software you can use with your printer. You will also learn about the consumables used in 3D printing, including the types of filament available. To round out the discussion on getting started, I present a short overview on buying a delta printer, including whether to build or buy, and what to consider when buying a used printer.

■ **Note** Henceforth I will use "3D printer" and "printer" interchangeably since I will be talking only about 3D printers.

What Is 3D Printing?

Mastering the mysteries of 3D printing should be the goal of every 3D printing enthusiast. But where do you find the information and how do you get started? This section presents the basics of 3D printing, beginning with the process of 3D printing and followed by a discussion on how the printer assembles or prints an object, and finally, it takes a look at the consumables involved in 3D printing. I will expand on many of these topics in later chapters.

The 3D Printing Process

The 3D printing process, also called a *workflow*, involves taking a three-dimensional model and making it ready for print. This is a multistep process starting with a special form of the model and software to break the model into instructions the printer can use to make the object. The following provides an overview of the process, classifying each of the steps by software type. I discuss each in greater detail in Chapter 3.

An object is formed using computer-aided design (CAD) software. The object is exported in a file format that contains the Standard Tessellation Language (STL) for defining a 3D object with triangulated surfaces and vertices (called an .stl file).

The resulting .stl file is split or sliced into layers, and a machine-level instruction file is created (called a .gcode file) using computer-aided manufacturing (CAM) software. The file contains instructions for controlling the axes, direction of travel, temperature of the hot end, and more. In addition, each layer is constructed as a map of traces (paths for the extruded filament) for filling in the object outline and interior.

The printer uses its own software (firmware) to read the machine-level file and print the object one layer at a time. This software also supports operations for setting up and tuning the printer.

Now that you understand how a 3D printer puts the filament together to form an object, let's take a look at how the object is printed by the printer.

How an Object Is Printed

It is important to understand the process by which objects are built. Knowing how the printer creates an object will help you understand the hardware better, as well as help you tune and maintain your printer. That is, it will help you understand topics such as infill, shells (outer layers), and even how parts need to be oriented for strength.

The process is called *additive manufacturing*[3] and is used by most 3D printers available to the consumer. Conversely, computer numeric control (CNC) machines start with a block of material and cutaway parts to form the object. This is called *subtractive manufacturing*.[4]

Both forms of manufacturing use a Cartesian coordinate system (X, Y, and Z axes) to position the hardware to execute the build. Thus, the mechanical movements for 3D printing are very similar to the mechanisms used in CNC machines. In both cases, there are three axes of movement controlled by a computer, each capable of very high-precision movement.

Additive manufacturing has several forms or types that refer to the material used and the process used to take the material and form the object. However, they all use the same basic steps (called a *process* or workflow, as described earlier) to create the object.

The most common form of 3D printing for hobbyists and enthusiasts is called *fused filament fabrication* (FFF). Since the majority of 3D printers available today for consumer purchase are FFF, I will only discuss FFF in depth in this book. To simplify our discussion, henceforth I consider 3D printing to be synonymous with the FFF process. In fact, all printers discussed in this book are FFF-based.

When a 3D printer creates an object, the material used to print an object comes in *filament form*[5] on a large spool to make it easier for the printer to draw material. The filament is then loaded into an extruder that has two parts: one to pull the filament off the spool and push it into a heating element, and another to heat the filament to its melting point.

The part that pulls the filament and feeds it to the heating element is called the *cold end*, whereas the heating element is called the *hot end*. Sometimes manufacturers refer to both parts as the *extruder*, but others distinguish the extruder from the hot end (but they sometimes don't call it a cold end). Delta printers typically separate the parts with the first part fixed to the frame and the second on the axis mechanism (called the *effector*). Just one of the many nuances to 3D printing I hope to explain!

■ **Tip**　Never buy filament that isn't on a spool or a similar orderly delivery mechanism. Improperly wound filament can introduce a maddening number of extrusion failures.

This is where 3D printers can differ. That is, they vary slightly in the mechanism used and the materials used to form the object. Table 1-1 lists some of the forms available, describes how the material is used to build the object, and tells what materials can be used.

---

[3]For more information, visit http://en.wikipedia.org/wiki/3D_printing.
[4]Also called *machining*; see http://en.wikipedia.org/wiki/Machining.
[5]Like fishing line, or as my wife says, "fishing twine."

Table 1-1. *Types of Additive Manufacturing*

Type	Build Process	Materials
Filament	Objects built layer by layer, where material in filament form is extruded from a heated nozzle.	Various plastics, wood, nylon, and so forth.
Wire	An electron beam is used to melt the wire as it is unspooled to form an object, layer by layer.	Most metal alloys.
Granular	Various processes are used to take material in a raw, granular form using a laser, light, or electricity to fuse the granules and build the object.	Some metal alloys and thermoplastics.
Powder	A reactive liquid is sprayed on a power base to form solid layers. Some variations use a multistep process to fuse and then bind materials.	Plaster and similar granular materials. Emerging solutions can use metal.
	Another form uses light or laser to cure powder to form solid layers. Printers of this type typically use SLA/DLP projectors for the light source.	Resin.
Laminate	Material is laid over the object and fused with a heated roller. A laser is then used to cut out the shape.	Paper, metal foil, plastic film.

If this sounds like nothing more than a fancy hot glue gun, you're right! The process is very similar, but unlike the hot glue gun that relies on human power to pump glue sticks (however inaccurately) into the heating element, 3D printers use a computer-controlled electric motor called a *stepper motor* to precisely control how much and how fast the filament is fed to the hot end. Most extruders use a direct drive mechanism where the drive pulley is driven by the stepper motor. This allows for faster retraction to avoid stringing (thin wisps of filament trailing the hot end).

Figure 1-1 shows a drawing of how the extrusion process works, including a pictorial representation of the components discussed in this section.

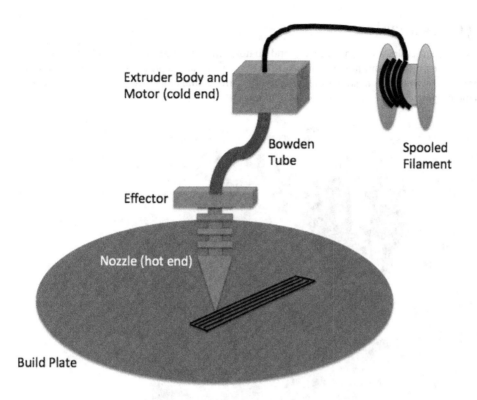

Figure 1-1. *FFF extrusion with nomenclature*

The drawing shows a mock-up of the extruder and a spool of filament. As you can see, the filament is pulled into the extruder (cold end) and then pushed into the nozzle (hot end) via a special PTFE tube (also called a Bowden tube). Once heated, the filament is extruded onto a *build plate* (a very flat surface used as the base for the object). Typically, the outer edges of an object are printed first, and then the interior edges are printed, and finally, the interior of the layer is printed as either a solid layer (for outermost layers) or as a fill-in matrix for inner layers.

Notice that the filament from the spool is much larger than the heated extrusion. This is because most nozzles (the small part where the filament exits the heater block) have a very small opening ranging from 0.2 millimeters (mm) to 0.5mm or larger. Notice in the drawing that I've exaggerated how the layer is built from multiple lines of heated filament. Although grossly simplified, this is effectively how a 3D printer takes filament and builds a layer of the object.

WHERE DID FUSED FILAMENT FABRICATION ORIGINATE?

FFF is also known as *fused deposition modeling* (FDM). FDM was developed by S. Scott Crump in the late 1980s, and further developed and commercialized by Stratasys Ltd. in the 1990s. Indeed, FDM is a trademark of Stratasys Ltd. (the owners of MakerBot Industries). Since the majority of 3D printers use this process (the process is not trademarked, only the term *FDM*), FFF is used to avoid confusion with the Stratasys trademark.

3D Printing Consumables

The ongoing costs of consumables for 3D printing depend on how much printing you do, what types of filament you use, and even what color filament you want. That is, if you want to print an object in a variety of colors, you will have to buy a number of spools of filament. For example, the object shown in Figure 1-2 uses six colors, which means you will have to buy six spools of filament.

Figure 1-2. Complex 3D print

This object is an excellent example of what you can achieve with your 3D printer. The nutcracker stands nearly 15 inches tall and is assembled from a number of pieces that snap and click together. Printing time will vary, but you can expect it to take 20 or more hours to print all the parts.

I don't recommend starting with this as your first print, but once your printer is calibrated and printing well, you will be ready to print objects like this fantastic novelty. You can find this object in the Thingiverse online repository (`thingiverse.com/thing:579567`).

WHAT'S THINGIVERSE?

Thingiverse is one of the most popular object repositories you can use to find and publish objects for 3D printing. Indeed, Thingiverse is a repository for more than just 3D printing. You will find objects and files for laser cutting, as well as CNC machining—although the majority of entries are for 3D printing.

On Thingiverse, you can search for objects by name, and order the results by popularity or newest creations. You can also create an account and publish your own objects. If you're looking for something to print, check out Thingiverse. Chances are you will find a lot of things you will want to print. To get started, navigate to Thingiverse.com and search for "Mini Kossel". You'll find hundreds of things, including the full list of plastic parts to print your own Mini Kossel plastic kit.

There are two basic consumables in 3D printing aside from things like lubrication and maintenance parts, which you will learn more about in an upcoming chapter. The most obvious is the raw material—filament. However, you will also need to have supplies to treat your print surface so that objects will adhere to it without lifting. *Lifting* is a term used when part of the object pulls away from the print surface (also called *curling*). If the lift is bad enough, it can render the part useless.

Let's look at filament first, and then discuss print surface treatments in detail. Proper preparation of the print surface is one of the keys to achieving high-quality prints.

Filament

There are many forms of filament and more being created every year. Filament comes in a variety of sizes (usually 1.75mm or 3.0mm)[6] and dozens of different colors. You can get filament that has a slight sheen or even a flat (think matte) finish, filament that glows in the dark, and even filament that has small bits of metal flake to make it appear to sparkle in the light. Indeed, you can build up quite a palette of colors to express your creativity. Filament is normally wound on a plastic, wooden, or corkboard spool.

■ **Note**   The diameter of the filament required is governed by the size of the extruder. Printers come with either a 1.75mm or 3.0mm hot end. Check your documentation before ordering new filament.

The most common types of filament are plastics called *polylactic acid* (PLA) and *acrylonitrile butadiene styrene* (ABS). Each type of filament has certain heating properties and requirements for build platforms. Table 1-2 lists the more common filaments available, along with their abbreviations and brief descriptions. The melting point (in this case, the temperature that the filament becomes soft enough to extrude) is listed in degrees Celsius.

---

[6]These sizes can vary a bit. For example, 3.0mm filament is usually 2.9mm +/- 0.1mm for most suppliers.

Table 1-2. *Filament Types*

Type	Abbrev.	Melting Point (Celsius)	Description
Polycarbonate	PC	155	Impact resistant. Can print clear.
Aliphatic polyamide	Nylon	220	Low friction. Somewhat pliable.
High-impact polystyrene	HIPS	180	Similar to ABS but can be dissolved with limonene. Sometimes used for support material.
Acrylonitrile butadiene styrene	ABS	215	Flexible, easy to modify (carve, sand, etc.).
Polyethylene terephthalate	PET	210	Made from food-grade substrate. Completely recyclable.
Polyvinyl alcohol	PVA	180	Dissolves in cold water. Used for support material.
Laywoo-D3		180	Wood blend. Similar to PLA. Looks like light pine when printed.
Polylactic acid	PLA	160	Derived from plants and biodegradable.

■ **Note**   Actual melting points for your printer and filament may vary slightly.

No matter what type of printer you buy or build, the choice of filament will be dictated by the printer hardware. Specifically, the following components determine which filament the printer will support:

- Size of extruder and hot end
- Hot end heating characteristics, such as the maximum heat range
- Heated print bed support

The size of the extruder feed mechanism and the size of the hot end will determine whether you can use 1.75mm or 3.0mm filament. The material used to make the extruder body and the heating characteristics of the hot end will also factor into which filament you can use. Lastly, whether the printer has a heated print bed will also determine which filament you can use.

A heated print bed helps the filament adhere to the print bed. Filaments that require a heated print bed (those that perform best with a heated print bed) are ABS, HIPS, nylon, and PC. PLA and other filaments with a lower melting point typically don't require a heated print bed. However, it can be shown to help prevent lifting with PLA.

If you are planning to build a printer or want to be able to print with a number of filament types, you should look for a printer that has a hot end that can heat efficiently to 265 degrees Celsius (or higher), and has a heated print bed option.

Another, less frequently cited criteria is the sort of gases that the filament exudes when heated. Some filament produces a noticeable odor when heated. Some have an odor that is neither harmful nor noxious (to some), whereas others have an odor that can cause irritation for those with sensitivity or are allergic to certain chemicals.

Some filament, like ABS, can be extruded in an open environment and are not susceptible to air movement that can cause the object to cool too quickly (none can withstand the effects of the air currents from a house fan, for example). Cooling ABS too quickly can cause print failures. Other filament, like PLA, retains heat and requires a small fan to cool. Figure 1-3 shows one example of how a fan is used when printing PLA. The photo shows a fan nozzle mounted on a Mini Kossel. A squirrel cage fan is mounted above the hot end and connected via a flexible hose.

Figure 1-3. *Using a fan when printing with PLA*

Most printers and kits on the market today are designed to print in PLA or ABS. Since ABS has a higher melting point than PLA, a printer that has a small fan to cool the filament can print ABS and PLA.

ABS VS. PLA: WHICH IS BEST?

The choice of whether to print with ABS or PLA can sometimes be emotionally charged. Those enthusiasts who have perfected their printing of either choice can be quite insistent that theirs is the best choice. Rather than supply yet more rhetoric, I will present arguments for and against each. With this information, you can make your own choice. That is, provided you haven't locked in on a printer that prints only one type of filament (not that there is anything wrong with that).

ABS is a very good choice if you plan to create objects that are going to be in close proximity to heat sources like a hot end. ABS is also somewhat flexible and can withstand bending that would break PLA objects. It is also easily modified—you can cut it with a hobby knife and glue it together with either ABS glue or acetone. In fact, ABS dissolves in acetone and can be smoothed with acetone vapor. You can make your own ABS glue by dissolving a small amount of ABS in acetone. As the acetone evaporates, it leaves hardened ABS that forms a strong bond. Lastly, ABS flexes well—forming strong bond layers.

However, ABS exudes a very noticeable odor that can cause some people irritation. It is always a good idea to use a fume extractor when printing with ABS. In fact, some people build special enclosures or fume hoods to vent the gases to the outside. While more flexible than PLA, ABS is not as rigid and can wear more quickly than PLA. For example, gears are best made from PLA, since gears made from ABS can wear out quickly. If your printer came with ABS gears, check them often for wear, and replace them when tolerance becomes too great (the gears have excessive play).

Lastly, ABS requires a heated print bed and Kapton tape or similar for the best bond. This fact alone makes ABS harder to print objects with no warping. Furthermore, Kapton tape can be a bit of a challenge to get to stick to a glass plate without air bubbles or wrinkles. There are many techniques that can help, and that alone should be enough to conclude that ABS is more difficult to use.

PLA is a very good choice for those who plan to use their printers in their home or office. The odor it exudes smells a lot like pancake syrup when overheated, so unless you abhor that type of breakfast food, it is not an unpleasant experience. PLA is harder and more rigid, making it a good choice for components that must be strong and do not permit too much flexing. It is recommended to use a fan when printing PLA. A fan forces air over the filament as it is extruded. This helps the filament cool more quickly, forming a stronger bond and reducing lift. PLA is also more forgiving when it comes to adhering to the print bed. PLA adheres well to common blue painter's tape, which is much easier to apply than Kapton tape. The ease of printing makes PLA a good choice for beginners.

However, since PLA does not flex well, it isn't a good choice for clamps and similar objects that must flex. Also, since PLA has a lower melting point than ABS, PLA is not a good choice for extruder bodies and similar parts for printers that print ABS.

So, which is best? That depends. If you are starting out, you might want to stick to PLA until you've mastered some of the calibration techniques for achieving high-quality prints. On the other hand, if you want to build things that you can customize or use *adaptive prototyping*,[7] you may want to choose ABS. Again, it is your choice, and now that you know the major ins and outs of each, you can make an educated choice.

You may be wondering if it is possible to switch from one type of filament to another. The answer is simply, "Yes, you can." The only issue is making sure that the old filament is completely removed from the nozzle before loading and using the new filament. The same is true for changing colors of filament.

I like to run at least 200mm of filament through the hot end to ensure that all traces of the old filament are removed. When you are changing from one filament type to another, be sure to use the higher temperature of the two to ensure that you do not have any residue of higher-temperature filament in your hot end. You can adjust the temperature setting once you have cleared the nozzle.

An alternative technique is to use what is called the *cold-pull method* to clear the nozzle of old filament. It is also a great way to clear a blocked nozzle. You start preheating the nozzle and pull up on the filament (unlatching any Bowden tubes or extruders first) while the nozzle heats. I and others have found that using Nylon 618 from Taulman to cold pull works better than using ABS or PLA.[8]

Once the nozzle reaches about 80% of the recommended temperature, you should be able to pull the filament clear of the nozzle. This will remove most of the old filament, allowing you to clear the nozzle with less new filament. I recommend this technique when switching from one filament type to another, such as switching between ABS and PLA. Be sure to allow the hot end to cool before inserting new filament.

---

[7]Which goes something like this: cut, drill, sand, glue, repeat.
[8]See http://bukobot.com/nozzle-cleaning.

Print Surface Treatments

There are several types of print surfaces. The filament type dictates which of these you can use. For example, the best surface for PLA is blue painter's tape, and the best surface for ABS is Kapton tape. These are surface treatments that work best for PLA and ABS filament and are considered the standard for each. However, I will discuss one alternative for ABS that is used to combat lifting.[9]

Some enthusiasts have discovered alternative print surface treatments, such as a glue-like coating, hair spray, different materials for the print surface, and even some different forms of tape. Some of these may work for you, but I would suggest starting with blue painter's tape and Kapton tape. I suspect some of the alternative treatments are remedies for symptoms like too much airflow (too cool), poor cooling (too hot), and similar issues. That said, some have had success using Elmer's disappearing purple glue (http://elmers.com/product/detail/e523) for ABS printing.

Under normal conditions, you should not have to use these alternative treatments (but you're welcome to experiment). Don't make the mistake of thinking blue painter's tape, Kapton tape, or ABS juice is inadequate or the source of your problems. Many printing enthusiasts use these surface treatments successfully every day. Fix what is broken first before applying any unorthodox techniques.

There are some additional considerations if you have a printer that permits you to choose the print surface itself. For example, aluminum is better for using blue painter's tape, and glass is a good choice for Kapton tape. However, glass works well for both. The following sections present various surface treatments. I include notes about the surface so that you can consider which is best for your needs.

■ **Tip** I like to have a different print surface for each surface treatment. For example, I have one for blue painter's tape, another for Kapton tape, and a third for Kapton tape plus ABS juice (see the following sections).

To get the most out of your surface treatment, you should ensure that the surface is clean and free from any dirt, smudges, and oils from your hands, and that it is dry. If your print surface is glass or aluminum, clean the surface with acetone followed by 90% or better isopropanol (also available as rubbing alcohol in most pharmacies), which cleans the surface well—without leaving any residue like soap and other cleaners. You may also use window cleaner, but make sure that it is safe to use on your print surface first. If you use a water-based solution, make sure that it is completely dry before printing.

If you are replacing the surface treatment, make sure that you remove all the old treatment first. Using several layers of surface treatment—more specifically blue painter's or Kapton tape—is not recommended. Although it saves you time and money from having to remove the Kapton tape first, you may discover they don't stick well to one another, which can result with the part lifting the top layer of tape, despite adhering well to the top layer. The same is true for multiple layers of the same type of tape. Use only one layer of tape at a time.

Blue Painter's Tape

If you visit your local hardware or home improvement store, or even a specialty paint store, you will find a number of tape products that are specifically designed to mask out areas for painting (also called *masking tape*). The best tapes for painting are those that prevent paint from bleeding along the edge, which helps painters create precise lines when painting with multiple colors or around trim, electrical components, and just about anything they don't want painted.

There are several types of painting masking tape. Some are nothing more than common masking tape (tan or brown in color), others are blue, while others are a combination of tape and plastic sheeting.[10] While some

---

[9]It is as close to a magic cure as you're likely to get for ABS lifting.
[10]Never, ever attempt to use painter's tape that is made of plastic of any variety. It will not survive application on a heated print bed and may make a mess of your prints because it may stick to your objects.

are certainly better than others, they all have one attribute that is a must for painters: they can be removed easily without peeling away the paint or wallpaper to which they were adhered. The type of tape used in this book is called *blue painter's tape*. It is called that because, well, it's blue and it is used for painting.

GOT THE BLUES?

There are some new vendors making painter's tape, and some of these are not—gasp!—blue! Indeed, I have found green and yellow painter's tape—called FrogTape. The green is equivalent to typical blue painter's tape. The yellow is a low-adhesion version for sensitive surfaces. Some people have reported mixed results with the green tape. I have found it works OK with a heated print bed, but it is not as good as blue painter's tape without a heated print bed because parts do not stick to it as well. However, the yellow is not as good for 3D printing because it can become loose and pull off with the part.

Blue painter's tape is a very good surface material for print beds. It works well for PLA and can work fine for ABS if a heated printed bed is used (but not as good as Kapton tape for ABS). The tape comes in a variety of widths and can be applied to glass or aluminum easily, and can be removed and replaced quickly without special applicators or tools.

■ **Note**   Objects printed on blue painter's tape have a matte finish for the bottom and show the stippling of the tape. If you want a gloss finish, you can sand the bottom and apply an even layer of acetone to change the finish. It won't look the same as the other sides, but it will be closer. This is one thing to consider when designing prints using multiple parts. To avoid the telltale tape side, you can try to orient the parts so that the "tape" sides mate together. The nutcracker in Figure 1-2 was designed specifically to avoid showing the tape side of the parts.

Parts can be removed easily once they have cooled, and the tape can be reused a number of times. Due to its lower cost, removing parts is not a stressful affair, even if you tear the tape. If you use several narrow strips vs. a single, wide piece, you can just cut away one strip or a part of a strip and replace that portion.

■ **Tip**   Objects can be removed from blue painter's tape more easily once they have cooled. If you try to use tools such as a scraper or razor, you will likely cut or tear the tape. It is best to wait until the part is cool. This is another good reason to have multiple build surfaces—you can allow one part to cool while printing another.

But not all blue painter's tapes are created equal. I recommend avoiding the really inexpensive, little-known manufacturers. Some of these may be just fine, but if they do not adhere well to the print surface, it can make a lifting problem worse. Similarly, if they adhere too well, they may not be easily removed from the print surface, making it harder to replace the tape.

Another consideration is whether the tape has the manufacturer's logo imprinted on the tape surface. You should avoid using these tapes if you plan to print with light-colored filament. This is because the logo can transfer to the filament. For example, I used a major manufacturer's "best" blue painter's tape for printing white PLA. When I removed my objects from the printer, I discovered the logo was prominently displayed on each of my objects. If you use dark colored filament, you may not notice, but I would still avoid tape that has logos imprinted on the surface.

You will have to do your own cost analysis based on the cost of the tape in your area, but generally, you should look for a balance of cost, width, and adhesive qualities. For example, I use two-inch-wide tape that features a non-bleed edge and does not have any logos. It costs a bit more, but makes for a good bond to glass and has a much better durability than cheaper brands.

HOW WIDE IS WIDE ENOUGH?

In general, it is best to get the widest tape you can find. However, be sure to do some comparative shopping. For example, I once found some four-inch-wide blue painter's tape, but it was priced nearly four times the cost of the two-inch tape and was only 75% as long as the two-inch rolls. In this case, wider is not cheaper. Also, really wide tape can be harder to apply if your print bed surface is not removable, especially if there are frames or electronics that prevent you from accessing the print surface easily. Thus, I use two-inch-wide tape and make several passes to cover the entire surface. This, for me, is the most economical choice.

Applying blue painter's tape to your print surface is really easy. You simply cut a length of tape a bit longer than your print surface and apply the tape to the surface one row at a time until the surface is completely covered. Don't worry about overhang—you can cut that away with scissors or a hobby knife after the surface is covered. I like to leave a bit of an overhang so that I can more easily remove the tape. But don't leave so much as to affect movement of the printer axes. That is, blue painter's tape overhang can curl on heated print beds. If you leave so much that it curls and strikes the hot end, it could stick and peel away the tape—or even obstruct the nozzle, causing extrusion failures.

___

■ **Tip** Always shut down your printer and allow the print surface to cool to room temperature before removing or applying tape. If you apply tape when the surface is hot, it may not stick well, or bubble, wrinkle, or separate when cool.

___

Since most delta printers have circular print surfaces, applying tape in narrow strips should start in the center and work outward. This allows you to avoid a case where there is a much narrower slice of tape on one side.

The hardest part of applying the tape is getting the seams even and as close as possible. Fortunately, the tape can be removed easily, so if you need to adjust it, you can. I like to start by holding the length of tape just beyond the print surface or at least near the edge.

Position one side of the tape so that there is no gap, and then slowly lower the other side, keeping the tape straight and tight against the edge of the previous strip. Again, this is easier to describe than do, but once you've practiced it a couple of times, you'll get the hang of it.

Once I have the tape applied, I trim the edges and use a flat edge to press down across the seams. For example, you can use a putty knife that can flex to slide over the seams to press them flat. This allows you to firmly adhere the tape to the print surface, even if there is a small bit of overlap. Plus, the knife can be used to remove parts once cooled.

Figure 1-4 through Figure 1-8 present the process for applying blue painter's tape. I used a glass print surface for a Mini Kossel. The procedure is the same for glass, acrylic, and similar materials. Similarly, if you have used Cartesian printers or delta printers with a square print surface, the procedure is exactly the same.

Take care with cutting away overhang if your print surface is soft (like Plexiglas). In that case, you may not want to use a hobby knife to trim the edges. That is, if you slip and cut the blue tape, you may also mar the print surface.

Also, if your print surface is attached to a heated print bed or a Kapton heater (as shown in the figures), take extra care to avoid getting the solution on the wiring or electronics. If you do get some solution on the wiring, allow it to dry completely before reinstalling or powering on your printer. Also, be careful when trimming the excess tape so that you do not accidentally cut the insulation on the wires or damage the thermistor.

Figure 1-4. *Applying the tape in rows*

Notice in Figure 1-5 that I pulled the tape taught and aligned the outer edges. This helps avoid creating wrinkles and ensures that the seam is even across the surface. Notice that I also left a little overhang.

Figure 1-5. *Align one side first*

Figure 1-6. *Align the other side*

In Figure 1-7, I apply the finishing touches of trimming the excess and smoothing the seams. If your tape overlaps, you may see the effect on the bottom of your prints.

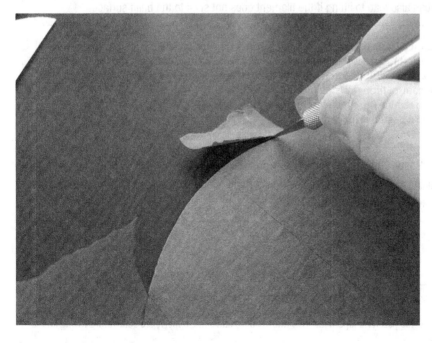

Figure 1-7. *Cut away the excess tape*

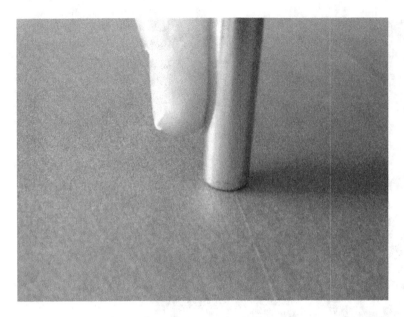

Figure 1-8. *Smooth over the gaps*

■ **Caution** Try to avoid overlapping the tape. The thickness of the tape may be enough to cause the nozzle to strike the tape on the first layer, which can lead to problems such as lifting, or at the very least a crease on the underside of your object. Similarly, avoid gaps between the strips of tape. Gaps will cause creases on the bottom of your prints, but can also lead to lifting if the filament does not stick to the build surface.

Printing with blue painter's tape requires no special settings on your printer. So long as the Z-height[11] is set correctly (the width of a standard weight sheet of paper), filament should stick to the tape easily. Blue painter's tape is great for printing with PLA and can also be used for printing ABS if there is a heated bed (but this may be harder to control lifting). Using blue painter's tape with PLA and a heated bed works equally well; however, it is known to reduce the effectiveness of the adhesive, so you may have to change the tape more often when using with a heated print bed.

■ **Tip** Using blue painter's tape with ABS requires a very precise Z-height setting. I have found I need to set the Z-height lower when using ABS on blue painter's tape than Kapton tape. ABS doesn't stick as well to blue painter's tape as it does to Kapton tape.[12]

---

[11]The initial height of the nozzle above the print surface when Z = 0 (lowest position).
[12]This is one of those YMMV situations. It is harder to control lifting and adhesion problems, and for that reason alone I'd recommend waiting to use blue painter's tape with ABS until you've had some experience controlling lifting and similar adhesion problems.

You should change the tape when you see distortions on the surface. After several prints (perhaps as few as five, but more likely several dozen), you may also start to notice a change in the color of the tape. Some discoloration is fine, so long as the tape is still attached to the print bed. You are most concerned about any damage from removing parts or distortion of the tape surface, which can happen over many prints.

This is especially so if your slicing software positions the objects in the center by default. In this case, the center of the tape will wear out sooner. On the other hand, even if there is no distortion, if your prints start losing first-layer adhesion—or worse, you start experiencing lifting at the edges and corners, you should replace the tape and double-check your Z-height.

If you used two-inch-wide tape like I do, you may be able to replace only a strip or two of the tape. That is, if you've only printed in the center and the size of the objects printed do not extend past the center two strips, just replace those. You do not need to completely strip the surface every time. This is also another good reason to choose tape that isn't as wide as your print surface—you can replace only those areas that are worn.

Kapton Tape

Have you ever seen the inside of a modern laptop, tablet, or smartphone?[13] Did you notice some transparent yellow tape in there? Most likely you were seeing Kapton tape. Kapton is a brand-name tape made by DuPont. Kapton tape is a polyimide film with an adhesive on one side. It is highly heat resistant across a range of temperatures, from –269°C to +400°C (degrees Celsius). In the 3D printing world (and likely others), the name Kapton has become synonymous with the product (like Xerox). Indeed, you may find several vendors who sell polyimide film, but do not call it Kapton tape (for obvious trademark/product restrictions).

Kapton tape is best used for printing ABS. It may also work for other higher-temperature filaments. Kapton tape is more difficult to apply because the adhesive is designed to stick really well. In fact, the adhesive is stronger than the film itself. Thus, if you apply Kapton tape to a dry aluminum or glass print surface, you may not be able to remove it without tearing the film. Figure 1-9 shows a typical roll of Kapton tape.

---

[13]Every Apple device I've seen has several pieces inside.

Figure 1-9. *Kapton tape roll*

■ **Note**   Objects printed on Kapton tape will have a smooth finish on the bottom. Some don't like this because it is different from the other sides of the object.

Removing parts from Kapton tape can be a bit of a challenge. For the best results, you should wait until the parts cool completely before attempting to remove them. They remove more easily when cool. There are a number of techniques for removing parts from Kapton tape, including using a sharp knife, or a craft blade, or a putty knife to pry the parts off. Any of these will work, but you risk damaging the Kapton tape. Given that Kapton tape is relatively expensive and harder to apply, you may want to use these tools as a last resort.

The technique I use for small objects is an adjustable wrench tightened around the object perpendicular to the print bed. I apply slight force to the wrench to twist the object—just enough to flex it—and the object usually pops off, or that side pops loose enough for me to use a dull plastic blade to pop the object off the print surface.

▪ **Caution**   Do not attempt the following without wearing thick gloves and eye protection. If you get this wrong, you can break your glass print bed!

Another technique that works for objects that are really stuck to Kapton tape on normal glass is to remove the glass print surface and place it on a towel on a workbench or a desk. Move the print surface so that half is on the desk and half is not. Press down very softly, gradually increasing pressure until you hear a pop. Do not use quick, energetic pressure—this can break your glass print bed! Repeat this for each edge or until enough of the part is free for you to pry it off.

Like blue painter's tape, you will find Kapton tape in a variety of widths. However, unlike blue painter's tape, I prefer the wider widths because it is harder to get pieces to align well enough to avoid gaps or overlap. Once again, you have to do some comparative shopping, as the wider widths can be a bit more expensive than the narrower widths. I use 200mm-width rolls and make two passes (two strips) when applying the tape. This leaves only a single seam down the center of the print surface for my larger printers and can easily cover the print surface of smaller delta printers, such as the Mini Kossel or Mini Rostock.

Applying Kapton tape requires some practice and a fair amount of patience. I have found a technique that works well for most print surfaces. It works best for glass and aluminum. I would not recommend using it on porous print surfaces or in situations where you cannot remove the print surface (some delta printer kits have a fixed aluminum build plate). The technique I use is as follows. Figure 1-10 through Figure 1-14 show the process in action.

1. Remove the print surface and place it on a flat, water-resistant surface. I like to put a couple of paper towels down first to absorb extra liquid.

2. Use a mixture of 1 drop of baby shampoo to 4 ounces of distilled water.

3. Spray a liberal amount of the water on the print surface. Use a spritzing sprayer to distribute the water as evenly as you can.

4. Cut a long strip of Kapton tape that is at least 2 inches longer than needed.

5. Spray a small amount of the water on your fingers and carefully grip the tape on each end.

6. Hold the tape over the print surface and allow it to droop, forming a "U" shape.

7. Slowly and evenly (without pulling), lower your hands so that the tape spreads out evenly.

8. If the tape isn't applying evenly, remove it and try again. The water solution will make the tape much easier to remove. Spray more water if the tape is sticking to the glass.

9. Using a rubber or similar soft-edge squeegee, start in the center of the tape and press lightly and outward to one edge to squeeze out the water. Repeat for the other direction. If there are large bubbles or wrinkles, carefully lift the tape back to the point where the anomaly begins and reapply by pulling (but not stretching) to remove the crease.

10. Continue to squeeze out all the water that you can. It is OK if you cannot get all the bubbles out. Small bubbles (say, about 4mm–5mm in diameter) are fine and will disappear as the water dries.

11. Repeat the process for the next strip, carefully aligning the tape next to the applied strip. You will find the water makes it easier to remove and even move the tape so that it joins the first strip.

12. Use the squeegee to remove as much water as possible. Go over the seams again with the squeegee to remove water trapped near the edge.

13. Use a hobby knife to cut off all the excess Kapton tape.

14. Dry the print surface with paper towels, place the print surface in sunlight, and allow it to dry. Any small bubbles will disappear in a few hours or, at most, overnight.

Figure 1-10. *Getting ready*

■ **Tip**   It is fine to spray a lot of water on the surface. The water keeps the tape from sticking to the glass.

Figure 1-11. *Applying the water mixture*

Figure 1-12. *Apply one strip at a time*

■ **Tip**   Starting in the center, use smooth, even strokes to press the water out to the edges.

Repeat the process until the entire surface is covered. Try to get the strips as close together as possible. Overlap should be avoided. If you do leave a small gap, make sure that it is no more than a few tenths of a millimeter at most. Any more than that and you will get a ridge on any objects that cross the gap.

Figure 1-13. *Go over the seam(s)*

Figure 1-14. All done!

Printing with Kapton tape requires a very precise Z-height—more so than blue painter's tape. You should check your Z-height for the first few prints on newly applied Kapton tape (if not at least once per day of use).

Although ABS sticks very well to Kapton tape, it is not a cure for lifting. Some people have switched from blue painter's tape to Kapton tape in order to solve lifting problems, only to discover it made it worse. This is most likely because the print surface wasn't the problem. For example, if ABS is subjected to cooling air currents, the higher layers can shrink faster than the lower layers (which are heated by the print bed), forcing the lower layers to bend and curl—hence, lifting.[14]

■ **Note** Delamination of layers can occur not only from cooling too fast, but also when printing on a layer that has cooled. In this case, the temperature of the two layers is too low for a sufficient bond.

---

[14]It can also cause larger objects to develop cracks where layers separate during cooling.

To get the most out of printing ABS on Kapton tape, you should use a heated print bed set to a range of 90°C to 110°C. The proper temperature may take some experimentation to get right and can vary based on the filament used. I have some lighter-color filament that requires lower heat on the print bed. The best thing to do is start at 100°C and watch how well the first layer adheres. If there is some lifting on smaller-diameter parts or the edges, increase the heated print bed by 5 degrees and run another print. This isn't a terribly scientific process. I tend to use 100°C to 110°C when I print with ABS on Kapton tape, using the lower range for large objects and the higher for smaller objects or objects with thin protrusions. You can set these values in your slicer program.

Replacing Kapton tape is required less frequently than blue painter's tape. It is more likely you will damage the tape when removing objects before the adhesion properties degrade. Even then, you can revive Kapton tape by using a small amount of acetone and a lint-free cloth to remove any ABS from the surface. I have had Kapton print surfaces last for more than 40 hours of printing. In fact, I have yet to wear out the tape without first damaging it.

ABS Juice

If you are printing with ABS and want to improve your first-layer adhesion, or you don't want to use Kapton tape (or you ran out), there is a surface treatment called *ABS juice*.[15] You can apply it to glass or on top of Kapton tape.

Simply dissolve about 10mm–20mm of thin ABS scrap from discarded skirts, brims, rafts, and so forth (filament can take a long time to dissolve) per 10ml of acetone in a glass jar with a lid. To apply, spread the solution evenly on a glass surface, allow it to dry (it only takes a few minutes), set your Z-height, and start printing. This technique will significantly reduce lifting problems with ABS on Kapton tape and is a great alternative to building a full enclosure to reduce drafts.

The proper mixture of ABS juice should be watery and free of clumps (the ABS is fully dissolved). Application can be made with a cotton tip, a cloth, or a paintbrush. You should apply the juice in a thin layer. It is OK if there are streaks of juice because this will not affect adhesion, and some users have actually reported that it helps adhesion. I've found it helps with the removal of parts. The proper application should make the glass opaque and it should have a slight tinge of the color of filament used. For example, you should see a very faint blue glaze when using blue filament juice. Figure 1-15 shows a print surface treated with ABS juice.

■ **Tip**   For better flow, you can apply the ABS juice to a heated surface of around 50°C.

---

[15]Not to be confused with ABS slurry, which is a thicker concoction used to glue parts together.

Figure 1-15. *ABS juice applied*

When you mix your juice, you should use the same color filament that you use to print. This is because each time you remove an object from the print surface, the layer of juice normally comes off because it is stuck (bonded) to the first layer of your print. Thus, if you want to print a blue object, you should use blue juice. This is one reason some do not like to use juice—you have to remix it whenever you change filament. This is a drawback, but if you are like me, you tend to keep the same color of filament in the printer for several prints, so it isn't that much of a burden. Figure 1-16 shows what happens when you remove parts from a juice-treated print surface.

Figure 1-16. *Parts removed from juice-treated surface*

■ **Tip** An alternative to the acetone-based solution is methyl methacrylate-acrylonitrile butadiene styrene (MABS), which is a hybrid of ABS and acrylic. It produces a milky-white ABS juice that dries clear, allowing it to be used for any color of ABS. However, MABS may not be as easily obtained as acetone.

Notice that the juice has pulled completely away with the parts. The really great thing about ABS juice—aside from the fact that it helps to reduce (or in my case, completely eliminate) lifting—is that you can simply reapply more juice over the print surface where you removed the parts, and keep on using the surface. There is no need to completely remove and resurface!

If you ever wanted to remove the juice from a glass print surface, a simple razor tool can be used to scrape off the juice. If you have painted windows in your home, you already know what to do! You can also use a rag and acetone to wipe away the juice. This works best when the juice is thin. If you decide to use a thicker layer, it may require more elbow action to remove the juice with acetone alone (but it can be done).

When mixing and storing the juice, be sure to use a jar that has a seal that can withstand acetone vapor. I use jars with a spring-loaded lid and a rubber gasket. Acetone vapor will damage and in some cases destroy synthetic gaskets. Another option is to use an empty nail polish bottle. It can withstand the acetone and even has a small brush inside.

Clearly, if you want to store juice, make sure your container can withstand the corrosive effects of acetone. On the other hand, if you only plan to use a little juice, you can either allow the acetone to evaporate (leaving a layer of ABS in the bottom that can be reused) or rinse out the jar with more acetone when you are done.

If you use a paintbrush to apply the juice, make sure to use one made from animal hair. If it dissolves or the bristles stick together,[16] it isn't made with hair! I use a paintbrush that is cut straight across the edge (in other words, not round or angled) and is a half-inch wide. When I apply the juice, I make sure to use long, even strokes in the same direction. This helps form a smooth layer with just enough ridges to make removing the parts easy.

■ **Caution** When using a paintbrush that has lacquer or a similar coating on the handle, be sure to avoid getting any juice on the brush handle. The acetone can make the surface tacky. It can also dissolve paint. The best brushes to use are those made with bare wood handles and animal hair bristles.

The problem with using a paintbrush—beyond the construction of the brush—is cleaning it between uses. I use two jars for acetone. One contains my ABS juice mixture and another is pure acetone. I use the second jar to clean my brush after every use. I simply swish it around a few times, and then dry the bristles with a paper towel and allow it to dry. This method will work well if your juice is thin. If you make it too thick, it may be difficult to clean the brush properly.

Some people prefer to use cotton swabs or cotton tips rather than paintbrushes. Whatever works best for you is fine. The point is to get the juice on the glass as evenly as you can. Again, streaks are OK provided they are not wider than a millimeter or so.

There is one other thing I'd like to mention about ABS juice. Recall that you apply it directly to a glass surface. You can use it on other surfaces, but it isn't nearly as good, and in some cases it can make the surface unusable. For example, I would not apply juice directly to a heated bed (some printers have no glass covering over the heater) because it can damage the circuit board. I would also not use it on an aluminum surface, but some people have reported success with this.

---

[16]Animal hair does not dissolve in acetone.

Applying the ABS juice over Kapton tape may sound wasteful or perhaps eccentric, but it is neither. It is a matter of convenience. Not only does it mean that I can remove the juice completely by removing the Kapton tape, it also means that I can use the juice sparingly by using thinner layers. Not only that, but if I accidentally tear the Kapton tape, I can fill in that tear (if it is small) with a bit more juice. So in a way, it means I can repair torn Kapton with ABS juice.

I have also experimented with applying the juice only near the edges of the object. What I do is let the printer lay down the outer border of the object. The outer border is set up in the slicer and is used to clear the nozzle of filament before starting the print. It is a great way to demarcate where the objects are on the print surface. Once the printer is stopped, I move the axes away and apply juice (about 10mm wide) around the inner perimeter. This saves a little juice while reducing lift.

Whether you use ABS juice directly on Kapton tape (as is recommended) or apply it on top of glass, you will find it a better alternative than using walls or similar barriers to reduce lifting. I will talk more about how to control lifting in a later chapter.

■ **Caution**   Remember, acetone is corrosive and can be harmful if ingested or inhaled. Use care when handling acetone because it can cause skin irritation. Prolonged exposure can cause dry skin. Small amounts are not normally harmful. Perhaps worse, acetone is flammable. Never use it near a flame or devices that can spark. Always have a fire extinguisher nearby when working with flammable liquids.

Cartesian vs. Delta Printers

If you haven't seen, used, or owned a 3D printer, you may not be aware that there are distinct differences between a delta printer and other Cartesian 3D printers. There are several designs of 3D printers other than Cartesian and delta, but I will compare Cartesian and delta prints since these form the vast majority of designs used today.

Aside from the vertical orientation of all the axes, the most noticeable difference between Cartesian and delta printers is that the Cartesian printer has a rectangular build volume and the delta has a cylindrical build volume. You may see some delta designs that use a rectangular build plate, but the build volume is still cylindrical. Most delta printers will have a circular or hexagonal build plate. The reason for the cylindrical build volume is the unique geometry of the vertical axes. Delta printers also typically have a taller build height than Cartesian printers—another byproduct of the vertical axes orientation.

Another difference is in the orientation of the home position [0,0,0] for the axes. A Cartesian printer typically orients the home position in the forward, left position with all three axes at their starting position. Conversely, a delta printer orients the [0,0,0] position in the center of the build area. Thus, Cartesian printer axes travel from 0 to max, whereas the delta printer axes (just the X and Y axes) travel from –max to +max. For a delta printer with a 300mm diameter build plate (assuming it can utilize the entire area), the X and Y axes travel from -150 to +150. The Z axis on delta printers move from 0 to max.

In most 3D printers, each axis moves on a single plane (a Cartesian printer); the axes are independent and do not affect the resolution (movement) of the other planes. A delta printer, however, uses very small movements for all three axes in order to move to a specific location on the X-, Y-, and Z-planes.

A Cartesian printer allows movement of a single axis without affecting the movement of the other axes. That is, you can move the X axis from one position to another without changing the Y or Z axis. A delta printer would have to change all three axes in order to reposition on the X axis alone (or the Y axis).

This is because each axis on a delta printer can only move in the vertical direction. The mechanism of each axis is formed from two parallel arms attached to a single plate, or effector. All three axes therefore are connected together. Thus, in order to effect movement, all three axes must move in harmony. They can be a wonder to behold as they reposition the effector.[17]

The simplest movement is the Z axis. In this case, all three axes are moved at the same time. To move the effector and therefore the hot end up in the Z axis, all three axes are moved the same distance away from the build plate. Similarly, to move the hot end down in the Z axis, all three axes move in the same distance toward the build plate.

To move the effector (hot end) to a specific X or Y location at a set Z position, the delta printer uses algorithms to resolve the movement of each axis. While not precisely accurate, but analogous, each axis can be thought of as forming a parallelogram using a pair of right triangles with the axis as the vertical side, an imaginary line from the axis to the effector, and the parallel arms the hypotenuse. In order to resolve the X and Y position, the triangles must change in shape; that is, the vertical and horizontal lines must change in length because the hypotenuse is fixed (the parallel arms). However, since the horizontal lines are all attached together, the only side that needs to change is the vertical side. Since the hypotenuse is fixed, changing the length of one side changes the other and moving the axis up or down does this.

This is also known as a *limited degrees of freedom* concept. That is, the geometry is designed to fix endpoints to the effector, thereby providing three degrees of freedom. The effector cannot move in any direction other than horizontal along the X and Y plane, and moving all three axes at the same time raises or lowers that plane.

While somewhat simplified, this is how delta printers resolve movement in the X, Y, and Z axis. You will see exactly how the mathematics for this works in a later chapter. Now let's turn our attention to a discussion about getting a delta printer.

Getting a Delta Printer

Whether you are looking to buy your first delta printer or looking to move on to a newer model with more features, this section will guide you in the right direction. I will discuss the classes of printers and present advice on whether to buy or build a printer. I will also present some advice for those considering building their own delta printer and even those seeking to buy a used delta printer. Let's get started with a discussion of the options for getting a 3D printer.

Categories of 3D Printers

Unlike conventional ink-on-paper printers, there are few delta printers that have become available in retail stores. That is, you won't likely find a delta printer at your local big-box home electronics store (but you may soon). However, if you are in Orange County, California, you can visit the MatterHackers retail store in downtown Lake Forest (matterhackers.com/retail-store).

For those of us living elsewhere, where do you go to find a delta printer? Why, the Internet of course! A quick Google search for "delta printer" will result in many different forms of delta printers—from ones that resemble a mash-up of random parts to well-implemented professional models. But how do you know which one is right for you?

---

[17]Actually, I find all 3D printers mesmerizing. It's just that the delta does it with a bit more class and a bit of whimsy thrown in for good measure.

I will answer these questions by first discussing the options available. I have classified the various 3D printers and vendors into three categories. Although there are certainly other options available (like inventing your own 3D printer, as well as other types of 3D printers, like a UV-cured resin printer), the vast majority of the FFF printers fall into one of these categories. I describe each of these in more detail in the following sections.

- *Professional grade*: Mostly closed-source options with advanced features and paid support

- *Consumer grade*: Commercial offerings available as a kit or preassembled

- *Hobbyist grade*: Pure open source designs for DIY enthusiasts

Professional Grade

The first category contains those vendors that offer 3D printers manufactured for commercial sale to consumers. That is, they offer printers of their own design with mass-produced parts (from minor parts to the entire unit) that arrive with a warranty and support options. Such vendors have elaborate, professional web sites where you can not only buy their products, but also purchase parts and even get help using the products.

While these qualities may (and often do) apply to other 3D printer categories, these printers are typically built with a higher level of quality and precision. Vendors typically do not offer a full parts catalog; rather, they typically offer only those parts that are considered wear-and-maintenance items. As you can expect, they are typically more expensive. What you get for the extra cost is directly reflected in the quality and ease of use of the product.

For example, a professional-grade 3D printer normally does not need much in the way of setup and configuration. You won't eagerly unbox your new purchase and find a 300-page assembly manual. In fact, some printers arrive so well packed that it takes longer to get it out of the box than it does to get it to print!

That doesn't mean commercial printers are ready-to-print out of the box. You can assume any printer you buy will require some amount of setup to use it the first time. This may include some minor assembly, but normally doesn't require more than a few simple hand tools that are often included in the box. You can also expect to have to adjust the printer periodically.

An example of a professional-grade delta printer is the Orion Delta Desktop 3D Printer from SeeMeCNC,[18] as shown in Figure 1-17.

---

[18]See openbeamusa.com.

Figure 1-17. *Orion Delta Desktop 3D Printer (courtesy of SeeMeCNC.com)*

The Orion Delta Desktop 3D Printer arrives fully assembled, but requires attaching a few minor components—none of which are difficult or require any special skills. You also have to spend some time unwrapping and removing the printer from its packaging. This will likely take you longer than attaching the miscellaneous bits. A short instruction manual that details every step needed is provided. Within a short time, you will have your new printer unboxed and ready to print.

In general, you will find a commercial 3D printer to be a rewarding buying and owning experience. They do cost more, but the higher cost may be worth considering if you need to get started printing objects quickly.

■ **Note** In my book *Maintaining and Troubleshooting Your 3D Printer* (Apress, 2014), I ranked the Orion printer in the consumer-grade category; but after using the product, and from reviews from long-term users, it is clear that this printer is more of a professional-grade printer. In fact, most high-end delta printers can be classified in either category because they share the same qualities.

Consumer Grade

The next category contains those 3D printers that are available as partial kits (some parts preassembled), full kits (requires you to do all the assembly work), or fully assembled. They aren't full, professional offerings since vendors typically don't offer the same level of services and support (although some do). Even for those that do offer professional services, the level of assembly is the main feature of this class of printer.

Don't be tempted to think that self-assembly means lower quality. This is generally not true; rather, the self-assembly aspect has more to do with shipping costs. Furthermore, some of the printers in this category are priced competitively with some of the printers in the professional-grade category. However, it is the kit format that permits vendors in this category to offer some of their 3D printers at lower prices, because it saves the cost of labor required for an assembly line. This is likely to be the case for small (and growing) companies. The kit form therefore offers you a price break in exchange for a few hours of your time.

If you purchase a 3D printer that comes as a kit, you can expect it to be fairly easy to assemble, requiring a small number of tools and a moderate level of skill. These printers aren't quite as simple as assembling a tricycle, but can sometimes require the same level of patience required for assembling furniture from Scandinavia. The time it takes to assemble varies, but in general you can expect assembly to vary from a few hours to an afternoon or three. Of course, your own skills, patience, and time constraints will play a factor in how long it takes you to assemble the kit. I like to double the vendor's estimate, and then add 50% more for those "oh, drat" moments.

So what do 3D printers in this category have in common besides the fact that they require some assembly? As you may surmise, it has to do with how the product is offered and the level of support available. Some vendors offer the same level of services as professional-grade vendors, but more often, vendors in this category have limited support on their web sites and either do not offer any paid support or do not offer any phone support. Although this may not be an issue for some, if you are concerned about getting help with your printer, you may want to examine a vendor's web site carefully, and before buying one of their 3D printers, ask if they provide any level of support.

Another aspect of 3D printers in this category is the material used in construction. While most use commodity components (e.g., stepper motors, bolts, etc.), the material used for the major frame components can range from laser-cut wooden platforms, like the SeeMeCNC line of printers, to the metal components found in the OpenBeam USA Delta printers.

None of this should affect or prevent you from buying a consumer-grade 3D printer. If you have some mechanical and electronics skills, as well as the desire to tinker, and you don't mind having to spend a little time putting the printer together yourself, you can save some money and have some fun at the same time!

An example of a consumer-grade delta printer is the Kossel Pro 3D Printer from OpenBeam, as shown in Figure 1-18.

Figure 1-18. *Kossel Pro 3D Printer (courtesy of openbeam.com)*

The Kossel Pro 3D Printer uses high-quality bespoke components that are well designed and go together easily. Although assembly can take some time, the documentation provided is very good and most of the tedious assembly (like the hot end) has been completed. The quality of this printer is quite high and if not for the extended assembly and configuration time, the printer could be classified as professional grade.

In summary, consumer-grade 3D printers are a good option for those who want or can handle a 3D printer that requires some assembly, for those who don't mind working on the printer, and for those who don't need technical support (free or otherwise). These 3D printers are a mix of customized designs with some open source derivations. The quality of the printers ranges from a bit below (but still considered good) to comparable with professional-grade 3D printers. They are sometimes cheaper than professional-grade 3D printers and parts are more readily available. Some vendors offer warranties, but those that do have shorter warranty periods than professional-grade vendors. Lastly, consumer-grade 3D printers require more time and skill to operate and maintain.

Hobbyist Grade (RepRap)

The vendors in this category offer 3D printers that are implementations of one or more RepRap designs. They are open source and almost entirely DIY. That is, the printers require assembly from scratch. However, you can find complete kits, as well as some vendors who sell assembled units.

These kits are not designed for those who want to open the box and start printing. This is one of the tenets or perhaps rules of the RepRap world—you are expected to have the technical skills to put it together. Those with less skill can assemble some kits, but most kits require some mechanical skills, soldering, and a zeal for tinkering.

If you do not have these skills and you don't want to learn them, or if you don't have the time to devote to assembling your own 3D printer, you may want to consider a consumer-grade printer kit or an assembled 3D printer. You should also consider the fact that RepRap 3D printers require a fair bit of maintenance and tinkering to get working well. Thus, you may still need to repair and maintain it.[19]

Most of the vendors in this category do not offer much in the way of services, but most at least make their manuals and assembly guides available for download. Although a few offer phone support, most will answer your questions via e-mail within a day or so.

The main reason for this is that the vendors are striving to make RepRap printers more widely available. They've done all the hard work for you by sourcing the various parts and ensuring that the parts work together. Consequently, most vendors allow you to pick and choose options when ordering their kits.

For example, if you decide to use a different electronics board, you can usually specify that when you order the kit. Similarly, you can often find kits that have part of the components omitted, permitting you to buy only what you need. I find this very convenient because it allows me to upgrade a RepRap printer from one iteration to another, reusing the motors, electronics, and extruder. If you are thinking about getting another printer because your old one is a bit dated or it doesn't have some of the latest features, look for vendors that offer partial kits so that you can save some money and get a new printer in the bargain.

■ **Tip**   If you are considering sourcing your own kit or want to learn more about other, Cartesian RepRap designs, you may want to read *Maintaining and Troubleshooting Your 3D Printer* (Apress, 2014). It contains a detailed discussion on sourcing components.

The Mini Kossel is an excellent choice for those who want to build a delta printer from scratch. The design is very well-thought-out and assembly is much shorter than a traditional Cartesian RepRap. Furthermore, the design allows for a host of customization and options that you can explore. For example, you can add a heated bed, an LCD panel, cooling fans, and more.

You can find Mini Kossel kits and parts from a variety of vendors from online auction sites to online retailers such as TriDPrinting (`tridprinting.com/BOM/Kossel-Mini/`), which sells individual parts, Blomker Industries (`http://blomker.com`), which sells complete kits, and Maker Geeks[20] (`makergeeks.com/mikofudiypae.html`), which sells parts and complete kits for a variety of 3D printers.

The Mini Kossel is just one of several RepRap delta printer designs. I will discuss some of the other designs in a later chapter. However, I consider the Mini Kossel the most refined of the RepRap delta printers and therefore the best choice in this class of printer. Figure 1-19 shows an example of a RepRap delta printer. In this case, it is a heavily modified Mini Kossel.

---

[19]While your mileage may vary, all 3D printers need maintenance and repair to ensure proper operation.
[20]If you want a premium heated print bed, check out the aluminum Mini Kossel option.

Figure 1-19. *Mini Kossel RepRap Printer*

In summary, RepRap printers are pure and simply DIY. The vendors that support RepRap 3D printers typically offer kits or parts only, and little or no online technical support. Most provide excellent documentation for their kits, but seldom include any help for assembly. Did I mention that they're DIY?

A RepRap kit is a good choice for someone who wants to learn how the printers work or someone who wants to tinker. Due to the lower cost of the kits, a RepRap kit can be a good way for someone to enter the 3D printing world, but success or failure lies in the hands of the buyer. You can find a lot of help on the Internet, including the RepRap wiki (`reprap.org`) and the deltabot mailing list (`groups.google.com/group/ deltabot`), but you should not expect to be able to pick up the phone and ask your vendor for help. Did I mention it's DIY only?

Build or Buy?

The answer to the question of whether to build your own printer or buy a ready-to-go printer lies in your assessment of your skills and your desire to learn. If you are confident you can handle any electrical or mechanical task needed to build a 3D printer, and you have the time necessary to devote to the task and to learn new skills, then a 3D printer kit is an option you will want to consider. On the other hand, if you don't have the skills or you don't have the time to learn those skills, much less the time to build the printer, you may want to consider buying a printer that is ready-to-print.

Reasons for Building Your Own Delta Printer

There are two main reasons why you would want to opt to build your own printer. First, you enjoy working on a project that requires you to spend a lot of time during construction and configuration. Second, you want to save some money. Other reasons include wanting to build a 3D printer with specific unique features or you want to be able to upgrade the printer in the future.

If you want to embark on a build option, you should plan to spend anywhere from a single afternoon (for some assembly-required kits) to about 40 to 60 hours or more for a built-from-scratch delta printer. Although this estimate may seem very high (and some would say it is), realistically you should anticipate it taking more than a long weekend to complete—and that's if you have all the parts and they all work! In addition, you should plan to spend some time configuring and calibrating your new printer. In my own experience, from someone who has built quite a few 3D printers, building a Mini Kossel from scratch is easier and faster than most Cartesian RepRap printers. It should be noted that the skillset is exactly the same for building a delta or a Cartesian 3D printer.

However, you should not try to rush through the build, but take your time to get things right. You will be glad you did. Once you have your printer whirring away, laying down plastic to make a whistle or another small gewgaw, you will be glad you took the time to get it right. So if you want a challenge and time isn't an issue, building your own printer is a good option.

Currently, there are far more kits than there are completed or partially completed delta printers for sale. Thus, it is likely you will encounter more people who have built their own delta printer than those who have bought assembled printers. But that trend is changing with the efforts of vendors like SeeMeCNC and OpenBeam (but there are many others on `kickstarter.com`).

Reasons for Buying a Delta Printer

Ready-to-print delta printers encompass all the professional-grade class of 3D printers and any 3D printer in the consumer-grade class that comes mostly assembled or can be ordered assembled.

There are several reasons for choosing a professionally assembled delta printer. One reason is time. If you need to get started printing objects quickly and do not have time to learn how to build (and then configure and calibrate) your own delta printer, either from a kit or from scratch, you will want to choose a professional- or consumer-grade option.

Another reason you may want to buy a printer that is ready-to-go concerns quality. The print quality is generally better than what you may achieve if you built your own delta printer. This isn't always the case, however, and it is more often applicable to professional-grade options. Regardless, if quality is a concern, you may want to buy a printer with a good reputation for high-quality prints.

Additionally, a ready-to-print option is easier to use and more reliable. That is, a ready-to-print option means all the hard work of configuration and calibration has been done for you. Although you may need to spend some time to get the printer set up properly once you've unboxed it, this is typically a small fraction of the time required to build your own delta printer, because you don't have to invest the time required to get everything fit together and working. This goes far beyond the mundane mechanics of the assembly.

Perhaps the most important factor in buying a ready-to-go printer is technical support. If you do not have or do not want to learn the skills required to diagnose or fix problems with your delta printer, you should buy your printer from a vendor that offers a support option, or at the least a very good warranty and a support forum and help line.

Buying a Used 3D Printer

If your budget limits your buying power or you are looking for a bargain, a used printer may be a good choice. You can often get a slightly used delta printer for about 75% of the price of a new one. However, like all used purchases, you need to do your homework to ensure that you are getting a well-maintained and reliable printer.

The following lists several considerations and some advice on how to buy a used delta printer. If you follow this advice, you should be able to find a good printer to fit your budget.

- *Online auction sites are an excellent place to look for a 3D printer.* If you apply a little patience and avoid the temptation to join a bidding frenzy, you will find the printer you want at the price you are willing to pay.

- *Set your expectations based on your budget.* Remember, real bargains are hard to come by. If the price is too good to be true, chances are there is something wrong with it.

- *Find the printer with the lowest usage.* I've seen cases where used printers have no more than a few hours of use. Avoid printers with hundreds of hours of use, or are broken, or advertised as non-working or needs work.

- *Beware of highly modified printers.* Buying a well-tuned printer is a good idea, but don't pay extra for all the add-ons and upgrades. It is possible those upgrades could be useless or even detrimental to your print quality. Some people will raise the price thinking the extras are worth more, but this is generally not the case.[21]

- If you are seeking a professional-grade printer, check to see if there is an extended warranty and that it can be transferred to you (most cannot).

- Ask if the seller is the original owner. If the printer has passed among several owners, you may want to pass on it as well. Similarly, if the seller professes he knows nothing about it, do not buy it for any price short of the absurd. Chances are that if you encounter a problem, the seller will politely refuse to help you (some state this up front in fact).

- Check for the original accessories. Look for printers that come with the original manuals and all accessories. Consumables may not be included, but the original tools and whatnot should.

- Be very careful if buying from a seller who doesn't have the original shipping box. This shouldn't be a deal breaker, but you should insist on shipping insurance and ask the seller to explain how they plan to prepare the printer for shipping. You should also ensure that they secure the axes for shipping.

- Ask to see hi-res photos of printed objects. Check the quality carefully. If you see any anomalies or quality issues, don't buy the printer.

- Good communication is the key to a good sale. If the seller is willing to exchange e-mails and answer questions promptly, it is a good sign. Don't buy from a seller who won't return your e-mails, dodges questions, or takes a long time to respond.

- Lastly, ask the seller whether he will take the printer back for a full refund if there is something wrong with it. You may have to pay return shipping but the peace of mind of getting a refund is worth paying a bit more for the reassurance.

---

[21]This is especially true for motorcycles and sports cars. Adding thousands of dollars of accessories will only net you about 10% of the cost of those accessories.

Summary

A delta 3D printer is a very different take on 3D printer designs. Delta printers solve a number of problems with Cartesian printers (but have a few of their own, as you will see in a later chapter), have a smaller footprint, and can achieve higher movement rates. As a plus, they're really neat to watch when printing.

In this chapter, you discovered how 3D printing works, learned about the software or workflow for 3D printing, and looked at the consumables used in 3D printing. I also discussed the options for getting your own delta printer.

The next chapter examines how the delta hardware mechanisms work in greater detail. I will remove the veil that obscures the magic in the machine.

CHAPTER 2

Delta Printer Hardware

The delta 3D printer design, despite the radically different axes arrangement, uses the same basic hardware as a Cartesian printer. For example, there isn't anything special about the stepper motors, electronics board,[1] or even the hot end. The differences are in how the axes are arranged (all three are vertical), and that the print bed is typically round (older designs use square or rectangular build surfaces) and the frame is typically triangular. These qualities alone are what give the delta printer its unique vertical form with a small footprint.

Note Internet lore[2] defines delta printers by their triangular or prismatic frame shape. However, not all delta printers have that shape. Some have cylindrical frames that resemble a cylinder more than a prism, and early designs employed rectangular frames.

In this chapter, you discover how a delta printer works; how delta printers are constructed, including all the components for the frame, axes, electronics; and more. You will also look at a few variants of delta printer designs.

While all delta printer designs share the same axes arrangement, they can vary greatly in how they are constructed. For example, the frame can range from printed components attached to wood pieces, entire frames made from wood, frames that incorporate aluminum extrusion uprights attached to wood or printed parts, as well as smooth rods for the towers.

Before you learn more about the hardware, let's see how a delta printer works. That is, how it can resolve positioning the hot end to a specific location within the build volume.

Anatomy of a Delta Printer

In this section, I explore the components that make up a delta printer from the perspective of how the components work as part of the whole. I will discuss the hardware that makes up these components in the next section. Knowing how the components work will give a much better insight on how the printer is constructed. Not only will this help you understand your printer better, but it can also help you should you decide to build your own delta printer.

---

[1]Some earlier firmware did not support delta printers. Fortunately, Marlin and Repetier-Host fully support delta printers.
[2]It's on the Internet, so it must be true, eh?

I begin with the axes arrangement and how the printer can position the hot end within the build volume. Following that, you learn about the extruder, electronics, and build plate. To get started, let's review the names of the various components that make up a delta printer. Figure 2-1 shows a mock-up of a typical delta printer with the components labeled. This image depicts the major components of the delta design. This is not a complete or even dimensionally accurate drawing, but it does illuminate the components that I will discuss.

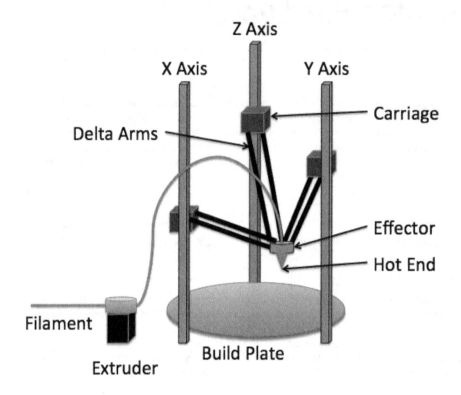

Figure 2-1. *Anatomy of a delta printer*

Starting from the lower-left corner, you see the following:

- *Extruder*: Also called the *cold end*. Responsible for feeding the filament to the hot end.

- *Build plate*: Where the printed parts are formed. Some build plates are heated.

- *Axes*: Arranged vertically and labeled counter-clockwise as X, Y, and Z.

- *Carriage*: Attaches to the axis mechanism and provides a mount point for the delta arms.

- *Effector*: The base where the hot end is mounted.

- *Delta arms*: Attaches to the carriage and the effector using a pair of parallel arms.

- *Hot end*: A special heater that heats the nozzle for melting (glassing) the filament for extrusion.

Now that you have the terminology down, let's see how the axis mechanisms work.

Axes

Each axis is mounted so that travel is in the vertical direction. A carriage is mounted on the axis movement and forms one side of a link of parallel arms that connect the carriage to the effector. Thus, as the axis moves up and down, the carriage moves along with it.

Recall that the combination of delta arms, effector, and axis movement forms a right triangle, as shown in Figure 2-2. Here you see that the delta arms forms the hypotenuse of a right triangle, formed by the vertical axis, and an imaginary line drawn from the axis to the effector.

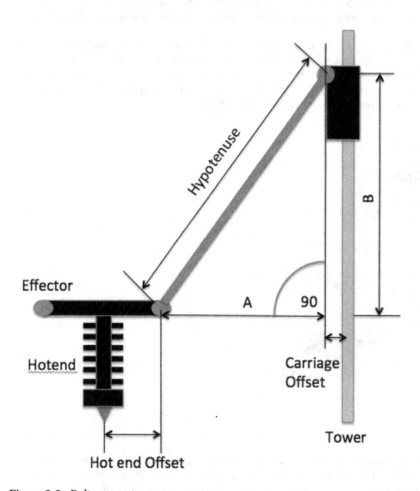

Figure 2-2. Delta geometry

Notice that there are two offsets you must also consider. There is a small distance from the center of the axis movement to the mount point for the delta arms on the carriage. There is also a short distance, as measured from the delta arm mount point on the effector to the center of the nozzle on the hot end. Thus, any calculation must also consider these measurements when positioning the effector.

▪ **Note**   Figure 2-2 shows only one axis, but the measurements and angles defined are the same on all three axes.

So how does the printer (the firmware) figure out where to position the effector using this data? It's a clever use of trigonometric equations made easier given the axis, delta arms, and effector form a right triangle.[3] With this information you can calculate how much to move the one side (B) in order to move the effector (side A). In this case, you know the hypotenuse is always the same length (the delta arms), so to calculate a movement you use the formula for calculating the sides of a right triangle by using the sum of squares.

But this is only half of the calculations needed. You also need to know where each tower is located in relation to one another. If you envision looking down from the top of the printer, the axes are located as shown in Figure 2-3. Notice the angles formed by the imaginary triangles superimposed over the build plate. You can simplify the math a bit if you consider that the delta arms form a parallelogram, and thus you need only calculate the triangle representing the center of each pair of arms.

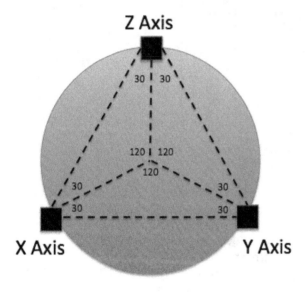

Figure 2-3. *Location of towers*

Notice that the triangles formed allow you to know where the towers are in relation to one another. In fact, once you know the radius of the circle formed from intersecting with each tower (also called *delta radius*), you can calculate the location of each tower using sine and cosine functions. Listing 2-1 is an excerpt from the Marlin firmware (located in Configuration.h).

---

[3]See themathpage.com/atrig/solve-right-triangles.htm.

Listing 2-1. Calculating Location of Towers

```
#define DELTA_TOWER1_X -SIN_60*DELTA_RADIUS // front left tower
#define DELTA_TOWER1_Y -COS_60*DELTA_RADIUS
#define DELTA_TOWER2_X SIN_60*DELTA_RADIUS // front right tower
#define DELTA_TOWER2_Y -COS_60*DELTA_RADIUS
#define DELTA_TOWER3_X 0.0 // back middle tower
#define DELTA_TOWER3_Y DELTA_RADIUS
```

Here you see that the Marlin firmware uses the Y tower as the starting point for the calculation (an arbitrary assignment, as the calculations would be the same for any origin).

Now that you know where each tower is located in relation to one another, you can calculate any movements by using the location of the tower, the original position of each axis, and the Cartesian location of where you want to move. Listing 2-2 shows the calculations from the Marlin firmware (located in `Marlin_main.cpp`).

Listing 2-2. Calculating the Delta Movement

```
void calculate_delta(float cartesian[3])
{
  delta[X_AXIS] = sqrt(DELTA_DIAGONAL_ROD_2
                       - sq(DELTA_TOWER1_X-cartesian[X_AXIS])
                       - sq(DELTA_TOWER1_Y-cartesian[Y_AXIS])
                       ) + cartesian[Z_AXIS];
  delta[Y_AXIS] = sqrt(DELTA_DIAGONAL_ROD_2
                       - sq(DELTA_TOWER2_X-cartesian[X_AXIS])
                       - sq(DELTA_TOWER2_Y-cartesian[Y_AXIS])
                       ) + cartesian[Z_AXIS];
  delta[Z_AXIS] = sqrt(DELTA_DIAGONAL_ROD_2
                       - sq(DELTA_TOWER3_X-cartesian[X_AXIS])
                       - sq(DELTA_TOWER3_Y-cartesian[Y_AXIS])
                       ) + cartesian[Z_AXIS];
}
```

As you can see, the firmware calculates solutions for all three axes. In this way, the printer moves all three axes simultaneously to reposition the hot end. Pretty cool, eh?

There is a little bit more involved in calculating the position for each axis. If the printer supports auto bed leveling (Z-probing), there are additional calculations performed after these to refine the positions. Not to mention the adjustments made for the carriage, effector, and hot-end offsets. However, for our discussion, consider these calculations as those responsible for positioning the effector.

Let's look at an example of the calculations. In this example, you position the printer to the Cartesian values [0,0,0][4] and you want to move the effector to position [–40,20,15]. Furthermore, you want to see how the preceding calculations resolve to movements of the three axes. I use a Kossel Pro printer as an example, but you can use your own delta printer. However, if you are in the process of building your printer, or if you have not configured or calibrated the printer, you may want to read the next two chapters and then return to this exercise; or simply follow along as I demonstrate the math.

Begin by moving the hot end to the bed center position. You can use your printer controller software or LCD to do this. Next, use a small section of masking or blue painter's tape and mark the location of each carriage on the towers. Figure 2-4 shows an example of marking the X tower on my printer. Be sure to position the tape so that it does not interfere with axis movement.

---

[4]The actual Z position is the minimal Z-height. For example, the nozzle is normally positioned 0.15mm – 0.25mm above the print bed at Z = 0.

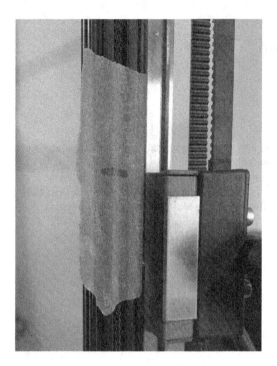

Figure 2-4. Marking the carriage position

■ **Note**   While not purely scientific, the following will demonstrate how these calculations resolve the position of each axis to effect movement within the build volume.

Next, move the effector to the left 40mm (X = –40) and forward 20mm (Y = 20), and then raise the effector 15mm (Z = 15). Once in position, measure the distance that each axis has moved. Don't worry about being accurate because this isn't a scientific test, rather a demonstration. Figure 2-5 shows how I measured one of the axes.

TOWER AND AXIS NAMING

In a Cartesian printer, each axis moves separately in a single plane. Thus, it is correct to simply refer to each movement of the axis in the X, Y, or Z direction. However, in the delta coordinate system, each axis is oriented vertically, and thus the X and Y axes mechanisms do not move in the same plane. Only the Z tower can be considered in the same plane. But that is not correct either. Recall that it requires movement from all three axes to effect a movement in the X, Y, and Z planes.

Thus, you refer to each axis movement as A, B, and C or alpha, beta, and gamma corresponding to the X, Y, and Z towers. You may find some delta literature that refers to these as the A, B, and C towers. When you measure the axis movement, not the position of the effector, you refer to the axis movement as A, B, and C.

Figure 2-5. *Measuring axis movement*

When I measured my towers, I found the following:

```
X Tower (A) = 25.5mm
Y Tower (B) = -17mm
Z Tower (C) = 23mm
```

Notice the signs I used. When the axis moves "up," it is moving in the positive direction. Thus, if the carriage is located above your mark, you measure that as a positive value; when the carriage is below the mark, you measure it as a negative value.

Now let's do the math. Rather than solve the equations by hand, I wrote a short Python script to perform the calculations. Listing 2-3 shows the code I created. You can download source code for this book from apress.com/9781484211748?gtmf=s. I simplify the code a bit to make it easier to read, but the calculations are exactly the same as the preceding ones.

Listing 2-3. Cartesian to Delta Simulation

```python
import math
import argparse

DELTA_DIAGONAL_ROD = 300.0
DELTA_SMOOTH_ROD_OFFSET = 212.357
DELTA_EFFECTOR_OFFSET = 30.0
DELTA_CARRIAGE_OFFSET = 30.0
DELTA_RADIUS = (DELTA_SMOOTH_ROD_OFFSET-DELTA_EFFECTOR_OFFSET-DELTA_CARRIAGE_OFFSET)
DELTA_PRINTABLE_RADIUS = 127.0
```

```python
SIN_60 = math.sin(math.pi/3)
COS_60 = 0.5
DELTA_TOWER1_X = -SIN_60*DELTA_RADIUS
DELTA_TOWER1_Y = -COS_60*DELTA_RADIUS
DELTA_TOWER2_X = SIN_60*DELTA_RADIUS
DELTA_TOWER2_Y = -COS_60*DELTA_RADIUS
DELTA_TOWER3_X = 0.0
DELTA_TOWER3_Y = DELTA_RADIUS
DELTA_DIAGONAL_ROD_2  = (DELTA_DIAGONAL_ROD*DELTA_DIAGONAL_ROD)
Z_MAX_POS = 280.67

X_AXIS = 0
Y_AXIS = 1
Z_AXIS = 2

delta= [0.0,0.0,0.0];
current_pos = [0.0,0.0,0.0]
difference = delta

parser = argparse.ArgumentParser(description='Provide Cartesian coordinates.')
parser.add_argument('source', nargs=3, type=float,
                    help='Cartesian values for starting position.')
parser.add_argument('destination', nargs=3, type=float,
                    help='Cartesian values for ending position.')
args = parser.parse_args()

def sq(d):
  return d * d;

def calculate_delta(cartesian):
  delta[X_AXIS] = math.sqrt(DELTA_DIAGONAL_ROD_2
                      - sq(DELTA_TOWER1_X-cartesian[X_AXIS])
                      - sq(DELTA_TOWER1_Y-cartesian[Y_AXIS])
                      ) + cartesian[Z_AXIS];
  delta[Y_AXIS] = math.sqrt(DELTA_DIAGONAL_ROD_2
                      - sq(DELTA_TOWER2_X-cartesian[X_AXIS])
                      - sq(DELTA_TOWER2_Y-cartesian[Y_AXIS])
                      ) + cartesian[Z_AXIS];
  delta[Z_AXIS] = math.sqrt(DELTA_DIAGONAL_ROD_2
                      - sq(DELTA_TOWER3_X-cartesian[X_AXIS])
                      - sq(DELTA_TOWER3_Y-cartesian[Y_AXIS])
                      ) + cartesian[Z_AXIS];
  print "  Cartesian =", cartesian, "\n  Delta =", delta

print "Delta kinematics conversion simulation:"
print "From:"
calculate_delta(args.source)
current_pos[X_AXIS] = delta[X_AXIS]
current_pos[Y_AXIS] = delta[Y_AXIS]
current_pos[Z_AXIS] = delta[Z_AXIS]
```

```
print "To:"
calculate_delta(args.destination)
difference[X_AXIS] = delta[X_AXIS] - current_pos[X_AXIS]
difference[Y_AXIS] = delta[Y_AXIS] - current_pos[Y_AXIS]
difference[Z_AXIS] = delta[Z_AXIS] - current_pos[Z_AXIS]
print "Difference:"
print "  X Tower:", difference[X_AXIS]
print "  Y Tower:", difference[Y_AXIS]
print "  Z Tower:", difference[Z_AXIS]
```

Notice that I copied in a number of definitions for various values. I retrieved these directly from the firmware (located in Configuration.h), converting them to Python (a minor syntax difference). If you want to do this for your printer, you will have to change these defaults to match. You will see where these values are located in Chapter 3.[5]

To use this code, you execute it passing in six values. The first three are the starting position, [0,0,0], the next three are the ending position, [–40,20,15]. The code then calculates the delta values for each and then calculates the difference, producing the distance each axis must travel to reposition the effector (hot end). Listing 2-4 shows the results of running this script.

Listing 2-4. Delta Simulation Results

```
$ python delta.py 0 0 0 -40 20 15
Delta kinematics conversion simulation:
From:
  Cartesian = [0.0, 0.0, 0.0]
  Delta = [258.43247580557676, 258.43247580557676, 258.43247580557676]
To:
  Cartesian = [-40.0, 20.0, 15.0]
  Delta = [283.878796387054, 241.2401422282287, 281.23603165424475]
Difference:
  X Tower: 25.4463205815
  Y Tower: -17.1923335773
  Z Tower: 22.8035558487
```

Notice here the values produced for X, Y, and Z. Recall that I measured values 25.5, -17, and 23. Clearly, the calculations worked because the measured values were approximately the same as those shown in the output. Try it yourself by choosing other values.

If the code and calculations described here are still a mystery, don't worry because all these are built into the firmware, and thankfully not something you have to calculate yourself. However, as you will see in Chapter 5, it is good to know how the printer calculates positions so that you can move the hot end (effector) to a position located at the base of each tower. This is needed for calibrating the towers and endstop positions.

Now that you understand how a delta printer uses three vertical-axis mechanisms to resolve any X,Y,Z position within the build volume, let's look at the hardware components that make all this magic work.

---

[5]Yes, this is a bit of horse-before-the-cart, but I feel it is important to understand how the mathematics works in a general sense, which should help you understand what all these values are and how they affect the calculations.

Hardware Components

The hardware and materials used to construct delta printers varies greatly, despite some fundamental concepts. You can find printers that are made from wood, others constructed with major components made from plastic, and some that are constructed from a sturdy metal frame, but most will be made using a combination of these materials. Not only do the materials used in constructing the frame vary, so do the mechanisms used to move the print head and extrude filament, but not nearly as much as the frame.

A delta printer is a special type of machine called a *robot*. You may think of robots as anthropomorphic devices that hobble around bleeping and blinking various lights (or bashing each other to scrap in an extremely geeky contest), but not all robots have legs, wheels, or other forms of mobility. Indeed, according to Wikipedia, a robot is "a mechanical or virtual agent, usually an electromechanical machine that is guided by a computer program or electronic circuitry". As you will see, delta printers fit that description quite well.

The following sections introduce the hardware as follows: the hardware used in extruding plastic (extruder or cold end and the hot end), delta arms, axes, types of electric motors used, build platform, electronics, and finally, the frame. Each section describes some of the variants you can expect to find, and some of the trade-offs for certain options.

Extruder

The *extruder* is the component that controls the amount of plastic used to build the object. On a delta printer, the extruder is normally mounted in a fixed position on the frame[6] (also called the *cold end*) and connected to the hot end via a Bowden tube. I have seen at least one delta printer that mounted the extruder on the effector, but that design is an exception because the goal is normally to reduce the weight of the effector, delta arms, and hot end to allow for faster movement.

When the hot end is at the correct temperature for the filament used, the extruder pushes the filament through the Bowden tube, and as the effector is moved, the plastic is extruded through the nozzle.

Figure 2-6 shows a photo of a 3D printer extruder assembly. The filament is fed into the top of the extruder. This is a direct-drive extruder that does not use any gears (although geared stepper motors can be used if you need a different ratio). Thus, there is a stepper motor attached to the extruder that turns the filament drive gear. This is called an EZStruder from SeeMeCNC (`http://seemecnc.com/collections/parts-accesories/products/ezstruder-cold-end-kit`).

---

[6]There are delta printers with an extruder directly on the effector, and others where the extruder is suspended on elastic strings just above the effector with a very short Bowden tube.

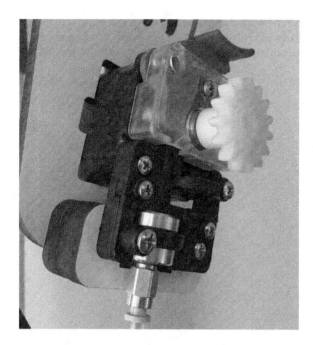

Figure 2-6. *Extruder assembly (EZStruder by SeeMeCNC)*

Figure 2-7 shows an example of a different extruder. This is an Airtripper extruder (`thingiverse.com/thing:126778`), which is a very popular choice for 3D printer builders.

Figure 2-7. *Extruder assembly mounted on a Mini Kossel*

49

Figure 2-8 shows an example of a filament drive gear. Notice the splines or grooves machined into the pulley. These help the pulley grip the filament. Indeed, as you will learn in Chapters 6 and 7, these grooves can become clogged with filament, causing the extruder to slip. This is a common source of problems and a frequent maintenance task.

Figure 2-8. *Filament drive gear*

In almost all cases, extruders use a tension mechanism to help the extruder grip the filament. For example, the EZStruder uses a spring-loaded arm and the Airtripper extruder uses a door with an idler pulley (in this case, a small sealed bearing). The extruder shown in Figure 2-8 is a modification of the original Airtripper design that uses springs instead of a flexible hose to keep tension on the drive pulley.

Now that you have an idea of how the extruder heats and extrudes plastic to form objects, let's talk briefly about where all that plastic goes—the hot end!

Hot End

The hot end, if you recall, is responsible for accepting the filament fed from the extruder body, and heating it to its melting point. You can see one of the latest hot-end upgrades for 3D printers in Figure 2-9. This is an E3D v6 all-metal hot end (`http://e3d-online.com/E3D-v6/Full-Kit`).

Figure 2-9. *E3E v6 hot end (courtesy of MatterHackers)[7]*

This hot end can be used with higher heat ranges and provides a very good extrusion rate for PLA, ABS, and other filaments. Notice the fan and shroud. This hot end, like most all-metal hot ends, must have a fan blowing across the cooling fins at all times. That is, the fan is always running.

There are dozens of hot end designs available for 3D printers. This may seem like an exaggeration, but it isn't. My research revealed several sites listing 10 or even 20 designs. The site that seems most complete is at `https://sites.google.com/site/3dprinterlist/home/hot-ends`. You will find links to details about each of the more than 50 hot ends listed—and this list is a bit out of date because there are even more available.

With so many hot-end designs, how do you know which one to choose or even which one is best for your printer, filament, and object design choices? Fortunately, most hot-end designs can be loosely categorized by their construction into two types: all metal and PEEK body with PTFE (polytetrafluoroethylene) liner. There are some exceptions, like an all-metal design with a PTFE liner; but in general, they either are made from various metals, such as brass for the nozzle, aluminum for the body (with cooling fins), and stainless steel for the heat barrier, or use a liner of some sort. The most popular PEEK variant is called a J-head hot end. Most delta printers come with either an all-metal hot end or a J-head hot end.

If you have a choice of hot ends, you may want to consider using an all-metal hot end. An all-metal hot end offers several advantages, including the following:

- A higher operating temperature range that allows you to use a wider variety of filament.

- The print quality is generally cleaner given that the fins allow a smaller heat zone and thus better retraction and less oozing.

- Most have fewer parts, and therefore are easier to maintain.

Now let's revisit the axis movement and discover the hardware used to raise and lower each axis.

---

[7]See `matterhackers.com/store/printer-accessories/v6-hot end-full-kit-1.75mm-universal`.

Axis Movement

A 3D printer gets its name from the number of planes it uses to construct objects. Technically, the axes movement is called a *three-dimensional Cartesian coordinate system*. Recall that the delta printer has its X axis oriented left to right, the Y axis front to back, and of course, the Z axis up and down.

Since the origin is in the center, as the printer moves the X axis to the left, its position is recorded as a negative value; and as it moves to the right, the position is increased, and when it is to the right of the origin, the values are positive. Similarly, the Y axis is positive toward the rear of the build plate and negative toward the front. Figure 2-10 depicts a cube that illustrates the planes of movement with a cylinder, representing the build volume of a delta printer superimposed. Notice that in the drawing, the end points of the axes are labeled with a plus or minus sign. This is representative of how the printer moves.

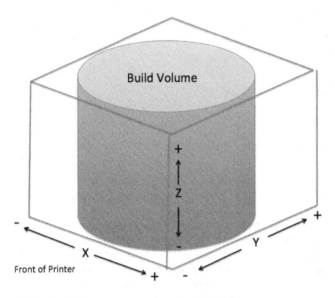

Figure 2-10. *Axes movement and orientation*

So how does the printer move the axis and how does it work? This is an area that can vary among delta printers, but fortunately there are only a few different mechanisms. Some use smooth rods with bearings to support the mechanical parts of the axis, whereas others use wheels running in tracks. Bearings can be made from plastic, oil-infused bronze, or special ball bearings (called *linear bearings*). Still others use a special rail with recirculating ball bearings. This is called a *linear rail*. Movement of the axis is accomplished with an electric motor and either a belt or a cable. I will explain each example mechanism in the forthcoming sections.

Whichever mechanism is used to move the axis, the geometry of that mechanism must be known and entered into the firmware. For example, the size of the drive pulley (the one mounted on the electric motor) and the number of teeth per millimeter of the belt are critical for determining how far the firmware must turn the motor to move the axis a fraction of a millimeter.

Smooth Rods

The earliest form of vertical delta printer axis mechanisms used a pair of smooth rails with linear roller bearings, brass bushings, or even bushings made from Nylon or PLA (and thus printed). Figure 2-11 shows a carriage from an earlier Rostock printer designed by Johann C. Rocholl (`https://github.com/jcrocholl/rostock` or `thingiverse.com/thing:17175`).

Figure 2-11. *Linear bearings on smooth rods (courtesy of Johann C. Rocholl)*

Notice that the linear bearings are attached to the carriage using zip ties. Other forms of carriages have used clamps or press-in options to secure the bearings. Also notice that the delta arm mounts are built into the carriage design.

While this solution results in a very secure mechanism, rods can be more expensive, depending on the quality of the material. That is, precision ground smooth rods may be too expensive and a bit of overkill for most home 3D printers. Cheaper drill rod quality items may be much more economic. In fact, you can often find lower prices for drill rods if bought in bulk.

In addition, the linear bearings can be expensive too. Even if you use printed bearings or less expensive bushings, smooth rods have an inherent problem.

The longer the rod, the more likelihood the rod will have a slight bend or imperfection that causes the carriage to ride unevenly, which is transmitted to the effector. While this is not a serious problem unless the bend is significant, it can result is slightly lower print quality. You can check this easily by rolling the rods on a flat, smooth surface looking for gaps between the rod and the surface.

Another disadvantage of smooth rods is that the frame formed by the rods is not stiff enough and can twist unless braced with wood or metal supporting framework. Thus to get the frame stiff enough to remove flexing, you end up with a much bulkier frame with more material.

■ **Note**   The Rostock design was inspired by `heliumfrog.com/deltarobot/delta.html` and `http://reprap.org/wiki/Helium_Frog_Delta_Robot`.

Linear Rails

Linear rails are much more rigid than smooth rods. Linear rails use a thick 15×10mm steel bar with grooves milled on each side. A carrier is mounted on the rail, suspended by a set of steel ball bearings (most use recirculating arrangements, but some versions use linear ball bearings). The rail is drilled so that it can be mounted to the frame rail using a number of bolts. Figure 2-12 shows a linear rail mounted on a Kossel Pro.

Figure 2-12. *Linear rails (courtesy of Seattle Automationz, LLC)*

Linear rails are very rigid and can provide additional rigidity to the frame of a delta printer. This is advantageous for the Kossel Pro because it uses the same 1515 extrusions as the Mini Kossel, which can flex if used in longer segments. The linear rails help stiffen the frame greatly.

Notice that there is an additional carriage that mounts to the linear rail carrier. The added complexity is the delta arm mount point positioned farther from the frame rail than the smooth rod version. This only means the offset is a bit larger, but otherwise isn't a problem.

Linear rails are also very precise and do not require any adjustment other than periodic cleaning and a small amount of lubrication. However, linear rails are the most expensive option among the popular options for delta axis mechanisms. You can get linear rails in a variety of lengths.

■ **Note**　Linear rails are also used in Cartesian printers. For example, the fifth-generation MakerBot printers use linear rails.

Roller Carriages

An alternative to the expensive linear rods is the use of Delrin-encased bearings that ride in the center channel of an aluminum frame extrusion. Some solutions use Nylon rollers. 3D printer enthusiasts have also had success using hardware-store-quality shower and screen door rollers. Figure 2-13 shows the roller carriage on a SeeMeCNC Orion printer.

Figure 2-13. *Roller carriage (courtesy of SeeMeCNC)*

Notice that there are four rollers (two in the front, two in the rear). The pair of rollers on one side are fixed, and the pair on the other side use concentric cams to allow adjusting the tension of the rollers. Also notice that the roller carriage is larger than the linear rail. Indeed, the linear rail is mounted on the inside of the frame rail, leaving the sides and rear open; whereas the roller carriage requires use of both sides, as well as the inside of the frame rail. This limits the types of attachments that you can use on the frame.

However, this isn't always the case. For instance, the roller carriages shown in Figure 2-13 block all four sides of the frame rail, which makes mounting anything on the rail within the axis travel range impossible. This isn't the case if you use roller carriages for the Mini Kossel (`thingiverse.com/thing:110283`).

While this solution is a lot cheaper (perhaps by half), it is harder to set up because the rollers must be adjusted so that they press against the rails with enough tension to prevent the carriage from moving laterally or rotating, and yet not so much as to bind when moving along the channel.

I have found that the rollers need adjusting periodically and can be affected by environmental changes. This is made worse by carriages made from materials such as wood. Thus, while linear rails need occasional cleaning and lubrication, roller carriages require more frequent adjustment. They may or may not need periodic lubrication but that depends on whether the roller bearings used. Since delta printer axes are vertical, cleaning the channel isn't normally an issue but is something you should inspect from time to time.

Recirculating Balls on Frame Rails

An interesting alternative to the expensive linear rails, and even the roller carriages, is a printable carriage that uses Delrin balls that ride in a recirculating channel. Johann C. Rocholl included this carriage in his Mini Kossel set of printable parts (`https://github.com/jcrocholl/recirculating`). Figure 2-14 shows an example of the carriage riding on an OpenBeamUSA 1515 aluminum frame extrusion. Thus, this solution only applies to the Mini Kossel (or similar designs using 1515 extrusions[8]).

---

[8]You could scale or modify this design to accommodate other frames, provided there is a center slot or channel.

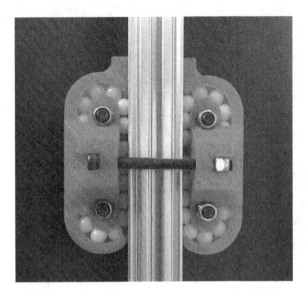

Figure 2-14. *Recirculating ball carriage on frame rails*

Not shown in this photo is an enlarged plate that mounts to the carriage on the interior side of the printer. Thus, this is a view of the exterior of the carriage (to show the recirculating mechanism). Since the dimensions are the same as the linear rail carriage alternative, you do not have to make any alterations in the firmware should you decide to experiment with replacing your existing mechanism with recirculating carriages.

This alternative works great for the Mini Kossel built from the OpenBeamUSA extrusions, but is a bit louder than the other solutions. This is because the Delrin balls tend to make a clicking sound as they recirculate. I've experimented with fine-tuning the ball channel, and that helped, but if you make the channel too small, the balls can bind.[9]

Like the roller carriage option, this solution also requires careful attention to keeping proper tension to keep the balls rolling smoothly. However, it does not need lubrication.

Delta Arms

Recall that each axis is connected to the effector via a carriage and a set of parallel arms (delta arms). The delta arms of most new delta printers are either 3D printed, injection molded, or assembled from joints glued to carbon fiber tubes.

There are several types of rod ends that are used. These include ball ends (e.g., Traxxas), concave magnets with steel balls (or similar), 3D printed or injection-molded joints, and joints with captured bearings. Except for the magnet option (discussed in more detail in Chapter 8), most delta printers include one of these types of rod ends. For example, the Mini Kossel design typically uses the Traxxas rod ends, the SeeMeCNC printers use injection molded parts (arms and joints), and the Kossel Pro uses injection molded parts with captured roller bearings.

The original Rostock and variants typically have printed arms. The Rostock Max v2 and Orion have injection-molded arms. The Kossel Pro, OpenBeam Kossel RepRap, and many Mini Kossel kits have carbon arms made with carbon fiber tubes. I have seen some examples with threaded rods, but these tend to be pretty heavy and may limit movement speed.

---

[9]Nobody wants that!

Stepper Motors

A stepper motor is a special type of electric motor. Unlike a typical electric motor that spins a shaft, the stepper is designed to turn in either direction a partial rotation (or step) at a time. Think of them as having electronic gears where each time the motor is told to turn, it steps to the next tooth in the gear. Most stepper motors used in 3D printers can "step" 1.8 degrees at a time. Figure 1-20 depicts a typical stepper motor.

Another aspect of stepper motors that makes them vital to 3D printers (and CNC machines) is the ability to hold or fix the rotation. This means that it is possible to have a stepper motor turn for so many steps, and then stop and keep the shaft from turning. Most stepper motors have a rating called *holding torque* that measures how much torque they can withstand and not turn.

Four stepper motors are used on a typical delta printer. One each is used to move the X, Y, and Z axes, and another is used to drive the extruder (E axis). Figure 2-15 shows a typical Nema 17 stepper motor (http://reprap.org/wiki/NEMA_17_Stepper_motor).

Figure 2-15. *Stepper motor*

Most stepper motors have a drive pulley mounted directly on the shaft, as you saw earlier in the discussion on extruders. However, some application, like the extruder included in the Mini Kossel design, use a geared extruder motor like the one shown in Figure 2-16. This stepper contains a set of planetary gears, giving the output a 5:1 ratio for more torque.

Figure 2-16. *Geared stepper motor*

Notice the cylindrical section on top of the motor. This contains the gear mechanism. Also notice that the shaft is considerably larger than a typical Nema 17 stepper motor (8mm vs. 5mm).

Build Plate

The build platform or build plate (sometimes called *print bed*) can be made from glass, wood, Lexan, aluminum, and composite materials. Glass is the most common choice. It is to this surface that the first layers of the object are extruded. Some build platforms include a heater element, called a *heated build plate*, placed under the glass. The heated plate is used to help some filament stick to the build plate. A build platform with the heated element is called a *heated build platform*. Figure 2-17 shows a heated build platform.

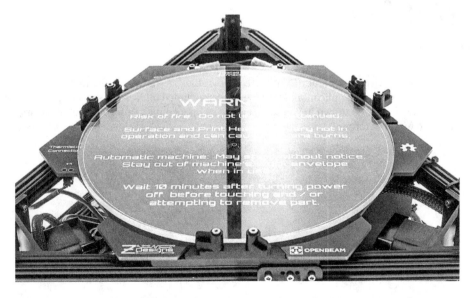

Figure 2-17. *Heated build platform (image courtesy of Seattle Automationz, LLC)*

Notice that the heated print bed is comprised of a thick printed circuit board (PCB) that includes a heating element and a thick circular plate of glass on top. Spring-loaded clamps hold the glass in place when printing.

One consequence of the mathematics and axis movement is that the valid movement area (without crashing into the towers) forms a rounded triangle. That is, the valid points where the printer can position the hot end, which you call the *build volume*. However, most delta printer designers have chosen to restrict the build volume to a cylinder to simplify things a bit. This is why you may notice some delta printers with manual Z-probes (such as the Mini Kossel and Kossel Pro) position the effector beyond the edge of the build volume (visually, the print bed) for deploying or retracting the Z-probe. These positions are still valid mathematical solutions.

Z-PROBE MECHANISMS AND THE BUILD PLATE

Most Z-probe mechanisms use a plunger mechanism that opens or closes a limit switch. The probe is moved from one position to another by repositioning then lowering and raising the effector until the switch is engaged. Thus, the Z-probe is connected to the effector.

However, there is another form of Z-probe that uses force resistor sensors (FSR) placed under the build plate. There are typically three FSRs wired such that if either is triggered, the electronics registers it in the same way as the limit switch. The FSR is triggered by the hot end as it is lowered (slowly) until it comes into contact and presses down on the print surface.

While most firmware supports FSR Z-probing, I have found it is a bit trickier to set up and tune than the plunger-type mechanical probes. Part of this has to do with how you do the Z-probing. That is, you must do it when the nozzle is hot and when there is no filament oozing from the nozzle. Also, if your print surface treatment is soft, it can absorb some of the force and therefore require more fiddling to get a proper initial Z-height. For more about using FSRs for Z-probing, see http://reprap.org/wiki/FSR.

Electronics

The component responsible for reading the G-codes and translating them into signals to control the stepper motors is a small microcontroller platform utilizing several components. Most notably are the microprocessor for performing calculations, reading sensors (endstops, temperature), and controlling the stepper motors. Stepper motors require the use of a special board called a *stepper driver*. Some electronics packages have the stepper drivers integrated, and others use pluggable daughterboards.

Most delta printers use a commodity-grade electronics board (RAMPS, RAMBo, etc.). The most common choice for smaller delta printers such as the Mini Kossel is RAMPS, which uses an Arduino Mega, a special daughterboard (called a *shield*) , and separate stepper driver boards. However, you may also see Printrboard (http://printrbot.com/shop/printrboard-rev-f/) and Azteeg X3 (panucatt.com/Azteeg_X3_Pro_p/ax3pro.htm) boards used. Another example is the Smoothieboard (http://smoothieware.org/smoothieboard), which has a 32-bit processor and dedicated firmware named Smoothieware (http://smoothieware.org/).[10]

The SeeMeCNC delta printers use the RAMBo electronics option, which is a single-board alternative to RAMPS that offers a better layout of the various connections. Figure 2-18 shows the RAMBo electronics board.

---

[10]Johann C. Rocholl suggests, "I predict it is going to completely replace RAMPS and Marlin in the next couple years."

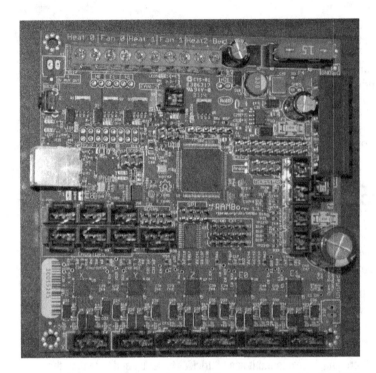

Figure 2-18. *RAMBo electronics board (image courtesy of SeeMeCNC.com)*

The electronics board is where you load the firmware, which contains the programming necessary for the printer to work. This is either a variant of Marlin (Mini Kossel, Kossel Pro) or Repetier-Host (Orion, Rostock Max v2). As discussed previously, this source code is compiled and then uploaded to the electronics board.

Now that I have discussed the axes and how they are moved, as well as the electric motors that move the component, the extruder, the hot end, the build platform used to form the object, and the electronics, it is time to discuss how a frame holds all these parts together.

Frame

Delta printers share a common design for the frame. While there are some differences in how the top and bottom portions are constructed and that there are several types of materials used, most designs use metal beams (sometimes called *rods*) or aluminum extrusions for the vertical frame components. I have seen at least one design that used an all-wood frame, but that was a custom design and not a popular choice.[11]

Recall that the delta printer has a base that secures the build platform, steppers for the axes, as well as a top section that holds the idler pulleys for the axes. Most designs incorporate the electronics, power supply, and other electronics in the lower section.

While the vertical axes use aluminum extrusions, the choice of frame material can vary among delta designs. The best frames are those that are rigid and do not flex when the extruder is moving or when the printer moves an axis in small increments. As you can imagine, this is very important to a high-quality print.

---

[11]All wooden frames are more susceptible to environmental conditions, such as varying humidity and temperature making it a less than ideal material choice. Note that Melamine dramatically reduces these effects.

Some printers, such as the Mini Kossel and Kossel Pro, use the same aluminum extrusions to form the base and top of the printer. The Mini Kossel uses printed vertices bolted to the extrusions. The Kossel Pro uses aluminum vertices bolted to the extrusions. While both form very stiff components, the Kossel Pro is noticeably stiffer. Figure 2-19 shows the Mini Kossel top vertex and Figure 2-20 shows the same vertex on the Kossel Pro.

Figure 2-19. *Mini Kossel top vertex*

Figure 2-20. *Kossel Pro top vertex*

■ **Note**   I refer to the aluminum extrusions as *frame components* when bolted together with the vertices.

Notice that the printed vertex incorporates a channel for the horizontal frame components as well as a channel for the vertical-axis frame component. The small, round cap on top of the vertical frame component protects the belt tensioner and prevents accidental scratches or dings from collisions. Once you've dinged enough cabinets, you'll want a set of these (thingiverse.com/thing:705791).

Notice that the Kossel Pro uses an additional steel plate bolted to the top of the vertex. This isn't so much for rigidity, but it provides a secure mounting point for the belt tensioner.

The SeeMeCNC printers use a set of laser-cut melamine (two sheets of melamine with a wood core) that resists changes to environmental factors. The parts are cleverly designed to bolt together to form a very strong unit. The lower section is large enough to contain all the electronics, as well as the power supply and stepper motors. The top section is also very strong and contains the belt tensioners, as well as mounts for the extruder and a spool holder on top. Figure 2-21 shows the lower section of the Rostock Max v2 printer.

Figure 2-21. *Melamine frame section (courtesy of SeeMeCNC)*

Notice how the frame components are bolted together. The sections are laser cut to accept the nut for each of the bolts and hold securely; once tightened, they form a very strong connection. Notice also the X and Y tower mounts that incorporate the stepper motors and pulleys. Finally, notice that the section is large enough to house a full-sized PC power supply.

Now that I have discussed how delta printers are constructed, let's look at three variant designs for delta printers.

Design Variants

In this section, I present three popular delta variants that represent excellent examples of good delta printers. I introduced these printers in Chapter 1. Here I present more information about each printer, including its capabilities, and a short review. Keep in mind these are only three examples of delta printers. While there are many others available, most are some variant of a Rostock or Mini Kossel. Thus, these printers represent what I consider the best examples of delta printers available.

SeeMeCNC Rostock Max v2

The Rostock Mac v2 is an iteration[12] of the original Rostock by Johann C. Rocholl, manufactured and sold by SeeMeCNC (http://seemecnc.com/products/rostock-max-complete-kit). The most significant aspect of this variant is the massive build volume. You can print objects up to 1300 cubic inches of build volume (an 11-inch diameter and a height of 14-3/4 inches). Indeed, with a spool of filament on the top-mounted spool holder, the printer itself is over 4 feet tall—presenting a very impressive profile.

I mentioned previously that the printer is constructed using laser-cut frame pieces bolted to large aluminum extrusions for the axes. However, the printer also uses injection-molded delta arms, joints, carriage mounts, and effector. There are also Lexan panels covering the upper and lower axis towers, making the overall package clean and modern looking. Figure 2-22 shows the Rostock Max v2. You can get the printer in either white or black Melamine panels.

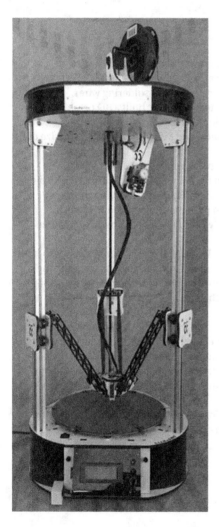

Figure 2-22. *Rostock Max v2*

---

[12]Perhaps an evolution.

Notice that the printer comes with an LCD panel mounted on the front face of the lower panel. The base is large enough to house all the electronics and provides a solid foundation for the axes. The following provides an overview of some of its best features:

- Made in the USA by SeeMeCNC

- EZStruder mounted below the top-mounted spool holder

- 1.75mm filament, dual-heater hot end

- Removable 0.5mm nozzle (other sizes available)

- RAMBo by UltiMachine electronics

- Repetier-Host firmware

- Large heated build plate with thick Borosilicate glass

- Customizable electronics and hardware[13]

The Rostock Max v2 comes in kit form only. It is a nontrivial build given the number of parts and the moderately complicated hot-end assembly. Soldering, mechanical, and general electronics skills are required. That is, you should be familiar with using crimping tools, stripping, and soldering wires.

Although that may sound challenging, and it can be for those who have never built a 3D printer, SeeMeCNC provides a detailed, lengthy assembly manual with all the steps explained in clear language and reinforced with photos. I printed the manual so that I could make notes, and I was impressed by the size of the manual. It is very well done.

SeeMeCNC also hosts one of the best user forums I've seen (http://forum.seemecnc.com/). If you get stuck or have questions, one visit and a short query later, you will have your answers. Furthermore, the customer and technical support is also among the best in the business, easily overshadowing the larger vendors. For example, I made a mistake assembling one of the Lexan panels and managed to break it.[14] SeeMeCNC sent me a new one the very next day and I received it only two days later. It doesn't get better than that.

Calibration is easy and the manual makes the steps very simple. In fact, SeeMeCNC uses macros to help set the endstops and calibrate the axes. I explain this in much greater detail in Chapter 5. As for using the printer, once properly calibrated, the print quality is excellent. The hot end has operated flawlessly without extrusion failures or extraneous artifacts (e.g., lumps of filament on the part), and mechanical noise is moderate. It just works.

This printer has everything you need for great-looking prints. The only thing I found missing is an auto bed leveling (Z-probe) feature. However, I found there was no need for this, as the print surface is very flat with no visible imperfections. Indeed, when testing the maximum build diameter, I found that the hot end tracked evenly across the entire print bed. To understand this significance, consider that I have spent countless hours tuning and adjusting print beds on other printers, whereas the Rostock Max v2 was dead-on without any bed adjustment whatsoever!

In fact, I found the Rostock Max v2 to be a high-quality, professional-grade delta printer (despite the kit factor). If you need a delta printer with a large build volume and you can handle the assembly, the Rostock Max v2 will provide many hundreds of hours of reliable printing.

---

[13]Look closely at the photo. Notice the custom spool roller on top.
[14]While I normally test-fit panels such as this, my one lapse ended in a spectacular part failure. Always test fit your parts before installing them, especially tension-fit mounts.

Kossel Pro

The Kossel Pro is a consumer-grade edition of the Mini Kossel made by OpenBeamUSA (kosselpro.com) and sold by MatterHackers (matterhackers.com/store/printer-kits). But it is much more than that. The printer is of very high quality and in all ways is a step up from its RepRap Mini Kossel ancestor.

Interestingly, OpenBeamUSA also offers a lower-cost version called the OpenBeam Kossel RepRap, which is a smaller version of the Kossel Pro that uses more plastic parts and fewer specialized parts. However, the OpenBeam Kossel RepRap shares many of the same parts as the Kossel Pro and it can be upgraded to the Kossel Pro with the purchase of an upgrade kit. Both printers are sold in kit form.

The most significant feature of this printer is the frame. As I mentioned previously, it uses the same OpenBeam 1515 aluminum extrusion that is popular with the Mini Kossel, as well as milled aluminum vertices and linear rails. There are very few plastic parts, all of which are high quality and injection molded. Another impressive feature is the effector, which incorporates a Z-probe, an always-on fan for the hot end, two part-cooling fans, as well as an LED light ring. Figure 2-23 shows the Kossel Pro. The Z-probe alone is a work of art.

Figure 2-23. *Kossel Pro*

At first glance, this printer has all the most-requested features. Indeed, the Kossel Pro has an impressive list of features, as follows. The only thing I found oddly missing is a spool holder—there is not even a mount. However, due to the origins of the OpenBeamUSA components, it isn't hard to find a spool holder that works. I created one myself from parts I found on Thingiverse (see Chapter 8).

- All-metal frame

- EZStruder mounted on the lower frame

- Designed to print ABS or PLA

- J-head 1.75mm hot end

- Custom-built electronics

- Marlin firmware

- Large heated build plate (optional) with thick Borosilicate glass

- Designed to print ABS (if heated build plate equipped) and PLA

Despite that this printer comes only in kit form, the build is very easy. In fact, one of the objectives of OpenBeamUSA is to make the printer easy to build quickly. This is achieved by using only bolt-on or plug-in wiring and components. In fact, the main wiring harness for the hot end, Z-probe, and light ring uses a single wiring bundle with molded connectors eliminating the need for any soldering. Furthermore, most of the tools you need are included in the kit.

I found the build a pleasure to work on. All of the parts are clearly labeled, and for the most part only fit together one way. There are some exceptions, so pay attention to the documentation! If there is any wrinkle, it is the documentation. While technically complete at the time of this writing, the documentation continues to evolve and I am happy that it is improving.

The Kossel Pro and OpenBeam Kossel RepRap are very new designs and are only just now moving from Kickstarter funding to full-on production. Thus, some things are still evolving and may change slightly. Fortunately, many of the minor issues in the first run of production kits have been solved. There is a small army of eager enthusiasts sharing the latest information about the printers.

Unlike the Rostock Max v2, there is no fine adjustability in the axis (i.e., endstops). This is partly because the assembly requires precise placement of the components during the build, and bolstered by superior-quality components and auto bed leveling (Z probing). However, I would have liked to dial-in the tower calibration rather than relying on auto bed leveling for any minor imperfections.

In using this printer, I found the mechanical bits superb examples of what printers should strive to be, but the print quality is not at the same level as other options. More specifically, it took me several experimental prints and numerous adjustments to get good print quality, but it will require a bit more tuning to perfect print quality. This is partly because the default settings in my software are not optimal for this printer (it's too new) and partly because the firmware needs some tweaking.

For example, the effector-mounted part-cooling fans are a bit on the small size. I found I needed to run them at 100% to get better cooling for printing with PLA. If I could change one thing (and I may in the future), it would be to exchange the small axial fans with centrifugal fans. See the sidebar "Got Fans" in Chapter 8 for more details.

However, I would be remiss if I did not point out that this is a very new printer design, and many of the early adopters are experimenting along with me and sharing their results and findings. In fact, like the SeeMeCNC forum, the creators of the Kossel Pro routinely post and answer questions on the forum (http://forums.openbeamusa.com/forums/openbeam-kossel-reprap-and-openbeam-kossel-pro.7/).

Given that the printer is made from high-quality parts, maintenance should not be an issue. Indeed, as you will see in Chapter 7, none of the parts require any significant adjustment or lubrication. Other than adjusting belt tension and keeping the printer clean and lubricated (and only a tiny bit is needed), the printer should prove to be very low maintenance.

This printer is also a great platform for tinkerers due to the use of the OpenBeamUSA extrusions. These allow the bolting of all manner of accessories onto the frame. For example, in Figure 2-23 I show a spool holder (not included in the kit) and a mount for my MatterControl Touch.

I really like this printer. It is a sophisticated black-on-black, serious-looking delta printer that always gets a look when friends stop by. If you want a high-quality delta printer that has a moderate-sized build volume, and you want to experience building your own from a kit without the tedious soldering and electronics work, the Kossel Pro is an excellent choice. Given the documentation and the ever-expanding and improving user forums, I expect this printer to be a very popular choice for those who want a printer with better quality, reliability, and maintainability than the RepRap variants.

Mini Kossel

The Mini Kossel is one of the newest RepRap delta printers (`https://github.com/jcrocholl/kossel`), also designed by Johann C. Rocholl. As I mentioned in Chapter 1, the Mini Kossel is a hobbyist-grade (RepRap) printer that is entirely DIY. While you can buy kits that include all the parts, most people source their own parts or buy subcomponents from various vendors.

In fact, the Mini Kossel has been copied and modified by many people. I find a new variant of the Mini Kossel almost weekly. Some have minor changes, like using a different extrusion for the frame or a different carriage mechanism (see the earlier discussion on axis movement), but others have more extensive changes, such as alternative frame vertices and use of injection-molded parts, and a few have even increased the build volume.[15]

And due to its RepRap roots, on 3D printing forums such as Thingiverse (`thingiverse.com`) you can find all manner of useful add-ons, upgrades, and even a few embellishments. I have built several Mini Kossel printers and continue to improve them by experimenting with new designs—both my own and others (some work well, some not so much). You can find my designs on Thingiverse under my alias "oliasmage" (`thingiverse.com/oliasmage/designs`).

The Mini Kossel is one of the most (perhaps the most) popular delta printer variants available, other than the original Rostock. Figure 2-24 shows one of my heavily modified Mini Kossel printers.

---

[15]I saw one described as a Mini Kossel XL. What?

Figure 2-24. *Mini Kossel*

In Figure 2-24 you can see that I've added a mount for my MatterControl Touch, onboard power supply, spool holder, RAMPS box, power box, part-cooling fan, and many other things not shown or hidden by other parts.

Since this design is a pure RepRap, DIY endeavor, listing standard features isn't helpful because there are so many options that you can choose. For example, you can choose your own hot end (1.75mm or 3mm, all-metal, peek, etc.), optionally add a heated build plate, add cooling fans, and so on. Indeed, there is almost no limit to what you can do with this little printer.

About the only thing I can say that is standard on most variants of the Mini Kossel is a small size. The printer is only a little over two-feet tall and takes up very little room. Although the build volume is quite small (about 5 to 6 inches in diameter and 6 to 8 inches tall), it is large enough to print most moderate-sized parts one at a time.

Building the printer is pretty easy if you have basic mechanical and electrical skills. The build time is only slightly less than what would be required for the Rostock Max v2, but because there are fewer parts, the build is a bit faster and the frame is less complicated to assemble.

While some vendors offer the Mini Kossel in kit form, few offer any form of help beyond the basic assembly.[16] Fortunately, there are numerous articles, blogs, and independent forums that offer a lot of help. I would start with a visit to the Mini Kossel wiki (http://reprap.org/wiki/Kossel) and then search for topics you need help with, such as "Z-probe assembly" or "Mini Kossel calibration". Another helpful forum is the RepRap general forum (http://forums.reprap.org/list.php?178), but enthusiasts building all manner of delta printers use this forum, so be aware that some of the information may not apply to the Mini Kossel. You can also check out the deltabot mailing list (https://groups.google.com/group/deltabot). When in doubt, ask.

Not surprisingly, given its small size and use of standard components, the Mini Kossel is the cheapest of the delta printers available today. If you opt to go without a heated print bed and use the less expensive axis components, you can find kits for under $500, and even a few around $400. I managed to source one of my Mini Kossel printers at about $300, but I opted to use some used parts from other Cartesian printers (e.g., motors, RAMPS).

If you are looking for a delta printer to start with, or want to experience building a delta printer from scratch or as a companion to a fleet of Cartesian printers, the Mini Kossel is an excellent choice. Build one for yourself or invite a friend to build one together.

Which Is Best?

The answer is "it depends."[17] Each printer represents an excellent choice. The answer lies in what you want to do with it. All require assembly, so that levels the field a bit, however, the Rostock Max v2 is the most difficult to assemble and the Kossel Pro the least.

■ **Tip** Chapter 4 focuses on building delta printers. If you have never built a 3D printer and are contemplating one of these kits, be sure to read through Chapter 4 before you buy or begin your build.

What sets them apart has to do with how much you want to tinker and modify. If you are the type who likes to change any component whenever you get a good idea (or sometimes not such a good idea), you will want to stay with the Mini Kossel. On the other hand, if you want a printer that has everything (except a spool holder), you should choose the Kossel Pro.

If you are choosing a printer on criteria such as customer support, documentation, and reliability, you will want to choose the Rostock Max v2 or perhaps the Kossel Pro, as the RepRap variants are purely DIY (you may get help from the Internet, but sometimes it can be a burden to sift fact from fiction).

Lastly, if you want build volume, the Rostock Max v2 has the largest, followed by the Kossel Pro, the OpenBeam Kossel RepRap, and the Mini Kossel, which has the smallest build volume.

---

[16]Which, with few exceptions, are normally very terse.
[17]I know, I know. It sounds like I don't want to choose, but in this case it's true.

WHY THE INTERESTING NAMES? DO THEY MEAN SOMETHING?

You may be wondering about the names of some of these printers. The original Rostock, and hence all the modern variants, was named after the town in northeast Germany where Johann C. Rocholl was born. Since the Mini Kossel is a RepRap design and most original RepRap printers were named after dead biologists, the Mini Kossel (and by inheritance, the Kossel Pro) is named after Albrecht Kossel, who was also born and studied in Rostock, Germany. Albrecht Kossel was a German biochemist and a pioneer in the study of genetics.

Summary

Delta printers represent a very different approach to 3D printing than Cartesian printers do. While they both share much of the same hardware, a delta printer's axes mechanism is something magical to behold. This and the fact that delta printers have higher move rates and smaller footprints make delta printers more enthusiast- and hobbyist-friendly than some of the Cartesian options. Indeed, I've found I use my Cartesian printer less and less, favoring the delta printers for critical prints.

In this chapter, you discovered how delta printers work and learned about the mathematics of delta printers, the types of hardware used in the frame and axes, and the electronics, including the hot end and the heated build plate. Lastly, you explored three types of delta printers that you can buy today.

In the next chapter, you will discover the software side of 3D printing, including how models are turned into objects and how the printer is controlled via the firmware.

CHAPTER 3

■ ■ ■

Delta Printer Software

As you discovered in Chapter 1, there are three pieces of software involved in a typical 3D printing workflow:[1] software required to create the object and export it as an `.stl` file (CAD), another to convert it into a G-code file that a printer can read (CAM), and finally, the firmware loaded into the "brain" of the printer itself that reads and executes the `.gcode` file. However, there is a bit more to 3D printing software.

For example, while CAM software is responsible for slicing the object for printing, advances in 3D-printing software has resulted in the combination of CAM operations with a fourth category of software—the printer control application. This software allows you to connect your computer to your printer (via a USB connection) and perform many operations, such as moving the axes, turning the hot end on/off, and aligning the axes (called *homing*).

Since most of the newest and best CAM software choices include printer control features, I limit the discussion to software that includes both the CAM and printer control operations. Some of these have their own built-in slicers (MatterControl and Simplify3D), but others utilize an existing slicer (CAM) like Repetier-Host, which uses Slic3r. If you want to know more about slicing applications, see my book, *Maintaining and Troubleshooting Your 3D Printer* (Apress, 2014).

There is also software that you can load on a smaller device and use it to control your printer remotely. I call this category simply *remote printing*. Solutions in this category are designed to run on a small, low-power and low-cost tablet or a small computer, such as a Raspberry Pi. This software is really handy because it can add features such as printing over a network, video monitoring, and remote access to printers that do not include these features.

Some 3D printing manufacturers have created software that spans the entire workflow (or tool chain). That is, newer releases have started to include basic CAD features; however, most focus on the CAM, printer control, and remote printing features. While some are touted as "all in one," most do not include CAD features. Examples include those from major 3D printer manufacturers such as MakerBot Industries' Desktop (makerbot.com) and Ultimaker's Cura (http://wiki.ultimaker.com/Cura). Other examples are from 3D printing software experts such as the Repetier-Host suite (repetier.com), MatterHacker's MatterControl (mattercontrol.com), and Simplify3D (simplify3d.com). Each of these is an interface to the CAM software (the slicer) and each provides a printer controller feature. Repetier-Host and MatterControl are free, but Simplify3D is commercially licensed software.

---

[1] Often called a *tool chain* because of the way you must use one piece of the software at a time to process and print an object.

■ **Note** When I discuss aspects of a type of software in general, I use the term *software*. When I speak of an implementation of the software, I use the terms *program* and *application*.

If you are about to purchase or have already purchased a printer that does not come with software, do not despair! Much of the 3D printing world has adopted the open source philosophy, and as a result there are several free options to choose from for each software category. In the following sections I discuss each of these, as well as show some examples from each category. I also explain the types of files you will generate from each step.

Let's get started by diving into CAD software, which is arguably one of the most complex steps in the 3D printing tool chain.

Computer-Aided Design

Simply put, *computer-aided design* (CAD) is software that permits you to use a computer to create an object. CAD software typically includes features to realize an object in various 3D views, manipulate the object surface and interior details, as well as change the view of the object (scaling, rotating, etc.).

■ **Note** CAD is also referred to as *computer-aided drafting*, but in this case it refers to the drawing aspect alone. I spent several years learning the art of mechanical drawing.[2] Computer-aided drafting revolutionized that aspect of the engineering discipline. In fact, learning computer-aided drafting software is what got me interested in the engineering disciplines.

Advanced CAD software has features that allow you to create a number of objects and fit them together to form a complex mechanical solution (called a *model*). Advanced CAD software includes additional features that test fit, endurance, and even stress under load. An ultimate example would be the software that automotive manufacturers use to construct engines. I have seen examples of such software that can animate all the moving parts and even suggest ways to improve the individual components.

There are many CAD applications available with a wide range of features. To be used with 3D printing, they must, at a minimum, permit you to design shapes in three dimensions; define interior features, like holes for mounting the object; and provide basic tools to add a surface or facing to the object.

CAD applications save the models in a specific, sometimes proprietary, format. This limits the possibility of using several different CAD applications to manipulate an object. Fortunately, most permit you to import models and objects from various file formats.

More importantly, the software must permit you to create an object that is manifold (has an inside and an outside surface with no gaps). This is important because the slicer needs to be able to create paths for the filament to follow, and gaps or holes means that there is a break in the path. Attempting to force the slicing and printing of a non-manifold object will result in an undesirable end result.[3]

---

[2]I still have my mechanical drawing tools. I can even letter properly when forced to do so. I remember distinctly practicing my letters for hours in preparation for a final exam—and I still remember the hand cramps incurred in the process.
[3]I tried it once with a whistle and ended up with a solid block in the shape of a whistle—it filled the interior with solid plastic. It was a tragic waste of a filament.

■ **Tip**   If your slicer program displays an error that your object is not manifold, you can use an online tool from NetFabb to fix the holes. Visit `http://cloud.netfabb.com`, select your object, enter your e-mail address, agree to the terms and conditions, and click "Upload to cloud". After a few moments, you will get an e-mail with a link to the fixed object. I have fixed a number of objects like this. While you are there, check out the cool online 3D printing tools they offer.

Remember, CAD applications for 3D printing must be capable of creating a standard tessellation language (`.stl`) file so that the CAM software can read the file, slice it, and create a printer instructions (`.gcode`) file for forming the object in three dimensions.

CAD Software Choices

There are a lot of applications that provide CAD features that you can use to create 3D objects. You can find some that are open source, some that are free to use (but limited in some way), and those that you must purchase. Most have a graphical user interface (GUI) that allows you to see the object as you build it. As you will see, there is one that uses a C-like programming language to build a script to create the object. Some applications are available for online use. Furthermore, some are easy to use, whereas others take a lot of time to learn. In general, the more features the software application has, the more difficult it is to use.

If you are just starting out, you may want to try an application with fewer features until you get the hang of it or outgrow its features. Table 3-1 lists some of the more popular CAD solutions, and includes for each the cost basis, the degree of difficulty to learn it (how long it takes to create your initial object), and the type of interface. This is not an exhaustive list, but rather a list of the software choices that I know exports or saves files in `.stl` format.

Table 3-1. *CAD Software for 3D Printing*

Name	URL	Cost/License	Interface	Difficulty
Blender	`www.blender.org`	Open source	GUI	High
123D (Autodesk)	`www.123dapp.com`	Free (limited) Paid (unlimited)	Web	High
SketchUp	`www.sketchup.com`	Free (limited), Paid (pro version)	GUI	Medium
FreeCAD	`www.freecadweb.org`	Open source	GUI	Medium
TinkerCAD	`https://tinkercad.com`	Free (limited), paid levels	Web	Low
NetFabb	`www.netfabb.com`	Paid	Web	Low
OpenJSCAD	`www.openjscad.org`	Open source	Web	Medium[4]
OpenSCAD	`www.openscad.org`	Open source	Text	Low[5]

---

[4]This uses JavaScript language to define 3D models. If you're a Java fan, the difficulty with be low. Others may have to learn or adapt to the JavaScript language.

[5]This requires learning the language and library of functions, which may be a challenge to those unfamiliar with programming languages.

Rather than discuss each of these in detail, which would be well beyond the scope of this book, in the following sections I briefly discuss the first (most difficult/full-featured) and last (easiest) options available.

Blender

The Blender CAD application (blender.org) is a veritable Swiss Army knife of CAD software. Not only can you create highly detailed 3D models, you can also create 3D animation and more! For 3D printing, it's really overkill for most of the types of objects you will create. On the other hand, if you plan to develop complex models for commercial use, or to create parts for a complex solution, you will want to take a hard look at this application. Figure 3-1 shows a screenshot of the Blender application.

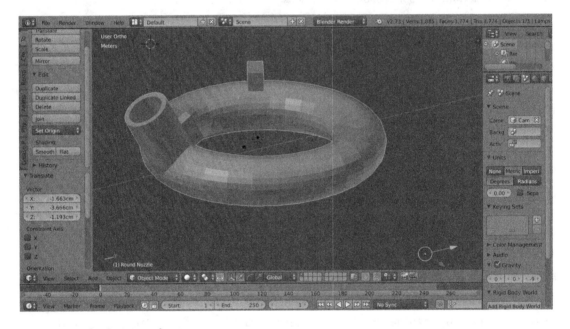

Figure 3-1. *Blender CAD software*

The example shows the editor window, into which an object has been loaded. In this case, it is a circular fan duct. Although I did not have access to the original CAD file, I was able to use Blender to import the .stl file so that I could modify it. For example, I may have wanted to modify the file to add a new bolt arrangement, or to make it smaller, or to join it with another object, and so forth. In this case, I wanted to add three solid blocks on top of the duct so that I could mount it to my effector. I was experimenting with using wire clips that were heated and pressed into the plastic. It worked OK, but I felt it was too wobbly. Regardless, this shows how it is possible to modify an object, even if you do not have the original CAD file.

If I had modified the object, I could save the object (model) and export it to a different .stl file, slice it, and print it. Clearly, this is a useful feature if you need to modify an object but do not have the CAD software with which it was created. Perhaps best of all, it is open source!

I rated this application with a high level of difficulty for several reasons. First, there are a dizzying number of features to learn and hundreds of menu choices. It is definitely not something you can sit down and learn in an afternoon. However, it is a first-rate CAD solution—one that you would do well to master if you plan to design highly complex objects.

The good news is that there are a number of books available to learn Blender. If you want to master Blender, I recommend spending some time with its included documentation and seeking out one or more of the following books:

- *Beginning Blender: Open Source 3D Modeling, Animation, and Game Design* by Lance Flavell (Apress, 2010)

- *Blender Foundations: The Essential Guide to Learning Blender 2.6* by Roland Hess (Focal Press, 2010)

- *Blender 3D Printing Essentials* by Gordon Fisher (Packt Publishing, 2013)

OpenSCAD

This solution is on the opposite side of the difficulty scale. Indeed, if you know a little programming (or at least the concepts of writing executable scripts), you can create simple objects very quickly without reading tome after tome of instruction manuals.

To build an object, you begin by defining a base object (say a square) and add or subtract other shapes. For example, to build a standoff for mounting a printed circuit board (like an Arduino or a Raspberry Pi), you start with a cylinder (the outer perimeter) and then "subtract" a smaller cylinder (the inner perimeter). Although this sounds simple, you can use this very simple technique to create very complex objects.

In fact, this is the process that was used to create the plastic parts for many RepRap 3D printer designs. Figure 3-2 shows an example of one of the models that Johann C. Rocholl created for the Mini Kossel.

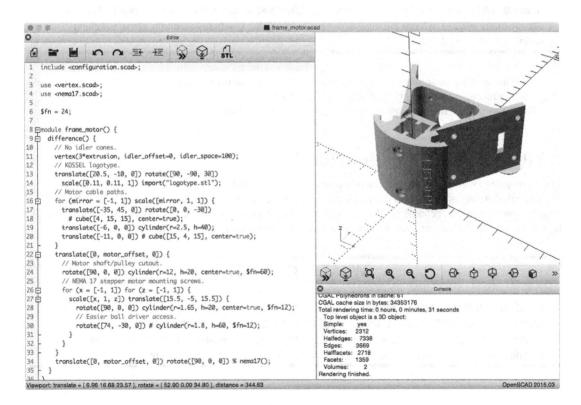

Figure 3-2. *OpenSCAD example (GPL v3)*

Take a moment to observe the figure. Notice that there are three parts to the interface. On the left is the code editor window where you enter all the statements for defining your objects. On the right, at the top, is a view of the model (generated when the script is compiled) and below that is a list of feedback and messages from the OpenSCAD subprocesses and compiler.

As you can see, you can create very complex objects and even several in the same file. When you save the file, you are actually only saving the statements and not a rendered model. This enables you to save a lot of disk space (CAD-based files can be quite large), but you must compile the script to visualize the object(s).

OpenSCAD allows you to export the compiled model in a variety of formats that can be opened by other CAD applications for further manipulation. More importantly, you can generate the required .stl file for use in a CAM (slicer) application, permitting you to use OpenSCAD as the first stop in your 3D printing tool chain.

Even if you do not know the language, it is not difficult to learn and there are many examples on the web site (www.openscad.org) to help you get going. You can also study the many complex parts for the Mini Kossel to see the techniques used. For example, the frame motor mount shown in Figure 3-1 uses many advanced techniques, as well as a couple of modules. Once you learn the basics of OpenSCAD, these techniques will become familiar.

GOT CODE SKILLS?

Although I am an expert software developer, I recognize that not everyone thinks in code like me. Thus, when I create OpenSCAD files that I plan to share with others, I keep the script as simple as possible to allow others to adapt them to their needs. I do this so others don't feel intimidated by advanced code techniques like those shown here. Like most software scripts and programs, there are usually many ways to achieve the objective—some simplistic, others not so much. There's nothing wrong with keeping it simple.

If you are looking for something to get started quickly, you will want to consider using OpenSCAD until you need the more advanced features of the larger CAD applications.

Now let's examine the next step in the tool chain—slicing (CAM).

Computer-Aided Manufacturing

There are many aspects to CAM, but the one process you need for 3D printing is the ability to take a 3D object definition (an .stl file) and convert it into a file that contains instructions for the printer to build the object, layer by layer (a .gcode file). More specifically, the slicer uses numerical control code in the standard tessellation language to create canonical machining function calls in the form of G-codes.

WHAT IS G-CODE?

G-code is a shorthand notation for a set of machine functions that govern the movement of the various parts of the machine. Although 3D printers read G-code files, the codes themselves are not limited to 3D printers. In fact, the codes cover a wider range of machines, including CNC machines. Moreover, the G-code definition has been modified to include new codes specifically for 3D printing.

The codes are formed by a letter that signifies the class of command, a number (index), and one or more parameters separated by spaces (optional). There are codes for positioning the hot end, setting the temperature, moving the axis, checking sensors, and many more. Let's look at a few examples in Table 3-2, and then see what a .gcode file looks like in Listing 3-1.

Table 3-2. *Common G-Codes*

Code	Description	Parameters	Example
G1	Travel to new location	X, Y, Z coordinates Additional parameters for extrusion, federate, and endstop sensing	G1 X10 Y10 Z10 F3500
G28	Travel to X, Y, and Z zero endstops. This is the homing command.	None	G28
G29	Auto Z-probe (auto bed-leveling)[6]	None	G29
M104	Set temperature of hot end.	Snnn: temp in Celsius	M104 S205
M105	Get temperature of hot end.	None	M105
M106	Turn on fan.	Snnn: fan speed (0–255)	M106 S127
M114	Get position of all axes.	None	M114
M119	Get status of all endstops.	None	M119

The G-code file is a text file that contains all the machine instructions to build the file, including the setup and teardown mechanisms as defined by the slicer. Listing 3-1 shows an excerpt of a .gcode file. Notice that the first lines are preceded with a semicolon; this indicates a comment line that is commonly used to define the parameters for the print operation in plain English. Notice that the comments indicate layer height, solidity of the top and bottom, density, and much more; this makes it easy for you to determine the characteristics of the file without having to translate the G-codes.

Listing 3-1. Example G-code File

```
; generated by Slic3r 1.1.7 on 2015-03-08 at 13:33:43

; layer_height = 0.25
; perimeters = 3
; top_solid_layers = 3
; bottom_solid_layers = 3
; fill_density = 0.2
; perimeter_speed = 30
; infill_speed = 60
; travel_speed = 130
; nozzle_diameter = 0.4
; filament_diameter = 2.97
; extrusion_multiplier = 1
; perimeters extrusion width = 0.53mm
; infill extrusion width = 0.53mm
```

---

[6]Johann C. Rocholl's Marlin variant permits the use of a Z parameter to set first layer height.

```
; solid infill extrusion width = 0.53mm
; top infill extrusion width = 0.53mm
; first layer extrusion width = 0.50mm

G21 ; set units to millimeters
M107
M190 S105 ; wait for bed temperature to be reached
M104 S215 ; set temperature
G28 X0 Y0 ; home all axes
G29
G1 Z5 F5000 ; lift nozzle
M109 S215 ; wait for temperature to be reached
G90 ; use absolute coordinates
G92 E0
M82 ; use absolute distances for extrusion
G1 F1800.000 E-1.00000
G92 E0
G1 Z0.250 F7800.000
G1 X16.090 Y17.406
G1 F1800.000 E1.00000
G1 X10.040 Y21.806 F540.000 E1.12918
G1 X9.350 Y22.246 E1.14331
G1 X8.870 Y22.486 E1.15258
G1 X2.290 Y25.416 E1.27696
G1 X1.780 Y25.616 E1.28642
G1 X1.000 Y25.836 E1.30042
G1 X-6.050 Y27.336 E1.42489
G1 X-6.860 Y27.456 E1.43903
...
```

If you would like to know more about G-code and the various commands available, see http://reprap.org/wiki/G-code for a complete list of codes supported by most 3D printer firmware.

Today CAM software has grown beyond the basic slicing capability; it incorporates printer control features, as well as a host of other features that help you get the most out of your printer. Thus, I will now focus the discussion on the latest software available for 3D printing. While I still classify them as CAM software, they are much more than that, and it is reasonable to call them simply *3D printing environments* or *3D printing software*.

Using CAM Software

Before you look at some examples of CAM software, let's discuss the general flow or process of how you use the software to print. Software can vary greatly in how the functions are implemented, how the screens are arranged, and even how the buttons and parameters are named. Regardless, they all share the same basic flow.

Installation is usually not an issue, as most software installs easily. However, on Windows platforms, it is possible that you may need to install a driver or configure your system to be able to connect to your printer. See the installation documentation of your chosen software for more information.

Once installed, the workflow is as follows. First, you load a .stl file (or object) and place it on the build plate. Some software automatically centers the object on the build plate, but others allow you to place it where you like. You can also add several objects to the build plate and print them at the same time.

Next, you choose or set the print settings, such as print quality, layer characteristics, heating, cooling, infill, and more. You also choose parameters for the filament. Most software applies your settings to all the objects on the build plate. However, Simplify3D, allows you to apply different settings to each object or subgroups of objects.

Optionally, although I highly recommend this step, you can preheat your build plate and extruder, perform auto Z-probing (bed leveling), and other changes or axis movements to ensure that your printer is ready for printing.

Once you are satisfied with the settings and the printer is ready, you then engage the slicer feature (most software includes this automatically when you click Print).

Finally, you click the Print feature and start your print.

As you can see, modern 3D printing environments make it really easy to select an object, choose the print settings, and print the object.

CAM Software Choices

Unlike CAD software, there are fewer choices of CAM software specifically designed for printing with delta printers. That is, not all CAM software has settings that allow you to specify the unique hardware constraints of delta printers.

Indeed, some CAM software has only rudimentary, if any, support for delta printers. The biggest issue is that the origin for delta printers is the center of the build plate [0,0,0], and the X and Y axes move in both negative and positive directions based on the radius of the build volume. (This is unlike a Cartesian printer, where the origin is at the minimal position for each axis and axes move in the positive direction.)

You can see this in how the software configures the printing parameters. If there is no provision for a circular build plate, much less a cylindrical build volume, it is likely that the software won't work with delta printers. Even software that claims support for delta printers (via the cylindrical build volume) may not be easy to configure. That is, you may not be able to set the build volume, axes homing, or maximum Z-height. I've seen this more with software designed for specific Cartesian printer designs. What this means is that if you are using a CAM solution with your Cartesian printer, you may not be able to use it with your delta printer.

Although you may be able to slice and generate files for your delta printer, you may not be able to control your delta printer. For example, MakerBot's Desktop (`makerbot.com/desktop`) does not support delta printers.[7] Similarly, whereas Cura supports delta printers, configuring support for delta printers involves some tricky settings. And although Slic3r can be used to slice files for delta printers, its defaults may need to be overridden to get the object placed correctly on the build plate.

Fortunately, there are a few full-featured CAM software solutions that are designed for 3D printing with delta printers, and which also include support for controlling the printer, as well as slicing and preparing the model for printing. Printer control for delta printers is not that much different from that for Cartesian printers, but a few software applications do not work well with delta printers.

Recall that CAM software is largely the slicing operation portion of the tool chain. However, CAM software has evolved considerably, such that the slicing operation is included in the generation of the print file. Indeed, they have evolved into fully featured 3D printing environments.[8] However, if you still need or want an independent slicing application, you look for one of the following:

- Slic3r (`http://slic3r.org`): Wildly popular among RepRap enthusiasts. Very customizable.

- Skeinforge (`http://fabmetheus.crsndoo.com/wiki/index.php/Skeinforge`): Simple interface, but can be tedious to use.

- KISSLicer (`http://kisslicer.com`): The Free edition has minimal features for 3D printing. The Pro edition adds multiextrusion and advanced model control.

---

[7]In fact, it is designed exclusively for MakerBot printers.
[8]Yippee! Gone are the days of pokey, nonintegrated applications!

Table 3-3 lists some of the most popular CAM software for use in 3D printing with delta printers (I excluded software that does not fully support delta printers). In the following sections, I discuss some of the software mentioned in Table 3-3. If your CAM of choice is not listed here, ask the vendor if it supports delta printers.

Table 3-3. *CAM Software for 3D Printing*

Name	URL	Cost/License	Notes
Repetier-Host	repetier.com	Paid but offers a free version[9]	Simple interface, but can be tedious to use. Has been gaining popularity since its release.
MatterControl	mattercontrol.com	Open source with paid add-ons	Full-featured 3D printing software has an intuitive interface and supports many printer designs.
Cura	http://ultimaker.com/en/products/software	Open Source	Supports delta printers, but a little finicky to set up (requires multiple steps). Very popular choice for Cartesian printers.
Simplify3D	simplify3d.com	Paid	Advanced, professional-grade 3D printing software.

The following sections discuss the software listed in Table 3-3. I start with a basic example, followed by one of the newest full-featured 3D printing applications, and close the discussion with a professional-grade commercial software offering. As you shall see, these applications are listed in order of their feature set and complexity.

I do not include a step-by-step guide to using any of the software beyond the general workflow description in Table 3-3; instead, I describe the capabilities of each so that you can decide which meets your needs and expectations. Each software vendor's web site offers a complete walk-through in its getting started documentation.

■ **Caution**   Resist the temptation of jumping into new 3D printing software, thinking it will solve your print-quality issues. Using 3D printing software with a poorly calibrated or improperly configured printer will result in frustration and disappointment.

Repetier-Host

Repetier-Host is popular among RepRap enthusiasts. You can place objects on the build plate in any position (rather than always centered), manipulate them, and even slice them using your choice of slicing application (either Slic3r or Skeinforge). You can choose to include both when you install Repetier-Host; simply configure Repetier-Host to connect to either one.

---

[9]Repetier-Host was open source but is no longer. See http://forums.reprap.org/read.php?267,313864.

Fortunately, Repetier-Host is made for a wide variety of printers, including delta printers. It has a much more technical feel to its interface than other examples, but not overly so. In other words, it's a bit nerdy. 3D printing veterans will appreciate the level of detail in feedback, logging, and printer control. It is easy to install and provides a dizzying amount of information about your printer and current print job. Figure 3-3 shows the Repetier-Host main window.

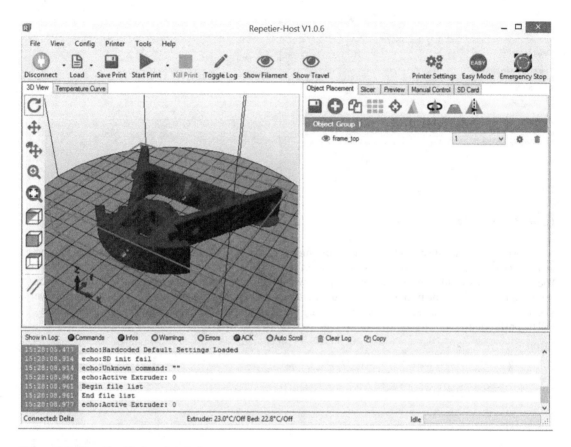

Figure 3-3. *Repetier-Host main window*

The interface is divided into several parts. Toolbars are located at the top and left for common operations, such as connecting to the printer, manipulating the build plate views, and so forth. In the center left is the build plate view. This is a 3D view that is very easy to zoom and rotate to orient the view. You can also see a temperature graph that includes graph lines for each extruder and the build plate (if available).

To the right is a multitab panel that provides controls for loading and manipulating objects, slicing the objects (using Slic3r or Skeinforge), and working with the G-code (including a nifty print preview). There is also a printer control panel. I will present an example of each of these.

The slicing pane allows you to configure the slicer used to generate the G-code. The software provides a very easy way to choose which profiles to use; for example, with Slic3r you can choose the specific profiles for each category. You can also change the slicer you want to use, as well as override slicer settings such as support, cooling, and layer height. This could be handy if you want to print a file in different filaments, add supports, or turn on cooling without reslicing the object. Figure 3-4 shows the Slicer pane.

Figure 3-4. *Repetier-Host Slicer pane*

The better CAM software solutions include a nice print preview feature. This allows you to see the layers in a rendered example of the object. That is, you can see how the object is going to be printed, layer by layer. You also get to see estimates for how long the print will take and an estimate for how much filament will be used. Figure 3-5 shows the print preview feature in Repetier-Host. You can use sliders to see a range of layers, or even a single layer. You have the option of adding the print moves so that you can see where the nozzle will be positioned.

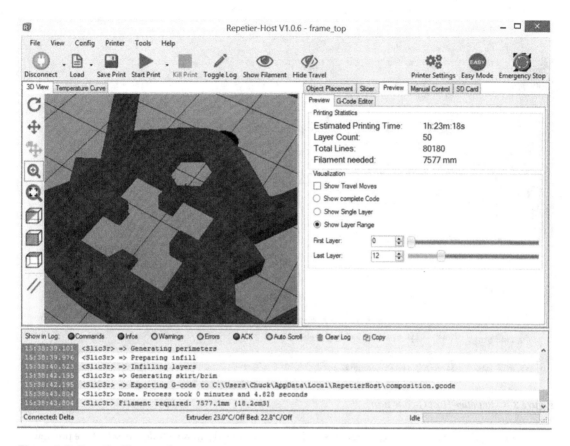

Figure 3-5. *Repetier-Host preview pane*

■ **Caution**   Tread lightly when editing the G-code file!

The G-code pane is one of the most interesting for-experts-only features; it provides the ability to edit the G-code directly. I have not found another application that permits you to do this. Thus, if you know what you are doing, you can change the G-code without reslicing. For example, I often print the same object in PLA and ABS (for various reasons). However, since the temperature settings and a few other parameters (like filament thickness) are different, I can simply change those settings and not run the slicer again. Very nice! Figure 3-6 shows the G-code pane.

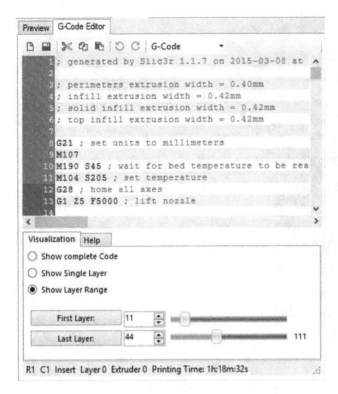

Figure 3-6. Repetier-Host G-code pane

This feature also allows you to preview a G-code file. Simply load a new G-code file, select the preview options, and visualize it in the 3D viewer—even while another print is still in progress.

You can control your printer via the print control panel. There are controls for all the normal operations, from moving the axes to dynamically changing the speed of the printer. Figure 3-7 shows the Repetier-Host print control panel.

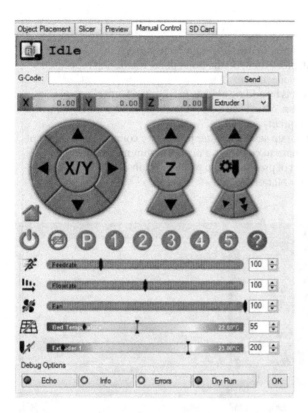

Figure 3-7. *Repetier-Host print control pane*

The ability to view all the messages to and from the printer is yet another interesting feature of Repetier-Host. You can see the actual G-codes scroll by as they are sent to the printer. Although this is fascinating at first, it can become a bit of a novelty. Fortunately, you can turn off classes of feedback messages to clean up the display.

There are other handy features, such as a set of calculators for calculating the parameters for axis mechanics in the firmware. You can configure the software for multiple extruders and multiple printers, as well as how each connects, however, the connection options are limited to direct USB (serial) or TCP/IP connections. There is also a tab for viewing files on the SD card if your printer has an SD drive. You can even select a file for printing.

Perhaps the feature I like most is the ability to create different profiles for several printers. Although this only saves the connection and general settings, it is nice for those of us who have several printers of various designs.

Finally, there are some niggles. Although the software runs on Mac OS X, Linux, and Windows, some platforms do not support all the features. On the Mac, the print control panel layout is quite different. Despite this minor issue, Repetier-Host is a good choice for most 3D printing enthusiasts. It does all the basic things you would expect from an all-in-one 3D printing solution, but as you will see, it is a bit more basic than other examples.

MatterControl

MatterControl, by MatterHackers, is a relatively new entry in the all-in-one 3D printing software category. Like Repetier-Host, you can choose objects to print, place them on the build plate, rotate, and reposition them. But it goes a lot further than Repetier-Host, as you will see.

Most obvious is the ability to organize your objects by adding objects to a library. MatterControl also stores historical information about your past print jobs. What I like best is the ability to fine-tune your prints and printer to achieve much greater control of print quality.

More specifically, MatterControl allows you to set up several printer profiles for connecting to different printers. However, unlike Repetier-Host, where you have to configure a printer communication and its hardware manually, MatterControl features a long list of preconfigured printer options, including those for delta printers. Figure 3-8 shows the main interface for MatterControl.

Figure 3-8. MatterControl main window

The main window is split into two panes. On the left are the Queue, Library, History, and About tabs. The print queue is a nice feature that allows you to prepare multiple print jobs and print them when ready.

The Advanced Controls button opens a host of advanced settings that allow you all manner of customization. There are three levels of settings, ranging from basic, which uses well-known defaults, intermediate for those that need to tweak layers, infill, and speed, as well as an advanced mode that lets you change just about anything. I discuss only the advanced view since that is the mode I use by default.

There are three sections on the Advanced Settings pane: a settings panel, which allows you to change a vast array of settings for controlling the print, a control panel for controlling the printer, and a configuration panel, which allows you to customize the application as well as turn on some advanced features. I will discuss each of these panels briefly.

The settings panel is a most impressive layout of parameters and settings. You can change settings for layers and parameters, infill (including multiple patterns), speed, skirt and raft, supports, and more. In fact, there is also a feature that permits MatterControl to attempt to fix problems with your object, including bad edges and misaligned polygons (sides). Other controls allow you to automatically center objects on the print bed, or provide support for multiple extruder control, or adjust the height of the first layer separately from the default layer settings. Figure 3-9 shows an excerpt of the settings panel.

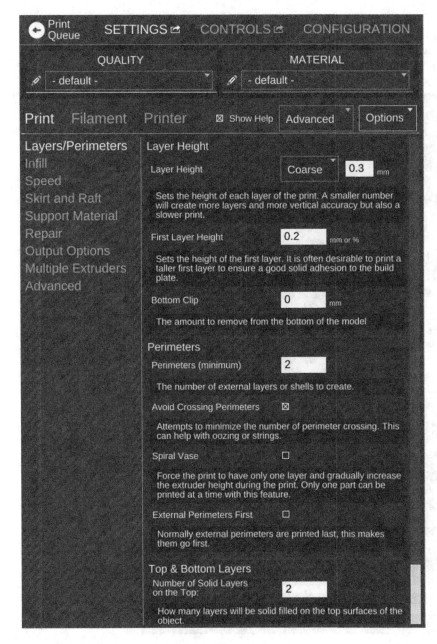

Figure 3-9. *MatterControl Advanced Controls panel*

Notice that near the top there are two drop-down boxes for quality and material. These allow you to define profiles so that you can perform quality fine-tuning, as well as profiles for various filament choices. This is really handy because filament can vary in heating, size, and other characteristics. Profiles allow you to fine-tune your printer to adapt to changes among your filament inventory.

You will also see that there are subpanels for print, filament, and printer. These subpanels allow you to further drill down and fine-tune your settings. You can set heating characteristics for filament, change the printer configuration, and more. You can also enter custom G-codes to be executed before, after, or during pausing and resuming print.

The next panel is the printer control panel. Here you will find controls for setting temperature, moving the axes, turning on the print cooling fan, and dynamically controlling the speed of the print and filament. You can also define macros to execute a batch of G-code commands. For example, I set up a macro to initiate auto bed leveling (Z-probing). Figure 3-10 shows the printer control panel.

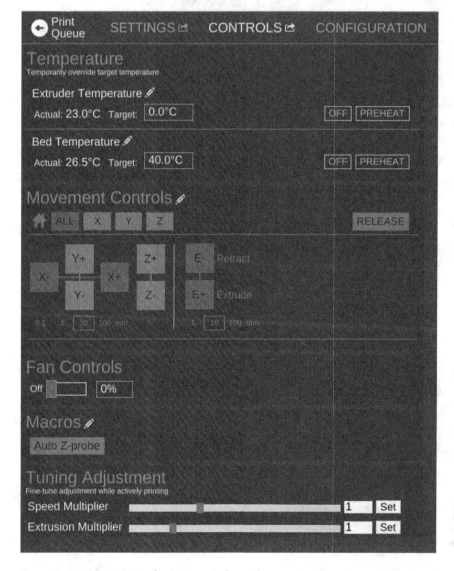

Figure 3-10. *MatterControl printer control panel*

The configuration panel lets you work with the application settings, such as the printer's hardware settings for the printer. It also displays a terminal for entering and executing ad-hoc G-code commands, as well as application settings such as color and language. You can also change the slicer if you so choose, but I've found that the default slicer is superior to the Slic3r, and given the vast array of advanced options, more tunable. Figure 3-11 shows the configuration panel.

Figure 3-11. *MatterControl configuration panel*

Cloud-based 3D print monitoring is one of the advanced features that MatterControl supports. It notifies you when your print completes. You need to create an account to use this feature, but account creation is free. To log in, click the sign in button in the far upper right of the main window. If you have the MatterControl Touch (see upcoming section), you can also connect to the tablet for transferring files. I have used the cloud monitoring to great satisfaction. When my print is complete, I get a text on my phone (via SMS), and an e-mail!

On the right of the main window is a 3D view of your object on a simulated build plate. What's really cool about this is it allows you to rotate the object so you can see it from all angles. You can also tilt the display to see the part from any angle. If you want to see a preview of the layer-by-layer build, you can do that with the Layer View tab. Figure 3-12 shows an example of the layer view. As you can see, there are controls you can use specify a layer or range of layers to view. It also shows you statistics on how long it will take to print, how much filament will be used, and the volume of the print. You can display the part in 2D or 3D and rotate it in any direction.

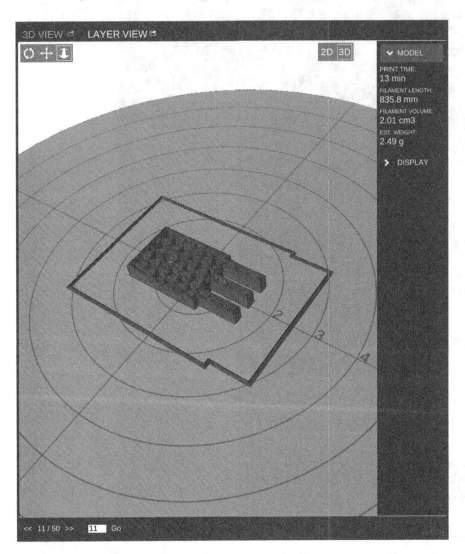

Figure 3-12. MatterControl layer view

If all of those features didn't convince you to try MatterControl, consider this: MatterControl keeps an historical record of each print, including the settings for each run. Thus, you can reprint an object from a while ago and rest assured that it will print exactly the same way as the first time. This feature is unique to MatterControl. I have not found another solution that does this quite this well. I cannot tell you how many times I've needed to reprint an object or a replacement part, only to discover I didn't remember how I initially printed it! You don't want to print a part with lower quality, especially if it originally failed due to stress or wear.

■ **Tip** To find out more about MatterControl, visit their documentation at mattercontrol.com/articles/mattercontrol-getting-started.

Finally, there are some very nice tools included. You can create text objects on the fly, connect to the MatterHackers 3D printing store, and for a small one-time fee (currently $15), convert 2D images into 3D. This feature is great for creating stencils or giving depth to 2D shapes.

The only niggle I can find with this software—and it is a very minor niggle—is that it is not integrated into the shell for your platform. For example, running on Mac OS X, the application is not aware of the various Mac OS X windowing and system features. Thus, it appears to run in isolation from the host operating system. I would not let this dissuade me from using MatterControl as my go-to application, however.

■ **Tip** For a complete examination of the MatterControl software, including how to set it up and configure it for maximum print quality, see the book *3D Printing with MatterControl* (Apress, 2015).

Simplify3D

Simplify3D is a fee-based 3D printing software suite. It boasts and lives up to claims of having the fastest slicer. Its slicing capabilities are very impressive and worth the cost of $140 per license (for two installations). True, it is not cheap by any measure, but as you will see, it is a very impressive application. It has nearly all the same features as the other choices, but it goes even further in the customization category than MatterControl.

More specifically, it allows you to apply different print settings (called a *process*) to each object on the build plate. This means that you can print one object at low quality while printing others at higher quality. This feature can be very handy, and if crafted well, allows you to save a bit of filament when printing a bunch of objects.

The interface is split into three parts: an area where you manage the build plate and configure the print settings, a print preview, and a window for controlling the printer. I first discuss the main window and its many features, and then I return to the printer control panel. Figure 3-13 shows the main window.

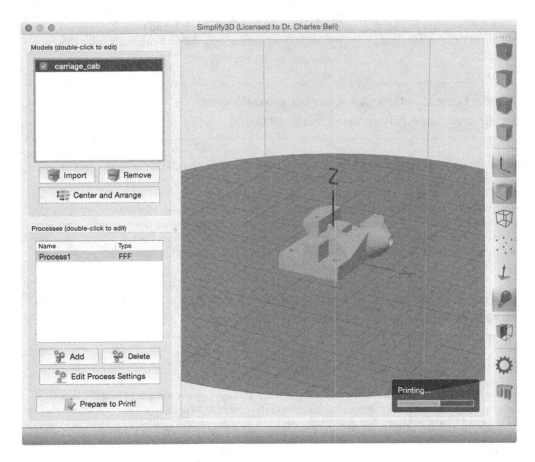

Figure 3-13. *Simplify3D main window*

Notice in Figure 3-13 that a print is underway. The software provides excellent feedback of the print process. In fact, its print estimates are the best I've seen in 3D printing software.

There are three areas that make up the main window. To the right is the build plate along with a toolbar that allows you to change the camera view and show the objects as a solid, wireframe, point cloud, or face normals (or any combination thereof). You can also launch the machine control panel, show a cross section, and define custom supports.

The custom supports feature is one the best and most unique of the Simplify3D. It is very powerful and allows you to create a minimal number of supports that are placed in key areas. If you have ever printed something with the supports enabled, and then had to spend a lot of time cleaning away the supports, you will appreciate this feature. I found it easy to use and the supports break away cleanly.

The models section in the upper left allows you to choose the objects to include in the print. You can load a set of objects and select (or unselect) the ones you want to print. Below that is another selection area that you use to define one or more processes to apply to the objects on the build plate. That is, you can define a different process for each object. I discuss processes in more detail later. Figure 3-14 shows the print preview window.

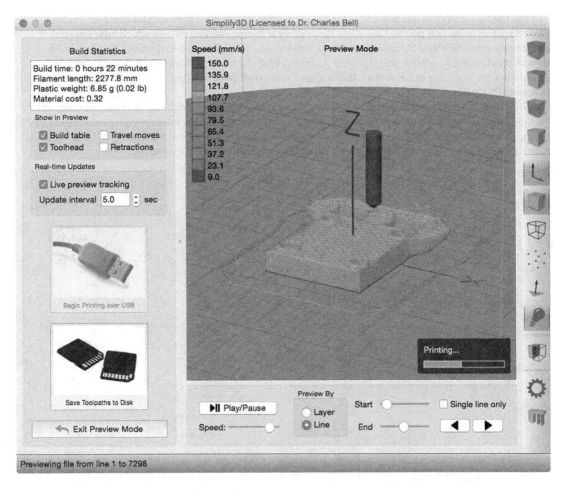

Figure 3-14. *Simplify3D print preview panel*

To initiate the print job, you click the Prepare for Print button, which opens the print preview window. You can select to either send the print job to the printer (via USB) or save the print file (G-code) to disk. When you start the print, you can return to the main window to set up your next print. This is another feature that I find very interesting. It is not as sophisticated as MatterControl's print queue, but it at least allows you to prepare for the next print.

In the upper-left print preview window, you can see the statistics for the print; below that are the buttons (rather large actually) that allow you to print via USB or save the G-code file to disk. Interestingly, Simplify3D uses some uncommon terminology for some things. Case in point is the Save Toolpaths to Disk, which is normally described as Generate, or Slice, or Save to G-code, or some similar variation.

■ **Note**   You may need to get used to some differences in terminology in Simplify3D. Some common operations have odd names. Fortunately, there aren't that many.

But the best feature of this window is the ability to animate the print preview and show or remove aspects such as retraction points. Like other 3D printing software, you can choose which layers to start and stop the preview. Once the print has started, this window turns into a virtual printer that draws the objects, synchronized with the actual printer. Although a bit of a novelty, I've found this feature to be a nice alternative to staring at the printer. It also allows you to continue working and checking on the virtual progress of the print.

When you are ready to print or work with the printer directly, there is an interactive printer controller window called the *machine control panel* that you can use to manipulate or monitor your printer. You can also open the machine control panel at any time from the main window or the print preview, but it will open automatically when you start a print. Figure 3-15 shows the machine control window.

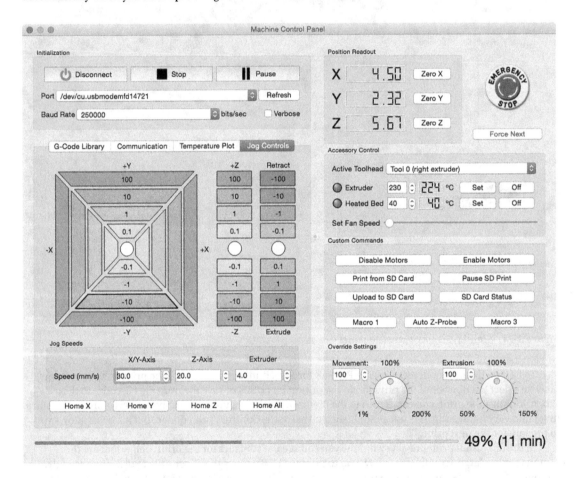

Figure 3-15. *Simplify3D machine control panel*

As you can see, there is a lot going on in this window! Not only do you find controls for connecting to the printer, you also find the normal printer control mechanisms, as well as controls to set temperature and fan speeds, disable/enable the motors, and interact with the printer's SD card—even printing from the SD files. At the bottom, there are also controls for adjusting the printer and extruder speed. Lastly, the progress bar at the bottom presents yet another feedback for checking print progress.

While it appears a bit comical, there is also an emergency stop button that is helpful for when things go wrong (and they sometimes do). Other than that curious control, the window is laid out well and is very easy to use. In fact, I like this window so well that I plan to forego installing an LCD panel on my next delta printer. This window has all the controls I need, and since I typically keep my newest printers under careful watch when using, I don't mind leaving my computer connected while printing.

Now let's return to the process feature, or more simply,[10] how to change the print, filament, and printer settings. You can open the process window by clicking the Edit Process Settings in the main window. Remember that you can make multiple processes and use them in the same print job.

There are two modes to making changes to processes. Figure 3-16 shows the basic view where you can set only higher-level features, such as the type of filament, which includes PLA and ABS, as well as PVA and Nylon. These choose a different set of defaults based on the filament. Aside from choosing the filament type, you can also choose the print quality (again, using a set of defaults), infill percentage, and raft and supports.

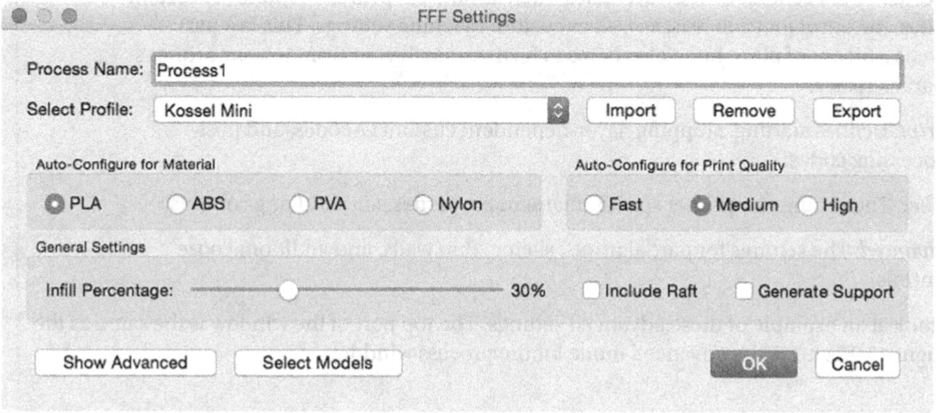

Figure 3-16. Basic process settings

Interestingly, the advanced mode is where Simplify3D really shines. Indeed, this feature alone may be worth the purchase price. There are far too many features to discuss in this chapter, so I focus on only one aspect to demonstrate the depth of control you have over your print. But first, I explain each of the tabs available.

When you turn on the advanced mode, you see a multitab area with the following 11 tabs:

- *Extruder*: The extruder settings, including parameters for the nozzle size and extrusion width control. There is also a section named Ooze Control that groups together settings for preventing stringing and artifacts.[11] You can define multiple extruders as well.

- *Layer*: The settings to create layers, including the number of shells, first layer overrides, and the general layer height.

- *Additions*: Adds skirts and rafts, along with custom settings for each.

---

[10]Another example of odd names for things.
[11]In a rare departure, this is actually a perfect name.

- *Infill*: The settings for infill percentage, including controls for overlap, width, skipping infill on some layers, and more. This is one area you want to focus on for stronger prints with less infill.

- *Support*: A vast array of controls for generating supports. Includes settings for how the supports print, which extruder is used, as well as settings for affecting how well the supports separate from the object. A little extra time spent here can save you from a lot of time with a hobby knife, cleaning up your prints.

- *Temperature*: The temperature settings for the extruder(s) and heated print bed. You can also set a different temperature for a range of layers to reduce or increase heat to help prevent cracking and other cooling related maladies.

- *Cooling*: Like the temperature, you can set the fan speed at different layer heights.

- *G-code*: Offers general G-code overrides, such as how the printer responds to certain codes, the offset for each axis, as well as custom machine settings. This last part seems a bit out of place but it also helps to further match your print to your printer's characteristics.

- *Script*: Defines starting, stopping, layer-dependent custom G-codes, and post-processing codes.

- *Other*: The settings for printer speeds, filament properties, and bridging controls.

- *Advanced*: The settings for partial prints, slicing, thin walls, and additional ooze controls.

Now let's look at an example of these advanced settings. The top part of the window is the same as the basic option. Figure 3-17 shows the advanced mode for the process window.

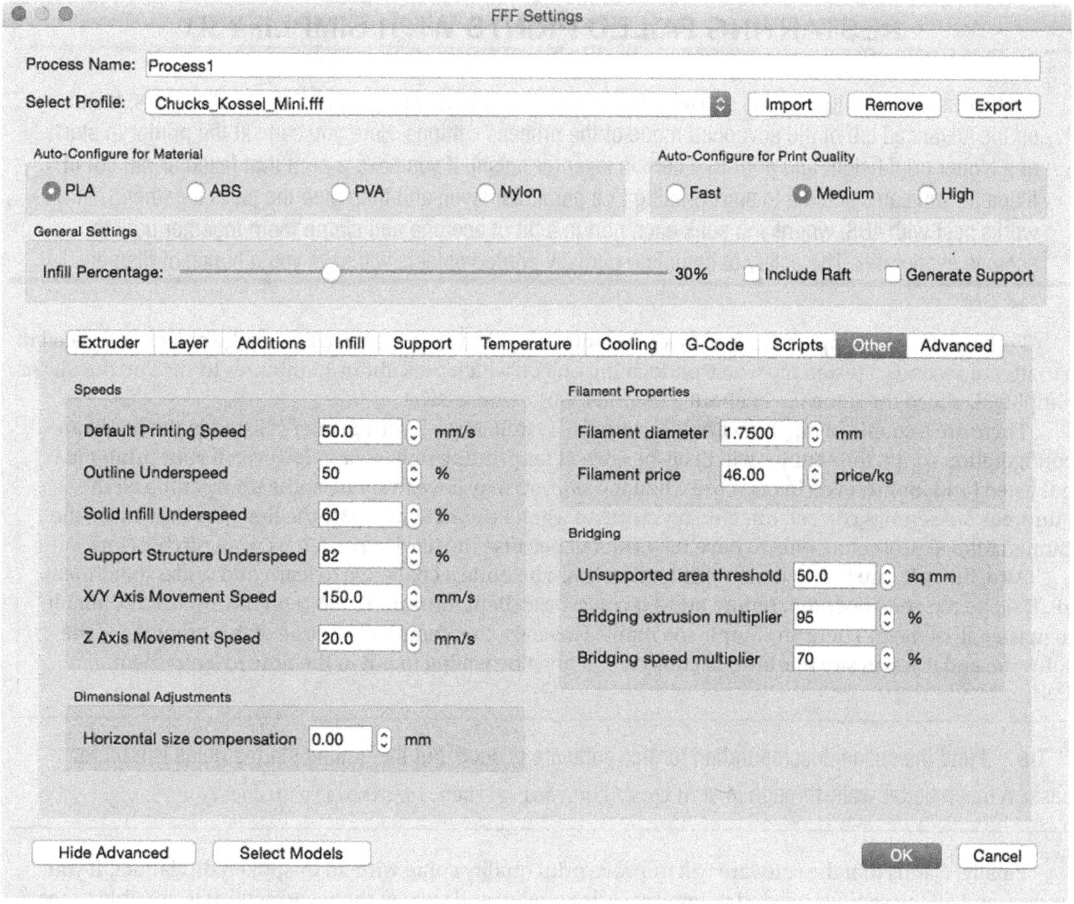

Figure 3-17. *Advanced process settings*

Figure 3-17 shows the Other tab of the advanced mode process settings. As you can see, here's where you find the settings for controlling the speed of the printer, settings for the filament's properties, including its price to estimate the cost of the print, and settings for bridging.

The last section, Bridging, is an example of the unique and fine control that Simplify3D provides. Being able to produce accurate, non-drooping, stringless bridging can really improve the quality of some prints. I should also point out that the filament cost estimate is really cool and helps answer the question that all 3D printing enthusiasts eventually get: "How much did it cost to print that whistle?" Now you can tell your wise-cracking friend exactly how much it cost!

■ **Tip** The default measurement is meters per minute. If you want millimeters per second, you have to first change the setting in the Preferences dialog.

RESTARTING FAILED PRINTS WITH SIMPLIFY3D

Another fantastic feature of this software is the ability to start and stop a print at specific layers, found on the Advanced tab of the advanced mode of the process settings. Here you can set the printer to start at a higher print height and print to a certain layer (or finish). If you have a print that failed or ran out of filament, you can calculate to start printing at a particular layer, and then glue the parts together. This works best with ABS, where you soak each part in a bit of acetone and clamp them together until the acetone evaporates. The ability to complete partially printed objects will save you a bunch of filament.

Perhaps the most impressive feature of this software is its very fast slicer. Even large objects are sliced in a matter of seconds. I tested my worst-performing object, which took about 15 minutes to slice on the Slic3r. Simplify3D sliced the same file in about 2 seconds. Quite impressive!

There are a couple of niggles with this example, as well. First, if your printer is listed in the hardware configuration script, the settings will likely be correct for printing right away. However, if your printer is not listed (and for me, even in one case when it was), you may have to spend some time getting all the hundreds[12] of settings correct. Imagine my surprise when I tested Simplify3D the first time and chose the canned Mini Kossel setup, only to have the print fail because the hardware metrics were off (by a lot).

Also, the software has so many settings that it can be quite a challenge to learn and understand them all. Despite the good documentation, and even a few excellent third-party blogs on the topic, it is difficult to master all of them. There are simply too many. However, this complexity is one of the strengths of the software, and if you desire this level of control, you must be willing to put in the time to learn them.

■ **Tip**   I find the online documentation for this software is good, but the getting started guide is a bit too basic. A much better walk-through is at `http://jinschoi.github.io/simplify3d-docs/`.

Finally, claims that the software will improve print quality come with an unspoken disclaimer. If you understand all the settings needed to improve print quality and you set them correctly, it is possible to see a very slight improvement in quality. It took me about a dozen or so tries to prove this, but I must conclude that it is possible; however, I fail to believe that the average-to-intermediate 3D printing enthusiast will see such an improvement. A series of frustrating trial-and-error sessions rather than out-of-the-box higher print quality is more likely.

Figure 3-18 shows two objects. The one on the left was printed with MatterControl on default settings, and the one on the right was printed with Simplify3D on default settings. After tweaking to improve quality, I was able to eliminate the slight artifacts (e.g., stringing) on the MatterControl print, and to achieve a slightly tighter print pattern on the Simplify3D print.[13] Interestingly, the differences in default settings were more noticeable when using higher resolutions (better quality settings). Simplify3D's higher resolution default settings produce a better print, but I was able to match the quality with a few modifications to settings in MatterControl.

---

[12]Yes, hundreds. I am not exaggerating.
[13]Even still, the better prints claim isn't a game changer in my opinion. Yes, you can get better prints but not dramatically so. However, as always, your mileage may vary.

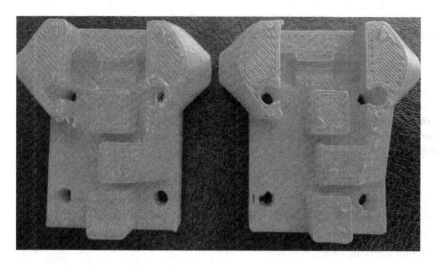

Figure 3-18. *Better prints with Simplify3D*

As you will see in Chapter 6, removing stringing involves adjusting the retraction and heater settings. Similarly, generating tighter prints can be achieved by adjusting the overlap settings for layers. Notice in Figure 3-18 that the runs in the MatterControl print are not as easy to see as those in the Simplify3D print. Once I adjusted the layer settings in Simplify3D, I was able to generate a better print than the default print for MatterControl, but it is not easy to see.

All that said, I still contend that this software is a good choice for experts. I would not suggest that beginners use it unless they own one of the more popular and fully supported printers. If you are considering this software, check the vendor's hardware support page first (`http://simplify3d.com/software/supported-printers/`). If your printer is listed, you are likely to be OK. If it isn't, be prepared to spend some time configuring the software.

How Do They Compare?

You may be wondering how these examples compare. I've made some references to this in the descriptions, but here I discuss the differences so that you can decide which application you may want to try. Although this discussion is nowhere near complete in regard to all possible software options, knowing the differences among these three software applications can help you decide which to try.

Table 3-4 lists several features and qualities, and how I judge among each. I omitted things that are equal among all the choices, such as documentation and installation ease.

Table 3-4. *Comparison of 3D Printing Software*

Topic	Repetier-Host	MatterControl	Simplify3D
Ease of use	Medium	High	Low
Print customization	Good	Better	Best
Delta printer support	Adequate	Excellent	Good
Advanced features	No	Yes	Yes
Target audience	Novice-Intermediate	Novice-Expert	Expert
Support	Good	Excellent	Good (e-mail only)

■ **Note**   These assessments are from my point of view as an expert 3D printing enthusiast. Others may have slightly differing assessments.

Clearly, it is difficult to say there is one that is better than the rest. However, having used all three extensively, I can say that MatterControl is my go-to choice. I feel it is much more mature and easier to customize than Repetier-Host, and not as complicated to use as Simplify3D. However, novices may find Repetier-Host adequate for some time, whereas advanced 3D enthusiasts may need the high level of customization that Simplify3D provides.

■ **Caution**   Whichever software you choose, take care to ensure that it is set up correctly for your hardware. Using software with the wrong hardware settings can result in an axis crash or a hot end crash. With delta printers, attempting to move the effector beyond the maximum (or minimum) travel of the delta solution can result in collisions with the frame and other hard parts.

If you decide to use Repetier-Host or MatterControl, you can use them for free. However, both accept donations, and if you like the software, you should consider donating toward keeping the features and improvements coming. Furthermore, both vendors are interested in getting feedback from their users, so feel free to tell them how you like the software and what features you would like to see in future releases.

Firmware

Object generation (CAD) and machine controller/slicing (CAM) will get you only so far. It is at this stage where the printer takes control. The software (called *firmware* because it is loaded into non-volatile RAM) on the printer is therefore responsible for reading the G-code file and providing controls for managing prints, controlling temperature, resetting the printer, and so forth.

If you purchased a complete delta printer like the SeeMeCNC Orion, you do not have to worry about the firmware—it is already loaded and configured for you at the factory. Similarly, if you built your printer from a kit, the choice of what firmware to use may have already been made for you.

You may still need to load the firmware, but typically all the hard work has been done for you. Consult your printer documentation for more information about the specifics of loading the firmware. On the other hand, if you are building your own printer from scratch or are considering changing the firmware on you printer, you need to know what options are available for delta printers.

One of the first things you need to know is that the firmware comes to you in the form of source code that you must configure and compile. There are some cases where this has been done for you, but the firmware listed in this section must be compiled. However, one of the choices has a configuration tool that you can use to create a custom download of the source code, which you can then compile.

In this section, I introduce the process and mechanics of working with and configuring the firmware, as well as some specifics about example firmware. I cover only two choices in this section—Marlin and Repetier-Firmware—because they seem to be the most popular by far.

■ **Note**   Although I only cover two examples here, there seems to be a new variant popping up every month; so if you want to know the very latest, you may want to consult online forums (`http://forums.reprap.org`).

Configuring Firmware

To configure your firmware, you need to use a compiler or integrated development environment (IDE). Since most delta printers use some form of an Arduino-derived microcontroller, you will use the Arduino IDE to compile the software. Once compiled, you can upload the software to the printer.

▦ **Tip** Check your vendor's web site for specific instructions for compiling and uploading their firmware of choice.

The Arduino IDE can accomplish both steps with one click. First, you connect your printer via a USB cable. Then in the Arduino IDE, select the board under the Tools menu (typically Mega 2560) and select the serial port under the Tools menu. Finally, click the Upload button to compile and upload the firmware. But this is the easy part. The real challenge is making sure all the variables (also called *options*) are set to the correct values.

Setting all the correct variables and constants can be a challenge. If you purchased your printer as a kit or without the firmware loaded, you should have received instructions on what values to set in this file. Consult your printer documentation or your vendor's web site for help.

The specifics for each delta printer can vary greatly. That is, each printer requires a different set of parameters and may require different changes to the configuration. Rather than diving into that realm here, I will talk more about configuring the firmware for a specific example in Chapter 4.

Marlin

The Marlin firmware has been around for a long time and has grown considerably. This is mainly due to the fact that the software is open source and many people have contributed code and features.[14] In fact, there are many variants or branches of this firmware. Most of these are customized versions that have been modified for specific hardware, or features that are unique to a particular printer vendor or design.

For example, the main Marlin repository is located at https://github.com/MarlinFirmware/Marlin. There is also a fork for the Mini Kossel created by the designer (Johann C. Rocholl) at https://github.com/jcrocholl/Marlin. If you are building your own Mini Kossel, you may find the Mini Kossel fork a good starting point. However, I should point out that sometimes these branches do not back port changes made to the main branch and therefore may not be up-to-date. Thus, if you plan to include advanced features that are not part of the standard bill of materials (BOM) or the build configuration, you may want to either wait to add those features or use the latest version from the main repository.

All the settings you need to change are located in two files, Configuration.h and Configuration_adv.h. Configuration.h contains basic settings, such as board type, temperature sensor type, axis scaling, and endstops. Configuration_adv.h contains settings such as thermal and mechanical settings. These are the only files you need to modify, and in most cases you may not need to change the advanced file. Listing 3-2 shows a small portion of the Marlin source code. In this case, it is an excerpt from the Configuration.h file. I show only a few parts of the file for delta printers—it is quite a bit larger than this!

▦ **Note** Older versions of the Marlin firmware had all the settings in the Configuration.h file.

---

[14]Owners of the specific branch act as gatekeepers and only accept code that they approve.

Listing 3-2. Configuration.h: Settings for Delta Printers

```
...
//============================================================================
//=========================== Delta Settings ================================
//============================================================================
// Enable DELTA kinematics and most of the default configuration for Deltas
#define DELTA

// Make delta curves from many straight lines (linear interpolation).
// This is a trade-off between visible corners (not enough segments)
// and processor overload (too many expensive sqrt calls).
#define DELTA_SEGMENTS_PER_SECOND 200

// NOTE NB all values for DELTA_* values MUST be floating point, so always have a decimal
point in them

// Center-to-center distance of the holes in the diagonal push rods.
#define DELTA_DIAGONAL_ROD 250.0 // mm

// Horizontal offset from middle of printer to smooth rod center.
#define DELTA_SMOOTH_ROD_OFFSET 175.0 // mm

// Horizontal offset of the universal joints on the end effector.
#define DELTA_EFFECTOR_OFFSET 33.0 // mm

// Horizontal offset of the universal joints on the carriages.
#define DELTA_CARRIAGE_OFFSET 18.0 // mm

// Effective horizontal distance bridged by diagonal push rods.
#define DELTA_RADIUS (DELTA_SMOOTH_ROD_OFFSET-DELTA_EFFECTOR_OFFSET-DELTA_CARRIAGE_OFFSET)
...
```

■ **Tip**   Most vendors have or document the proper settings for their printers. Check their web sites and forums if you have questions about any of the settings.

If this file is scary, or if you think you're in way too deep, do not despair! While it requires you to know all the specifics of your hardware, like the mechanics (and mathematics) of each axis, there are a great number of people who have done this before. If you get stuck, consult the forums and similar online sites. With a little digging, you can find the correct values to use for just about any hardware configuration.

The latest version of Marlin comes with several example configurations. Look in the example_configurations folder for these files. You will find an example for delta printers. Copy these to the main Marlin folder (before you start the Arduino IDE) and use that as your starting point.

Repetier-Firmware

The nice folks at Repetier (repetier.com) have created both a 3D printing environment (Repetier-Host) and a 3D printer firmware (Repetier-Firmware). The firmware traces its origins to a variety of early 3D printer firmware efforts. It is most similar to Marlin (which is really evident when you see the source code files), but it has a very different approach to how it implements certain features. Yet, the biggest difference is the Repetier-Firmware configuration tool (`www.repetier.com/firmware/v092/`). This web site allows you to step through the setting of the firmware variables in a guided form. You can use the results from the hardware calculator to complete the process. Once all the settings are complete, you can download a customized source code bundle that you can simply compile and upload. If you need to make minor changes, you can do so in the source code files or re-run the configuration tool by first uploading your own configuration.

Figure 3-19 shows an excerpt of this tool in action. In this case, it highlights the dimensions section for delta printers.

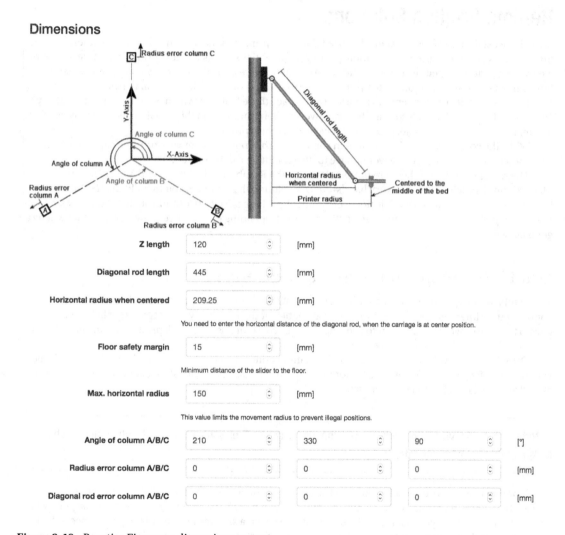

Figure 3-19. Repetier-Firmware dimensions excerpt

As you can see, it is very comprehensive, and if you compare it to the source code in Listing 3-2, it is much easier to understand and use. Indeed, most people have no idea what some of these settings are. A drawing goes a long ways to help! However, do not despair, as I will explain these in more detail in Chapter 4.

This configuration tool may be very attractive if you have never worked with 3D printer firmware before or you don't want to dive into the gore and guts of the source code to ferret out the settings you need. All you need to do is follow the guided tour! Also considering its online help forum, this firmware may be a better option for most delta printer enthusiasts.[15]

Remote Printing Solutions

If you have used some of the latest full-featured Cartesian printers or have seen a demo of their features, you may come away quite impressed.[16] Remote printing capabilities such as wireless printing, remote access via a network connection, remote camera, and so forth can be quite appealing if you want to print something but cannot be in the same room as the printer—due to noise or other environmental reasons.

In general, delta printer vendors have yet to embrace these features, which is a pity if they appeal to you. However, all is not completely lost, as there are two excellent solutions to this problem. Fortunately, for delta printer owners the answer is no, you do not have to buy a new printer!

While the solutions are quite different in some ways, they both add network printing capabilities and camera access that you otherwise would have to do without on a delta printer.

The two choices I cover here are the OctoPrint for the Raspberry Pi (OctoPi) and MatterHackers' MatterControl Touch. OctoPi is a very hands-on, DIY solution that requires you to build the hardware and install the software by hand (but it is not overly difficult); whereas MatterControl Touch is a turnkey solution that uses a tablet. Now let's see how each of these work. Depending on your needs, one or the other will be a good choice.

OctoPi : OctoPrint Running on a Raspberry Pi

The OctoPrint software (http://octoprint.org) is a 3D printer network print server that allows you to control your printer remotely. OctoPrint is also available for the Raspberry Pi (https://github.com/guysoft/OctoPi), which allows you to use a lightweight computer as a network print server to control your printer. In fact, you can set it up to be wireless!

OctoPi is not a CAM application, but rather a remote print controller. You upload sliced files (G-code files) via a web interface, and then select the file for printing. You can also print files stored in the printer's SD card, as well as send files to be stored on the OctoPi.

▪ **Note** OctoPrint works only with printers that use G-codes. Thus you cannot use it with printers such as MakerBot that use other formats.

More specifically, you use a Raspberry Pi computer to run a special version of the OctoPrint software that enables you to print and control your printer over the network. As a bonus, if you add the Raspberry Pi camera (or equivalent), you can monitor your printer to watch a streaming video of the print process. You can also set up time-lapse photos so that you can make a short video of your build. How cool is that?

---

[15]However, I still prefer getting my hands dirty in the source code.
[16]Or perhaps say the same thing I did the first time I saw remote printing, "Meh."

WHAT IS A RASPBERRY PI?

The Raspberry Pi is a small, inexpensive personal computer. Although it lacks the capacity for memory expansion and can't accommodate onboard devices such as CD, DVD, and hard drives, it has everything a simple personal computer requires. That is, it has USB ports, an Ethernet port, HDMI (and composite) video, and even an audio connector for sound.

The Raspberry Pi has an SD slot that you can use to boot the computer into any of several Linux operating systems. All you need is an HDMI monitor (or DVI with an HDMI-to-DVI adapter), a USB keyboard and mouse, and a 5V power supply—and you're off and running.

The board is available in several versions and comes as a bare board costing as little as $35.00 (for the version with Ethernet). It can be purchased online from electronics vendors such as SparkFun and Adafruit. Most vendors have a host of accessories that have been tested and verified to work with the Raspberry Pi. These include small monitors, miniature keyboards, and even cases for mounting the board.

Getting Started

Setting up the Raspberry Pi to run OctoPi is not very difficult. It involves assembling the hardware (installing the Raspberry Pi in the case, and plugging in the camera and the Wi-Fi module), and creating a boot image on an SD card. There are a lot resources for accomplishing these steps. In fact, there are so many options for Wi-Fi cards, cameras, and other peripherals that a step-by-step tutorial could not cover them all.

Thus, rather than give you a tutorial on how to set up an OctoPi, I refer you to https://github.com/guysoft/OctoPi for more details. Links on this web site take you to well-documented (and current) techniques for creating the SD boot image. The good news is that the boot image you need is available on the OctoPi site, which contains everything you need. Just create the boot image, plug it in, and you're good to go.

■ **Note** You do not have to perform the development steps, just follow the "How to use it?" section.

I should also note at this point that you want to check with your vendor for whatever peripherals you need to buy, especially Wi-Fi USB dongles, to ensure that they work with Raspbian, upon which the OctoPi software is installed. A good resource to determine if your hardware choice works is at http://elinux.org/RPi_VerifiedPeripherals.

Once you have the SD boot image created and the hardware assembled, it's time to power things up.

If you need additional help or want to manually install OctoPi, visit https://github.com/foosel/OctoPrint/wiki/Setup-on-a-Raspberry-Pi-running-Raspbian.

Using OctoPi

To connect to the OctoPi server, you should first ensure that the network cable is plugged in, wait for the Raspberry Pi to boot, and if using Wi-Fi, wait until it connects. This can take about 3 to 5 minutes. If you have access to the Raspberry Pi LEDs, wait until all the networking LEDs illuminate or begin blinking. Once fully booted, open your browser on your laptop and use the URL octopi.local to connect.

The first thing you need to do is set up access control for connecting to the printer. Figure 3-20 shows the OctoPi access control window. Use the user account you created to log in to OctoPi so that you can ensure that you are the only one with access to your printer.

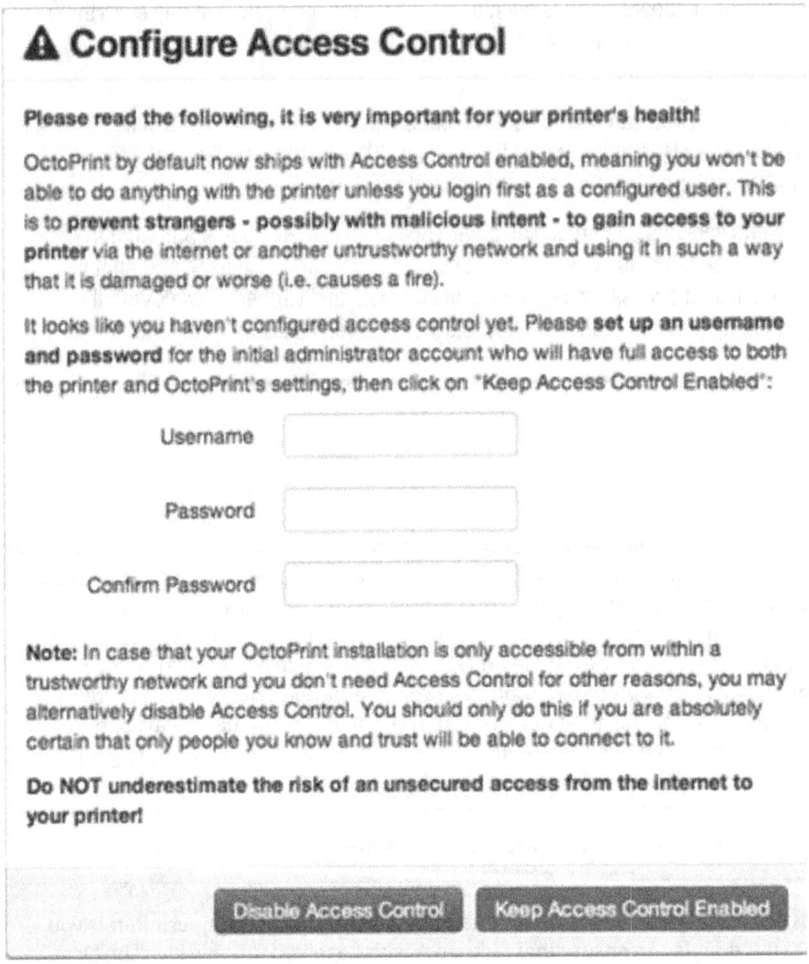

⚠ Configure Access Control

Please read the following, it is very important for your printer's health!

OctoPrint by default now ships with Access Control enabled, meaning you won't be able to do anything with the printer unless you login first as a configured user. This is to **prevent strangers - possibly with malicious intent - to gain access to your printer** via the internet or another untrustworthy network and using it in such a way that it is damaged or worse (i.e. causes a fire).

It looks like you haven't configured access control yet. Please **set up an username and password** for the initial administrator account who will have full access to both the printer and OctoPrint's settings, then click on "Keep Access Control Enabled":

Username

Password

Confirm Password

Note: In case that your OctoPrint installation is only accessible from within a trustworthy network and you don't need Access Control for other reasons, you may alternatively disable Access Control. You should only do this if you are absolutely certain that only people you know and trust will be able to connect to it.

Do NOT underestimate the risk of an unsecured access from the internet to your printer!

Disable Access Control   Keep Access Control Enabled

Figure 3-20. *Access control window (first run)*

Once logged in, you will see the main window, as shown in Figure 3-21.

Figure 3-21. *OctoPi main window*

Before you can print, you need to upload one or more G-code files to the server. I have uploaded a test cube to the server. I have also activated the printer's extruder heater, which along with the heated build plate is depicted in the Temperature tab (see Figure 3-21). Notice that you can set the temperatures on this tab.

Figure 3-22 shows the Control tab. As you can see, there are controls for moving the axes, homing, and more. Notice the coolest part of this—the camera view! When you use this tab, you see a streaming, live video feed from the Raspberry Pi. You can use this page to watch your printer over the network.

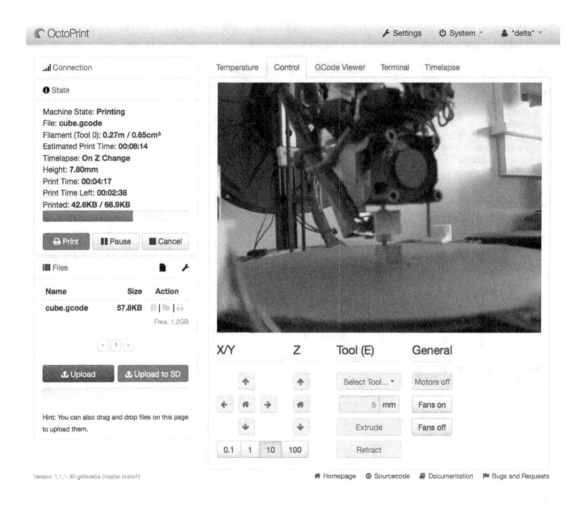

Figure 3-22. *Control tab*

The GCode Viewer tab lets you view the layers of the file you are printing. You can also get a bunch of statistics about the print from the links on that page.

The next tab is a terminal viewer that you can use to watch the G-codes sent to the printer, as well as any messages received from the printer. This is the same sort of information you see at the bottom of the Repetier-Host application.

The last tab is the Timelapse tab. Here you can set up a time-lapse capture and manage existing time-lapse movies. You cannot change the time-lapse settings if there is a print in progress or if a printer is not connected. You must therefore wait until after you have connected to a printer and before you start to print to turn on the time-lapse feature. The default setting is to record a snapshot in a frame of the movie on each Z-axis change. This creates a small, fast movie of your print.

To see a time-lapse movie, wait until the print is done and then visit this tab. If the movie isn't ready yet, you may have to refresh the page after a couple of minutes. OctoPi names the movie using the name of the object you printed. To view the movie, click the tiny icon to the right of the file name. The first one deletes the movie. Figure 3-23 shows the movie in progress.

Figure 3-23. *Time-lapse movie*

Notice how the movie has the OctoPrint icon branded on it. If you'd like, you can turn this off in the Settings dialog (see the link in the upper-right corner of the dialog).

Well, that's it! When you complete this project, you will have a fully functional network-enabled printer. What you've done is move the printer controller software from your computer to the small Raspberry Pi (which is clearly up to the task), letting you control your printer without tying up a USB connection on your laptop. Oh, and you get some really cool video capabilities in the bargain!

If you have not tried this project, I encourage you to do so at your first opportunity. You may want to wait until your printer is fully calibrated, but as you can see, the OctoPi has all the controls you need to run the preflight tests—even over the network! How cool is that?

So what does it cost? If you buy the Raspberry Pi, camera, case, power supply, and wireless network adapter, you are looking at about $125 to $150 in expenses. While that isn't exactly free, it is much cheaper than buying a new printer just to get networking access!

MatterControl Touch

MatterControl Touch is a remote printing solution unlike anything else. MatterHackers has loaded its MatterControl software on an Android tablet. Yes, you get all the power of the excellent MatterControl 3D printing software on a small, portable touchscreen. How cool is that?

You can buy MatterControl Touch at `matterhackers.com/store/printer-accessories/ mattercontrol-touch`. It costs $299 and comes with the tablet, power supply, and USB adapter. The tablet comes preloaded with a cool tablet stand that you can print right away. In fact, I'd make it the first thing you print! Figure 3-24 shows my MatterControl Touch on its freshly printed stand.

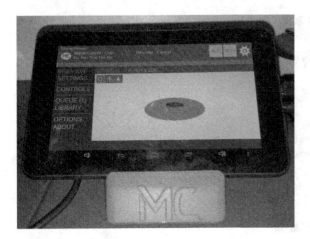

Figure 3-24. *Printed tablet stand*

Getting Started

Setting up the MatterControl Touch is really easy. All you need to do is plug in the power, USB cable, and power on the tablet. MatterControl will launch automatically. Once launched, just plug in your printer and power it on. A setup wizard will launch, prompting you to configure your Wi-Fi connection and printer (manufacturer and mode). From here, it's like using MatterControl on your computer. Everything is where you expect it to be, albeit a bit compressed to fit on the smaller screen.

■ **Note** You cannot use the tablet without the power adapter plugged in. At first, this seemed very strange, but given that the USB cable powers most 3D printing electronics, it makes sense to require the tablet to be powered on. Otherwise, the printer will drain the tablet battery very quickly.

Using MatterControl Touch

Once again, MatterControl Touch runs MatterControl. If you have used MatterControl, you know how to use the MatterControl Touch! Thus, a detailed explanation of its features can be found in the previous section on MatterControl. Rather than rehash that information, let's take a look at the MatterControl Touch in action and some of its unique features.

For example, Figure 3-25 shows MatterControl Touch printing a test cube. Here you can see the application looks very similar to MatterControl on a computer—because it is the same.

Figure 3-25. *Printing a test print*

However, unlike the desktop version, MatterControl Touch goes into a sort of screensaver mode after a few moments, showing the print status (see Figure 3-26). I really like this feature. Typical LCD panels do not offer this data, making the MatterControl Touch a clear replacement for LCD panels. As the screen suggests, just tap the screen to return to the application.

Figure 3-26. *Print status report*

You really appreciate the power of the application when you realize that all the controls you are used to on MatterControl are included. Figure 3-27 shows an example of the advanced settings panel. As you can see, all the power of MatterControl is at your fingertips. This means that you don't need to load only G-code files onto the tablet, like you would with OctoPi. Instead, you can configure and slice your object right there on the tablet.

Figure 3-27. *Same settings as MatterControl*

Since the tablet has a camera, MatterControl Touch adds the ability to take a photo of your print. You can do this anytime you want and you can also have a photo taken when the print completes. This requires you to point the tablet in the direction of your printer, but that is a minor inconvenience.[17]

One feature I really like about MatterControl Touch that OctoPi doesn't have (perhaps yet) is the ability to notify me when a print is complete. Indeed, if you have cloud support turned on, when a print completes, your MatterControl Touch can send you an SMS (text) message and an e-mail. Figures 3-28 and 3-29 are examples of the communications you receive.

---

[17]Actually, I have a design for mounting the MatterControl Touch to my delta printer. See thingiverse.com/thing:731012.

Figure 3-28. *Print complete text*

From: MatterControl Notifications >   Hide

To: drcharlesbell@gmail.com >

MatterControl: Your 3D Print is Complete
March 3, 2015 at 4:11 PM

Your 3D print 'cube' is ready.

If you believe you've received this notification
by mistake please contact
support@matterhackers.com

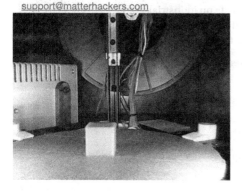

Figure 3-29. *Print complete e-mail*

If you consider all the power that comes in such a small package, MatterControl Touch is one of those game changers in the 3D printing world. If you want to be able to control your printer as if your computer were attached with all the features of MatterControl, there is no better choice.

Which Is Best?

Once again, depending on your needs, either OctoPi or MatterControl Touch is a good solution. However, I feel that the power of the MatterControl software alone makes MatterControl Touch the best choice. OctoPi works very well, but since MatterControl Touch is a fully assembled, ready-to-go solution that requires no more setup than MatterControl itself, and the feature set from MatterHackers with remote connectivity planned in a future release, for most people it is the best choice.

Indeed, the only thing I find lacking on MatterControl Touch is the remote access that OctoPi provides. Once that is in place, MatterControl Touch will be more powerful and more versatile than OctoPi. Then again, if you have a dozen printers and want to add remote printing capability to all of them, OctoPi will be a little cheaper, provided you don't mind getting your hands dirty building it.

Object Repositories

If you are thinking that learning a CAD program is a lot of work, you're right, it can be. Learning Blender can be a steep curve, but if you favor a GUI with advanced features, the learning curve comes with the territory. The other GUI-based CAD programs have varying demands for learning to use, but most require you to learn a specific set of menus and tools. On the other hand, OpenSCAD is easier to use if you think in code, and therefore you may not need to use a complex GUI and all of its trappings to design your own objects.

But what if you don't have the time or the inclination to design your own object? Wouldn't it be great if there were a place where you could download .stl files of interesting and useful objects for printing? That's exactly what developers were thinking when they created object repositories. I find them so useful for finding objects to print, or for inspiration in designing objects, that I've gotten in the habit of checking these repositories at least once per day.

Although they are not software, object repositories play an important role in the 3D printing tool chain. Object repositories are online web sites devoted to allow enthusiasts to share 3D designs. Some are designed for 3D printing specifically, but most support many forms of 3D objects, such as CNC, laser cutting, and more.

Some are sponsored by 3D printing manufacturers, such as MakerBot and Ultimaker, but they are open to everyone to use—regardless of the brand of printer that you own. Some, like Shapeways and Sculpteo, allow you to buy, share, sell, and order objects and even prints made on industrial-grade 3D printers.

There are several object repositories available and more added every year. I encourage you to visit these repositories and others like them to find objects for printing and to share your own objects with the world:

- Thingiverse (`Thingiverse.com`), sponsored by MakerBot Industries: An online maker-centric community

- YouMagine (`youmagine.com`), sponsored by Ultimaker: An online 3D printing community

- Shapeways (`shapeways.com`) : A 3D object marketplace

- Sculpteo (`sculpteo.com/en/`) : A 3D object marketplace

- Yeggi (`yeggi.com`): A 3D printing search engine

Most of these repositories permit you to search and download any objects that are made publically available, but require an account to post your own objects or comment on others. The following is a short discussion on two of the more popular repositories.

Thingiverse

Thingiverse is a place where anyone can upload and post information about their objects (ones they have created or modified by permission) for anyone else to view and use. It was created by MakerBot Industries, but can be used by anyone, and indeed many non-MakerBot owners have accounts and post objects regularly. Most of the objects on Thingiverse are open source, so you need not worry about intellectual property violations—but always read the license! Figure 3-30 shows a snapshot of the Thingiverse web site.

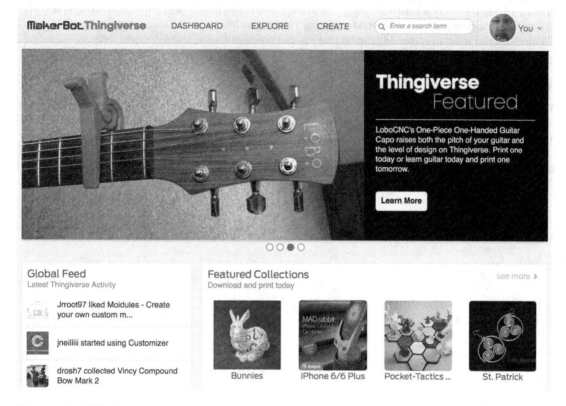

Figure 3-30. Thingiverse

The site is free to browse, search, and download objects. You don't even need to create an account! Once you find an object you want to use (print), simply click the Download button and save the files to your hard drive. Most files are in the .stl format, so you need only to slice it and print it.

Registered users can create objects, mark objects to print later, tag things that they like, organize things into collections and keep a virtual file, and keep tabs on any objects uploaded. You can also share with others the objects you have printed (made). It is always nice to find a thing you like and see examples of it printed by others.

■ **Tip** The best objects are those that a lot of people like. Watch for things that have been made often. This is indicative of a well-designed (and useful) thing.

When you find a part you want to see in more detail, simply click it. You will then see a detailed page with a list of photos of the thing (a 3D view and one or more photos that the creator has uploaded). The page also includes a menu or tabs (varies among platforms) that include entries for a description of the object (thing info), instructions for assembly (optional), a list of the files available, and a comments section where anyone can comment or ask the creator questions. There are also statistics on the number of people that have liked the object, added it to a collection, or printed (made) it.

There is even a Thingiverse app for your iPhone or Android device so you can see what has been added since your last visit. Simply go to the site, click the Explore menu item, and choose Newest. I find myself checking for new objects at least once a day. I've found many useful objects and inspiration for other objects. Thingiverse is a great asset. I recommend searching Thingiverse before you create any object yourself. Chances are you will find something similar that you can download, slice, and print right away!

YouMagine

YouMagine is an object repository by Ultimaker, where anyone can search, retrieve, and with an account, post their own objects. Although there are features similar to Thingiverse for sharing things (objects), YouMagine also has an online discussion forum where 3D printing enthusiasts can participate in chats about current topics. Thus, YouMagine kicks things up a notch by including collaboration among like-minded people. Figure 3-31 shows a snapshot of the YouMagine main screen.

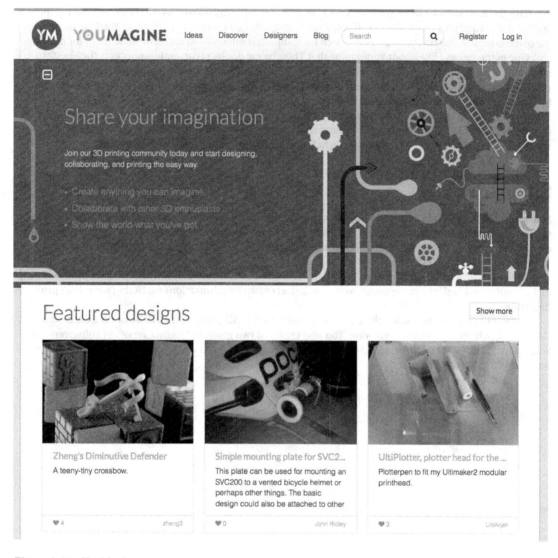

Figure 3-31. *YouMagine*

The collaboration feature is very advanced. When you click the Ideas button, you are taken to a list of the current ideas being discussed. You can join or start your own ideas, but you will need an account. Once logged in, you can join any of the chats and discuss an idea with the owner and others. This is a really powerful way to leverage the 3D printing community to help you develop an idea. You will be surprised how helpful most people are![18]

---

[18]Of course, there are always a few who can be contrary but most are very helpful. Peer pressure seems to keep the worst naysayers at bay.

The discover feature allows you to see what designs are trending, as well as what categories are popular and even the latest postings to the site. If you want to keep abreast of what is going on in YouMagine, this is the place to look. Naturally, you can also search for things that interest you and download them for printing.

One of the things I like about YouMagine that Thingiverse doesn't (currently) support is the ability to integrate social media such as Twitter, Facebook, Google+, and e-mail. That is, you can tweet about a design you like, post it on your Facebook page, share it on Google+, and even e-mail yourself or your friends a link to the design. Perhaps it is just me, but that is really nice.

Finally, like Thingiverse, you will find YouMagine a handy resource for finding things to print, discussing new designs, and even collaborating with other 3D printing enthusiasts. Whichever object repository you choose to use (if not both), it will help you take your enthusiasm to a new level.

Summary

Software for 3D printing has come a long way since the days of a mix-matched set of discrete applications, scripts, and manual file editing. Modern 3D printing software is far more sophisticated and streamlined than ever before. Aside from CAD features, 3D printing software today contains all the features one could need to operate a 3D printer to perfection.

Even the firmware has grown to an impressive feature set. Firmware that works with delta printers include advanced bed leveling features, as well as a host of small optimizations for tuning your delta printer hardware.

In this chapter, you examined the types of software used in 3D printing with delta printers, including CAD, CAM, printer control, and firmware. You also explored two growing Internet services (Thingiverse and YouMagine) for sharing and storing 3D designs. In the next chapter, you will learn some tips and tricks for building your own delta printer.

CHAPTER 4

■ ■ ■

Tips for Building a Delta Printer

Building your own 3D printer can be a really cool project. Building a 3D printer requires basic mechanical skills and the ability to work with wiring (crimping and soldering). It also requires a certain set of tools to build the printer. There are a number of things you can do to help make the build more productive and successful. I cover all these topics and more in this chapter, starting with the tools and skills required.[1]

Tools and Skills Required

You don't have to be a master mechanic or an electrical engineer to build a delta printer. You don't even have to have a garage full of machinery or drawers full of gleaming chrome tools. However, you do need a certain number of small hand tools to build a typical delta printer.

Most commercial- and professional-grade printers require fewer tools. However, for more complicated builds, you will need a few more tools. The main reason for this is RepRap and similar DIY kits tend to be unrefined and require more work, such as building cables, soldering, and cleaning parts for assembly.

In this section, I cover the tools you need to build a typical RepRap delta printer (or one you design yourself). Depending on your printer choice, you may not need all the tools. However, I do suggest you acquire all the tools on the required tools list.

The printer kit you buy may determine what tools you need. For example, if you are building a Kossel Pro, you only need a good quality hobby knife and a pair of needle-nose pliers to complete the build. Furthermore, the Kossel Pro requires fewer tools than the Rostock Max v2, and the Mini Kossel (RepRap designs) requires the most tools. You should consult your vendor's documentation if you want to minimize the number of tools you need to buy to build your printer.

CAN YOU HAVE TOO MANY TOOLS?

I still remember the massive garage my parent's neighbor maintained. He was a retired engineer who had every imaginable tool and machine to work wood and metal. Today such a garage would cost a small fortune, and while I'd love to have such a setup, reality suggests you can only have so many tools. If you don't have any desire or need to perform maintenance on your own car, motorcycle, boat, or anything with an engine, buying the tools listed in this chapter will provide the tools you need to properly build and maintain your delta printer. Besides, if you don't know how to use certain tools, or you don't have the time to learn, you can indeed have too many tools.

---

[1]Much of the information in this chapter appears in my book, *Maintaining and Troubleshooting Your 3D Printer* (Apress, 2014). This chapter is a condensed version of that material with a specific focus on delta printers. If you need more information than what is included here, see my other book.

A Word About Tool Quality

I should also point out that there are different quality tool brands available to buy. At the top are those tool brands like Snap-On and Mac tools, followed by Craftsman and Kobalt, and finally, the generic hardware and department store brands (sometimes unbranded).

If you are going to build a lot of printers or you want tools to work on your car or motorcycle, where precision is very important, you may want to consider the top-quality brands. However, for most 3D printer enthusiasts, store brands such as Craftsman and Kobalt are more than adequate.

■ **Tip** Watch for occasional in-store sales. Stores often run sales on overstock items—especially after a holiday like Christmas or Father's Day. Indeed, most of my tools were bought at 40%–50% off the regular price.

Required Tools

The vast majority of tools that you will need to build and maintain your delta printer are common hand tools (screwdrivers, wrenches, pliers, etc.). There are a few tools that you may want to have that would make the job easier. There are also a few tools that I recommend having in case you'd like to build more than one printer or if you want to experiment with upgrading your printer. I divide the tools into three categories: required (general and building), recommended, and optional.

■ **Tip** You cannot go wrong if you prefer to buy a complete toolset for small projects.[2] You may also want to buy an electronics toolkit since few mechanics kits include these. The two sets should contain most of the tools listed here (plus a few more) and could be cheaper to buy as a set—especially if you find them on sale. Just throw the hammers away.

Most of these tools are commonplace items. Rather than describe each, I focus on those that are less common or are likely to be tools that you have not encountered before. In other words, you won't find them in your kitchen junk drawer.

General Tools

This section describes those tools I feel are essential for every 3D printer owner. While some printers require fewer tools than others, the following list is what your basic 3D printer toolkit should contain. I list the tools first, and then discuss some of the less common tools later.

- Needle-nose pliers

- Small flat-blade (slotted) screwdriver

- Small and medium-sized Phillips screwdrivers

- Side cutters

- Hex wrenches: 1mm, 1.5mm, 2.5mm, 3.0mm

---

[2]Avoid toolkits designed for working on cars, trains, RVs, semitrucks, or anything larger than your body. The tools included will be far too heavy-duty for working on delta printers.

■ **Tip**   Try to find those with ball ends (sometimes "ball head" or just "ball"), which allows you to use them at an angle.[3]

- Digital caliper with metric scale

- ESD tweezers

- Hobby knife set

- Rulers (metric), (1) 300mm or more, (1) 100mm–150mm

■ **Note**   Some vendors include tools with their products. For example, the Kossel Pro kit contains three very nice hex wrenches (1mm, 1.5mm, and 2.5mm). Similarly, the Rostock Max v2 comes with a nifty part-removal tool.

The digital caliper is used in a variety of ways. It makes setting up your printer easier and more precise. That is, the caliper can reliably measure small distances. It can also measure depth—outside and inside dimensions. It is also very handy to use when modeling or creating objects that will be mounted to other objects. For example, you can use a digital caliper to measure the thickness or depth of mating surfaces. Figure 4-1 shows a typical digital caliper from Kobalt. When you use a digital caliper, always make sure to close the jaws and press the zero or reset button to calibrate the scale to zero, as shown in the photo.

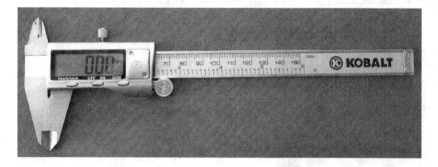

Figure 4-1. *Digital caliper*

Electric static discharge (ESD)–safe tweezers are another handy addition. I prefer tweezers with an angled head. You can use these to safely remove excess hot filament from the nozzle and build plate without fear of a static discharge (or getting burned).

A hobby knife set (known by its more common name, X-Acto)[4] is another very handy tool every 3D printer owner must have. You will need a hobby knife to remove plastic filament from your objects, and to cut and reshape objects, and more.

---

[3]In fact, you will need these to build a Mini Kossel.
[4]Just like Xerox is a synonym for copier, X-Acto knife is a synonym for a small, sharp, and guaranteed-to-make-you-bleed if you're careless hobby knife.

Tools for Building a Delta Printer

There are also a number of tools you will need if you plan to build your own delta printer or if you plan to upgrade your existing printer. While you may not need to use some of the following tools unless repairing your printer, you should consider adding these items to your toolkit eventually.

For example, if you are not planning to build your own 3D printer, you can wait until you see these tools on sale, so that you can save some money and have the tools when you need them in the future.

- Wire stripper

- Soldering iron and solder

- Multimeter

- Ceramic screwdriver

- Wrenches: a combination of 5.5mm, 6mm, 6.5mm, 7mm, 7.5mm, 8mm, 10mm, 12mm, and 13mm sizes

- Square

- Crimpers

There are several types of wire strippers. In fact, there are probably a dozen or more designs out there. But there really are two kinds: ones that only grip and cut the insulation as you pull it off the wire, and those that grip, cut, and remove the insulation. The first type is more common, and with some practice, do just fine for most small jobs (like repairing a broken wire); but the second type makes a larger job—such as wiring 3D printer electronics from bare wire (no prefab connectors)—much faster. As you can imagine, the first type is considerably cheaper. Figure 4-2 shows both types of wire strippers. Either is a good choice.

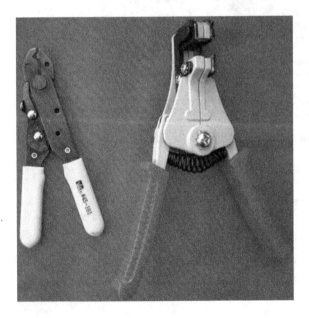

Figure 4-2. Wire strippers

A soldering iron is required for some delta printer kits—especially those that do not have prefabricated electronics and cables. If you are going to build a printer that requires you to solder wires together, or maybe a few connectors, a basic soldering iron from an electronics store is all you will need.

On the other hand, if you plan to assemble your own electronics, you may want to consider getting a good, professional soldering iron such as a Hakko. The professional models include features that allow you to set the temperature of the wand, have a wider array of tips available, and tend to last a lot longer. Figure 4-3 shows a well-used entry-level soldering iron. Maker Shed (makershed.com/collections/soldering-tools) has a variety of inexpensive soldering tools.

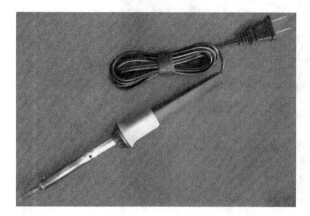

Figure 4-3. *Entry-level soldering iron*

■ **Tip** For the best results, choose a solder with a low lead content in the 37%–40% range. If you use a professional soldering iron, adjust the temperature to match the melting point of the solder (listed on the label).

A multimeter is another tool that you will need when building your own printer. You will also need it to do almost any electrical repair on your printer. Like soldering irons, there are many different multimeters available. And like soldering irons, the prices of multimeters range from inexpensive basic units to complex, feature-rich, incredibly expensive units.

For most 3D printer tasks, including building most kits, a basic unit is all you will need. However, if you plan to build more than one delta printer or want to assemble your own electronics, you may want to invest a bit more money in a more sophisticated multimeter. Figure 4-4 shows a professional multimeter from BK Precision.

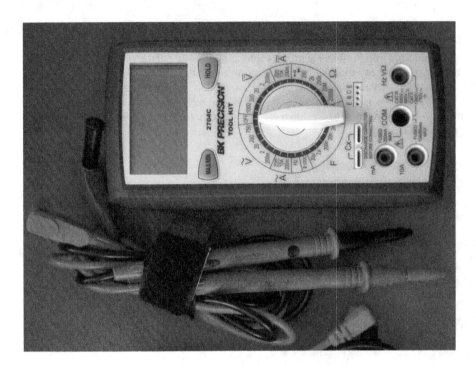

Figure 4-4. *Advanced digital multimeter*

You probably won't need more than a basic unit. You will need to measure voltage and resistance at a minimum. Whichever meter you buy, make sure that it has modes for measuring AC and DC voltage, continuity testing (with an audible alert), and checking resistance.

A ceramic screwdriver is used to adjust small potentiometers found on some electronics components. Since it is ceramic, it does not conduct electricity and therefore makes it safer to adjust potentiometers while the electronics are powered-on. The primary reason for having one of these screwdrivers is to adjust the stepper motor driver voltage. You would need to do this during a build if you purchased a RAMPS (or similar) electronics set that is not prematched to your stepper motors. If you have to replace a failed stepper motor with a different model, you may need to adjust your stepper motor driver.

I have listed a number of wrench sizes, but the ones that you will need depends entirely on the printer you have. For example, if you own a Kossel Pro, you may not need any of the wrenches. Before buying a set, check the vendor's bill of materials and build instructions, or observe your printer first. You can save some money by buying only those wrenches you need. On the other hand, if you plan to build a delta printer now or in the future, the sizes listed should cover most printer designs.

■ **Tip**   The SeeMeCNC Rostock Max v2 uses SAE hardware, but fortunately most bolts are Phillips head, with only a few nuts that aren't in a nut trap. Thus, a good adjustable wrench will work well.

An adjustable wrench can be a good compromise if you want to keep your toolkit small. A medium, six-inch adjustable wrench will do for most printers. However, keep in mind that cheap adjustable wrenches may be more trouble than they are worth since they tend to not hold their settings very well and can slip under moderate force. So if you want to get one, get one of the better brands (like Craftsman or Kobalt).

A small carpenter's square can be very helpful when assembling frame components by keeping the frame parts at the proper angle. For example, if there are frame components that are mounted 90 degrees to other components, the square can be used to keep the parts at the proper angle when tightening the hardware.

One of the more difficult things you may need to do when building a delta printer (or any 3D printer) is crimping a connector for the electronics board. The three most common types of crimps you will need to do are those for connecting a thermistor (ferrule connectors), adding terminals for connecting a power supply, and building connectors for the electronics board.

Figure 4-5 shows a typical budget ferrule-crimping tool. Notice that it has a ratcheting jaw that compresses the ferrule from four sides.

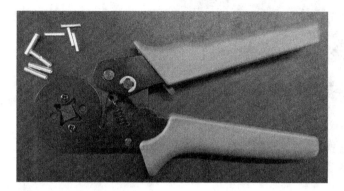

Figure 4-5. *Ferrule crimper*

Although crimping ferrules can be done with such a special tool, given how easy it is to compress ferrules, you can use a normal pair of needle-nose pliers. I find this adequate for the way ferrules are used in building 3D printers, and if you're careful, you can get a good crimp. You can use this technique if you only have a couple of crimps to make. However, using pliers to crimp other types of connectors is not a good idea. You will not be able to get a firm enough crimp with pliers.[5] Thus, you should use terminal and multiconnector crimping tools to crimp the other two types of connectors you may encounter.

Figure 4-6 shows a typical budget crimping-and-wire-cutting tool, as well as examples of the terminal co. nnectors it is designed to crimp. These are typically end connectors for blade terminals and screw terminals, such as those used for typical terminal mounts (like those on LED power supplies).

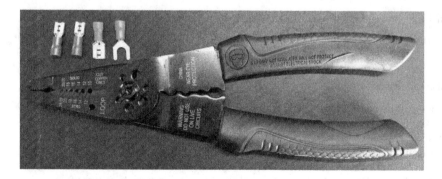

Figure 4-6. *Terminal crimper*

---

[5]That being said, I've used pliers a few times when I didn't have a crimp tool handy. However, these connections eventually work loose, especially if the wiring is under stress. It is best to use the crimping tool.

The following SparkFun site has a complete, detailed discussion of crimping these connectors: https://learn.sparkfun.com/tutorials/working-with-wire/how-to-crimp-an-electrical-connector.

Figure 4-7 shows a different crimping tool designed to crimp smaller connectors for what is commonly referred to as 0.1" terminal pins, which gets its name from the spacing of the pins (which happens to be the same as most electronic breadboards). The jaws are specially designed to curl the tabs on the connector to make a tight connection. If you have to crimp more than a couple of these connectors, you should get one of these tools.

Figure 4-7. *Multiconnector (0.1") crimper*

The following document has a complete, detailed discussion of crimping these connectors: www.hansenhobbies.com/products/connectors/Connectors.pdf.

Recommended Tools

The tools mentioned in the previous sections are the minimal sets you should have for working with and building delta printers. This section lists and describes some additional tools you should consider adding to your kit if you plan to make 3D printing a hobby. While not explicitly required, they can improve your experience over the long term. Some may seem obvious, but others not so much. I'll describe the benefits of using each.

- Fire extinguisher

- Electric screwdriver and bits

- Drill bits

- Heat gun (also called a hot air gun)

At the top of my list of recommended tools is a fire extinguisher. You may think it a really strange thing to have in your 3D printer kit, but let me assure you it is the proverbial ounce of protection. I have not had the need to use one myself with any of my printers (thankfully), but I have encountered people who have. Indeed, I've read a couple forum posts about cases where the heaters on the printers have run away and caused overheating, and in at least one case, a small fire.

Considering the fact that the nozzles on 3D printers routinely heat to temperatures in excess of 180 degrees Celsius, and even the heated print beds run at over 60 degrees Celsius, there is a lot of heat generated. Even if your printer is made mostly of metal, the electronics and plastic parts can still burn, or at least give off noxious fumes when smoldering. It is best to not take chances.

One tool that you will find very handy if you plan to build more than one printer, or you plan to build a printer with a lot of bolts, is an electric screwdriver. Although not expressly required, it will save you a lot of work. One task where this is evident is assembling the frame and attaching the effector. There are several bolts that take more than a few turns to install (or remove). An electric screwdriver can make this a lot faster and relieves you from the stress of turning the screwdriver manually.[6]

If you plan to get an electric screwdriver (only a cordless rechargeable will do), get one with a variety of bits, such as a Phillips, slotted, hex, Torx, or the like. You can often find these at reasonable prices in most hardware and home improvement centers. On the other hand, if you do not want an electric screwdriver, you should consider a ratcheting bit driver instead. You can get them with various bit assortments.

You may also want to consider getting a drill bit set. There are many uses for drill bits. When building a printer, you may need to drill out some plastic or wood pieces if the holes are not quite large enough (or you need to enlarge holes because you only have SAE bolts—because your hardware store thinks metric bolts are just a fad). You may also want to have some drill bits on hand to work with your own objects. Sometimes printed objects can be distorted (for a variety of reasons) where holes may need reaming a bit. A drill bit of the correct size makes short work of that task.

Sadly, it is almost impossible to find metric-sized drill bits in most hardware and home improvement stores in the United States. Fortunately, the SAE sizes included in most drill bit sets will do. The following lists the frequently used sizes and their metric equivalent (not exact in some cases). This is another example of where a digital caliper can help. Use it to measure your drill bits to make sure that you have the correct size before drilling through something that took hours to print.

- 1/8 inch = 3.175 millimeters

- 11/64 inch = 4.366 millimeters

- 13/64 inch = 5.159 millimeters

- 1/4 inch = 6.350 millimeters

- 5/16 inch = 7.938 millimeters

The last recommended tool is a heat gun (sometimes called a *hot air gun*). If you plan to do any wiring more than crimping pins to build connectors, you will want to use shrink-wrap to cover them. A heat gun is the best tool for applying heat to shrink wrap to make it constrict. You can also use a lighter or a butane torch (or similar), but I do not recommend these for novices because it is far too easy to burn the wrap and wiring.

The next section lists some other tools you may want to consider having, but these tools are not strictly necessary to build, use, or maintain delta printers.

Optional Tools

The following is a list of tools that you may need at some point. In some cases, it is a tool of convenience, and in other cases, it is a tool of necessity if you perform a certain task often.

- Canned air
- Small brush/sweeper
- Vacuum
- File set

---

[6]For those of us suffering from repetitive stress injuries, an electric screwdriver is a must.

- Sandpaper

- Small level

- Butane torch

- Scissors

Although it may sound strange, a can of compressed air can help clear away debris and dust from your printer. In fact, it is the only method I consider safe for cleaning dust from electronics. You can also use canned air to cool objects more quickly (tread lightly here—cooling parts too fast can cause cracking). You can find canned air in most hardware, home improvement, and some department stores.

Similarly, for cleaning your print bed and surrounding areas, I recommend a small brush—like those used by artists, mechanical engineers, and architects.

■ **Caution**   Never attempt to clean your build plate while the printer is on or the bed is hot!

Perhaps the best optional tool is a small vacuum. This can be somewhat of a personality thing. For example, I am of the type that doesn't like dirt and debris on my work surfaces. Thus, I clean my printers and work surfaces after my printer(s) has cooled.

■ **Caution**   You should never use a vacuum around a printer that is actively printing. The suction will affect the cooling of the part and can hasten or increase warping and lift. Wait until the printer has stopped and cooled before getting that annoying extra bit of plastic off the build plate.

Once you have printed for some time, you will notice that small bits of filament seem to litter the area around and underneath your printer. Whether this is from your working with shaping plastic parts or from just the usual excess print, a vacuum will make short work of the cleanup.

Two other tools that you may want to work with plastic or wood parts are a file set and sandpaper. I use a small metal file set that includes a number of files with different profiles—flat, round, triangular, and so forth. You may need to file parts for fit. Often the areas needing to be modified are interior areas. A file can make reaching these areas much easier than sandpaper. If you plan to buy sandpaper, look for medium and fine grades. You generally do not need the coarser grades, and unless you plan to paint your parts, you won't need the finishing grades.

A butane torch can be very handy when making your own parts. If you plan to make parts that bolt together and you plan to make nut traps (small pockets to hold a nut in place), you can use a butane torch to heat up the nut before placing it in the part. Thus, you can make the nut traps a bit smaller, and once the heated nut is in place, it will not come loose or fall out (a common hassle for wood or acrylic parts with nut traps).

A butane torch can also be used to heat a part for flexing. For example, some parts may need to be heated before bearings are inserted so that you don't break the part. A heat gun can do the same thing, and honestly is a bit easier to use.

Scissors are needed if you plan to print on Kapton tape. Unless you have found a source that I am unaware of, Kapton tape comes in rolls that you must cut to length. I'll talk more about the specifics of how to apply the tape in a later chapter. If you do plan to use Kapton tape, look for scissors that are nonstick. The nonstick coating helps prevent the tape from sticking to the scissors when you cut it.

WHAT, NO HAMMERS?

It is very rare that you would need a heavy metal hammer (or any metal hammer) to build a delta printer. Conversely, you may need a small mallet made of wood, plastic, or rubber to press together some components (those intended to be pressed together, that is), but in general, no metal hammers are needed.

Now that I've talked about the required, recommended, and optional tools, let's now discuss the skills you need for building a delta printer.

Skills

The skills needed to build a delta printer are somewhat dependent on the type of kit you buy. I will highlight the skills needed to build a typical RepRap kit (e.g., a Mini Kossel), but let's consider the skills needed for kits that come with all the necessary components.

The skill area where most kits differ is in mechanical skills. Fortunately, if you can successfully negotiate tightening a bolt with a wrench, pliers, or a screwdriver, then you have the basics covered. More specifically, most kits come with instructions that guide you through the mechanical assembly, which rarely requires more than bolting parts together and using zip ties to attach pieces.

Similarly, if you are building a printer based on a kit that has the electronics preassembled and the wires cut to length, you may not even need to solder anything. Indeed, it is likely you won't have to do anything more difficult than plugging in the wires to their respective points on the electronics board.

Mechanical

RepRap delta kits are unlikely to be optimized or refined for ease of assembly. Indeed, most require you to solve fit issues with the frame components in particular. For example, kits with wooden frames may require you to sand or cut pieces for a better fit. Kits with plastic components sometimes need to have the pieces trimmed and holes reamed out to allow clearance for bolts.

Thus, the mechanical skills needed for a typical RepRap delta printer include simple mechanical assembly, cleaning plastic and wood parts of excess material, resizing holes for bolts, sanding, filing, drilling holes, and in rare cases, tapping holes for bolts. Thus, you should be competent with using a drill and similar handheld power tools.

Electrical

The electrical skills needed for RepRap delta kits can vary from nothing more than plugging in wires—as you saw with the Kossel Pro—to needing to solder components to printed circuit boards (PCBs).

Beyond plugging in wires, most kits require you to assemble cables either using crimped connectors, or by soldering together connectors or soldering wires. For example, some kits require you to use crimped connections for thermistors (temperature sensors), and possibly the resistor for the hot end (the heater) and heated print bed. Thus, you should have had practice with connecting wires together with solder, assembling connectors with crimped pins, and securing the connections with shrink wrap.

■ **Tip** If you do not know how to solder or it has been a while since you've used a soldering iron, you may want to buy the Learn To Solder Kit from Maker Shed (`makershed.com/products/make-it-learn-to-solder-kit`), which comes with a soldering iron, wire cutters, and supplies.

You may also need to be able to use a basic multimeter to measure resistance and check voltage and current. The most frequent case is adjusting the stepper drivers to match the current requirements (via the reference voltage) of your stepper motors.

■ **Caution** This is one area where most beginners fail to heed the instructions. Be sure to take the time to check and adjust your stepper drivers so that they are set correctly. If they are set too low, the steppers may fail to move or it may miss steps. If they are set too high, they become noisy and can overheat.

As you can see, the more do-it-yourself a kit is, the more skills it is likely to require to use it. Now let's look at some common (and some not so common) build tips to help make your delta printer build a success.

Delta Printer Build Tips

Building a delta printer isn't that different than building a typical Cartesian printer. Indeed, if you have built a Cartesian printer, especially a RepRap design, you've experienced nearly all the tasks you will likely encounter. Thus, much of what you read here will be familiar.

However, there are some techniques or procedures that are specific to delta printers. In fact, that is exactly what I present in this section: a set of tips and tricks you can use to help avoid some of the pitfalls associated with building a delta printer. I limit the discussion to the build tasks, and save the maintenance tips and tricks for a later chapter. I have arranged the tips into the following categories to make it easier to use as a reference:

- General notes
- Frame components
- Moving parts
- Electronics

I recommend reading through all the tips prior to starting your build. Even if you have already started building a printer, reading through the tips may help get you past a troublesome point.

The following is not intended to replace any set of instructions that your kit may contain or that your vendor provides. I think writing any set of general printer-building instructions is not helpful, given how often printer designs change—not to mention the many variants out there. However, there are a few things that are common to all builds. I include these in the following lists as well.

General Notes

This section includes tips for things you should do prior to starting your build.

Organize Your Small Parts

One of the most time-consuming things I've experienced is finding the right small part—be that a bolt, nut, washer, or that one small grub screw among 50 small screws of the same diameter. The best thing you can do when building your printer is to organize your small parts using a plastic storage bin with a number of small compartments. If you purchased a kit that has the hardware included, or perhaps you bought a hardware kit, it is worth the extra time to organize the small parts in this manner.

I use a storage bin with a hinged lid. This means that I can stop my work at any time, close the lid, and put the project away. If you plan to buy trays for small parts, get one that has a lid. This tip alone may help you avoid a most dreadful case of missing or scattered small parts if you drop something.

If you plan to build more than one 3D printer (that is, make it an obsession), you may want to invest in a set of storage trays for storing an assortment of bolts. For example, I have storage trays with a wide variety of 2mm, 3mm, 4mm, 5mm, and 8mm nuts, bolts, washers, and more. Not only does this make it easier to find the size bolt you need, it can also be cheaper in the long run to buy your small hardware in bulk. This could be considered overkill if you are building a single printer, but a necessity if you plan to build many. Figure 4-8 shows my 3mm storage tray.

Figure 4-8. *Storage tray for organizing bolts by size and length*

WHICH IS BEST: HEX, SLOT, OR PHILLIPS?

If you are sourcing your own printer kit, you may wonder which type of screws to use—socket cap (hex), slotted, or Phillips. I and many other builders use hex or hex-cap head bolts. Indeed, most kits come with them. They are easier to use because the hex wrench fits snugly in the cap head. But this is a matter of preference. It turns out it really doesn't matter so long as you have the correct size, thread, and lengths needed.

Read the Instructions

If your vendor has provided you with a set of build instructions, be sure to read through them, front to back, at least once. If this is your first delta printer build, read through the instructions several times so that you are familiar with each step.

This is important because it will decrease the possibility that you will miss a step or perhaps assemble parts in the wrong order, or worse—in the wrong orientation. If your manual is very detailed, it is even more important to read through it thoroughly. Do not be tempted to assemble by photo. That is, do not build your printer relying only on the photos as a guide. There is often much more information in the text; the photos are normally provided for checking your work and may not explain everything you need to know.

For example, if you fail to correctly orient some of the parts, especially the Rostock Max v2 or Kossel Pro, you could find yourself disassembling the entire frame to get that one lousy nut in place. Yes, it does happen. Reading the instructions can help avoid this and similar calamities.

Lastly, reading the instructions will help confirm you have the correct tools for the job. Most build instructions include a required tools list at the front, but I found at least one that had the tool list separated by chapter, with no master list. Check this against your own toolkit to make sure that you have everything you need. This too will help avoid frustration late in the build when you discover your own hex key is just a wee bit too small, forcing you to abandon your build in order to acquire another tool.

Use a Clean, Clear Workspace

This is one tip that can save you some consternation if planned in advance. Make sure that your choice of workspace for your build has no other small parts, tools, animals, or projects that can interfere with your build. It also helps to choose a workspace where you can leave your project in place should you not be able to finish it in one sitting.

It also helps to clean the workspace before you lay out your parts. You need not be able to eat off the surface, but it should be clear of any dirt, debris, grease, and other contaminants. Keep in mind that smooth rods, and certainly bearings, will come oiled. Placing these on a dirty worktop will result in transfer of the dirt to your printer. You do not want that.

As to how large a workspace you will need, most delta printer components can fit on a typical folding table–sized workspace (approximately 30"× 60"). However, I do not recommend using a folding table (especially if you may need to move the table) unless you can secure the legs or the table is very sturdy.

Your work habits may also be a factor. If you like to keep your workspace clear, you may want to store parts in boxes (or the shipping box) stacked in order of the build instructions. That way, you can remove only the parts needed. I found this particularly helpful when building the Kossel Pro. Keep in mind that every kit has stages where you will need to set aside a partial assembly. Leave some room for those.

Also, keep in mind the type of frame your printer uses. This is an important point if your workspace happens to be the family dinner table. Your family may not appreciate the character your metal frame printer inflicts on the wood surface. Thus, you should consider covering the workspace to avoid scratches, or choose a difference workspace to build your printer. You can also use self-healing cutting mats. Some have foam backing that protects the surface.

Lastly, make sure that all liquids, beverages, and other messy things are well clear of your work area and parts. Accidental spills can be quite a bother to clean up, especially if you need to dry off a hundred little bolts and nuts, or worse, your electronics board.

Check the Bill of Materials

If you purchased a kit with a bill of materials, lay that aside and refer to it as you unpack your kit. This helps to ensure that you aren't missing any parts, but it also helps you take inventory of the parts. Lay each part or package of parts on your workspace. Try to arrange them in order of the build instructions.

If your kit came with small hardware such as nuts and bolts, be sure to count them to ensure that you have enough to complete the build. Do this the same day you receive your printer kit. Contact customer service if you are missing any parts so that you won't have to stop in the middle of the build. Most vendors will send you extra in case you lose one or thirteen small nuts and washers.

Lay Out Your Tools

Once you have read the instructions and checked the bill of materials, you should assemble and lay out those tools you will need for the build. I like to keep mine in small trays to make them easier to get to and easier to put away, should I need to stop before I am finished. You could also use a pegboard (or something similar) mounted on your wall to keep your work surface clear and organize your tools at the same time.

It can be frustrating to spend a lot of time contorting your hands into position to place a nut on the back of a component, only to realize the bit driver is out of arm's reach or has the wrong bit installed. Keep your tools close by.

Don't Mix SAE and Metric

All jocularity about hardware stores and metric sizes aside, don't be tempted to force an SAE bolt in place of the proper metric bolt (or vice versa). While it is fine to use SAE bolts for some components and metric for others,[7] mixing them can be a problem. I recommend sticking with all metric hardware. It may be harder to find, but at least you only need one set of wrenches.

Keep Your Hands Clean

If your frame has laser-cut wood parts (like the Rostock Max v2), be advised that some of these parts may have ash on the cut edges that can transfer to your hands, and in turn, to other things—like your clothing, or face, or your white cat. If this doesn't bother you,[8] then you can safely ignore this tip. However, if it does, you should also consider the fact that small hardware, bearings, and rods often have a thin coat of oil applied by the manufacturer. Unless you want to transfer that oil to your plastic and wood parts, you might want to keep a damp washcloth (preferably one your spouse won't mind having oil get on it) and some paper towels to clean up after handling the parts.

---

[7]Unless, like me, your OCD condition simply won't permit such blasphemy.
[8]But I assure you that your cat won't think it is funny. Nor will your spouse.

No Duct Tape Allowed

That's right. Duct tape ("high-speed Bondo" to NASCAR fans[9]) is strictly prohibited. OK, maybe just one small piece—but that's all you get! Joking aside, there really is no (reasonable) reason to use questionable bonding practices such as duct tape to join parts of your printer together.[10]

On the other hand, zip ties may be an alternative worth considering. They are tidier and can be removed easily. In fact, I've used zip ties to secure parts on my printers when I didn't have the correct length bolt. If pulled tight, they can be very strong.

Give Me a Break!

If you find yourself getting frustrated or trying to rush through a build step, stop and give yourself a break. Sometimes stepping away from the problem—even overnight or over a weekend—can work wonders in solving your particular frustration. I recommend taking a break every two hours or so. Do something different during that time, like talking to your family and friends so they don't think you're a complete nerd. But they still might.

Don't Force Components Together

Test-fit all parts before bolting or snapping them together. Some parts fit together easily only one way, but can be forced together the wrong way. Just ask any parent the day after Christmas what this means.

Don't Stray from the Plan

If you are like me and are always thinking about ways to improve your printers, don't be tempted to alter the design or build midstream to add some gizmo or upgrade you found on Thingiverse. While these upgrades and convenience accessories may improve your printer, adding them before the printer is finished can be more trouble than you expect.

For example, if you add a new Z-probe in place of the one that came with the kit, and you encounter problems when calibrating the printer later on, how do you know there is something wrong with the kit and not your new addition? Also, if you need help from the vendor and you've deviated from their instructions, you may not find they are as sympathetic as you'd expect. And you should expect them to request you remove the upgrade as a first step in solving the problem. It is best to wait to add embellishments.

Keep an Engineering Logbook

Many developers, engineers, and scientists keep notes about their projects in paper notebooks or digital notebooks using apps like Evernote (http://evernote.com/). A voice recorder can also be handy in catching those impromptu ideas when you don't have time or it is too dangerous to use pen and paper. Some people are more detailed than others, but most take notes during meetings and phone conversations, thereby providing a written record of verbal communication.

If you aren't in the habit of keeping an engineering logbook, you should consider doing so. You will find a logbook especially handy for building a 3D printer if your build will take more than one sitting. Not only can you record what you've done—settings, measurements, and so forth, but you can also record your thoughts on what worked and what did not. Perhaps more important for a project that requires more than a few hours and a single session is having a place to write down where you are and what you need to do next.

---

[9]Guilty as charged.
[10]OK, maybe one (http://reprap.org/wiki/Duct_Tape_RepStrap), but that's pushing things.

Naturally, you can use any type of notebook you desire; but if you want to class up your notes a bit, you can purchase a notebook made especially for keeping engineering notes. These typically have subdued gridlines and sometimes text areas for recording key information like the project name and page number. Two of my favorite notebooks include the small project-sized notebooks from SparkFun and the larger Maker's Notebook from Maker Shed.

It's Not a Toy!

As tempting as it may be to buy your gifted son or daughter a delta printer kit and say, "Have at it, kid," you should resist this temptation. 3D printers are not toys. They have parts that can get hot enough to burn and scar human tissue. That does not mean your gifted offspring should be denied the pleasures of 3D printing. On the contrary, just make sure that you provide adult supervision during the build and use of the 3D printer.

Frame Components

This section contains tips that are related to assembling the frame of a delta printer.

Cleaning Bolt and Rod Holes

If the hole or shaft that a bolt or rod must pass through is too small, you can make the hole larger (also called *reaming*) by using a drill bit of the correct size. For plastic parts in particular, be sure to use a bit that is only marginally larger than the existing opening.

Some parts in delta printers require bolts to be snug in their slots. For example, the bolts in the optional roller carriages for the Mini Kossel need to be snug fit. Reaming these out so that the bolts slide in easily can affect how the carriage performs.

It is also important to use the drill bit manually instead of popping it into a high-speed drill and letting the bit eat away at the plastic. As tempting as this may be, it can be hazardous to the structural integrity of the part. There are two reasons for this. First, plastic parts are built with several layers on external surfaces. If you drill beyond these layers, you will expose the internal fill volume, which typically has a fill of 50% or less, and weaken the part. Second, a drill bit can easily bite into the plastic, putting excessive pressure on it. If the drill is spinning very fast, the bit can heat up and melt the plastic. Either of these can result in broken parts.

If the opening is significantly smaller, you may need to either use a smaller bolt, or correct the part and reprint it. It is always better to use a smaller bolt if possible.

■ **Tip** You can also use drill bits in an electric drill, but here you should place the drill in reverse to prevent the bit from biting into the plastic. If a bit bites too deeply, it can cause cracks and similar damage.

Test-Fit Parts Before Assembly

While there are many examples to the contrary, some printer kits are not laser or water-jet cut, milled, or printed with enough accuracy that all the pieces bolt together without any problems. That doesn't mean you will always need to cut, trim, or sand pieces to fit. However, it does mean you should test the parts first so that you don't discover too late that one of the seven tabs, grooves, or screw holes needs a bit of trimming to fit properly after tightening the first six. In addition, you should check each component, especially long metal parts, for straightness to ensure that there are no bends or other imperfections.

I would test-fit two, or no more than three, pieces together at a time. This gives you an opportunity to modify those parts individually, rather than trying to trim some area on a larger assembly that may be harder to hold, or to reach the area needing attention, or worse—force you to disassemble.

I once saw a wooden frame printer assembled so poorly that the frame itself could be flexed slightly from side to side. That's horrible for print quality given how 3D printers shake under the small, rapid movements of the extruder.

Once you have the parts mating well, you can assemble them and move on. A positive side effect of this practice is that the build is usually tighter, making for stronger joints and ultimately a bit better printer. The negative side effect is that the build could take a bit longer.

Measure Twice

Delta printers that use vertical frame members made from metal rods or extruded aluminum that are bolted to plastic connecting parts are assembled according to a specific measurement and alignment. If your printer requires measuring the position of a component, be sure to measure twice—once as you are assembling it and again after you've tightened the fasteners. This can help you avoid ill-fitting parts. You should also check the frame for alignment—that is, the parts are assembled with the correct orientation to one another (e.g., right angles are 90 degrees) and the parallel subcomponents are indeed parallel.

Nut Traps

If your printer is made from laser-cut wood, acrylic, or a composite, it is likely the design uses nut traps cut into one piece of the material. The idea is you use a bolt through one piece threaded into the nut held in place in the nut trap.[11] This works really well and is an excellent alternative to nails and other error-prone fasteners.

However, it can be maddeningly difficult to keep the nut in place if the nut trap is larger than the nut itself. In other words, the nut trap won't hold the nut in place long enough for you to thread the bolt. This makes it frustrating to work with nut traps in pieces oriented so that the nut falls out.

To combat this, you can place a small piece of blue tape (You did buy a roll, didn't you?) on the side facing the direction of the earth's gravitational pull (er, down). This way, you can put the nut in the nut trap and it won't go kerplunk! into the inner workings of your printer.

Another method is to use a pair of needle-nose pliers to place the nut in the nut trap and hold it there while you thread the bolt through. In this case, you grip the outer edge of the nut and hold it firmly.

Tighten, but Don't Overtighten

I sometimes get this question from inexperienced and experienced alike; "How tight do I make the bolts?" While there are tested limits for torque of each fastener (see the manufacturer's data sheet if you are curious), building delta printers is not like building a spaceship. You don't need a torque wrench.

However, you should be aware that too much torque can be bad. For example, don't tighten bolts and nuts on wood and plastic parts so much that you crush the material. In other words, your wooden frame should not appear to be using countersunk bolts. Nut traps in these materials are also vulnerable to damage when overtightening bolts. If you damage a nut trap in a laser-cut part, you may not be able to repair it without replacing the part.

---

[11]No, it does not involve squirrels.

To give you an idea of how much is enough, the parts you are bolting together should make for a strong connection without any play. Parts should not be loose or be capable of working loose from normal operation. If you find a bolt that does work loose, use a bit of Loctite to fix the bolt. Blue Loctite works best for these situations. You can also use a Nyloc nut, which can be removed and replaced without reapplying the solution. If you are assembling something that may never be disassembled, Loctite is a fine choice. However, if you need to disassemble the part, Nyloc may be a better choice.

Fixing Stripped Bolts

If you make a mistake and overtighten a bolt, you could strip it. That is, the threads can cross, making it difficult to remove the bolt. If this happens when the nut is in a nut trap made from plastic, it can also damage the plastic.

This most often happens with smaller 3mm and 2mm bolts. When it does happen, and you cannot get the bolt to unthread without damaging the plastic or wood, you can use a small metal file to cut the bolt off. You can also use a small bolt cutter to cut the head off. However, you should not use an electric hobby tool with a cutting wheel for bolts in plastic. The bolt could get hot enough to melt the plastic and ruin the part.

■ **Tip**   Always start bolts with your fingers, which allows you to feel how the bolt is threading. If you need to use a tool to start a bolt, stop and remove the bolt, and inspect the nut and part for anomalies. When I encounter this, I throw the nut away and try another. M3 nuts aren't precious enough to risk stripping a bolt.

Locate Lost Nuts and Other Small Bits

Given the small size of 2mm and 3mm nuts and bolts, and their proclivity for falling onto the floor and disappearing under furniture,[12] you may be tempted after the first dozen or so cases to just ignore it and let the vacuum cleaner find it later. Avoid this temptation and keep close tabs on the small hardware!

I did this once myself. I looked and looked for a missing 3mm nut and never found it. I even used a magnetic pickup to reach behind my workspace, but it simply wasn't there. That is, until I powered my printer on. Yes, you guessed it. That small nut had fallen into my electronics and shorted out my Arduino Mega board. Well, at least two good things came from this. I saw some very interesting smoke, complete with a small light show, and I learned the importance of always locating that lost little bit of metallic hardware.

■ **Caution**   Be mindful of metal chips and strands of cut wiring. These can also fall into your electronics and cause shorts when powered on.

---

[12]There are at least three that I have never been able to find.

Build Your Top and Bottom Frame As Completely As Possible

With a delta printer, the top and bottom frame components typically house most of the components for the printer. The bottom frame often has the electronics, power supply, and sometimes the cold end (extruder). Depending on the printer you chose to build, the top can also contain a number of components, such as the electronics, LCD, or a spool holder.

I've found completing installation of these components into the frame section as a unit much easier before you join them with the vertical frame components. If you need (as is often the case) to rotate the frame to get to a particular nut or bolt, it will be much easier if you don't have the two sections connected (or the towers connected to the bottom).

When I built my first delta printer, I often had to turn it upside down or on its side to complete some installation. Not only is this inconvenient, but if your build instructions had you align the towers or adjust some other frame component, mishandling your frame can undo that careful adjustment.

Add Extra Nuts

If your delta printer is built with aluminum extrusions that are designed to capture nuts (like the OpenBeam 1515 extrusions), you will want to add a couple of extra nuts in the channel for each exposed frame section. Sometimes your build instructions will tell you how many nuts you need to add, but not always.

This is important because delta frame vertices block some of the ends of the extrusions, making adding nuts impossible. Some designs, like the Mini Kossel or Kossel Pro, have frame sides with special cavities that allow you to add nuts, but the interior and exterior facing sides are still blocked. The only way to get nuts into these blocked channels is to loosen the frame, which is a generally bad since it requires you to recheck your alignment and can even affect calibration.

Not only will having extra nuts make assembly of required parts easier, it will also help you in the future should you decide to relocate a component or add an upgrade, or you just want to bolt something to your frame. I like to add nuts and secure them with grub screws so they don't rattle around while the printer is printing.[13] Figure 4-9 shows a photo of a set of nuts captured in the frame channel.

Figure 4-9. *Adding extra nuts to frame members*

---

[13]My mild OCD condition will drive me crazy trying to find a rattle like that.

The Moving Parts

This section concerns the mounting and alignment of the stepper motors, belts, and assorted bits for the moving parts of your printer.

Working with Oiled Parts

I will talk more about keeping your printer's moving parts oiled as part of a regular maintenance regimen, but it is also important for assembly. The smooth rods, bearings, and even some of the bolts and other hardware come from the factory with a light oil covering them. Resist the temptation to clean this away. Your smooth rods need to be damp with a thin layer of oil on most bearings. Naturally, this oil will transfer to your hands. I have already discussed the need to keep your hands clean, but handling the rods themselves makes that complicated.

However, you can wear tight-fitting rubber, Nitrile, or similar latex gloves when handling these parts. This allows you to work with the oily bits and still have clean hands for handling the other bits. I keep a box of Nitrile gloves on my worktop for just those occasions.

Keep Smooth and Threaded Rods Clean

A related tip concerns keeping the threaded rods, bearings, and smooth rods free of dirt and other debris. Using gloves can help in this endeavor, but the best way to keep them clean is to store them in a plastic bag or under a sheet of plastic during assembly. This way they won't accumulate dust and debris from your build, like particles of wood, bits of plastic, and so forth. If they do get dirt or dust on them, use a lint-free rag to wipe them clean. Reapply a thin coat of oil once a part is installed.

Belt Tensioners

Before cranking down your belt (or cable) tensioners until you get a high E note from plucking the belt,[14] leave a little slack until your printer build is complete. Chances are you will have to adjust them again anyway; so leaving a little slack saves you from having to do it twice. Plus, if you have to adjust the axis in any way during the build, you won't have to loosen it first.

Once the build is complete, the belts should be tight enough so that there is no slack, but not so much that they produce music. Too tight and it will bind the idler pulley and overheat or excessively wear the stepper motor.

Align Pulleys with the Belt

This is one area most instructions fail to illustrate or even mention. When building a printer that uses belts for axes movement, you need to align the pulley, idler, and fixed belt mounts so that the belt does not wander on the idler, or worse—the drive pulley. There is a very easy way to do this. Once you have the axis assembled, sight down the belt and check the alignment as it moves. The belt should not move to one side or the other. If it does, you must adjust the location of the idler or pulley.

The method I use is to loosen the idler and the pulley, and then move the axis back and forth (up and down for delta printers), adjusting the idler and pulley as needed. Once I get both aligned, I tighten them in place. This makes for a smoother moving axis and can also improve part quality.

---

[14]Which is entirely too tight.

Don't Stress the Plastic

During assembly it may be tempting to flex the axis to align the rods and the axis ends. This is normally the case for an axis that uses press-fit connections for vertical frame components, like the Mini Kossel (aluminum extrusion) or Rostock (smooth rods). If you need to do this, take care. Too much flex will likely result in broken plastic. If you hear a creak or crack, you've gone too far and have just broken the bond between the filament layers or the filament itself. I recommend using a file or drill to enlarge the opening until the part fits snugly, without resorting to the use of force. And never, ever use a hammer to pound metal parts into plastic.

Take Care with Mounting the Accessories

When upgrading your printer with cooling fans, spool holders, and similar features, take care to ensure that the mount does not interfere with moving parts. For example, if your delta printer uses roller carriages and you want to mount something on the vertical frame components, be sure to give the carriage enough clearance so that the rollers or the carriage are not obstructed.

Similarly, if you mount something on your effector, be sure that the effector (with delta arms attached) can move throughout the build volume and that the Z-probe deployment process continues to work correctly.

Sometimes you have to get a little creative to overcome these issues if space is a premium. For example, I designed a part-cooling fan for one of my Mini Kossel printers that used a hose to connect the fan to a nozzle suspended from the effector. This was the only way I could use a large fan and still mount it on the effector.

■ **Caution**   Do not attach anything to the delta arms. You may be tempted to zip tie wiring or other flexible things to the delta arms, but I do not recommend that. These items can add stress or bind the movement of the effector. It can also increase wear on the arm joints and can exasperate a backlash condition.

Electronics

This section contains tips for assembling the electronics for your printer. If you have little experience with electronics, you might want to reread some of these before working with the printer's electronics.

ESD Is the Enemy

You should take care to make sure that your body, your workspace, and your printer are grounded to avoid electrostatic discharge (ESD). ESD can damage your electronics. The best way to avoid this is to use a grounding strap that loops around your wrist and attaches to the frame of the equipment you are working on. You can also grasp a ground source such as a metal water pipe, but that may be inconvenient. Grounding straps are more convenient and are inexpensive.

Test Your Components Separately

Whenever possible, it is a good idea to test your electronics components prior to assembly. This can add significant time to your build, but it is worth it. This is especially true if you either bought your kit from several component kits or sourced them yourself. I used to trust that certain components—like power supplies and Arduino clone boards—were rarely dead on arrival (DOA); that is, despite being new, they don't work or work incorrectly.

Thus, it is a good idea to plug in the power supply and check its voltage when the item arrives. But be sure to test the components individually. If that power supply is putting out too much voltage, you could damage other components.

You can test your Arduino and RAMPS simply by installing the shield on the Arduino and connecting it to your computer (and loading the firmware). I sometimes do this when I use components from vendors that I haven't used in the past.

You can take this tip to an extreme and wire up all of your electronics, and then run tests like moving the axis (to see the motors spin), checking the hot end for proper heating, and even checking the LCD panel for proper operation. This process is called *bench testing*, and savvy electronics enthusiasts do this as a matter of practice.

If you do nothing else, I recommend testing the power supply. It is the one component that can quickly ruin a build—either by not working or working too well. A quick test can avoid that unpleasant (and depressing) moment of stolen eureka when you flip the switch on your newly built printer, only to have nothing happen.

Don't Rush Assembly

Rushing the assembly of your electronics can be very bad for the life of your equipment. For example, if you mistakenly plug in a component the wrong way, you could risk burning out the component, or worse—shorting out your RAMPS or similar board altogether. Especially if this is your first build, take your time and study the instructions carefully to make sure that you've got everything wired and connected properly.

You Cannot Use Too Many Zip Ties

Well, I suppose you can, but that would be a lot of zip ties! That aside, don't hesitate to use zip ties to tame your wiring to keep it clear of moving parts or parts that get hot—or that may otherwise interfere with the normal operation of your printer.

You should also avoid the temptation to cinch everything up before you've done the preflight checks. Imagine the frustration level incurred if you have to take your RAMPS apart to change the orientation of one wire connection.

Similarly, I would not let your wires lay about wherever they fall. Aside from keeping them away from moving parts, it makes for a more professional build to have all the extra wire bundled up and tucked away.

Cutting Wires to Length

You may also want to avoid the temptation to cut wires to length if your kit requires you to make your own cables or to attach the connectors. There are two reasons for this. First, if you discover you need to reroute a cable to add an accessory later, you may find the cable is too short to accommodate the accessory, forcing you to redo the cable. Second, if you ever have to replace your electronics board with another, where the connectors are in a different location, you may not be able to if the cables are too short. It is best to leave them a little long and bundle them with zip ties.

Cut Zip Ties Close to the Nub

This is something you may not think about. When you use as many zip ties as most printer kits tend to, the point where you cut off the excess can vary based on how fast you go through the build.

For example, if you are in a hurry to trim the zip ties, you may not position the side cutters close enough to the nub, leaving a small, often angled bit of tie sticking out. This isn't a problem with really small zip ties (but it might not look as nice), but with larger zip ties, especially those made from hard plastic, it can be a problem. I have scratched my hands and arms on zip tie nubs several times. I could have avoided those minor injuries if I had taken the time to cut the tie off closer to and flush with the nub. It also looks a lot neater.

Use High-Temp Wire for Heaters

The heaters on your printer (the extruder hot end and the heated build plate, if provided) can generate a lot of heat. You must use special wire designed for use in heater circuits. The wire is often labeled as being high temperature (or it gives a temperature rating). If you bought a kit, make sure that the vendor has included high-temperature wiring for the hot end and the build plate.

Use ESD Shielding for LCD Cables

I have found that some LCD panel components are sensitive to radio interference from other wires. I had this problem on one of my early Prusa printers. It seemed that if I got anywhere near the printer when it was printing, the LCD panel became corrupt. This didn't seem to affect the printer, and I traced it to a small electrostatic discharge. Despite grounding everything properly, this particular LCD panel was very sensitive to EMI. You can combat this by making sure that your LCD cables are routed away from wires carrying mains (5V or 12V) power.

The best method is to wrap the LCD cables in EMI shielding. I use peel-and-stick wire wrap that has a braided core and an aluminum inner sheet. McMaster sells a variety of shielding. The type I used is for EMI/RF (mcmaster.com/#standard-cable-sleeving/=rxbz4z).

Be sure to mark your cables! Once you wrap them in the shielding, it may not be obvious which end corresponds to one on the other end. I use a small permanent marker to mark both ends of one of the cables (most LCD panels use two cables). Figures 4-10 and 4-11 show the cable before and after the wrap is applied. You will want to keep the dark (black) side facing out.

Figure 4-10. Before wrapping the LCD cables

Figure 4-11. After wrapping the LCD cables

Insulate Mains

If your printer kit does not include a self-contained power supply or if you plan to use a typical LED 12V/30A power supply, you will need to take care with how you wire it for plugging into your household power—that is, the AC power connector should be deliberately protected.

A popular method is to use an AC plug with a switch, such as IEC320 C14 (or similar), and mount that to the printer in some manner—either as part of a cover for the power supply or as a separate mount. I've used both and I can say I feel a lot safer with those AC wires tucked away.

Even if you don't have an enclosure-like mounting point, keeping the higher voltage wires covered is always a good idea to avoid accidental experiments in hair follicle growth.

Another reason may be to avoid accidental shorts. For example, I have a cover I made for one of my Prusa printers that covers the end of my LED power supply. Incorporated into that design is the power plug and switch. When I mount the plug, the wires on the back that connect the switch and lead to the power supply get compressed. Clearly, if one of those connectors came loose, it could cause a short.

The best way to insulate these wires is to use heat-shrink tubing to cover the ends of the connectors. This ensures that all higher voltage wires are covered as much as possible.

Use Stress Relief

Cables that attach to moving parts such as the print bed, extruder, and some axes are sources for failures from repeated movement. For these areas, use a stress relief mechanism to keep the wires from flexing at a single point. One way to do this is to use plastic wire wrap around the bundled cables. This keeps the cables from flexing in one place, which can cause them to break. You can find plastic wire wrap at most hardware stores, as well as automotive parts stores.

■ **Caution**   When using plastic wire wraps, be sure to tie down the ends of the wrap so that the stiffness added doesn't create a flex point beyond the ends of the warp, thereby making the problem worse.

Spread the Load

If you are wiring your own power supply, be sure to use a different lead from the power supply for each major component. Use two leads for your RAMPS (most have two sets of mains power) and one for your accessories. If one of those accessories is a heater, use a separate lead for it. Some people wire the RAMPS to the same output lead from the power supply. Depending on how powerful your power supply is, it may not matter, but it is always better to distribute the load.

Wiring Endstops

If you are using standard endstops with three pins, take a look at the side of the endstop (or the documentation). You should see three sets of letters: NO, NC, and C, which represent normally open, normally closed, and common. You want to use the NO and C connectors for your wiring so that when the switch is triggered, it makes a connection between the C (common) and NO (normally open) pins. For all other endstops, check with your vendor for proper wiring.

■ **Note**   Some CNC experts suggest using NC and C, setting the firmware accordingly. This helps detect when wiring faults occur; otherwise, the axis mechanism can slam into a failed endstop. That is, by keeping the endstop closed, a wiring fault automatically triggers the endstop.

Route Wiring Safely

When routing your wiring, be sure to route all wiring away from moving parts such as belts, stepper motors, and the carriages. You should also avoid routing wiring away from heated parts. Use zip ties to secure wiring if you must pass near moving or heated components. Similarly, route your filament away from these obstacles if it must pass close by. I like to use an extra length of PTFE tubing to route the filament. Figure 4-12 shows an example of this technique.

Figure 4-12. *Routing filament and wiring away from moving parts*

Notice that the filament runs inside a PTFE tube secured to the bottom frame rail. Also notice that the wiring is routed behind the stepper motor and sensitive wiring is encased in a sheath (see arrow).

Check Your Wiring Twice

If you have been building your printer over several days or perhaps over an extended marathon build session (or you become impatient), it is very tempting to plug in the last few wires and throw the power switch. It is far safer to take a break and double-check your wiring. Twice. Unless your electronics use keyed or tabbed connectors that only go one way, it is very easy to get wiring backward.

Polarity isn't critical for endstops (unless they use more than two wires or require power), heaters, or thermistors, but it is critical for all powered components. Double-check all wiring and connections to ensure that you have the polarity correct and that the wiring is connected to the right pins. It is very easy on a RAMPS setup to miss a pin.

Also be sure to check that the wires are connected to the right places. You don't want to connect your thermistor to an endstop, or worse, a heater connector.

Flame Bad, Heat Good

I have seen experienced, well-educated electronics gurus use a match or a butane torch to shrink heat-sensitive material (also called *shrink wrap*). Don't do this! Use a heated air gun on shrink wrap. An open flame, even from a match, is not a well-controlled heat source and you can damage your wiring, frame, and especially plastic components instantly if you get the flame too close.

While professionals with years of experience may be able to get away with this,[15] hobbyists and novices will likely not fare so well, especially if you make a mistake. Keep in mind that open containers of acetone and similar substances can exude invisible, flammable vapors. A match or a torch can and will ignite these vapors if you are not careful.

---

[15]They would say, "Do as I say, not as I do."

Label Your Wiring

I like to use a bit of blue tape to label my wiring so that I keep things organized and to get them plugged in the correct spot! This is especially helpful if you route wiring through a common access port or hole in the frame. And it is made worse by kits that use the same colored wire for everything. Figure 4-13 shows an example of my crude, but effective wiring labels.[16] Once I've routed the wiring where it needs to go, I peel off the labels, but you don't have to. So long as they do not interfere with cooling or moving parts, you can leave them in place. Smaller labels are better; this one was made larger for illustration. You can find more sophisticated (and nicer) labels from some online 3D printer component vendors.

Figure 4-13. *Ad hoc wire labels*

Other Considerations

This section contains additional tips that you may find helpful when building and planning your delta printer build.

Electronics Fan Controller

I always run a fan on my printer electronics. I've found the stepper motor drivers and sometimes the power components tend to get hotter than I prefer (if you can feel the heat with your hand, it's way too hot). Not only can this result in odd behavior like missed steps or poor print quality, it can also result in overheated and failed electronics.

You can also use an infrared thermometer to measure heat in components. Not only are these touchless, but they help keep your hands away from parts that can burn you.

Electronics that are exposed are not as susceptible as electronics in an enclosure (most good enclosures incorporate a fan) or electronics that are cocooned in extra wiring. In both cases, you need a fan blowing across the cooling fins on your stepper drivers to ensure that they do not overheat.

---

[16]Yes, I have terrible handwriting. This reads, "Therm HPB" for thermistor, heated print bed.

However, while simply adding a fan is easy, you need to consider how you want to mount the fan. That is, you must consider which direction the fan is blowing air and ensure that the airflow does not blow across your print bed. This equates to extra cooling, which may be harmful if you are printing with ABS, as it can cause cracking and lifting.

It may surprise you to read that not all fans run at the same speed or have the same airflow qualities. While you should use a high-quality 12V axial fan, some move more air than others. I like to use the higher specification axial fans along with a small circuit to control the fan speed. Figure 4-14 shows the circuit drawing.

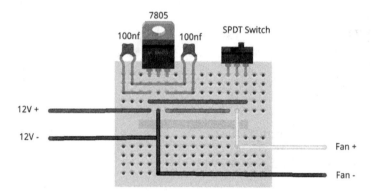

Figure 4-14. *Fan control circuit*

Notice that I use a 5V voltage regulator (7805), two 100nf capacitors wired across each side for cleaning the power, and the SPDT switch to wire 12V power to one side of the switch and the 5V output of the regulator to the other side. I then connect the center pole of the switch to the positive side of the fan. When the switch is in the left position, the fan is supplied 5V power and therefore runs at a lower speed. When the switch is in the right position, the fan is supplied 12V power and therefore runs at high speed.

I recommend building this circuit and testing it before wiring everything to a PCB. Once you have it working, you can transfer it to a PCB and mount it along with the switch on your printer. See the section on stabilizing print cooling fans in Chapter 6 for an example of how to do this.

Printed Part Scaling

Printed parts can be a source of frustration if the part is slightly out of scale. If the part is more than 1% to 2% too large or too small, you will want to consider reprinting it. If your printed parts came with your kit, contact your vendor and request new parts. This may not sound like a lot of variance, but consider 2% of a part that is 100mm wide results in a part that is 102mm wide, which is enough to cause assembly issues.

A related issue is when the holes in the part are not the correct size. Sometimes this is due to extrusion width issues or may be just a small undersize issue on scaling. In this case, reaming out the part as described previously can solve the issue.

However, if you find that you are removing a lot of plastic when resizing the holes, you may have a problem. If you remove enough material, you could reduce the integrity of the part and it could fail when you tighten a bolt, or it could be a source of a bolt that comes loose.

This issue is common for those printing their own parts for a Mini Kossel. However, it is also easy to fix. If you look in the folder with the Mini Kossel parts (https://github.com/jcrocholl/kossel), you will see a file named configuration.scad. Listing 4-1 shows the contents of the file.

Listing 4-1. Configuration File for Mini Kossel parts

```
// Increase this if your slicer or printer make holes too tight.
extra_radius = 0.1;

// OD = outside diameter, corner to corner.
m3_nut_od = 6.1;
m3_nut_radius = m3_nut_od/2 + 0.2 + extra_radius;
m3_washer_radius = 3.5 + extra_radius;

// Major diameter of metric 3mm thread.
m3_major = 2.85;
m3_radius = m3_major/2 + extra_radius;
m3_wide_radius = m3_major/2 + extra_radius + 0.2;

// NEMA17 stepper motors.
motor_shaft_diameter = 5;
motor_shaft_radius = motor_shaft_diameter/2 + extra_radius;

// Frame brackets. M3x8mm screws work best with 3.6 mm brackets.
thickness = 3.6;

// OpenBeam or Misumi. Currently only 15x15 mm, but there is a plan
// to make models more parametric and allow 20x20 mm in the future.
extrusion = 15;

// Placement for the NEMA17 stepper motors.
motor_offset = 44;
motor_length = 47;
```

Notice the line, `extra_radius = 0.1;`. Simply increase the value a bit (use 0.2 for slightly too small holes; 0.3 or 0.4 if the holes are really small), and then save the file and recompile the part and export it to an .stl file. Once you do that, your part will print with larger holes.

Notice that this file also controls things like the size of the bolts and nuts. You can change these values to control those too. However, if you have to change them more than a few tenths, you may have a more serious scaling issue and should check your parts for scale first.

Take Measurements

One thing that you can do that will help you with calibration is measure your printer once you complete the build. To configure the firmware, you need values like the length of the delta arms, offsets for the effector and carriage, height of the hot end, and so forth. I like to take these measurements and write them in my engineering notebook so that I don't have to hunt for them later, or worse, measure the printer every other step in the configuration process. Even if your vendor supplies these values, you can use them as a double check to make sure that they are correct.

Safe Build Plate

If you are building a new printer design or if you are upgrading a printer with a new effector, delta arms, hot end, or Z-probe, you may want to replace your print bed with a piece of cardboard. Find a nice, flat piece of cardboard and trace your build plate, and then cut the cardboard to shape. You can even mark the boltholes and drill them out. If you have a heated print bed, I would replace that with cardboard too. Replacing the print bed with a cardboard plate allows you to experiment with your new hardware without fear of crashing the nozzle into the glass and damaging the nozzle or glass.

Loctite Is Your Friend

I like to use blue Loctite[17] for all bolts that are subjected to vibration or that cannot be tightened well. Applications where this is a must are grub screws for pulleys, bolts for the effector, and delta arms that do not use Nyloc or lock washers (and sometimes even if they do). Blue Loctite keeps the bolt or screw from coming loose, but does not harden so much that it prevents you from removing the bolt or screw if you need to.

Summary

If you thought that building a delta printer was like assembling a child's bicycle or personal computer, you may be a bit surprised to see this chapter list a bunch of tools—some of which you may have never seen. Fortunately, I've listed all the tools that you are most likely going to need to build, use, and maintain a delta printer.

I also presented a set of tips and tricks for getting the most out of your build should you decide to build your own printer. If you were considering building a delta printer but were concerned about the skills needed and the general lack of instructions, I hope that this chapter has alleviated those concerns.

Well, that's about it. I've prepared you as much as one can to take on the challenge and succeed in your first delta printer build. Now, open those boxes, check the manifest, read the instructions, and start building![18]

The next chapter examines one of the most important things you need to do to get the most out of your delta printer—calibration. Too many people gloss over this step and become frustrated with their poorly performing printer. Sadly, a small amount of work is normally all that is needed to turn an improperly configured and calibrated printer into a good printer.

---

[17]You may also see it referred to as *thread locking glue* or *thread caulk*.
[18]To all you Klingon fans out there, Qapla'! (http://en.wiktionary.org/wiki/Qapla%27).

CHAPTER 5

Calibrating the Printer

Now that you have taken a look at the delta printer's hardware, including all the parts, the software to drive the printer, and tips for how to build your own delta printer, it is now time to dive into the one area that is often overlooked—calibration. Failing to properly calibrate your delta printer can make your 3D experience a misery.

Sadly, many enthusiasts jump directly from a fresh build to trying to print a complex object. If your printer is a professional- or consumer-grade ready-built printer, you might be able to get away with this. Once. However, even these printers will need some minor adjustments to get them to print well. In fact, SeeMeCNC's Orion delta printer manual recommends that you perform several adjustments to correct any possible misalignment or minor changes that occurred during shipping.

Calibration is especially important if you are working with a printer built from scratch or from a kit. As you saw in Chapter 4, it is important to complete the build with as much accuracy and consistency as possible. If the printer is not built with care and attention to detail, no amount of calibration will overcome poor assembly.[1]

Tip Your calibration efforts can be greatly improved if you start with a well-assembled machine.

Calibration-related inaccuracies can be subtle, and thus almost undetectable. They can also become serious and affect the quality of your prints. Significant inaccuracies can result in a wide range of problems, including inaccurate object size (too large, too small), excess filament (resulting in globs of filament), insufficient filament (weak layer bonds), and adhesion problems. I've read a number of articles and requests for help, and heard general misery from people who have struggled with one or more of these maladies. More often than not, the owner is treating the symptoms rather than the source of the problem. Proper calibration won't solve all of your printing woes, but it will go a long way toward improving your experience and the quality of your prints.

This chapter will reveal the entire set of calibration steps you need to take for a new delta printer. While some of these steps are for newly built printers, you should understand what is being done in case you ever build you own delta printer or have to disassemble your printer for maintenance or upgrades.

However, there is a bit of planning and foreknowledge needed to prepare yourself and your printer for successful calibration. I must also warn you that calibration, especially for a newly built printer, is a long process, but the payoff is well worth the effort.

---

[1]The most severe cases I've seen can be traced to skipping steps and rushing assembly. Take your time to get it right the first time.

Getting Started

If you want to succeed, you need to make a plan. Calibrating a delta printer is no exception. You first must establish a base configuration upon which you can begin the calibration steps. This includes ensuring that the printer is assembled correctly, that you understand and know the key measurements for configuring the firmware, that the firmware is properly configured (at least to known starting values), and that the motors are wired and move in the correct direction. It is so easy to get those stepper motor wires reversed!

This section examines each of these preliminary calibration steps to prepare for loading the firmware. Let's start with the mechanical bits and visit the firmware before you jump into testing the printer (called *preflight checks*).

Check the Frame

There are several choices for frame hardware and axis mechanisms that delta printer designs have incorporated. As you saw in Chapter 2, this includes printed components attached to wood pieces, entire frames made from wood, frames that incorporate aluminum extrusion uprights attached to wood or printed parts, and smooth rods for the towers. No matter how the frame is constructed, there are certain things that must be true for the frame to be properly assembled.

At a minimum, the towers must be square with the print bed (perpendicular), all must be the same height,[2] and firmly attached to their frame components. There should be no play, flex, or loose parts on any of the towers, lower or upper sections.

■ **Note** Some early and variant designs place the axis towers in nonequidistant points. That is, they do not form an equilateral triangle as viewed from the top.

I recommend checking your frame for any loose (or missing) bolts. Even if a vendor built the printer, it is still a good idea to check to make sure that everything is firmly attached and properly aligned. Perhaps more important is making sure that the towers are square.

To do so, use a small framing square, placing one side against the tower and resting the other on the lower frame section. Figure 5-1 shows an example of proper placement. If you find the tower is not square, loosen its mounting bolts, bring it into square, and retighten the bolts. The best way to hold the towers in the proper position is to use a small clamp to hold one side of the square to the tower, as shown. Repeat on all three towers.

---

[2]Designs that incorporate the upper frame section as part of a belt tensioning system (like the Mini Kossel) do not require extreme precision. However, the type-A and OCD among us insist on this maxim.

Figure 5-1. *Aligning the towers (courtesy of SeeMeCNC.com)*

For frames that have a fixed upper section (not part of the belt-tensioning mechanism) and an unadjustable endstop, recheck the distance between the upper and lower sections to ensure that they are all the same height. This may not be that critical if the endstops are adjustable, but it is best to get them all the same because it will aid in calibration later.

Owners of delta printers with fixed frame components that do not allow for adjusting the tower may still need to square the towers. For example, the Mini Kossel has lower frame parts that mount the towers in a fixed, 90-degree angle and is not adjustable from side to side (but can be adjusted up and down). However, since the part is connected to horizontal members that are not fixed other than via bolts, it is possible for these parts to be out of square slightly. In this case, you can square the vertical frame with the horizontal frame parts by loosening the bolts in the lower frame parts until the tower is square.

Once the towers are properly aligned and the upper and lower sections are equidistant, move on to setting the starting location for the endstops.

Set the Initial Position of the Endstops

The endstops on a delta printer are located at the maximum travel position of each axis. As you discovered in Chapter 2, they provide the origin of the axis movement. If they are not set correctly, one or more of the axes will move too far or not far enough, resulting in an incorrect delta movement calculation.

Some documentation suggests setting the position of the endstops by measuring the distance from the endstop to the lower frame, or if closer, the print bed. However, this step should be considered a coarse adjustment designed to provide a starting point and is not sufficient for proper calibration.

This is because the reference point—the frame or print bed—may not be in the same position on all three towers. Furthermore, the endstops can have minute differences in how they are positioned on a PCB (if using MakerBot-derived endstops) and can differ in how far the arm must travel before triggering. Even a small difference can cause delta movement problems. However, you have to start somewhere. Setting all three endstops to a known position will at least ensure that your delta printer moves correctly, assuming all other settings are correct.

To set the endstops, use a tape measure to measure the base of the endstop or PCB or move the axis carriage up until you hear the endstop click and measure from the base of the carriage to the lower frame or print bed if located directly under the tower. You measure from the lower frame because some delta printer designs use a floating upper frame as part of the belt adjustment mechanism (like the Mini Kossel). Figure 5-2 shows one method of measuring the distance.

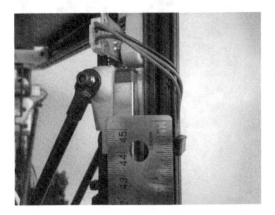

Figure 5-2. *Setting the initial endstop position*

Some firmware allow you to adjust the endstop position using an offset measured in steps. This can save you from having to move them physically during tower calibration. For example, if you are using Repetier-Firmware, you can use the following offsets in the firmware. However, the documentation for using these is not very clear. It is best to physically move the endstop.

```
#define DELTA_X_ENDSTOP_OFFSET_STEPS 0
#define DELTA_Y_ENDSTOP_OFFSET_STEPS 0
#define DELTA_Z_ENDSTOP_OFFSET_STEPS 0
```

Note that you will fine-tune the endstops when you calibrate the towers. For now, this initial adjustment allows you to complete the rest of the precalibration steps so that you can get the printer moving.

Calibrate the Stepper Drivers

There is one thing that you should do before you attempt to calibrate your axes. You should check the stepper drivers to make sure that they are sending the right voltage to your stepper motors. If the voltage is too low, it may skip steps. If it is too high, it will cause the motors to run hot and make much more noise. It is OK if you haven't done this step yet, but if you have, I highly recommend that you do it again as a double check.

The following presents procedures for setting Pololu A4988 stepper drivers. There are other stepper driver boards available. While the basic logical process is the same, the actual steps may differ for other boards. You should check your vendor's web site for the correct procedure if you are using other stepper drivers.

First, check your stepper motor specifications to see what operating amperage the vendor recommends. You should be able to find this on the data sheet for the stepper motor. Next, check your stepper drivers to see what value resistors are used. For example, Pololu stepper drivers normally have 0.05 ohm (50 milliohm) resistors (but you need to check your vendor's data sheet to know for certain). Finally, you can plug this data into the following formula to calculate the reference voltage (VREF):

```
VREF = Max_Amps * 8 * Resistors
```

For Pololu stepper drivers, the formula is as follows:

```
VREF = Max_Amps * 8 * 0.05
```

Let's suppose your stepper motors are rated at 1.0 amps. The reference voltage should be as follows:

```
0.4V = 1.0 * 8 * 0.05
```

To measure the VREF, power on your printer and locate the small potentiometer on the stepper driver. Figure 5-3 shows a Pololu stepper driver. I have highlighted the potentiometer with an oval and the ground pin with a square.

Figure 5-3. *Stepstick stepper driver module*

■ **Caution**   Watch where you put that probe! It is easy to accidentally touch the wrong pin.

To measure the voltage, use a multimeter set to measure DC voltage. If your multimeter has several settings, choose the one that measures up to 10 or 20 volts. Power on your printer and carefully place the positive probe on the center of the potentiometer and the ground probe on the ground pin. Read the voltage and compare it to your calculations.

If you need to increase the voltage, use a ceramic screwdriver to rotate the potentiometer clockwise a small fraction at a time. It only takes a small movement to increase or decrease the voltage. Measure the voltage again and repeat the process until you get the correct voltage. If you turn the potentiometer too far, you may cycle back around to 0 volts. Just keep turning the potentiometer, but do so using smaller increments. Repeat the process for each of your axes and the extruder printer driver.

Now that the basic hardware, preliminary hardware, and initial electronic settings are complete, you can dive into the firmware. But first, let's review the characteristics of delta printers and record some key measurements.

Confirm the Delta Kinematics

Before getting into the firmware settings, you need certain values or measurements for the delta mechanisms (also called *kinematics*)[3]. Let's first review the delta mechanism from the viewpoint of a single tower. Figure 5-4 shows the delta mechanism with labels for identifying the parts and measurements for the Marlin firmware.

---

[3]See http://en.wikipedia.org/wiki/Kinematics.

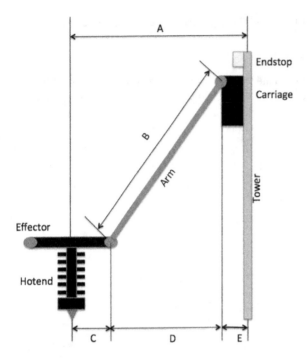

Figure 5-4. *Delta mechanism with labels: Marlin firmware*

The measurements needed for the Marlin firmware include those in Table 5-1.

Table 5-1. *Key Delta Measurements*

#	Description	#define in Configuration.h
A	Distance from the center of carriage mechanism to the center of the effector (hot end)	DELTA_SMOOTH_ROD_OFFSET
B	Length of the delta arms measured center to center of the joint	DELTA_DIAGONAL_ROD
C	Distance from the center of delta arm joint to the center of the effector	DELTA_EFFECTOR_OFFSET
D	Calculated distance from (A - C - E)	DELTA_RADIUS
E	Distance from the center of the carriage mechanism to the center of the delta arm joint	DELTA_CARRIAGE_OFFSET

If you are building your own delta printer and using the Marlin firmware, it is important that you take the time to get these measurements as close to accurate as you can. You will see later on that you can adjust these in the firmware.

If you are using the Repetier-Firmware, your measurements are a bit simplified. Figure 5-5 shows an excerpt from the Repetier-Firmware configuration tool (repetier.com/firmware/v091/).

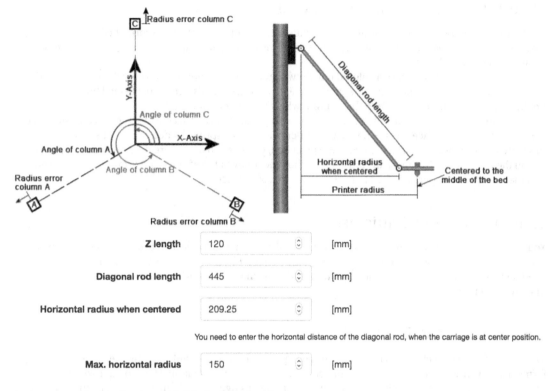

Figure 5-5. *Delta mechanism with labels: Repetier-Firmware*

As you can see, the measurements needed are a bit simplified compared to the Marlin firmware. Notice that there is no measurement for the DELTA_SMOOTH_ROD_OFFSET and DELTA_CARRIAGE_OFFSET. Some people find the configuration tool much easier to use than manually updating the source code. However, the configuration tool doesn't eliminate the possibility of having to change settings in the source code. Thus, I provide the definitions for these measurements in the Repetier-Firmware code in Table 5-2.

Table 5-2. *Key Delta Measurements: Repetier-Firmware*

Description	Configuration Tool	#define in Configuration.h
Length of the delta arms measured center to center of the joint	Diagonal rod length	DELTA_DIAGONAL_ROD
Distance from the center of the delta arm joint to the center of the delta arm joint on the effector	Horizontal radius when centered	DELTA_RADIUS
Distance from the center of the delta arm joint to the center of the effector	Max horizontal radius	DELTA_MAX_RADIUS

Determine the Print Surface Radius

Another measurement that is important is the radius of the printable area of your print bed. If you are using a heated print bed, this is the maximum radius that fits inside the heat zone. The heat zone is the area of the print bed that can be heated.

Most heated print beds have a colored line drawn around the border. This is more than simple border dressing. It demarcates the outer perimeter of the heated surface. That's right, most heated build plates do not heat all the way to the edge. Keep this in mind when setting your delta radius.

Regardless of whether you have a heated print bed, you also must also consider the mechanisms used to secure your print surface. That is, if you use binder clips, levers, spring-loaded arms, bolts, and so forth, to secure the print bed or a print surface to the print bed, you need to make sure that the printable radius is within these obstacles. Nothing can ruin a nozzle, hot end, or even the effector and arms faster than a hot end that strikes a hard part attached to the frame. So measure twice!

Examine Axis Mechanisms

You also need to know the values for your axis mechanisms. Since all three axes use the same mechanism,[4] you can calculate these values once and use them for each of the X, Y, and Z axis formulas. But wait, you need one more thing. You need a value for the extruder mechanism! Let's look at each of these in the upcoming sections.

Check the X, Y, and Z Axis

The X, Y, and Z axes mechanisms for delta printers typically use belts or cables. Fortunately, the same formula can be used for each and are calculated using the following equation. Here you derive the steps per millimeter using the number of steps the motor has per a single revolution, multiplied by the microstep setting for the driver. This value is then divided by the pitch of the belt (the spacing between the teeth) and the number of teeth in the drive pulley. Wow!

```
steps_per_mm = (motor_steps_per_rev * driver_microstep) /
  (belt_pitch * pulley_number_of_teeth)
```

For example, let's say you have a typical Nema 17 stepper motor common to almost all 3D printers. It has 200 steps per revolution and the driver microstep is 1/16th. You use the denominator for the value of the microstep. Now, let's say your drive pulley has 16 teeth and the belt pitch is 2.0mm (GT2). The steps per millimeter is therefore calculated as follows:

```
100 = (200 * 16) / (2.0 * 16)
```

■ **Note** You may be wondering where the idler pulley is in this equation. It isn't needed. In fact, despite what you may read on the Internet, the idler pulley is of no concern. The only possible concern is how large the idler pulley is in relation for belt travel or the carriage mechanism. For example, if the idler is so large that the belt rubs some part of the frame or carriage, it is too large.

---

[4]Strictly speaking, they don't have to be the same, but it makes things easier if they are.

Let's see another example, but this time you will use a T2.5 belt with 20 teeth on the drive gear. The steps per millimeter is calculated as follows:

```
64 = (200 * 16)  / (2.5 * 20)
```

The calculations for your delta printer should be very similar. If you built yours from a kit, check the documentation from your vendor to confirm your calculations.

Check the Extruder

Extruders for delta printers are normally Bowden setups where the cold end is mounted away from the hot end to reduce weight on the effector. As such, most extruders used in a Bowden setup are either direct-drive, where the drive pulley is mounted directly to the stepper motor, or they use a geared stepper motor. This section describes these two configurations.

You need the same values for the stepper motor, but also the gear ratio (the number of teeth in large gear divided by the number of teeth in the small gear), which you divide by the diameter of the filament drive pulley times pi. The formula is as follows:

```
e_steps_per_mm = (motor_steps_per_rev * driver_microstep) *
    (big_gear_teeth / small_gear_teeth) /
    (drive_pulley_effective_diameter * pi)
```

This is the one calculation that trips almost everyone up when building a delta printer. If you miscount the number of teeth in the gears or measure your drive pulley incorrectly, your calculation will be off a bit. This can result in either too much or not enough filament extruded during a print.

For example, your extruder may extrude only 95mm of filament when instructed to extrude 100mm. Since this is such an issue, I will go over the calibration of the extruder in much greater detail in an upcoming section. For now, let's get the calculation as close as possible.

■ **Tip** To measure the drive pulley diameter, use a digital caliber set to millimeters and measure the inside-most diameter of the drive pulley at the center of the hobbed area. This will provide a good starting point for finer calibration of the extruder. Some vendors provide this information on their web sites.

For example, using the same Nema 17 motor and a geared stepper motor with a ratio of 5.18:1 (the large gear divided by the small gear), and a drive pulley diameter of 7mm, you calculate the steps per millimeters as follows:

```
749.39 = (200 * 16) * 5.18 / (7 * 3.1416)
```

If you are using a direct-drive extruder, the calculation is a bit easier since you need not calculate the gear ratio:

```
145.51 = (200 * 16) * 1 / (7 * 3.1416)
```

If you have some other form of extruder or your stepper motor drive is different, you will want to spend time reading your vendor's documentation and recommendations.

Estimate the Z-Height

There is one last measurement you will need and that is the maximum Z-height. This is the maximum build height of your delta printer. However, you cannot determine this accurately until all the other calibration steps are complete. For now, you should choose a value that is about 20mm more than the measured distance.

Turn off your printer and slowly move all three axes to the maximum position. The best way to do this is to hold the effector and pull up slowly, keeping each axis moving upward. Stop when you hear the endstops click for all three axes. Next, use a ruler to measure the distance from the build plate to the tip of the nozzle. Note this value and add 20mm. Figure 5-6 shows one method of measuring the distance. Remember that it doesn't have to be 100% accurate at this stage, and it should be a bit more than measured. In this case, I used 225mm. You will fine-tune this later.

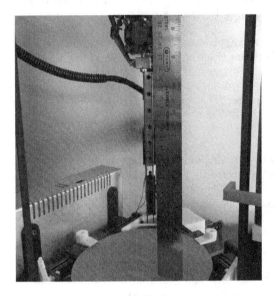

Figure 5-6. *Estimating the Z-height*

The reason you add a bit more and intentionally introduce inaccuracy is so that you can ensure that the nozzle will reach the build plate once the endstops are adjusted correctly. If you used the actual measurement and have to move the endstops up, the nozzle may not reach the print bed because the firmware will not move the Z axis any lower than the maximum Z-height specified. But don't worry, you will set this correctly once the firmware is configured and installed.

Now that you have all the measurements you need, let's plug those into the firmware.

Configuring and Loading the Firmware

If your printer vendor supplies firmware for you, you may not need to perform the steps covered next. However, if you need to reload the firmware or plan to make significant changes to your delta printer (axis mechanisms), you may want to follow along so that you are prepared for what you will need to do to get the printer working properly.

In this section, I present how to configure, compile, and install firmware on your delta printer. I present two popular open source firmware solutions for 3D printers that are known to work well on delta printers.

WHAT IS OPEN SOURCE?

Open source means that the software or hardware is free for anyone to use. Think free as in "free speech," not free as in free beer. Most open source products have a license associated with it, designed to define ownership and outline the permissions that users have. For example, if something is marked as open source, it may be that the license allows you to freely use and even distribute. The license may also permit you to modify the product, but requires you to surrender all modifications to the original owner. So while you can use it for free, it isn't yours to own. Always check the license carefully before using, distributing, or modifying the product.

These include Marlin (`https://github.com/MarlinFirmware/Marlin`) and Repetier-Firmware[5] (`repetier.com/downloads/`). The Marlin option is available as a download of the latest version, whereas the Repetier-Firmware offers an online configuration tool. Scroll down their download page to find the links for the configuration tool. You do not have to use this tool, but it is the recommended and best way to get going with Repetier-Firmware.

As you will see, the Marlin firmware is more hands-on and requires modifying the source code directly, whereas the Repetier-Firmware uses the online configuration tool to generate the initial settings. Whichever you choose, you will likely need to modify the source code, but at least the Repetier-Firmware makes it a bit less painful. Let's begin with the Marlin solution. I will use a Mini Kossel as the example for each.

■ **Note** There are many variants of firmware available on the Internet. This is especially true for Marlin. If your vendor provides such a variant, it is best to use that instead of downloading the latest and greatest version. This will help ensure that you get help from your vendor (and matches your documentation).

However, before I jump into the specifics of each firmware, I present a concise tutorial on the Arduino development platform. If you are already familiar with the Arduino IDE, you can skip to the firmware section of your choice.

Using the Arduino IDE

Both the Marlin and Repetier-Firmware run on an Arduino-compatible microcontroller. I present a short tutorial on using the Arduino IDE for compiling your firmware.

WHAT IS AN ARDUINO?

The Arduino is an open source hardware prototyping platform supported by an open source software environment. It was first introduced in 2005 and was designed with the goal of making the hardware and software easy to use and available to the widest audience possible. Thus, you don't have to be an electronics expert to use the Arduino. This means you can use the Arduino for all manner of projects—from reacting to environmental conditions, to controlling complex robotic functions, to controlling a 3D printer. The Arduino has also made learning electronics easier through practical applications. For more information about using Arduino, visit `http://arduino.cc`.

---

[5]Version 91 is the current stable version. If you want to use a later version, select it from the options provided on the web page.

The Arduino IDE is available for download for the Mac, Linux (32- and 64-bit versions), and Windows platforms. There is also a download for the source code so that you can compile it for other platforms, or even customize it for you own needs. The current version is 1.6.1. You can download the Arduino IDE from http://arduino.cc/en/Main/Software. There are links for each platform, as well as a link to the source code.

Installing the IDE is straightforward. For brevity, I omitted the steps for installing the IDE, but if you require a walk-through, you can click the Getting Started link on the download page, or read more about in *Beginning Arduino* by Michael McRoberts (Apress, 2010). Figure 5-7 shows the Arduino IDE with one of the sample sketches loaded.

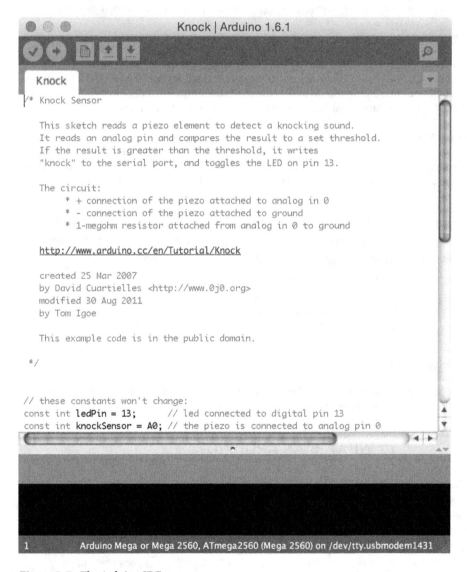

Figure 5-7. The Arduino IDE

Once the IDE launches, you see a simple interface with a text editor area (a white background by default), a message area beneath the editor (a black background by default), and a simple button bar at the top. The buttons are (from left to right) Verify, Upload, New, Open, and Save. There is also a button on the far right that opens the serial monitor. You use the serial monitor to view messages from the Arduino sent (or printed) via the Serial library. You see this in action in your first project.

Due to the differences in processors and supporting architecture, there are some differences in how the compiler builds the program (and how the IDE uploads it). Thus, one of the first things you should do when you start the IDE is choose your board from the Tools ➤ Board menu. For most 3D printers, you want to choose the Arduino Mega 2560 entry. Figure 5-8 shows a sample of selecting the board on the Mac.

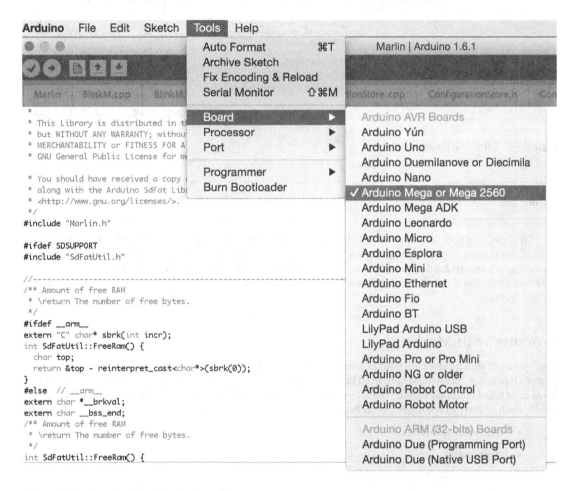

Figure 5-8. *Choosing the Arduino board*

Notice the number of boards available. If your 3D printer uses a different board, check the manufacturer's site for the recommended setting to use. If you choose the wrong board, you typically get an error during upload, but it may not be obvious that you've chosen the wrong board. Because I have so many different boards, I've made it a habit to choose the board each time I launch the IDE.

The next thing you need to do is choose the serial port to which the Arduino board is connected. To connect to the board, use the Tools ➤ Serial Port menu option. Figure 5-9 shows an example on the Mac. In this case, no serial ports are listed. This can happen if you haven't plugged your Arduino in to the computer's

USB ports (or hub), or you had it plugged in but disconnected it at some point, or you haven't loaded the FTDI drivers for the Arduino (Mac and Windows). Typically, this can be remedied by simply unplugging the Arduino and plugging it back in and waiting until the computer recognizes the port.

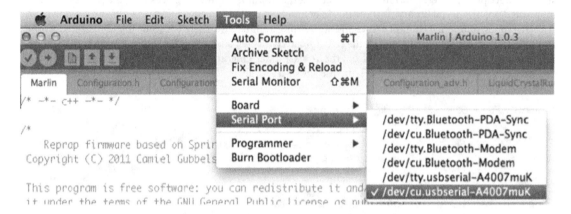

Figure 5-9. *Choosing the serial port*

■ **Tip**   See `http://arduino.cc/en/Guide/Howto` if you need help installing the drivers for Mac and Windows.

Go ahead and open the Arduino IDE. Choose the correct board and serial port if you have not done so already. Try out the blink sketch by opening, compiling, and uploading it to your Arduino. Once the sketch starts, you will see the hard-wired LED on pin 13 blink periodically. Once your IDE is installed and you are able to compile the simple blink sketch, you are ready to open the Marlin firmware and start configuring it for your hardware.

Working with Marlin

Configuring Marlin for use with your printer involves modifying the `Configuration.h` file in a number of places. Depending on the hardware used in your printer, you may need to modify only a few locations. The areas most often modified include the following (listed in the order they appear in the file)[6]. I explain how to modify each of these in the following sections.

- Author and Version
- Baud Rate
- Motherboard (electronics)
- Delta Settings
- Temperature
- Endstop Behavior

---

[6]The order of these tends to change from version to version, but they are generally in this order.

- Home Position

- Axes Movement

- LCD Panel

To download the latest version of the Marlin firmware, visit https://github.com/ErikZalm/Marlin and click the Download Zip button located on the right side of the page. Once the file is downloaded, unzip the file and copy or move it to your Documents/Arduino folder.

Begin by opening the Marlin firmware by navigating to the folder you unzipped and placed in your Documents/Arduino folder. Under that folder is another folder named Marlin. Within that folder is the Marlin.ino file. Double-click the file. This will automatically open the Arduino IDE. Alternatively, you can first open the Arduino IDE and then use the File ➤ Open menu to locate and open the file. Once the file is open, locate the Configuration.h tab and click it. You are now ready to edit the file.

■ **Note** The following sections refer to "the file", which is henceforth the Configuration.h file because there is no other file you should be changing for basic configuration steps.

I recommend making one change at a time and saving the file after each change. Use the File ➤ Save menu item to save the files.

■ **Tip** You can also copy the example configuration files in the Marlin/example_configurations/delta folder. You will find both a Configuration.h and a Configuration_adv.h file that are good starts for delta printers.

Author and Version

Changing the author and version is optional, but can be very helpful if you have several printers or if you plan to modify the printer at a later date. I don't change the date and time values. Rather, I allow the firmware to compile with the __DATE__ and __TIME__ directives, which are the defaults. This means the date and time will be filled in when the firmware is compiled.

However, I do change the author. This helps me identify printers that I have made custom firmware changes to (or I just set up myself). The following code shows the lines changed in the file. Find those lines and change the author to yourself.

```
#define STRING_VERSION_CONFIG_H __DATE__ " " __TIME__ // build date and time
#define STRING_CONFIG_H_AUTHOR "(CAB, Mini Kossel 1)" // Who made the changes.
```

■ **Tip** Use the M115 code to see these values in your 3D printer.

Baud Rate

The next area to change sets the baud rate of the serial (USB) connection. Most people choose 250000, but in some cases you may want to set it slower. Locate the code to change it as follows:

```
// This determines the communication speed of the printer
#define BAUDRATE 250000
```

Motherboard (Electronics Board)

The firmware must know what electronics board you are using. You can find a long list of the types of boards supported (called *motherboards*) in the boards.h file. Listing 5-1 shows an excerpt of the code that defines the list.

Listing 5-1. Selecting the Electronics Board

```
...
#define BOARD_RAMPS_OLD         3    // MEGA/RAMPS up to 1.2
#define BOARD_RAMPS_13_EFB      33   // RAMPS 1.3 / 1.4 (Power outputs: Extruder, Fan, Bed)
#define BOARD_RAMPS_13_EEB      34   // RAMPS 1.3 / 1.4 (Power outputs: Extruder0,
                                        Extruder1, Bed)
#define BOARD_RAMPS_13_EFF      35   // RAMPS 1.3 / 1.4 (Power outputs: Extruder, Fan, Fan)
#define BOARD_RAMPS_13_EEF      36   // RAMPS 1.3 / 1.4 (Power outputs: Extruder0,
                                        Extruder1, Fan)
...
```

Choose the entry from the list and make the change in the Configuration.h file, as follows:

```
// The following define selects which electronics board you have.
// Please choose the name from boards.h that matches your setup
#ifndef MOTHERBOARD
  #define MOTHERBOARD BOARD_RAMPS_13_EFB
#endif
```

Delta Settings

This is the area where some people get wrapped around the axle. If you followed the preceding sections and measured your delta mechanism (or got the information from your vendor), you should have no problems with this section. It is a simple matter of filling in the values from the table. The code you need to change is highlighted in Listing 5-2.

Listing 5-2. Setting the Delta Parameters

```
//===========================================================================
//============================= Delta Settings ==============================
//===========================================================================
// Enable DELTA kinematics
#define DELTA

// Make delta curves from many straight lines (linear interpolation).
// This is a trade-off between visible corners (not enough segments)
```

```
// and processor overload (too many expensive sqrt calls).
#define DELTA_SEGMENTS_PER_SECOND 160

// Center-to-center distance of the holes in the diagonal push rods.
#define DELTA_DIAGONAL_ROD 213.5 // mm

// Horizontal offset from middle of printer to smooth rod center.
#define DELTA_SMOOTH_ROD_OFFSET 143.275 // mm

// Horizontal offset of the universal joints on the end effector.
#define DELTA_EFFECTOR_OFFSET 30.0 // mm

// Horizontal offset of the universal joints on the carriages.
#define DELTA_CARRIAGE_OFFSET 30.0 // mm

// Horizontal distance bridged by diagonal push rods when effector is centered.
#define DELTA_RADIUS (DELTA_SMOOTH_ROD_OFFSET-DELTA_EFFECTOR_OFFSET-DELTA_CARRIAGE_OFFSET)

// Print surface diameter/2 minus unreachable space (avoid collisions with vertical towers).
#define DELTA_PRINTABLE_RADIUS 80.0
```

Notice that you see all the measurements from the table here, including the printable radius. Recall that this is the maximum area that your nozzle can travel around the print surface. Be sure to set this so that the nozzle does not come into contact with any hard objects. It may also be a good idea to double-check this whenever you add accessories such as print fans, nozzle fans, and Z-probes, which can limit your print radius if they protrude beyond the effector area.

Temperature

The next area to change concerns the temperature sensors. More specifically, the type of sensor that you have to measure the temperature of the extruder or print bed. Listing 5-3 shows the values and the code changes for a 100K thermistor, which is the most common type for RepRap kits. Check with your vendor for the correct sensor.

Listing 5-3. Setting the Temperature Sensors

```
//===========================================================================
//============================Thermal Settings ============================
//===========================================================================
//
//--NORMAL IS 4.7kohm PULLUP!-- 1kohm pullup can be used on hotend sensor, using correct
resistor and table
//
//// Temperature sensor settings:
// -2 is thermocouple with MAX6675 (only for sensor 0)
// -1 is thermocouple with AD595
// 0 is not used
// 1 is 100k thermistor - best choice for EPCOS 100k (4.7k pullup)
// 2 is 200k thermistor - ATC Semitec 204GT-2 (4.7k pullup)
// 3 is Mendel-parts thermistor (4.7k pullup)
// 4 is 10k thermistor !! do not use it for a hotend. It gives bad resolution at high temp. !!
```

```
// 5 is 100K thermistor - ATC Semitec 104GT-2 (Used in ParCan & J-Head) (4.7k pullup)
// 6 is 100k EPCOS - Not as accurate as table 1 (created using a fluke thermocouple)
(4.7k pullup)
// 7 is 100k Honeywell thermistor 135-104LAG-J01 (4.7k pullup)
// 71 is 100k Honeywell thermistor 135-104LAF-J01 (4.7k pullup)
// 8 is 100k 0603 SMD Vishay NTCS0603E3104FXT (4.7k pullup)
// 9 is 100k GE Sensing AL03006-58.2K-97-G1 (4.7k pullup)
// 10 is 100k RS thermistor 198-961 (4.7k pullup)
// 11 is 100k beta 3950 1% thermistor (4.7k pullup)
// 12 is 100k 0603 SMD Vishay NTCS0603E3104FXT (4.7k pullup) (calibrated for Makibox hot
bed)
// 13 is 100k Hisens 3950  1% up to 300°C for hotend "Simple ONE " & "Hotend "All In ONE"
// 20 is the PT100 circuit found in the Ultimainboard V2.x
// 60 is 100k Maker's Tool Works Kapton Bed Thermistor beta=3950
//
//    1k ohm pullup tables - This is not normal, you would have to have changed out your
4.7k for 1k
//                     (but gives greater accuracy and more stable PID)
// 51 is 100k thermistor - EPCOS (1k pullup)
// 52 is 200k thermistor - ATC Semitec 204GT-2 (1k pullup)
// 55 is 100k thermistor - ATC Semitec 104GT-2 (Used in ParCan & J-Head) (1k pullup)
//
// 1047 is Pt1000 with 4k7 pullup
// 1010 is Pt1000 with 1k pullup (non standard)
// 147 is Pt100 with 4k7 pullup
// 110 is Pt100 with 1k pullup (non standard)

#define TEMP_SENSOR_0 5
#define TEMP_SENSOR_1 0
#define TEMP_SENSOR_2 0
#define TEMP_SENSOR_BED 8
```

■ **Caution**   This is another area where novice 3D printer builders sometimes get confused. If you choose the wrong sensor type, your printer may heat the extruder to the wrong temperature, and may even overheat it. Take the time to make sure that you get this part right. Don't hesitate to contact the vendor to verify the setting.

Notice that there are four settings. The values support up to three extruders and one for the bed. If your printer does not have a second (or third) extruder, set those to 0. Likewise, if your printer does not have a heated bed, set that to 0 to turn off monitoring of the sensor. In this example, there is a single extruder and a heated bed, both with 100K thermistors.

■ **Note**   If your printer has multiple extruders, you should also change the #define EXTRUDERS 1 statement to indicate the number of extruders that are included.

Endstops

The next area can also cause some hiccups. This is partly because the variable names are a bit confusing. In this case, you may need to do several things, but it depends on your choice of electronics and the type of endstops.

For example, if you are using endstops that are normally open (true in the following code), you may need to reverse the logic, since by default they are treated as normally closed (false in the following code). The following shows the lines involved; the ones I changed are in bold.

```
const bool X_MIN_ENDSTOP_INVERTING = false; // set to true to invert the logic of the
endstop.
const bool Y_MIN_ENDSTOP_INVERTING = false; // set to true to invert the logic of the
endstop.
const bool Z_MIN_ENDSTOP_INVERTING = false; // set to true to invert the logic of the
endstop.
const bool X_MAX_ENDSTOP_INVERTING = true; // set to true to invert the logic of the
endstop.
const bool Y_MAX_ENDSTOP_INVERTING = true; // set to true to invert the logic of the
endstop.
const bool Z_MAX_ENDSTOP_INVERTING = true; // set to true to invert the logic of the
endstop.
```

As I said, this is one area that can be an issue. If you get the settings wrong, your endstops will not be triggered correctly. In a later section, you discover how to check the endstops for proper functioning. You learn how to use the M119 command to see the endstop status in the G-code console output.

There is one other portion of the code that you may need to change with respect to endstops, shown as follows. This defines how the endstops are used in the homing process. Delta printers typically have the endstops at the max position on each axis. If this is reversed, the axes will run toward the print bed when homing. You do not want that to happen because they will not stop and your hot end will crash into the print bed. It is best to check this in the firmware. Locate the following code and ensure that your settings are the same as shown.

```
// Sets direction of endstops when homing; 1=MAX, -1=MIN
#define X_HOME_DIR 1
#define Y_HOME_DIR 1
#define Z_HOME_DIR 1
```

Home Position

Recall that delta printers set their endstops at the max position of the axis and the home position is at [0,0,MAX_Z], which is the center of the print bed. To set this behavior in the firmware, you need to use the following settings (substituting your maximum printing height).

```
// The position of the homing switches
#define MANUAL_HOME_POSITIONS  // If defined, MANUAL_*_HOME_POS below will be used
#define BED_CENTER_AT_0_0      // If defined, the center of the bed is at (X=0, Y=0)

//Manual homing switch locations:
// For deltabots this means top and center of the Cartesian print volume.
#define MANUAL_X_HOME_POS 0
#define MANUAL_Y_HOME_POS 0
#define MANUAL_Z_HOME_POS 250  // For delta: Distance between nozzle and print surface after
homing.
```

Notice several things here. First, you set the bed center at zero using a special definition. If this is commented out in your firmware, uncomment it! Next, you set the position of each axis when homed. For X and Y this is 0, but for Z, it is your maximum Z-height. Notice here I set it to 250. This is a bit high for a Mini Kossel, but it allows me to move the Z axis low enough for fine-tuning later.

Axes Movement

The next segment of code to change is the place where you will need those values from the calculations in the last section. Since all the axes are the same, you can just set the values to be the same. However, you also set the extruder values in the same section. The following is the code to set the axis movement. Notice I use two decimals. Had any of my values needed to be expressed with more, I would likely use only four decimal places.

```
#define XYZ_FULL_STEPS_PER_ROTATION 200
#define XYZ_MICROSTEPS 32
#define XYZ_BELT_PITCH 2
#define XYZ_PULLEY_TEETH 16
#define XYZ_STEPS (XYZ_FULL_STEPS_PER_ROTATION * XYZ_MICROSTEPS / double(XYZ_BELT_PITCH) /
double(XYZ_PULLEY_TEETH))

#define DEFAULT_AXIS_STEPS_PER_UNIT   {XYZ_STEPS, XYZ_STEPS, XYZ_STEPS, 169.74}
#define DEFAULT_MAX_FEEDRATE          {200, 200, 200, 200}      // (mm/sec)
#define DEFAULT_MAX_ACCELERATION      {9000,9000,9000,9000}     // X, Y, Z, E ...
```

Notice that I set the stepper motor characteristics. The most important values here are the microsteps and the values for the belt and pulley size. Here I use a GT2 belt with a 16-tooth drive pulley. My stepper motors are set up for 200 steps per rotation and 32 microsteps. Your vendor may have a data sheet with recommended settings for the stepper motor, but the stepper driver and its jumper settings in this information is configured.

Wait a minute! You had me do all of these calculations for the X, Y, and Z axis, but I don't need them! While that is true, I wanted you to know how these calculations are done so that you understand what data is needed. However, as you can see, you still need that calculation for the extruder! Notice I plugged the number into the last position in the DEFAULT_AXIS_STEPS_PER_UNIT array. This is the calculation for my extruder.

LCD Panel

Finally, if your printer has an LCD panel, you must change the firmware to enable it, else your LCD will either power on but display lines of solid blocks, or perhaps display garbage, or partial or no data. Locate the code shown in Listing 5-4. It should be down the file a ways.

Listing 5-4. LCD Settings

```
//LCD and SD support
//#define ULTRA_LCD  //general LCD support, also 16x2
//#define DOGLCD  // Support for SPI LCD 128x64 (Controller ST7565R graphic Display Family)
//#define SDSUPPORT // Enable SD Card Support in Hardware Console
//#define SDSLOW // Use slower SD transfer mode (not normally needed - uncomment if you're
getting volume init error)
//#define SD_CHECK_AND_RETRY // Use CRC checks and retries on the SD communication
```

```
//#define ENCODER_PULSES_PER_STEP 1 // Increase if you have a high resolution encoder
//#define ENCODER_STEPS_PER_MENU_ITEM 5 // Set according to ENCODER_PULSES_PER_STEP or your
liking
//#define ULTIMAKERCONTROLLER //as available from the Ultimaker online store.
//#define ULTIPANEL  //the UltiPanel as on Thingiverse
//#define LCD_FEEDBACK_FREQUENCY_HZ 1000 // this is the tone frequency the buzzer plays when
on UI feedback. ie Screen Click
//#define LCD_FEEDBACK_FREQUENCY_DURATION_MS 100 // the duration the buzzer plays the UI
feedback sound. ie Screen Click


// The MaKr3d Makr-Panel with graphic controller and SD support
// http://reprap.org/wiki/MaKr3d_MaKrPanel
//#define MAKRPANEL


// The RepRapDiscount Smart Controller (white PCB)
// http://reprap.org/wiki/RepRapDiscount_Smart_Controller
#define REPRAP_DISCOUNT_SMART_CONTROLLER


// The GADGETS3D G3D LCD/SD Controller (blue PCB)
// http://reprap.org/wiki/RAMPS_1.3/1.4_GADGETS3D_Shield_with_Panel
//#define G3D_PANEL


// The RepRapDiscount FULL GRAPHIC Smart Controller (quadratic white PCB)
// http://reprap.org/wiki/RepRapDiscount_Full_Graphic_Smart_Controller
//
// ==> REMEMBER TO INSTALL U8glib to your ARDUINO library folder:
http://code.google.com/p/u8glib/wiki/u8glib
//#define REPRAP_DISCOUNT_FULL_GRAPHIC_SMART_CONTROLLER


// The RepRapWorld REPRAPWORLD_KEYPAD v1.1
// http://reprapworld.com/?products_details&products_id=202&cPath=1591_1626
//#define REPRAPWORLD_KEYPAD
//#define REPRAPWORLD_KEYPAD_MOVE_STEP 10.0 // how much should be moved when a key is
pressed, eg 10.0 means 10mm per click


// The Elefu RA Board Control Panel
// http://www.elefu.com/index.php?route=product/product&product_id=53
// REMEMBER TO INSTALL LiquidCrystal_I2C.h in your ARUDINO library folder:
https://github.com/kiyoshigawa/LiquidCrystal_I2C
//#define RA_CONTROL_PANEL
```

As you can see, there are a lot of LCD panel options. Fortunately, this is one of the best-documented areas of the code. Notice there are links to most of the LCD panels supported. Choose the one that matches your LCD and uncomment the #define as I have done. For example, RepRap Discount Smart Controller made the LCD panel I used for this example.

If you choose the wrong value, you most likely will encounter strange behavior on the display (wrong data, corrupted values, not refreshing, etc.), or the rotary button won't work. If this happens, check your setting, correct it, compile, and upload the firmware.

Now that you have the Marlin code configured, you must now compile and upload it to your printer.

Compiling and Uploading

I like to compile the firmware before I attempt to upload it. You can use the Compile button on the toolbar (the leftmost button) in the Arduino IDE to do this. Once you have changed all of your settings in the file, open the Marlin.ino file.

When you compile, you may see a few warnings in the other Marlin files. These are OK and are not normally an issue. What you want to make sure of is that there are no errors and that you see a successful compile message, like the one shown here.

```
Sketch uses 113,144 bytes (44%) of program storage space. Maximum is 253,952 bytes.
Global variables use 4,767 bytes (58%) of dynamic memory, leaving 3,425 bytes for local
variables. Maximum is 8,192 bytes.
```

■ **Tip** If you get an error about LiquidTWI2.h or similar missing libraries, Google for the library and download it into your Arduino libraries folder. Remember to restart the IDE before recompiling.

If you encounter errors, scroll up in the messages window and read the error messages. Try to find the first error listed. Since the only file you changed was Configuration.h, you should only see errors related to your editing of the file. If you get errors, consult the examples and correct them, and then recompile. Sometimes a single error can produce a number of false errors, such that when the first one is fixed the false hits vanish. For example, unbalanced curly braces or a missing semicolon can cause false errors in several lines.

Now that the firmware compiles, it's time to connect to your printer and upload the sketch. To do so, click the Upload button (second from the left). Even though you just compiled the code, the upload process will compile it again and begin transferring it to your printer's electronics. When it is done, you should see a message stating that the compile is complete, and the progress bar will disappear.

■ **Note** On some printer electronics boards, like the Brainwave board on a Kossel Pro, you may have to depress two buttons to initiate the firmware upload. Check your vendor's documentation for specific instructions for uploading firmware.

Once the upload is complete (the progress bar in the lower right of the edit screen is gone), check the LCD panel. After a brief reboot, you should see the initial information screen on the display. Your printer is now ready to use! You can now perform your preflight checks, as described later in this chapter.

■ **Note** Some electronics boards may require you to manually reboot or cycle power to initiate the new firmware bootup.

WHAT ABOUT THE REST OF THE SETTINGS?

You may be wondering what all the other bits in the file are. There are many, and many more in other files in the source code. Fortunately, the default settings are usually fine for most people. However, as you use your printer, you may want to tweak some of these settings. For example, you may want to adjust the speed the axes move or improve heater performance. While I don't cover everything in the file, a quick Google search can reveal all manner of advice on these settings.

Working with Repetier-Firmware

Configuring Repetier-Firmware for use with your printer involves using an online configuration tool that generates a `Configuration.h` file for you. When you download the firmware, you get all of your settings, so you don't need to open the source code (at least not yet). There are several sections to the online configuration tool. I explain how to modify each of these in the following sections:

- General
- Mechanics
- Temperature
- Features
- User Interface
- Download

To get started, visit `repetier.com/firmware/v091/` and click the General tab, located on the top of the page. Notice while you are here that you can upload an existing configuration and use the configuration tool to modify it. How cool is that?

The following sections present the minimal settings you need to make to get the firmware working. I use the Mini Kossel delta printer as an example, but the items I changed should be representative of most delta printers.

If you are switching from Marlin to Repetier-Firmware, you may find some of the names of the parameters a bit odd. That is, they are not the same as Marlin. However, if you read the labels, you can determine what each does without relying on the Marlin equivalents.

General

The general page is where you enter all the general parameters, such as motherboard, printer type, and baud rate. You also enter data for the delta mechanism on this page.

One thing that becomes clear when using the configuration tool is that the options are easier to see, and choosing them from drop-down lists makes it very easy. In fact, you find you can choose the board type as a typical 8-bit microcontroller or the newer Arduino Due. Similarly, you find a number of different printer types, including Cartesian and delta.

Best of all, you can choose the level of detail, including a minimal view that hides all defaults, the normal view that shows the most common parameters, and a maximum view that shows all the details. Most people are fine using the normal view.

If you are following along in this text while configuring your delta printer with the configuration tool, go ahead and click through some of the drop-down lists to see the many options. For now, let's see how to use this tool to configure a typical Mini Kossel delta printer. Figure 5-10 shows the upper portion of the configuration page.

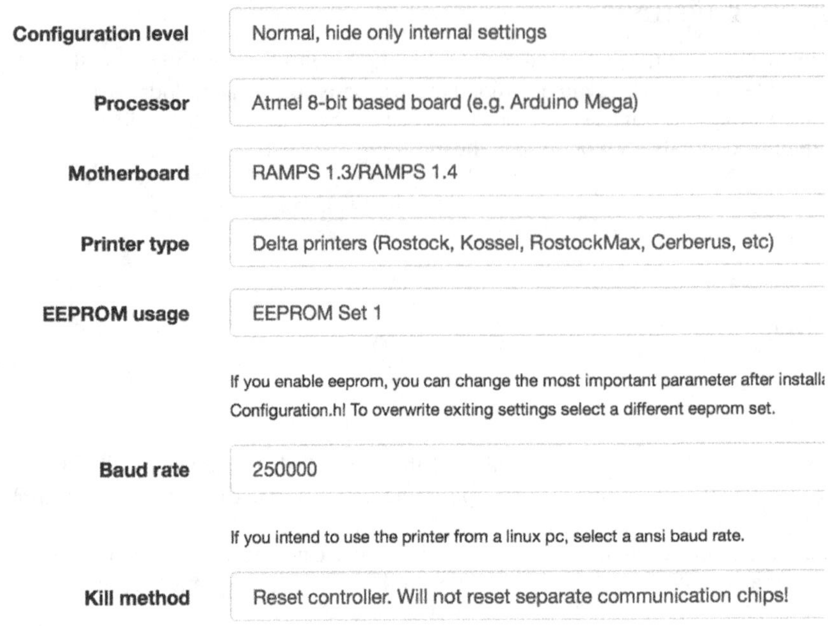

Configuration level	Normal, hide only internal settings
Processor	Atmel 8-bit based board (e.g. Arduino Mega)
Motherboard	RAMPS 1.3/RAMPS 1.4
Printer type	Delta printers (Rostock, Kossel, RostockMax, Cerberus, etc)
EEPROM usage	EEPROM Set 1

If you enable eeprom, you can change the most important parameter after install
Configuration.h! To overwrite exiting settings select a different eeprom set.

Baud rate	250000

If you intend to use the printer from a linux pc, select a ansi baud rate.

Kill method	Reset controller. Will not reset separate communication chips!

Figure 5-10. *General page: basic parameters*

■ **Note** Since the font is so small and the images quite large, I crop them to show more detail. Visit the web site to see the full details.

Here you can see that I chose the defaults, because I am building the firmware to run on a RAMPS setup using an Arduino Mega. Figure 5-11 shows the delta configuration items located at the bottom of the page. For brevity, I omitted the nice drawing of the delta mechanics.

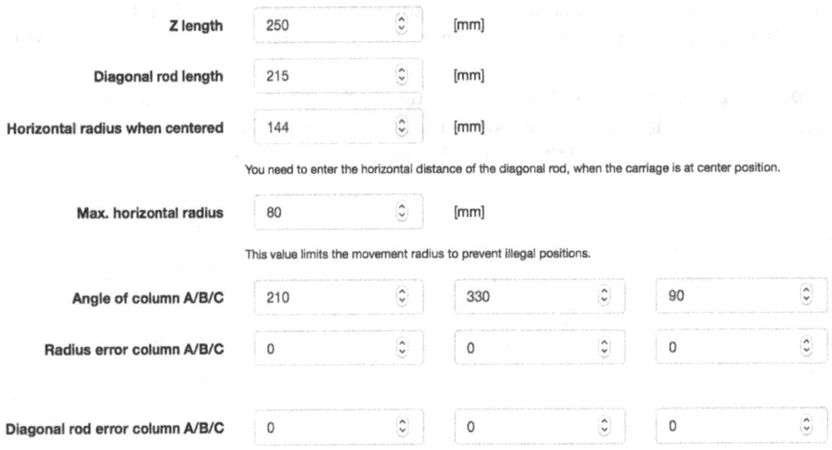

Z length	250	[mm]
Diagonal rod length	215	[mm]
Horizontal radius when centered	144	[mm]

You need to enter the horizontal distance of the diagonal rod, when the carriage is at center position.

Max. horizontal radius	80	[mm]

This value limits the movement radius to prevent illegal positions.

Angle of column A/B/C	210	330	90
Radius error column A/B/C	0	0	0
Diagonal rod error column A/B/C	0	0	0

Figure 5-11. *General page: delta parameters*

When you are satisfied with the options and values entered, click the Next Step button at the bottom of the page. Note that at any point you can use the Previous Step button to go back and check your entries.

Mechanics

This page is where you set the parameters for each stepper motor for each axis, as well as the endstops. Since the page has a separate section for each axis, you must enter the same values for each axis. Figure 5-12 shows the general section and one of the axis sections. Notice you can also invert the direction of the stepper motor. This is not the same as the homing direction, so be careful here.

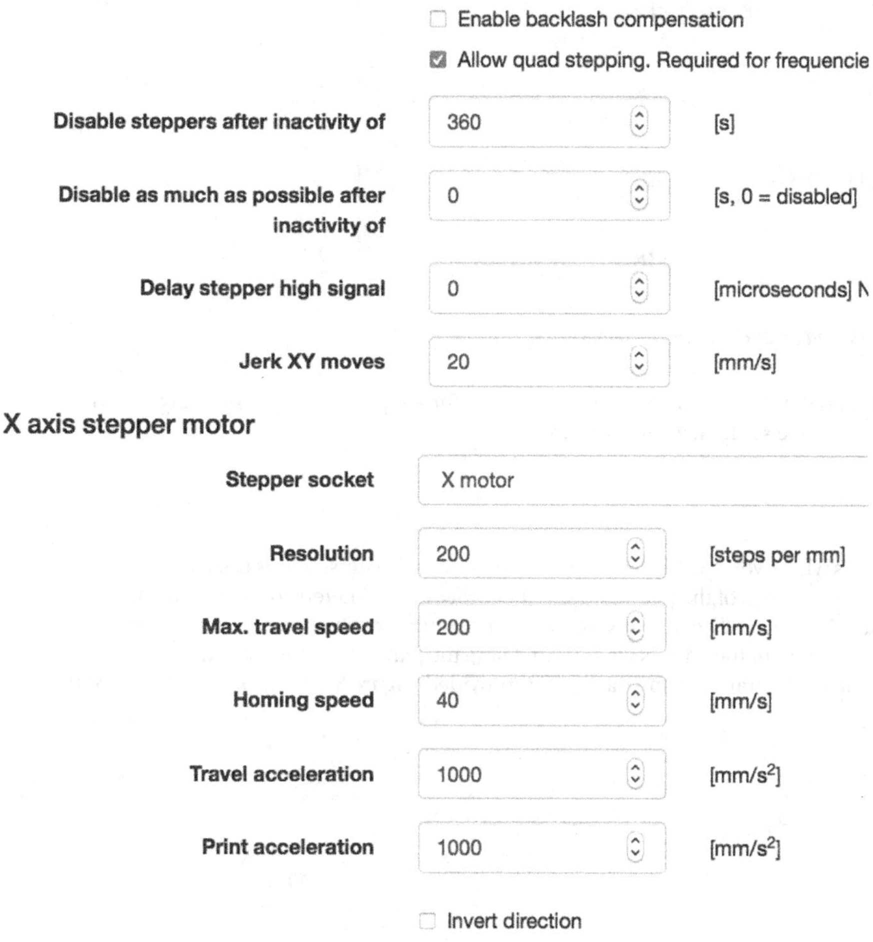

☐ Enable backlash compensation

☑ Allow quad stepping. Required for frequencie

Disable steppers after inactivity of	360	[s]
Disable as much as possible after inactivity of	0	[s, 0 = disabled]
Delay stepper high signal	0	[microseconds] ℕ
Jerk XY moves	20	[mm/s]

X axis stepper motor

Stepper socket	X motor	
Resolution	200	[steps per mm]
Max. travel speed	200	[mm/s]
Homing speed	40	[mm/s]
Travel acceleration	1000	[mm/s²]
Print acceleration	1000	[mm/s²]

☐ Invert direction

Figure 5-12. *Mechanics page: axis parameters*

At the bottom of the page is where you set up the endstop behavior. Figure 5-13 shows the values selected for a typical delta printer (a Mini Kossel).

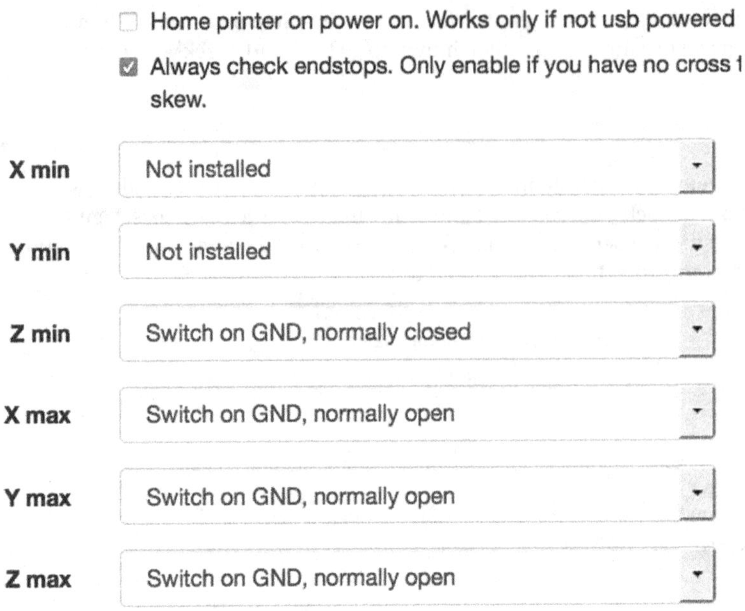

☐ Home printer on power on. Works only if not usb powered

☑ Always check endstops. Only enable if you have no cross 1 skew.

X min	Not installed	▾
Y min	Not installed	▾
Z min	Switch on GND, normally closed	▾
X max	Switch on GND, normally open	▾
Y max	Switch on GND, normally open	▾
Z max	Switch on GND, normally open	▾

Figure 5-13. *Mechanics page: endstop parameters*

Notice that I selected the Z min endstop. I use this setting for a Z-probe using a normally closed endstop. I discuss the Z-probe setup in a later section.

Temperature

The temperature page is where you specify the characteristics of the heaters. In this case, you also configure the extruder on this page. The top of the page contains a number of parameters for controlling max temperatures and extruder length. The defaults for these parameters are fine for most delta printers.

The section at the bottom of the page is where you define the parameters for the extruder. In fact, you can add extruders to the configuration using the buttons provided. Figure 5-14 shows the settings for the extruder.

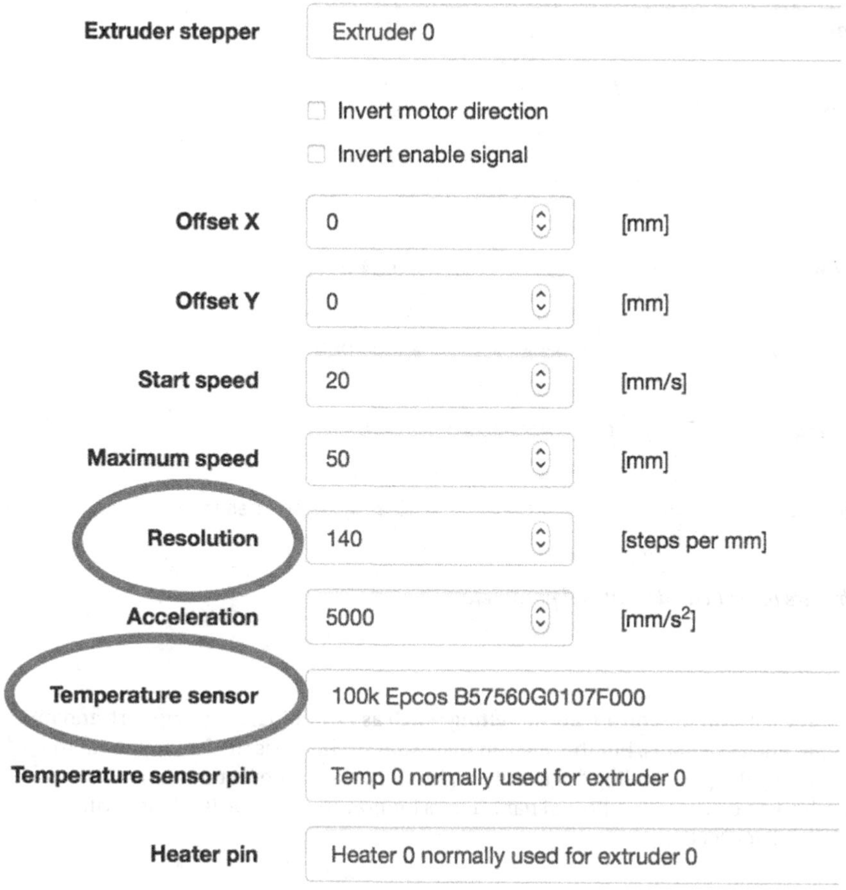

Extruder stepper	Extruder 0

☐ Invert motor direction
☐ Invert enable signal

Offset X	0	[mm]
Offset Y	0	[mm]
Start speed	20	[mm/s]
Maximum speed	50	[mm]
Resolution	140	[steps per mm]
Acceleration	5000	[mm/s^2]
Temperature sensor	100k Epcos B57560G0107F000	
Temperature sensor pin	Temp 0 normally used for extruder 0	
Heater pin	Heater 0 normally used for extruder 0	

Figure 5-14. *Temperature page: extruder parameters*

You only need to change two things in this section: the extruder resolution (steps per mm) and the thermistor for the extruder. I note these with circles in the drawing. Notice there are a lot of settings on this page, many of which you might want to use to calibrate the temperature, as described in a later section.

If you have a heated print bed, you can check that check box and enter the thermistor settings, as shown in Figure 5-15.

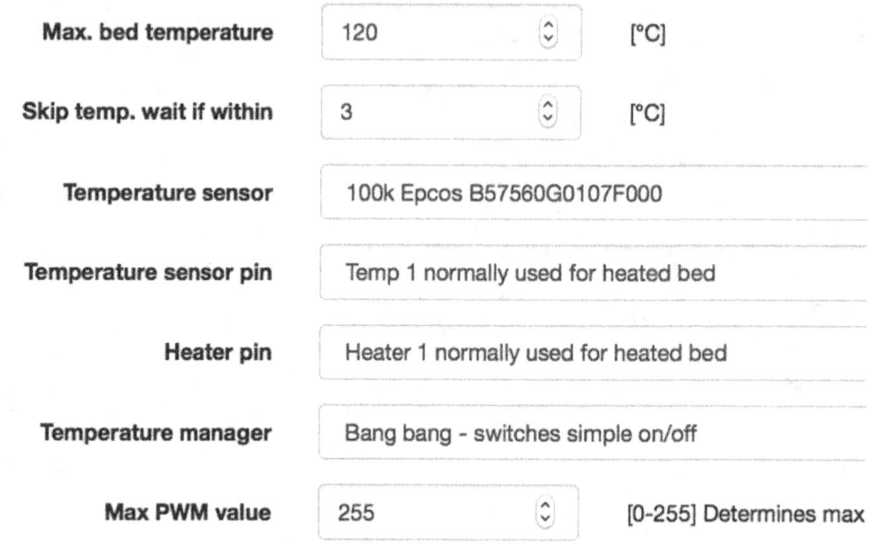

Max. bed temperature	120	◊	[°C]
Skip temp. wait if within	3	◊	[°C]
Temperature sensor	100k Epcos B57560G0107F000		
Temperature sensor pin	Temp 1 normally used for heated bed		
Heater pin	Heater 1 normally used for heated bed		
Temperature manager	Bang bang - switches simple on/off		
Max PWM value	255	◊	[0-255] Determines max

Figure 5-15. *Temperature page: heated print bed parameters*

Features

The features page is where you can turn on advanced settings such as Z-probing, servo support, and more. Most of these settings are fine as defaults, but the one you may want to change is the fan options at the bottom. Here you can specify the part-cooling fan details. Figure 5-16 shows the features page. Note that if you choose the Z-probe, you can specify a host of parameters for how the Z-probe is aligned with the extruder. I discuss this in a later section.

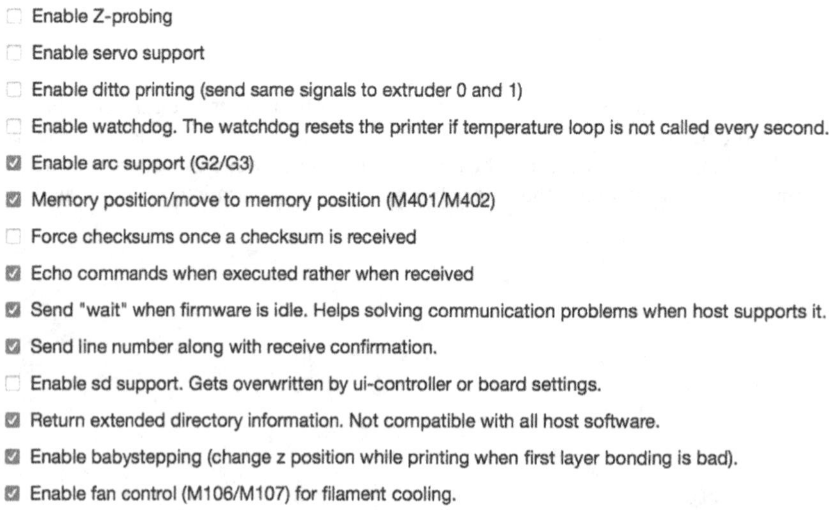

☐ Enable Z-probing

☐ Enable servo support

☐ Enable ditto printing (send same signals to extruder 0 and 1)

☐ Enable watchdog. The watchdog resets the printer if temperature loop is not called every second.

☑ Enable arc support (G2/G3)

☑ Memory position/move to memory position (M401/M402)

☐ Force checksums once a checksum is received

☑ Echo commands when executed rather when received

☑ Send "wait" when firmware is idle. Helps solving communication problems when host supports it.

☑ Send line number along with receive confirmation.

☐ Enable sd support. Gets overwritten by ui-controller or board settings.

☑ Return extended directory information. Not compatible with all host software.

☑ Enable babystepping (change z position while printing when first layer bonding is bad).

☑ Enable fan control (M106/M107) for filament cooling.

Figure 5-16. *Features page*

User Interface

The last page allows you to specify the type of LCD you have on your printer. Unlike Marlin, which only allows you to choose the LCD panel in the Configuration.h file (but you can do customize it by modifying other source code files), Repetier-Firmware allows you to set a host of things about the LCD, including languages, greeting, printer names, and more.

Download

Once you have entered all of your changes, you can choose to download the entire source code, including the configuration items that you just made, or download only the Configuration.h file, or download a JSON version of the changes. You can use either of the last two to upload to the tool and make changes.

Compiling and Uploading

Compiling Repetier-Firmware is very similar to compiling Marlin. You can use the Compile button on the toolbar (the leftmost button) in the Arduino IDE to do this. Once you have downloaded the source code and unzipped the file, navigate to the Repetier folder open the Repetier.ino file.

Like Marlin, you may see a few warnings in the other Marlin files. These are OK and are not normally an issue. What you want to make sure of is that there are no errors and that you see a successful compile message like the one shown here.

```
Binary sketch size: 131,378 bytes (of a 258,048 byte maximum)
```

Once the code compiles, connect a USB cable to your printer and click the Upload button (second from the left). Even though you just compiled the code, the upload process will compile it again and begin transferring it to your printer's electronics. When it is done, you should see a message stating that the compile is complete, and the progress bar will disappear.

■ **Note**   As of this writing, the Repetier-Firmware may not compile correctly with the latest Arduino IDE. If you use version 1.0.6, it will compile. See the Repetier online documentation at repetier.com/documentation/ Repetier-Firmware/rf-installation/ for the latest information about compiling the firmware.

Preflight Checks

Now that you have all of your hardware set at initial positions and the firmware installed on the printer, it is time to kick the tires a bit to ensure that the printer is working—at least on the most basic level.

This section is where you will conduct some simple checks to ensure that the basic parts of the printer are working. This includes tips for things you should do once your build is complete and before you begin calibrating it. Note that these tips assume the firmware is already loaded on the printer controller electronics. If it has not been loaded, come back to these tips once it is loaded.

Check to see that the electronics power on,[7] that each axis moves in the correct direction, that you can connect and communicate with the printer, and that the endstops are working correctly.

---

[7]I cannot tell you how many times a desperate friend or relative has asked me (and I reluctantly agreed) to fix a printer, computer, or kitchen appliance only to discover the source of their desperation was that they simply failed to plug the thing into a power source.

Smoke Test

The first thing I like to do when the printer is fully assembled and the basic adjustments are complete is called a *smoke test*.[8] Simply stated, this is plugging in the power supply and powering on the printer. Stand by the switch just in case, but you should be rewarded with an LED or two glowing, and if you have a LCD panel, it should illuminate too. In fact, if the firmware is loaded on the printer, you should see the menus appear on the LCD panel.

If you smell or see any smoke, or otherwise hear any strange noises, you should immediately cut the power and investigate. Similarly, if you see no effect—no LEDs, LCD, and so forth, illuminate—you should turn off the printer and unplug it to check your wiring. This could mean that the wiring has come loose, isn't plugged in properly, or you have a short somewhere. It doesn't take long for a short to cause major damage, so it is best to power off and check everything carefully before proceeding.

Assuming that you don't smell, see, or hear anything strange, and that any visual elements are illuminated, you can proceed to the next check.

Connect Your Controller Software

Now comes the fun part. Go ahead and power on your printer, and then launch your printer controller software (e.g., MatterControl or Simplify3D), insert the USB cable into your computer, and connect the other end to your printer. You can then press the connect button in the software to permit the printer software to talk to the printer. Recall that you use your 3D printing software or a printer controller application to manipulate the axes, turn on fans, and set heaters. I use examples of MatterControl in this section, but Simplify3D and Repetier-Host work the same way.

■ **Tip**   If you have not installed or configured your software, you should do so now.

If you cannot get the software to connect, check the port settings of the printer software and try again. If you still have problems, check the communication speed. Some versions of firmware (like Marlin) allow you to set the communication speed. Check your documentation for the correct speed or check your firmware configuration if you loaded the firmware yourself.

Use a USB cable to plug into your printer's electronics (typically the square-looking end or Type-A) and the other into one of your USB ports. Launch your software and connect to your printer. Figure 5-17 shows the connection made via MatterControl to a Mini Kossel printer.

---

[8]Don't worry. This does not involve tobacco of any variety—electronic or otherwise.

Figure 5-17. *Connected to the printer*

Check the Endstop Status

Endstops are one of the most simple components on your printer, and yet vital to its operation. Recall that the endstops are switches that, when closed, prevent the axis from moving. Failure to check the endstops for correct operation can result in the axis crashing into the frame or other bits that it should never come into contact with (like fragile wires, electronics, your fingers, small animals, and so forth—all very bad).

■ **Caution** Always double-check your wiring connections before changing the behavior of your endstops! It can be wildly irritating to switch the settings and retest, only to discover nothing has changed. If your wiring is wrong, no amount of fiddling with the source code will fix it.

Remember that your towers are labeled counterclockwise from the left as X, Y, and Z. Most people orient their delta printer with the side between the X and Y towers facing them. This isn't really important beyond a frame of reference, so if you choose a different orientation, just make sure that you know which tower is which.[9]

The best way to check your endstops is with a special G-code. The code you need is M119. Issue this command via your printer controller software. Listing 5-5 shows the commands issued via Repetier-Host.

---

[9]As in Oz, knowing which witch is which can keep you from being bewitched.

Listing 5-5. Checking Endstops with M119

```
> 4:33:11 PM: N89 M119 *59
< 4:33:11 PM: Reporting endstop status
< 4:33:11 PM: x_max: open
< 4:33:11 PM: y_max: open
< 4:33:11 PM: z_min: TRIGGERED
< 4:33:11 PM: z_max: open
> 4:33:20 PM: N99 M119 *58
< 4:33:20 PM: Reporting endstop status
< 4:33:20 PM: x_max: TRIGGERED
< 4:33:20 PM: y_max: open
< 4:33:20 PM: z_min: TRIGGERED
< 4:33:20 PM: z_max: open
> 4:33:34 PM: N113 M119 *9
< 4:33:34 PM: Reporting endstop status
< 4:33:34 PM: x_max: open
< 4:33:34 PM: y_max: TRIGGERED
< 4:33:34 PM: z_min: TRIGGERED
< 4:33:34 PM: z_max: open
> 4:34:16 PM: N154 M119 *10
< 4:34:16 PM: Reporting endstop status
< 4:34:16 PM: x_max: open
< 4:34:16 PM: y_max: open
< 4:34:16 PM: z_min: TRIGGERED
< 4:34:16 PM: z_max: TRIGGERED
> 4:34:23 PM: N162 M119 *15
< 4:34:23 PM: Reporting endstop status
< 4:34:23 PM: x_max: open
< 4:34:23 PM: y_max: open
< 4:34:23 PM: z_min: open
< 4:34:23 PM: z_max: open
```

Notice that the firmware returned the status of each endstop for each command. Also notice that I ran the command several times with different results. This is because I ran the command once when all endstops were open and again while triggering each endstop.

The first time, all endstops were marked open except the Z min, which is used for the Z-probe and is normally triggered (closed). The second time the X endstop is marked as TRIGGERED. This is because I manually pressed the X endstop to trigger it. You have to use two hands—one with the mouse ready to click the Send button, and another holding the endstop closed. I then repeated the process for the Y and Z endstops.

If the endstop you have closed does not register as triggered, check your connections to make sure that the endstop is connected properly. In rare cases, especially when using Marlin or similar firmware, you may need to change the configuration to match your endstop behavior. If you use normal endstops that make contact when closed (and you've wired it correctly), you should not have to adjust the firmware.

Once you confirm that the endstops are triggered when closed (if you're using a Z-probe like mine, the Z-probe endstop is open when the probe is triggered), you are ready to move on to checking the axes movement.

Recheck Axis Movement

Next, you will try moving the axes, one at a time, about 10mm in each direction. However, before attempting to move the axes, you want to place each axis in the center of its travel. You do this to ensure that the axes have plenty of room because each axis needs to move up or down, depending on the direction you move. Remember, on a delta printer, moving a single axis results in all three axes moving as the mathematics dictate. This is why you need the axes at the center of their movement.

Recall that a delta printer orients the axes such that X moves left to right, Y moves front to back, and Z moves up and down. Also recall that a delta printer has the home position as [0,0,MAX_Z] in the center of the print bed. Thus, X moves in a negative direction to the left and in a positive direction to the right. Similarly, you want Y to move in the positive direction when it moves toward the "back," and in the negative direction to the "front." To do this, you need to change the orientation of the Y axis because by default, Y moves negative to the rear and positive to the front. Think about it this way: positive moves away from the tower and negative moves toward the tower.

■ **Caution**   Do not home your printer unless you are certain the axis is moving in the correct direction. Homing a delta printer with one or two of the axes moving in the opposite direction can cause hardware failure! To protect the print surface, place cardboard or another protective covering on top of it when calibrating.

When moving the axes by hand, be sure to move the axes slowly because rapid movement can cause the stepper motors to generate an electrical current. If you move them too fast, you can accidentally power and perhaps damage your electronics. Once the axes are in the center, power on your printer and connect your 3D printer software. Locate the printer control panel or dialog. Figure 5-18 shows the printer control dialog for MatterControl.

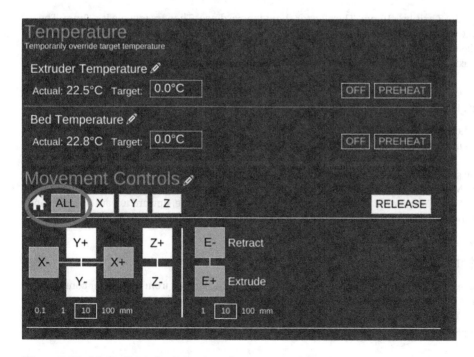

Figure 5-18. *MatterControl printer control*

Starting with the X axis, move the axis –10mm and observe how the effector moves. It should move to the left. If it does not, the stepper motor wires may be reversed. Try it again but move the axis +20mm. The effector should move to the right. If the effector is still moving in the opposite direction, you need to check your stepper motors to make sure that they are all plugged in the same way.

If one is plugged in wrong (plug is reversed), the effector will not move in a direct line and may move at an angle or another strange direction. If the axis moves in the exact opposite direction, all three axis cables may be reversed.

To correct the problem, power off your printer and unplug the USB cable. Carefully examine the cables and plug them in the correct way. You can then power on the printer, reconnect, and try the test again. The axis should move in the correct direction.

■ **Caution**   Never unplug any components, especially stepper motors, when the printer is powered on. Power the printer off before working with connections.

Next, try the Y axis. Move it –10mm and observe how it moves. It should move toward you. Similarly, try moving it +20mm. It should move away from you. If this is backward, don't panic! This is normal, as I explained earlier. Here you just need to reverse the direction of the Y axis in the firmware, as shown in the following. For example, the Marlin software has settings for reversing the axes direction in the Configuration.h file. I prefer to do this in firmware because I use multiple printers, and having it hard-coded is more convenient.

```
#define INVERT_X_DIR true    // for Mendel set to false, for Orca set to true
#define INVERT_Y_DIR true    // for Mendel set to true, for Orca set to false
#define INVERT_Z_DIR true    // for Mendel set to false, for Orca set to true
```

Next, move up the Z axis by +10mm. The effector should move down. Then try moving it –20mm. The effector should now move up. If it does not, you may have inadvertently reversed the settings in the firmware or the software. Make sure that the Z axis moves in the correct direction before continuing.

Now that the axis move in the correct direction, you can test homing the printer for the first time.

Home the Printer

The next step is to home the printer for the first time. You know that the endstops are set correctly and the axes are all moving in the correct direction. Always use the home-all feature to home all three axes to the top of the delta printer.

To do this, you should have a home-all button on your printer controller panel. Figure 5-18 shows the home-all button in MatterControl, indicated by the oval. Go ahead and press it, but keep your hand on the power button just in case. You should see all three axes move at the same time, upward toward the endstops. If this does not happen, cut the power and go back to the previous section to correct the problem.

Check Heaters

The next step is to test the heaters. You can turn on the hot end and heated bed from the printer controller software. Set the hot end to 200 degrees Celsius and the heated bed (if installed) to 30 degrees Celsius. Check them one at a time. You can use an infrared thermometer to ensure that they are heating. Remember, the temperature settings are in Celsius, so the hot end gets plenty hot enough to burn you.

■ **Caution** Some hot ends can smoke a bit when heated the first time. This is normal. Do not hose it down with your fire extinguisher. On the other hand, if the smoke becomes a small plume and you hear crackling or popping sounds, unplug your printer immediately and check your electronics for wiring faults.

Test Extrusion

The last preflight check you should perform is testing your extruder. Begin by inserting filament in your extruder, following the vendor's instructions. For example, Bowden mechanisms, common on delta printers, require loosening or opening the idler clamp on the extruder, and then removing the Bowden tube from the hot end side by pressing down on the press-fitting and pulling out the Bowden tube. You can then thread the filament past the drive pulley, through the Bowden tube, and press the filament into the hot end. Be sure that the filament travels all the way down to the nozzle before securing the Bowden tube and the extruder idler clamp.

■ **Tip** The press-fittings used in Bowden setups can loosen over time. It may be best to unscrew the brass fitting rather than repeatedly removing the Bowden tube.

Since you already have the heaters warmed up to temperature, go ahead and use your printer controller software to extrude a small amount of filament. Depending on how far you were able to insert the filament, you may need to extrude about 30mm to 50mm. But don't do that all at once. If your hot end isn't heating properly, you will only result in stripping the filament—filling the teeth of the drive gear with filament.

Once you've extruded a small pile of filament, it is time to celebrate by throwing your head back and letting loose the cries of triumphant success,[10] because you have just proven that your delta printer is alive! Don't celebrate too long. You've still got the calibration process to go through before you can print your first object. But you are nearly there!

Now that you have confirmed all of your hardware measurements, including the axes and the extruder, as well as the initial positions of the endstops and the initial Z-height, it is time to calibrate the printer to finalize these values and tune the printer for maximum print quality.

Calibrating the Hardware

You are now entering the part where most delta printer enthusiasts feel the most frustration. This is because they rushed through the preliminary calibration steps, especially the firmware configuration, or they are itching to print something and skim through these processes with too little attention to detail. I have also encountered some delta printer owners who found and followed instructions that were a bit less than accurate or were tied too closely to a particular delta design or variant. For these reasons alone, you should spend time getting your printer calibrated using the advice in the following sections.

This section discusses the hardware calibrations needed for a delta printer. The following processes detail those calibration procedures you need to perform to make sure that your printer hardware is set up correctly. You must complete these before you can calibrate and tune the delta settings. Always do these steps before calibrating the delta settings.

---

[10]Not to be confused with the Klingon death ritual, which warns the dead of the arrival of a warrior into Sto-vo-kor. This is more like Dr. Frankenstein, only geekier and less creepy.

Calibrate the Towers

This step is the most critical and one of the most overlooked. If you are frustrated by your delta printer digging into the print bed on one or two sides or inconsistent Z-height on one area, your towers are likely not calibrated properly. Fortunately, the process is easy, but depending on how your endstops are mounted or whether they can be adjusted, this may be a bit tedious and require several attempts to get right. You may even have to improvise a measuring device if your endstops are not accessible. But with a bit of patience, the payoff is a much better calibrated printer.

However, before you begin calibrating the towers, it is important to verify that the steps per millimeter settings are correct. If you do not know or you are not certain that the steps per millimeter are set correctly in the firmware, you can do the following:

1. Home all axes.

2. Lower the Z axis 200mm.

3. Measure the distance between the endstop and the carriage for each tower.

This measurement should be 200mm for each tower. If it is not, you should adjust belt tension and recheck; if it still off, check the steps per millimeter settings in the firmware (DEFAULT_AXIS_STEPS_PER_UNIT in Marlin) and correct as needed.

Once you are certain that the steps per millimeter settings are correct, you can calibrate the towers. The basic process is as follows. First, you home all axes. Then for each tower, you move the effector so that the hot end is near maximum printing radius and aligned at the base of each tower. However, you first need to move the Z axis down to within about 20mm of the print surface. You then lower the Z axis until the nozzle is approximately 0.1mm above the print surface (the thickness of a sheet of paper).

Fortunately, you can make this easy by using macros in your 3D printing software. I will show you how to do this with MatterControl. You can also do it manually, but macros make it easier to repeat the process—and repeat it you will, depending on how your endstops are adjusted. Figure 5-19 shows a mount I created for one of my Mini Kossel printers.

Figure 5-19. *Adjustable endstops (Mini Kossel)*

Sadly, some delta printer designs do not have endstops that can be easily adjusted. In fact, some don't have any way to adjust the endstops in small increments. These typically require you loosen the endstop or its mount, and then move the endstop up or down and retighten. These are by far the hardest to work with because it is very difficult to move the endstop a precise distance each time. If you have such a setup, be prepared to spend a bit more time on this task.

Fortunately, some delta printer designs have small screws or adjusters that can be turned in or out in small increments. These are much easier to calibrate. If your delta printer doesn't have these types of adjusters, you may want to consider this as a first upgrade—but wait until you confirm that your printer is printing correctly first! Figure 5-20 shows the endstop adjuster on a Rostock Max delta printer. The oval indicates the location of the adjuster.

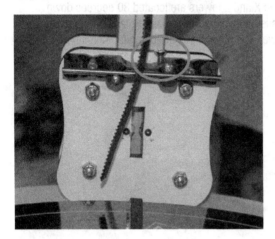

Figure 5-20. Endstop adjuster (Rostock Max courtesy of SeeMeCNC.com)

Macros for Tower Calibration

Let's write some macros to help perform these checks. Note that some enthusiasts write their macros to move the Z axis to 0, but since you have yet to determine the correct Z-height (because the towers are not calibrated), you need to move the axis close to the position, but lower it slowly. This part you will do manually using the printer controller feature (jog controls).

Table 5-3 shows macros for a delta printer with a printing radius of 90mm. Your printer may have different geometry, so be sure to check it. These are the X and Y coordinates for locating the nozzle at the base of each tower that is close to the tower itself. Notice that these are sets of G-codes. You will enter these in your 3D printing software next.

Table 5-3. Macros for Tower Calibration

Tower	G-codes
X	G28 G0 X-77.94 Y-45 Z25 F3000
Y	G28 G0 X0 Y90 Z25 F3000
Z	G28 G0 X77.94 Y-45 Z25 F3000

Notice in each macro that you home all the axes first, and then move to the location you want about 25mm above the print surface. Recall that this allows you to move the Z axis down slowly so as not to ram the print surface if the endstop is in the wrong position. The last parameter is the feedrate per minute, which controls how fast the axes will move.

WAIT! HOW DO I CALCULATE THE X,Y VALUES FOR THE X AND Z TOWERS?

If you do not know the correct values for the X and Y positions for your printer, they are easily calculated. Recall that the print surface origin is [0,0,0] and that the X and Z towers are located 30 degrees down from the imaginary X axis line. Also, the printing radius is the hypotenuse of a right triangle formed from the Y axis and X axis that intersects the base of the tower. The following figure demonstrates this.

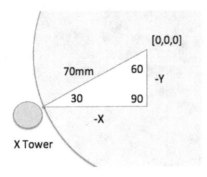

Now, recall from your trigonometry knowledge[11] that you can calculate the length of either side of the triangle if you know the angle and the length of one side. The following is an example using a printing radius of 70mm.

```
sin(30) = -y/70
sin(30) * 70 = -y
34.99 = -y
-34.99 = y
sin(60) = -x/70
sin(60) * 70 = -x
60.62 = -x
-60.62 = X
```

You can check this with the formula for summing the squares of the right angle sides.

```
34.99*34.99 + 60.62*60.62 ?= 70*70
1224.30 + 3674.78 = 4900
4899.08 = 4900
```

So as you can see, you are very close to the correct values. This small bit of inaccuracy is fine for calibrating the towers. Now, it's your turn to calculate the X and Y values for your own delta printer!

Now let's enter these in your software. To add macros in MatterControl, connect to your printer, click the Advanced Controls button, and then the Controls tab. Scroll down to the macros section and click the edit icon (a small pencil). This launches the macro dialog, where you can add and remove macros. Figure 5-21 shows the macro editor. Name the macro, enter the commands, and then click Save.

---

[11]See the mathpage.com/atrig/solve-right-triangles.htm.

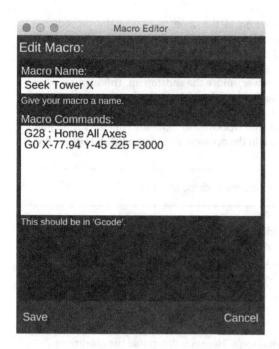

Figure 5-21. *MatterControl macro editor*

Once all the macros are created, you will see them in the macro section, as shown in Figure 5-22.

Figure 5-22. *MatterControl macro section*

Now it is time to use these macros to set your endstops.

Adjusting the Endstops

This is where things can get a bit tedious. Remember that you are trying to set the endstops for all the axes so that the nozzle arrives at the print surface at the same height for a given Z-height on all three towers. This sounds simple, but there is a small twist, as you shall see. The process you want to use is as follows. You do this for each tower (I like to start with the X tower).

1. Click the macro to home and move the axis into position at the base of the tower.

2. Place a small piece of paper under the nozzle.

3. Lower the Z axis until you can just feel that the paper is snug under the nozzle. Use small increments at first (0.1mm), and then switch to fine increments (0.01mm) when it gets close to the paper. Try pulling the paper from under the nozzle. When you can just feel friction, it's low enough.

4. Note the value of the Z-height.

189

You should have three Z-heights. Don't worry if they are not all the same; that's what this procedure is going to fix. I like to choose the axis with the highest Z-height as the target or reference tower. That is, I get to choose which axis I want to consider fixed and then get the other two to match. To adjust the other towers, you need to make small adjustments to the endstops as follows.

If the Z-height is too low (it is less than the reference tower), move the endstop up. This increases the Z-height for that tower. Conversely, if the Z-height is too high, move the endstop down. If you are working with a delta printer that has endstop adjuster screws on the carriages, for example, you would turn the screw counterclockwise to move the endstop trigger point down, and clockwise to move the endstop trigger point up. Confusing? Don't worry. If you get it wrong, just move it in the opposite direction until you get it right.

■ **Caution**   Adjust one tower at a time! Never adjust more than one endstop at a time.

Adjust one tower at a time, and then rerun the preceding process for that tower (and that tower only). Compare the measurement to your reference tower and adjust the endstop, repeating the procedure until the endstop is within 0.01mm to 0.05mm of the reference tower. Repeat this for the remaining tower.

Once all the tower endstops are set, you can set the Z-height.

Set the Z-Height

This is the last step in the tower hardware-based calibration steps. Here you determine the maximum Z-height possible, as measured from the center of the build plate to the home position (maximum travel of all three axes).

To do this, home all axes and then lower the Z axis down to within about 20mm of the print surface. Place a small piece of paper under the print surface, and then lower the Z axis slowly until the paper can be pulled out with a small amount of friction. Note the value of the Z-height.

Go back to your Arduino IDE and open your firmware to make the adjustment. Then compile and upload. Now when you home the axes and then lower the Z axis to 0, it should be at the correct position.

The following code is the Z-height setting in Marlin:

```
#define MANUAL_Z_HOME_POS 221.25
```

The following code is the Z-height setting in Repetier-Firmware:

```
#define Z_MAX_LENGTH 221.25
```

I recommend testing this to make sure that you didn't make a mistake. But don't simply lower the Z axis to 0, instead lower it to about 20mm above the print surface and then slowly lower the nozzle until it is within 1mm of the surface. Switch to the lowest Z axis step (0.01) and lower until the Z-height goes to 0. If the nozzle doesn't stop and touches the print surface, repeat this process until you get the correct Z-height.

Extruder

The extruder is the most challenging component to calibrate. Recall the number of variables in the formula. One of the variables is the diameter of the drive pulley or hobbed bolt. If this measurement is off, the extruder will extrude less or more filament than desired.

An improperly calibrated extruder can cause a range of problems that may tempt you to think there is something wrong with the objects you are attempting to print. For example, extruding too little filament can cause poor layer adhesion. Similarly, extruding too much filament can cause stringing and globs of filament being deposited during slower movement. There are other similar problems related to extruder calibration. However, if your extruder is calibrated properly, it becomes easier to diagnose problems related to filament size, heat settings, or slicer options.

■ **Tip**   For best results, use a light-colored filament and a dark marker.

To measure the amount of filament extruded, you measure the distance the filament travels as it enters the extruder. The basic process is as follows. I will describe the steps in more detail next.

1. Remove the hot end.

2. Load filament in the extruder.

3. Make a mark on the filament aligned with a nonmoving part of the extruder (e.g., the body or door).

4. Use a ruler to measure 100mm along the filament and make a second mark on the filament. Then measure 120mm and make a third mark.

5. Use your printer controller software to extrude 100mm of filament.

6. You're done if the filament stops at the second mark; otherwise, measure the distance. This is called underrun. You will subtract this from 100 to get the filament extruded. If it goes past the second mark, this is overrun and you measure the distance from the third mark and subtract that from 120.

7. Calculate a ratio based on your existing steps per millimeter for the extruder and modify it with the M92 ENN.NN command.

8. Advance the filament past the marks.

9. Repeat starting with step 3 until the extruder extrudes precisely 100mm of filament.

The first step is to unload your filament and remove the hot end. This saves you from wasting a lot of filament and avoids having to wait for the hot end to heat up. If you have already loaded filament and tested the extruder, that's great. You do not strictly have to unload the filament and remove the hot end, but it is a bit easier.

If you removed the hot end, you must use the M302 code to disable the cold extrusion prevention. This is because most firmware has a setting that prevents attempts to extrude filament if the hot end is cold. If you get the message "cold extrusion prevented," use the code. Otherwise, you have to heat the hot end before you can extrude.

With the filament loaded and the extruder idler closed and tightened, make a mark on the filament that aligns with a fixed portion of the extruder. This helps determine a baseline should you need or want to recheck the calibration after changing the firmware. A good choice is the extruder body or the extruder idler edge. Figure 5-23 shows how to do this with an Airtripper extruder.

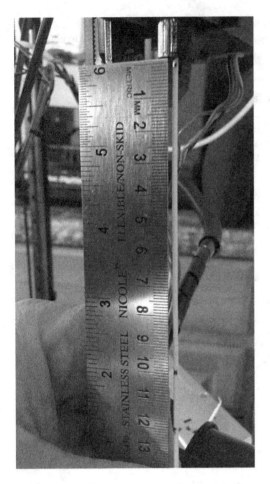

Figure 5-23. *Marking filament at 0, 100, and 120mm*

Next, measure a distance 100mm away from the first mark and mark the filament at this point. Make a third mark at 120mm. Make the 120mm mark distinct with a wider mark or maybe a different color. You will use the second mark if the extruder extrudes too much filament. This is because you won't be able to see the 100mm mark if there is an overrun.

■ **Tip**   I use different colored markers for each mark so that I can tell which mark is the starting, 100mm, or 120mm mark, and so that if I do the test a second or third time, I won't confuse the marks.

Using your 3D printer software, set the extruder to extrude 100mm of filament. Once the extruder stops, take a look at where the mark on the filament at the 100mm mark is in relation to your reference point. If it is aligned with your reference point, congratulations, you're done! If not, you must determine if you have an underrun condition where not enough filament was extruded or an overrun where the extruder extruded too much filament.

If underrun, the 100mm mark is above the reference point. Use a digital caliper or a small ruler to measure the distance from your reference point to the 100mm mark. Formulate a difference calculation using your existing extruder steps per millimeter. You can find this value by looking in your Marlin firmware files or by searching the log window in the Repetier-Host software. As part of the connection handshake, Repetier-Host requests the steps per millimeter settings using the M503 command. The following is an example of the data returned from the printer:

```
4:21:56 PM: echo:  M92 X200.00 Y200.00 Z200.00 E147.00
```

Let's say your extruder extruded 92mm of filament. Figure 5-24 shows an example of underrun.

Figure 5-24. *Extruder underrun*

In this case, there was an 8mm gap from the reference point to the 100mm mark (100 – 8 = 92), or you extruded 92% of 100mm. Using the steps per millimeter from the output of the M503 command run previously(147),[12] you can calculate the new steps per millimeter as follows:

```
159.78 = 147 / .92
```

On the other hand, if the 100mm mark is below your reference point, you have overrun. Figure 5-25 shows an example of overrun.

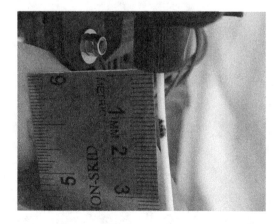

Figure 5-25. *Extruder overrun*

---

[12]You can also find this value in the firmware source code (`Configuration.h`).

In this case, measure the distance to the 120mm mark, subtract that from 120, and add 100. For example, if the distance to the 120mm mark is 10mm, the actual run of filament was 110mm or 110% of 100mm. Using the steps per millimeter from earlier, you can calculate the new steps per millimeter, as follows:

```
133.64 = 147 / 1.10
```

Once you calculate the correct value, use the M92 EN.NN command to set the new steps per millimeter for the extruder (E axis), and run the test again. Be sure to use the M500 command to write the values to EEPROM and update your firmware accordingly. Make a new mark for 0mm and for 100mm, and extrude 100mm. The 100mm mark should now align perfectly with your reference point. If it doesn't, and it is just a few millimeters off, try the process again to fine-tune the steps per millimeter of your extruder. Repeat until you get consistent results.

Now that the extruder is calibrated, let's discuss calibration of the filament, or in this case, ensuring that you supply the correct values to the slicer for calculating extrusion.

Filament

Filament can vary in size from one manufacturer to another, and in the case of moderate-quality filament, from one spool to another. I've found two manufacturers whose standards seem to be better than most. MakerBot Industries (makerbot.com) and IC3D printers (ic3dprinters.com) both manufacture filament of consistent size throughout the spool. You may find others, and when you do, you should stick with them.

Until you are satisfied that your filament is a consistent size, you need to check it periodically. At first, you should check it before every print, and once you find it is stable, check it only when you change filament, or weekly, whichever comes first.

Set the filament size in your 3D printing software or slicer application. Don't be tempted to just enter the generic 3mm or 1.75mm, because filament diameter (and even the same color) can vary from one manufacturer to another. Use a digital caliper to measure the thickness of your filament. Figure 5-26 is an example of measuring 1.75mm filament.

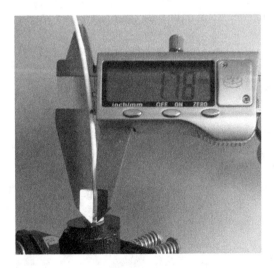

Figure 5-26. *Measuring filament diameter*

Notice that the filament diameter is not 1.75mm; rather, it is 1.78mm. Like the nozzle size, the slicer needs the diameter of the filament to fill out another variable in its calculation of how much filament to extrude. There is quite a bit more to it than that, but for these purposes, consider these the variables that you provide so that the slicer can do all the hard work.

■ **Tip**   You should get into the habit of measuring your filament diameter before each print. If it varies more than 0.01mm to 0.02mm, you should change it in your slicer settings. If you find your roll of filament varies throughout the roll, you may want to avoid buying from that vendor. Too much variation in the filament can cause poor prints or even extrusion failure.

Once you have measured your filament, enter that value in the filament settings section of your software. Figure 5-27 shows where to do this in MatterControl.

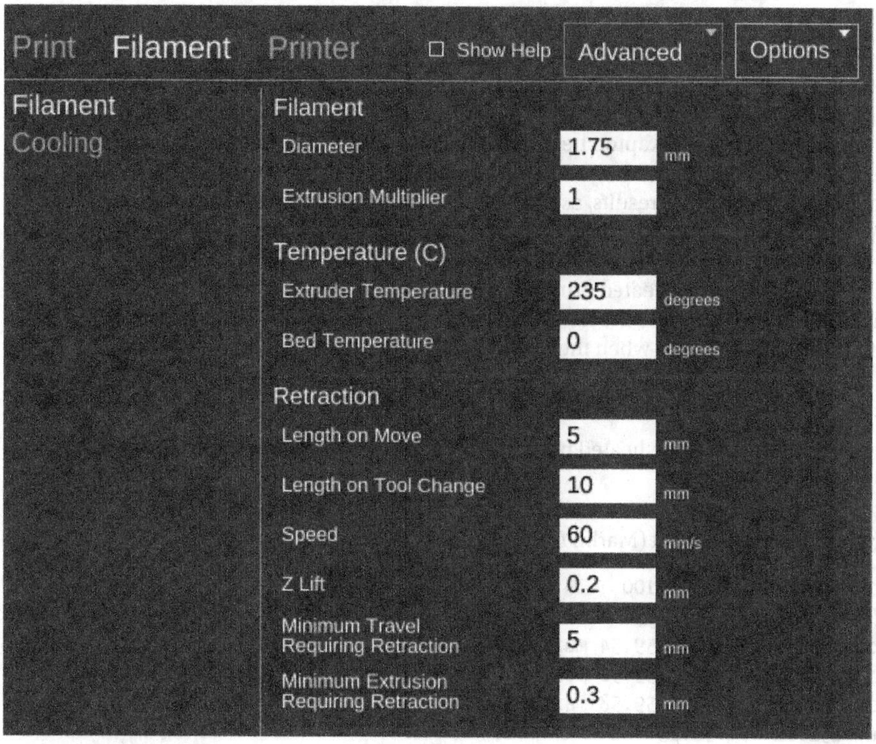

Figure 5-27. *Specifying filament diameter: MatterControl*

Next, you calibrate the temperature control. If you have experienced odd heating behavior, the next section should help you solve these problems.

Temperature

Calibrating the temperature is one aspect that is often overlooked. If your thermistors are correctly configured and the heaters are typical among those used in 3D printers, you may not need to calibrate the temperatures. However, if you encounter a situation where the heater takes too long to heat up, heats past the target, or fluctuates, you need to tune your heating characteristics.

Fortunately, there is a utility built into the G-codes that allow you to do this. In this case, you run a procedure built into the firmware to test the heater over several iterations. When it is complete, it generates a new set of values that you can use in the firmware to get the heater working better. The firmware calls this automatic proportional-integral-derivative control algorithm, or PID tuning. Sadly, only certain firmware has this code enabled. I will present an example using the Marlin firmware. Check your firmware for support of this feature.

There is a whole lot of math that goes into these values, but I don't feel the need to discuss it in any length. This is because the automatic tuning procedure tells you what needs to change. Thus, I only cover an example of how to change these values. If you want to read more about it, visit the wiki at http://reprap.org/wiki/PID_Tuning. The following command initiates the procedure:

```
M303 E0 S200 C8
```

The E parameter is the heater, where E0 is the extruder and E-1 is the heated print bed. The S value is the target temperature and the C parameter is the number of times to repeat the procedure. Use 8 or 10 for this value. Let's see this in action.

One of my Mini Kossel printers has a Kapton heater that is a bit strange in its heating characteristics. When I first built the printer, the heater would exceed the target temperature by more than 15 degrees, which is far too much and can cause unexpected results, especially for certain types of filament. Worst, over time it would fluctuate and not hold the temperature, dropping by about 5 degrees and then overshooting by about 5 degrees. In other words, it was hunting for the right temperature.

If you have similar trouble with your heated print bed, you can use the automatic PID tuning feature in the Marlin firmware to overcome this. Use the following command and enter it in your G-code editor or command window (for best results, do this when the printer is cold and try to eliminate air drafts):

```
M303 E-1 S60 C8
```

Here I am asking the printer to test the heated print bed at 60 degrees eight times. Listing 5-6 shows the results.

Listing 5-6. Temperature Autotune Report (Marlin firmware)

```
> 17:16:21 PM: N11 M303 E-1 S60 C8 *100
< 17:16:21 PM: PID Autotune start
< 17:21:41 PM:  bias: 55 d: 55 min: 59.54 max: 61.25
< 17:22:47 PM:  bias: 52 d: 52 min: 59.38 max: 60.59
< 17:23:44 PM:  bias: 49 d: 49 min: 59.58 max: 60.41
< 17:23:44 PM:  Ku: 151.01 Tu: 56.23
< 17:23:44 PM:  Clasic PID
< 17:23:44 PM:  Kp: 90.60
< 17:23:44 PM:  Ki: 3.22
< 17:23:44 PM:  Kd: 636.83
< 17:24:46 PM:  bias: 48 d: 48 min: 59.58 max: 60.41
< 17:24:46 PM:  Ku: 147.92 Tu: 62.52
< 17:24:46 PM:  Clasic PID
< 17:24:46 PM:  Kp: 88.75
< 17:24:46 PM:  Ki: 2.84
< 17:24:46 PM:  Kd: 693.63
< 17:25:47 PM:  bias: 49 d: 49 min: 59.46 max: 60.41
```

```
< 17:25:47 PM:  Ku: 131.72 Tu: 60.95
< 17:25:47 PM:  Clasic PID
< 17:25:47 PM:  Kp: 79.03
< 17:25:47 PM:  Ki: 2.59
< 17:25:47 PM:  Kd: 602.13
< 17:26:43 PM:  bias: 49 d: 49 min: 59.54 max: 60.37
< 17:26:43 PM:  Ku: 150.25 Tu: 56.36
< 17:26:43 PM:  Clasic PID
< 17:26:43 PM:  Kp: 90.15
< 17:26:43 PM:  Ki: 3.20
< 17:26:43 PM:  Kd: 635.11
< 17:27:39 PM:  bias: 49 d: 49 min: 59.58 max: 60.36
< 17:27:39 PM:  Ku: 160.36 Tu: 55.97
< 17:27:39 PM:  Clasic PID
< 17:27:39 PM:  Kp: 96.22
< 17:27:39 PM:  Ki: 3.44
< 17:27:39 PM:  Kd: 673.12
< 17:28:32 PM:  bias: 48 d: 48 min: 59.60 max: 60.23
< 17:28:32 PM:  Ku: 193.36 Tu: 52.56
< 17:28:32 PM:  Clasic PID
< 17:28:32 PM:  Kp: 116.02
< 17:28:32 PM:  Ki: 4.41
< 17:28:32 PM:  Kd: 762.21
< 17:28:32 PM:  PID Autotune finished! Put the Kp, Ki and Kd constants into Configuration.h
```

I used Repetier-Host and graphed the progress of the heater. Figure 5-28 shows the result of running this command several times and making the adjustments in the firmware. As you can see, I got a bit closer the second time.

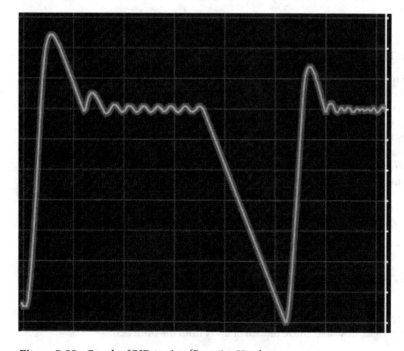

Figure 5-28. *Graph of PID tuning (Repetier-Host)*

To set the values in Marlin, open your `Configuration.h` file and locate the heated print bed PID code as follows. Here you can see I entered the values as suggested by the automatic PID tuning feature. You can also use the `M301` command to write the values, but I prefer to set them in firmware.

```
#ifdef PIDTEMPBED

    // kapton heater

    #define  DEFAULT_bedKp 116.02
    #define  DEFAULT_bedKi 4.41
    #define  DEFAULT_bedKd 762.21
```

Once I set these values in my firmware, my heated print bed behaved much better. It still overshoots the target temperature, but now it is by only a much more manageable 2 to 3 degrees instead of 15, and it cools down to the correct temperature and holds it for the entire print job.

Delta Movement Calibrations

The previous sections are all the adjustments needed to ensure that the delta printer hardware is properly calibrated. Next, you will calibrate the delta mechanism. You will also see how to set up a Z-probe mechanism. Let's begin with ensuring that the delta measurements are correct.

If your delta measurements are wrong, you may not notice any problems initially. On the other hand, you could notice a dramatic problem such as the effector moving outside of the printing radius, or worse, the hot end crashing into the print bed on one side. You could also have the case where the print surface is not even, and thus have problems setting a consistent first-layer height.

I address these issues in the next two sections. I start with confirming the delta kinematics, and then address one of the more subtle issues (print size), and conclude with a look at how to control first-layer height on an uneven print surface.

Confirm Delta Kinematics

If your delta measurements are off by more than a millimeter or so, you will notice some strange behavior. Even if you are able to print something, it may not result in a correct print. This can manifest as lopsided objects, uneven or curved sides, or erratic bed adhesion.

The best way to ensure that your delta kinematics are correct is to use a template to track how the X and Y axes are moving, that they are moving the correct distance, and that the print head remains parallel to the print bed (the nozzle is the same height on all portions of the print bed). I will talk about a special case related to convex or concave print surfaces.

Let's begin with checking the X and Y axis movement.

■ **Caution** Do not attempt the following until you have completed the previous calibration steps.

Confirm that X and Y Axis Movement Is Linear

If your delta measurements are not correct, you could encounter a situation where the X and Y axis do not move in a straight line when moving from one point to the next along the axis. For example, the X axis my move in a parabola—either left or right, or worse, move toward or away from the print bed.

Fortunately, at this point you should have checked and rechecked your measurements so that if they are wrong, they won't be off by that much. I like to test the delta movement before trying to print for the first time. To do this, I use a template with straight lines marked on it. I use the jog controls on my 3D printing software to move each axis to a point on the appropriate line, and then move along the line to ensure that the nozzle reaches the other side of the template while moving in a straight line. At the same time, I watch the nozzle to ensure that it appears to move parallel to the print bed. Figure 5-29 shows a template that I use.

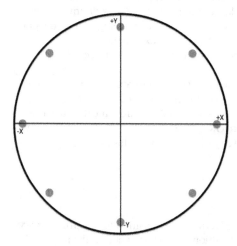

Figure 5-29. Axis template

Some print beds are slightly concave or convex. You'll check that in the next section. This is not normally noticeable. What I am talking about here is obvious descent or ascent of the axis as it moves. If this happens, stop and reexamine your delta measurements.

Notice the eight dark circles around the perimeter. You will use these to determine if the Z-height is consistent, and whether the print surface is concave or convex.

You can create a template like this with any drawing program. If your print bed is larger than a typical sheet of paper, just make it as large as you can to fit on the page. You can always use a ruler to extend the lines to the edges. This works best when you have blue painter's tape on the print surface.

Print out the template and home your printer. Then lower the Z axis until the nozzle is about 10mm above the print bed. Then place the template on the print bed and align the Y line with the Z tower (the one in the rear). It doesn't have to be exact, but if your print surface is removable or can be rotated, you can correct the orientation by rotating the print surface.

For example, you can move the Y axis to its maximum radius and align the Y line with the nozzle. This will ensure that the template is centered and oriented correctly. Once the template is oriented correctly, raise the nozzle another 10mm to 20mm to make sure that you have plenty of room. Now run the following procedure. But first, a bit of caution. Keep your hand near the power switch on your printer and be ready to turn it off should something not work or suddenly do something strange. You can always power it back on and try again.

■ **Caution** Keep your hand near the power switch when checking axis movement of more than a few millimeters. This will allow you to stop the printer should the axis move out of its range or head toward obstacles. However, keep in mind that the 3D printing software is feeding instructions to your printer until you stop it. Thus, if you turn a printer off and then back on before the software finishes, the axis will start moving again.

Move the axis to maximum negative printing radius. Note its position over the template. If the nozzle is not directly over the print bed, slowly lower it until it touches, mark the location, and then raise the Z axis 20mm to 30mm. Alternatively, you can just rotate the print surface until the nozzle is directly over the line.

Now, move the axis to the maximum, positive printing radius. While it is moving, watch how it moves. It should move smoothly, follow the line on the template, and position directly at the location you specified. If you do not see any anomalies, your axis movement is correct and you're nearly done.

However, if you do notice something wrong and you made a mark on the opposite side of the print surface, slowly lower it to the print bed and make a another mark, and then raise the Z axis 20mm to 30mm. Next, measure the distance from the mark to the line on each side. You should see two things. First, the mark should be on the opposite side of the line from the other. This indicates that the axis is moving in a straight line. Second, the distance on each side should be the same (or nearly so, depending on the accuracy of your marks).

Once you finish with one axis, check the other using the same process. If you rotated the template in the previous run, don't realign it. Either your template is not positioned correctly (it shifted left or right) or it is the wrong size. Don't worry. So long as the other axis moves the same way, ends up the same distance from the line and on the same side, and moves in a straight line, you're OK.

You check the Z-height in the next section. You will need to remove the template for the next procedures.

Confirm Consistent Z-Height

You set the Z-height in a previous section. You know the Z-height for the center position on the print surface [0,0,0],[13] but did you know that the Z-height is the same at other positions on the print bed? If the print bed is completely flat, it should be. Alas, but not all plate glass (or common glass) or aluminum print surfaces are perfectly flat. Some have a very slight convex shape, in which it is thicker in the center than the outer edges; whereas others are concave, in which it is thinner in the center than the outer edges. The following test will determine the shape of your print bed.

■ **Caution**   If you haven't set the initial Z-height as described previously, do that first.

Begin by homing your printer and then lowering the Z axis to its minimal position. Check that the nozzle is slightly above the print surface. Now raise the Z axis 10mm and move it to the maximum printing radius along the X or Y axis, and then slowly lower the Z axis. You should see the nozzle stop at the same height as it did at the center position.

If the nozzle touches the print surface, note the value of the Z axis. This represents how much higher the print surface is at this point; you may have a convex surface. If the nozzle does not touch the print surface, check the gap with a sheet of paper. You should be able to slip the paper under the nozzle with a small amount of friction. If the nozzle is higher than the print surface and the paper thickness (about 0.10mm), you may have a concave print surface. Figure 5-30 presents a graphical representation of convex and concave print surfaces (albeit a bit exaggerated).

---

[13]Technically, this is [0,0,0.1] given you set the first layer height to 0.01 (the thickness of a piece of paper).

Figure 5-30. *Print bed profile*

Checking the value at only one point is not sufficient. You need to do this at several places on the print surface to ensure that you aren't seeing an inconsistency in the glass; that is, a small portion that is not flat. Repeat the preceding process at max negative and max positive positions for the X and Y axes. I also like to measure the points at the midpoint of each quadrant. Notice the small dots in Figure 5-29. These are the points I like to use to test convex and concave print surfaces.

If you have a convex or concave print surface, the Z-height should be similar for all eight points. Naturally, there could be some variance but it should be consistently higher or consistently lower to confirm the shape of the print surface.

To correct the problem of convex or concave print surfaces, you adjust a parameter called DELTA_RADIUS in Marlin or PRINTER_RADIUS in Repetier-Firmware. For a convex print surface, you increase the value. For a concave print surface, you decrease the value. Only make the adjustment in 0.50mm increments. A little value goes a long way here. If the print surface is really off, you might want to use a higher increment. For example, the following shows a small adjustment made for a convex print surface in the Marlin firmware (Configuration.h).

```
#define DELTA_RADIUS (DELTA_SMOOTH_ROD_OFFSET-DELTA_EFFECTOR_OFFSET-
                      DELTA_CARRIAGE_OFFSET) + 0.50 // convex print surface
```

Compile the firmware and reload it, and then run the procedure again to check the effect. Your problem should be a bit better. Repeat the entire process until your nozzle is between 0.10mm and 0.175mm above the print surface on all checkpoints.

Remember, this is an act of extreme fine-tuning, and some would say it is correcting a poor-quality print surface (or print bed). It is also true that minor convex or concave shapes can be overcome by a Z-probe (auto bed leveling), but this is only true if your Z-probe mechanism samples many places on the print surface. However, the error is more likely caused by DELTA_RADIUS inaccuracies. This is because it is difficult to precisely measure DELTA_RADIUS. Thus, you may need to fine-tune until the first layer height is consistent across the print surface.

I should also point out that if your print surface is removable, and either convex or concave, chances are that it has the opposite problem if you turn the print surface over. Thus, if you correct for this problem, be sure to mark your print surface so that you don't accidentally turn it over. This will result in poor bed adhesion and can cause the nozzle to strike the print surface.

OK, you're done checking the axis movement and have confirmed that the delta kinematics are correct. Now it is time to set up that Z-probe!

Z-Probe

Now that you have everything else working, you can turn your attention to enabling a Z-probe mechanism. Since this is a fairly new feature, the exact steps vary for each type of mechanism. As mentioned in Chapter 2, there are a number of types of mechanisms available. Older models use an extra endstop mounted on an arm or plunger, but newer mechanisms use inductive sensors mounted on the effector, or force-sensitive resistors

(FSR) mounted under the print surface. I describe a popular option for the Mini Kossel that uses a plunger mechanism. Other probe setups can use the same procedure described here. If you have a probe that isn't a plunger or lever type, check your vendor's web site for specific instructions on setting up the probe.

To set up the Z-probe, either cover the print surface with blue painter's tape or put the template back on. You need to determine how far the probe is from the nozzle when it touches the print surface. To do this, you home the printer, deploy the probe, and then lower the Z axis until the probe triggers.

This requires monitoring the probe endstop condition. If your probe uses an endstop with an LED, this is easy—just wait for the LED to illuminate (or extinguish). If the probe uses a normal endstop switch, you will have to use the M119 command to check the status after each move.

Once you determine that the probe has triggered, you note the Z-axis position. This is the height of the nozzle above the print surface when the probe is triggered.

Next, make a mark on the print surface where the probe is touching the print surface. If the probe is an endstop on a lever, make the mark at the point where the lever touches the print surface. If is it a plunger, just mark where it strikes the print surface, raise the Z axis, and stow the probe. Be careful not to move the effector in the process.

Now lower the Z axis until the nozzle is just above the print surface. Next, use the job controls to position the nozzle directly over the mark for the probe. Note the values of X and Y. This the distance away from the nozzle. Now that you have these three values, you must plug them into your firmware. You will find these values in Configuration.h. I will show the values for Marlin. Repetier-Firmware uses the same names.

The correct values may have a different sign than what you wrote down. That is, if the probe is in front of the nozzle on the Y axis, you would subtract the value. Similarly, if it is located to the right of the nozzle on the X axis, you add the value. Since the probe is lower than the nozzle, you subtract the value. You can see this in the following code. In this case, you see that the probe is 5.1mm lower than the nozzle, located 24mm to the right of the nozzle, and 9mm in front of the nozzle.

```
#define X_PROBE_OFFSET_FROM_EXTRUDER 24.0
#define Y_PROBE_OFFSET_FROM_EXTRUDER -9.0
#define Z_PROBE_OFFSET_FROM_EXTRUDER -5.1
```

In Repetier-Firmware, the values are as follows:

```
#define Z_PROBE_X_OFFSET 24
#define Z_PROBE_Y_OFFSET -9.0
#define Z_PROBE_HEIGHT -5.1
```

Go ahead and put these values in the firmware, and then compile and reload it.

To complete the Z-probe setup, you need to have a way to deploy the probe. In this case, most Mini Kossel owners set up their printers to automatically deploy and stow the probe before and after the auto probing code. I show one such example here, but there are many ways to do this. Figure 5-31 shows a small bar I mounted to the frame. I use this to position the effector so that the lever on the probe catches the bar as it moves, thereby deploying the probe.

Figure 5-31. *Z-probe deployment bar (Mini Kossel)*

There is a bit of a trick to get this to work. I explain how to do this in Marlin. If you are using Repetier-Firmware, you can do this using G-code scripts entered in the Probe Start Script and Probe Finish Script text boxes on the features page in the configuration tool. I leave the exact codes for you as an exercise. Hint: Use G0.

Notice the arrow in the photo. The small lever on the probe strikes the arm mounted to the frame, and as the effector glides past, the probe is rotated and its spring-loaded mechanism forces it to deploy.

To enable the autodeploy mechanism in Marlin, edit the `Marlin_main.cpp` file. Yes, this is going deep into the code, but fortunately it isn't too gnarly, as you will see. Locate the method `engage_z_probe()`. At the bottom of that method are statements that position the effector at one location and then moves it to another location. I show how I did this in Listing 5-7.

Listing 5-7. Deploying the Z-Probe in Marlin

```
destination[X_AXIS] = 49;
destination[Y_AXIS] = -65;
destination[Z_AXIS] = 20;
prepare_move_raw();

feedrate = homing_feedrate[Y_AXIS]/10;
destination[X_AXIS] = 54;
destination[Y_AXIS] = -40;
destination[Z_AXIS] = 20;
prepare_move_raw();
destination[Z_AXIS] = 25;
prepare_move_raw();
```

The first portion of the code positions the effector so that the lever for the probe is in front of the bar I mounted. The `prepare_move_raw()` method executes the move. The next portion tells the printer to move the effector diagonally so that the lever is moved and the probe deploys. Lastly, I raise the Z axis 5mm to ensure that I clear the bar on the next move. Easy, yes?

To stow the probe, I use a portion of the print surface mount to lower the effector until the probe returns to its docking position, which is accomplished by the spring that presses the lever back into its docking position. Figure 5-32 shows the part I used to stow the probe.

Figure 5-32. *Z-probe stow point (Mini Kossel)*

To find the location, I moved the axes until I located the probe over the spot and then I recorded the values for X, Y, and Z. If you don't have any way to display these values, you can use the M114 command to read the current location of all the axes. I then entered those in the code. In this case, you are looking for the retract_z_probe() method. Listing 5-8 shows the changes. Note the location of the comment. This is the correct location.

Listing 5-8. Stowing the Z-Probe in Marlin

```
// TODO: Move the nozzle down until the Z probe switch is activated.
destination[X_AXIS] = 63;
destination[Y_AXIS] = 63;
destination[Z_AXIS] = 26;
prepare_move_raw();

// Move the nozzle down further to push the probe into retracted position.
feedrate = homing_feedrate[Z_AXIS]/10;
destination[Z_AXIS] = current_position[Z_AXIS] - 20;
prepare_move_raw();

feedrate = homing_feedrate[Z_AXIS];
destination[X_AXIS] = 0;
destination[Y_AXIS] = 0;
destination[Z_AXIS] = current_position[Z_AXIS] + 30;
prepare_move_raw();
```

Here I positioned the probe over the point and then lowered the Z axis. This presses down on the probe plunger, and therefore docks it. You will have to experiment with how far to lower the effector to get a proper dock. I finish by raising the Z axis to clear the stowing point and to ensure that the axis is high enough to start the auto probing procedure.

Once you have these portions of code fixed, recompile and reload the firmware. Then test the process with the G28 followed by the G29 codes. The first code homes the axes and the second initiates the auto probing code. If you want to auto probe before each print, add these codes to your 3D printing software G-code options to execute on print start.

Interestingly, if you observe your G-code console as the auto bed leveling procedure executes, you see that it reports the measurements at each probe location. It reports the X, Y, and Z values at each point. You can make a graph of this data if you want to see a topographical map of your print surface. The following is a partial set of data from one of my runs. Notice how the Z-heights reported are very close to the same value as my probe height. This indicates that my print surface is reasonably flat (but not perfectly so).

```
<- Bed x: 20.00 y: -40.00 z: 5.19
<- Bed x: 0.00 y: -40.00 z: 5.15
<- Bed x: -20.00 y: -40.00 z: 5.11
<- Bed x: -40.00 y: -20.00 z: 4.92
<- Bed x: -20.00 y: -20.00 z: 4.91
<- Bed x: 0.00 y: -20.00 z: 4.99
```

■ **Note**   The G28 command erases any auto bed leveling data collected with the G29 command.

You are now finally and mercifully ready to do some printing! Rather than trying to print a masterpiece, let's start with a simple cube and do one more calibration test to ensure that the scale of your prints is correct.

Check the Print Scale (Object Size)

OK, now you have a properly calibrated printer. It moves correctly, the nozzle is the same height across (around) the print bed, the extruder is extruding properly, correct temperatures are being reached, and you even have the Z-probe thingy working. You're done, right? Nope. There's one more check.

It is still possible that you could have a printer that prints objects slightly too small or slightly too big. I am not talking about printing something half or double the size. Most times it is only a small percentage difference, and indeed some slight variance is considered acceptable.

Aha, gotcha there, eh? You thought all of your wrenching and monkeying around with firmware was over. Well, it is, sort of. But you really need to check how the printer performs when printing objects. That is, if asked to print a 20mm cube, is the resulting object exactly 20mm in size on each side?

So how do these variances occur? Simply, it is a matter of small imperfections in your delta measurements. The most common solution is to change the DELTA_DIAGONAL_ROD value (the same in Marlin and Repetier-Firmware), which affects the size of the object on all three axes. However, once this value is corrected, you should not change it to overcome inaccuracies in other measurements.

HOW CLOSE IS CLOSE ENOUGH?

Depending on how you will use your printer, the objects you print may not need to be exact. For example, if your objects are used as parts to build another printer, so long as the object prints correctly and tolerances allow for slightly larger outer dimensions, you may not need to adjust your printer calibration settings. So how close is close enough? I think it depends on the printer. For instance, a factor of 0.2mm–0.4mm is acceptable for most entry-level and RepRap printers. For consumer- and professional-grade printers, 0.0mm–0.2mm is acceptable.

To correct this, you must print a series of calibration prints. A calibration print is a special object designed to test how well your printer performs on certain tasks. For example, you can print a cube to test the accuracy of your axes movement, print an object with several round holes to check precision, print an object with overhangs to test how well your extruder performs, print a hollow object to check bridging, and much more.

I recommend starting with the cube. It is the best way to see how well you've done in setting up your printer. This can be very rewarding for those who have built their own printers. The cube allows you to measure how well your axes are moving. That is, if you print a 20mm cube, you would expect to measure the resulting object and see that it is 20mm on each side.

Well, that's the goal. In reality, most printers are slightly off, but only by a tenth of a millimeter or so. Any more than that and you have to go back and perform axis calibration. The objects may be slightly off for several reasons. Most notable are that the filament has slightly different cooling properties or that there are small imperfections in the layers. Whatever the cause, it is generally acceptable for objects to be off by a few tenths of a millimeter.

You can find calibration cubes on Thingiverse or you can create your own using OpenSCAD. I discuss OpenSCAD in more detail in another chapter; however, creating a simple cube requires only the basics of using OpenSCAD. Let's do that now. If you have not installed OpenSCAD, do so now.

Begin by opening OpenSCAD. Notice that it launches with a new window. Type the following in the edit box on the left side of the screen. This will generate a cube 20mm on each side.

```
cube([20,20,20]);
```

Now you need to compile it. You can choose the Design ➤ Compile and Render menu item to compile the code and generate a rendering of the object. You should see the cube appear to the right. That's it! You've just written code to generate a 20mm cube. Cool, eh?

Now you need to generate a .stl file for use in the slicer. Choose the File ➤ Export ➤ Export as STL... menu and give the file a name, like cube_20 or similar. If you want to save the OpenSCAD file, you can do so, but given how simple the code is, you may want to skip saving it. You can always type the code again if you want to make a different cube. OK, you're all set! Now you just need to print the cube.

Open your 3D printing software and load the file you just created. Make sure that you have the right filament size specified and use a lower resolution (like 0.30mm) for the layer height. Check the extruder temperature to ensure that it matches your filament and the heated print bed settings in the same manner.

In MatterControl, you do this by clicking the Add button on the main window. Select the .stl file and click Open. Next, you can use the Advanced Controls to choose the print quality on the Print tab and the filament size on the Filament tab. When you're ready, return to the Queue panel and click Print. When the print is done, you should be rewarded with a fantastic, whimsical plastic cube. Now you need to measure the cube to check its size. Figure 5-33 shows a photo of a cube I printed and measured.

Figure 5-33. *20mm test cube*

Notice here that the size of the cube is very close to what was expected. In fact, I measured each side and found the sizes were 20.12mm, 20.15mm, and 20.15mm. In my opinion, there is no need to further calibrate this printer because it generates objects that are sized with a low error factor. That is, the error is a mere 0.6 percent (20.12 ÷ 20). If it were higher, say 1 percent, I would likely calibrate.

If you print several calibration test cubes and find your measurements are off by more than 0.2mm to 0.4mm, you may want to consider recalibrating your printer. You should also observe the print carefully for sides that are not flat or have similar aspects that can cause your measurements to be inaccurate. If you find these characteristics and your measurements are within about 0.2mm, you should not recalibrate until you explore solutions for those problems.

For example, if the first layers appear to be squished, it can cause your Z-axis measurement to be less than what you expect. In this case, it indicates the Z-height is too small, causing the first layer to smash into the print bed.

But before you do that, print a second (or even a third) cube to ensure that you are seeing consistent results. If so, try printing a larger cube. If the error factor remains constant from a small to a larger cube, I would not recalibrate because the inaccuracy may be related to other, less significant factors. However, if the inaccuracy scales with the cube, it is definitely a calibration issue. If you do decide to adjust your printer settings, be sure to adjust one axis at a time, reprint the cube, and check the measurements.

So how do you do this with a delta printer? The easiest way is to change only the DELTA_RADIUS value. You do this by calculating the difference in the size of the actual print versus the desired size. To correct this, you use a ratio of the measured to desired size to adjust the value.

```
NEW_DELTA_RADIUS = (measured_value / desired_value) * DELTA_RADIUS
```

For example, suppose you wanted to print a 100mm cube, but it prints only 95mm on each side. Let's say my DELTA_RADIUS is 145mm. The formula would then yield the following.

```
137.75 = (95.0 / 100.0) * 145.0
```

Thus, I would correct the code by subtracting the value from the original, or 145 – 137.75 = 7.25, and then subtract this from DELTA_RADIUS in the code as follows:

```
#define DELTA_RADIUS (DELTA_SMOOTH_ROD_OFFSET-DELTA_EFFECTOR_OFFSET-DELTA_CARRIAGE_OFFSET)
- 7.25
```

■ **Tip**   You can adjust DELTA_SMOOTH_ROD_OFFSET instead. This is located nearby in the code (a few lines prior in Marlin) and having more whitespace may make it easier to annotate than adding the adjustment to the longer DELTA_RADIUS definition.

As another example, let's say your test printed the cube 103mm on each side. You then use the formula to calculate the new value. In this case, I would add 4.35 to DELTA_RADIUS in the firmware.
149.35 = (103.0 / 100.0) * 145.0
Notice that to increase the size of the print, you decrease DELTA_RADIUS, but to decrease the size of the print, you increase DELTA_RADIUS.

■ **Note**   An alternative process is to use the scaling feature in your software to resize the object prior to printing. If you calibration is accurate (or acceptable to you), scaling the object may be easier than recalibrating your printer. It is also possible that the size of the object is incorrect, in which case recalibration may not be necessary.

If you decide to do this, you will enter the value in the firmware, recompile, and reload. You should try to print another object to ensure that your calculations are correct and to confirm that the size is closer to your desired accuracy.

■ **Tip**   A more correct adjustment may be to adjust the steps per millimeter. Refer to the stepper motor calibration discussion in a previous section.

OK, now you can throw your head back and let loose cries of triumphant glee! Not only have you successfully calibrated your printer, you've also succeeded in learning a great deal about how delta printers work. Well done!

Summary

Calibrating your printer involves a number of steps. You need to ensure that the firmware settings match your hardware, that your hardware is configured correctly, and that the extruder, filament, and temperatures are all set and working properly. If this is your first time calibrating a delta printer, no doubt it seems a bit complex, and the number of things that need to be adjusted is perhaps a bit surprising.

Fortunately, if you follow the processes described in this chapter, you should be able to get your delta printer calibrated properly so that print quality will be optimized. As mentioned, you should not have to do the more difficult steps, such as setting the Z-height or calibrating the towers, more than once unless you have repaired or otherwise disassembled your printer. You will see in an upcoming chapter the things you can do (maintenance) to maximize the effectiveness of your printer and to keep it calibrated properly and in good working order.

In the next chapter I discuss topics you are most likely to encounter once you start using your delta printer: what to do when things go wonky.[14] As you will see, there is a bit of an art to diagnosing printing problems.

---

[14]A highly technical term used to describe something without reason. Not to be confused with hinky, which means "not quite right."

CHAPTER 6

■ ■ ■

Delta Printer Troubleshooting

If you built your own delta printer, either from a kit or from scratch, chances are you learned a lot about how the printer works and what it takes to complete the assembly of a sophisticated robot.[1] Even if you didn't build your own delta printer, there is no doubt you have spent considerable time building your skills by learning how to get the most out of your delta printer.

There is one skill that I have found both inexperienced and experienced delta printer enthusiasts seem to learn the hard way—if at all: how to diagnose and correct problems. The source of the problem could be with the hardware, software, or to some extent the firmware, but almost all problems manifest in poor print quality. Knowing how to reasonably determine what is wrong in each of these areas is a bit of an art. However, this chapter is your gateway to that art form.

I sincerely hope you were not told that 3D printing is a carefree endeavor where the printer behaves spectacularly every time you use it. Sadly, that is not the case. All 3D printers, delta printers included, will have issues with print quality, or at least things will go wrong to cause issues with print quality at some time or another.

That is not to say all 3D printers will have problems, nor do I insinuate they will self-destruct when you least expect it.[2] Some printers will be better than others. I have read where people have had problems with every grade of printer. Most times the problem can be solved with a simple adjustment, replacing a worn or broken part, or by altering the software settings. Again, knowing what to focus on when trying to solve a problem is key, but knowing how to properly diagnose the problem will lead you to success much more quickly.

Keep in mind that you are seeking the best print quality possible. Anything that affects your print quality (or expectations of quality) is a problem that must be fixed. In some cases, the problem causes the print to fail (the part is unusable). In other cases, the part is still usable but may not be of sufficient quality. Also consider that most problems can have more than one cause. For example, layer shifting can be caused by loose axis mechanisms, improper voltage to the stepper motors, or failing electronics and software.

In this chapter, I visit many of the common things that can go wrong when using a delta printer. More specifically, I focus on the problems you will likely encounter with the hardware, software, and firmware. As you will see, some problems can have multiple possible causes, and in some cases, several causes can contribute to a print quality issue. I begin with a short discussion on troubleshooting techniques.

---

[1] Perseverance, unwillingness to accept defeat, loss of sleep, increased vocabulary, too many trips to the hardware store, and so forth.

[2] I once owned a beautiful British racing green MG that would spontaneously spew a random vital liquid or mechanical part when you least expected. It's the only car that I've stocked with a toolkit and spares.

Troubleshooting Techniques

Troubleshooting is not a new method, process, art, or science. Essentially, troubleshooting is determining the source of the problem and solving it. How you go about that can contribute greatly to the success of your solution. You may be able to fix your problem by randomly changing things until the problem gets better. Or you may instinctively know what to do.

Some have learned good troubleshooting techniques the hard way by suffering many failures and frustrations before adapting strategies that minimize failure and maximize success. That is, they learn the hard way to approaching problems with methodical, proven techniques. Others have learned good troubleshooting techniques from wise tutors. Others still, like myself, have learned from a combination of life experience and academic training. I hope that this section fills in some niche or void in your own experience. If nothing else, you should be able to use these techniques to greater success when facing problems.

The following sections describe several tasks you should do prior to trying to solve a problem. If you follow these tasks when approaching a problem, especially a problem with a 3D printer, you will find a solution more quickly with less frustration and fewer headaches.

■ **Note**   The information presented here assumes the problem is repeatable. Random failures can be very difficult to repair. Without the ability to re-create the problem, you won't know whether you have fixed the problem or introduced a new one.

Create a Baseline

A baseline will establish many things for you. First and foremost, it will allow you to set a standard or a set of observations that define the normal operation of your printer. A baseline is a set of observations made under normal (or initial) operation. Any observation that changes beyond normal parameters can be an indication that something is wrong.

Most people skip this step, and it is truly a pity because they often fail to notice when something is starting to wear or requires maintenance. For example, how would you know that the belts or cables need adjustment? You could wait until your printer starts skipping steps and ruining prints, but that seems silly. Wouldn't it be better if you measured the slack in the belts while the printer is operating correctly? If you have data like this, you would be able to tell when the belts needed adjustment. That is, you know you need to tighten the belts when the slack becomes considerably more than your baseline measurement.

A baseline for a delta printer is a list of observations about a fully configured and properly functioning delta printer. You should create this baseline as soon as you are comfortable with the print quality of your printer. You can record the observations before that—say when your printer is assembled—but if you make major changes to components during calibration, the values may become invalid.

You can capture all kinds of observations from measuring the length of travel for each axis, belt tension, frame size, and so forth. However, some of these may not be of much use because they measure things that should never change (although there is nothing wrong with recording them).

To give you a starting point, I recommend making the following observations for your printer and recording them in your engineering notebook (or suitable recording device). You may want to include these and any other observations you can think of. Consider all aspects of your particular printer, especially those components that have any form of adjustment.

- *Belt tension*: Establishes minimal tension values

- *Height of each endstop*: Established baseline for tower calibration

- *Actual vs. reported temperatures for the hot end and heated print bed*: Lets you check to see if heaters or sensors fail

- *Free play in delta arm joints*: Establishes a basis for wear or maintenance (if the tension is adjustable)

- *Tightness of frame components*: Establishes whether they become loose and affect printing

- *Thickness (diameter) of new filament rolls*: Lets you know if there is a quality problem with your filament

Once you have these values and any others you can think of recorded, you can refer to them when something goes wrong. The next sections discuss a process to follow when problems occur. Whether you record a baseline or not, the following process will help you to methodically find the best solution (or at least one that works). I discuss each in more detail later.

1. Observe and record relevant data.

2. Consider all possibilities.

3. Choose and implement a strategy.

4. Record the solution.

   a. If the problem is solved, stop and record the new baseline data.

   b. If the problem is not solved, return settings to their original values and return to step 3.

I present each of these using a concrete example of a layer shift during the printing of an object.

Observe and Record

The key to successful troubleshooting is making observations and recording them at the time the problem occurs. Recording your observations helps you understand what is wrong. Having a written record of the problems you encounter also allows you to diagnose and repair the problem more quickly should the problem reoccur.

Let's look at an example that can happen with delta printers. Suppose you notice your object layers are shifted a little. Figure 6-1 shows an example of this problem. There are many observations that you could make about this situation. More generally, I recommend starting with observing the state of the printer when you discover the problem. In this case, I discovered the problem after the print completed. If you see something like this occurring during the print, you may want to cancel the print since the part will likely be unusable.

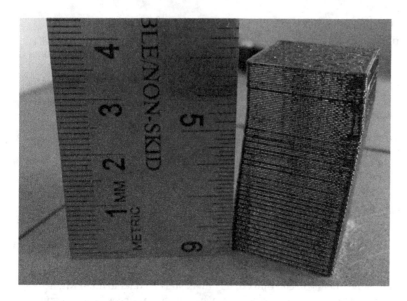

Figure 6-1. *Layer shift*

Specifically, I noted which direction the shift occurred (the direction of the "lean"). In this case, there were two bands of shifting: one for the first 30mm and another for the remainder of the print. Both occurred on the Y axis. I also noted the state of the axis mechanisms. Initially, all seemed well and nothing seemed out of place. Next, I homed all the axes and noted how they moved and whether there were any noises (beyond the usual), and if everything moved smoothly. I then checked the stepper motors for excessive heat. I performed a general check, without touching anything, to ensure that I didn't change anything by accident. Listing 6-1 shows the observations made when the layer shift occurred. Notice that I record a problem description, the date the problem occurred, and a list of my observations.[3]

Listing 6-1. Layer Shift Problem: Observations

```
Problem:  Layer shifted for about 30mm in one direction then shifted back.
Date: 24 April 2015

Observations:
- Occurred on Y-axis
- Stepper motors are warm but not more than expected
- No heat, odor, noise, or smoke from electronics
- Axis movement is normal, no binding
- Belt on Z axis was much looser than the other two
```

So how do you know what to observe? While you may be able to discern which observations are more likely to point to the problem—and only experience will give you this knowledge—you should record as many as you can. This may sound more like an art form than scientific analysis, and there is some truth to this. The best diagnosticians that I've met like to use their creativity when problem solving. This includes thinking of all possible things that can go wrong, as well as observations of the state of the machine when the problem occurs.

---

[3] I normally write these in my engineer's notebook so that if I encounter it in the future, I will know how to fix it.

Consider the Possible Causes

Once you have noted your observations, it is time to consider a list of causes. You should always try to think of as many causes as you can, because while sometimes the cause is obvious (e.g., user error), this isn't always the case. You should consider all the components involved. In the layer shift example, this includes all the components of the axis movement—from loose or broken parts—to failed electronics.

Although you may not know what to list, you should try to list anything that comes to mind. Experience or a good diagnostic chart like those found in the appendix will help you. I like to make a list of the possible causes and write them underneath the observations. Listing 6-2 shows the updated problem entry in my engineering notebook.

Listing 6-2. Layer Shift Problem: Causes Added

```
Problem:  Layer shifted several times.
Date: 24 April 2015

Observations:
- Occurred on Y-axis
- Stepper motors are warm but not more than expected
- No heat, odor, noise, or smoke from electronics
- Axis movement is normal, no binding
- Belt on Z axis was much looser than the other two

Potential Causes:
- Loose belt on Z axis
- Stepper motor failure
- Stepper driver failure
- Loose drive gear
- Obstruction in axis mechanism
```

The next step is to consider each cause in turn and decide which to explore first. I like to start with the most likely cause. From experience, it usually has something to do with the mechanics of the axis movement.

Determine the Cause and Implement a Strategy to Correct It

When considering potential causes to explore, one strategy is to first focus on those that are the most likely. If the problem is a new one (one you have not experienced before), you can start with any of the most likely causes.

Another strategy is to check those causes that are least likely to be the problem. In the layer shift example, this includes the stepper motor, stepper driver, and obstructions in the axis mechanism. All of these are easy to check. For example, you can see if there is something in the roller carriages channel (such as filament, tape, dirt, etc.) or something colliding with the carriage when you home the printer. As you test each possible cause, make a tick or check mark next to it on your observations list so that you know you've tested and eliminated it as a cause.

Regardless of which strategy you implement, you should follow the simple technique of adjust, observe, and readjust. More specifically, you make a change, test to see if the change fixed the problem, and if not, return the adjustment back to the previous setting. That is another very handy use of a baseline: How do you know what the initial setting was if you didn't record it? It also applies to anything you do, from adjusting belts and other mechanical items, to changes in software (as you saw in the last chapter).

This technique of adjust, observe, and readjust works well to successfully diagnose and repair. It reduces the chances of introducing other problems. If you did not use this technique, you may still fix the problem by changing several things at once, but you may not learn which repair fixed the problem. In this case, if the problem occurs again, you will not have learned how to fix it—only how to throw a box of wrenches at it.[4]

Choosing what to change is dependent on the cause you've decided to correct, and it is usually intuitive. Some causes may not require any changes; rather, you may just need to check something. For example, if you suspect the cause is a broken clamp, you can simply observe the clamp. If it isn't broken, loose, or so forth, then you can cross off that potential cause and move on to the next.

■ **Caution**   Change one—and only one—setting at a time. Changing more than one thing before observing the effects can lead to introducing other problems.

Once you choose a cause to try to fix, work on that cause and that cause alone. The best approach is to check and fix the cause, changing only one thing at a time. For example, if you choose to explore the possibility that the belt is loose, you first check the tension on the belt, and if slack, adjust it accordingly. But you don't go any further! Test the condition again before looking at another cause.

Record the Solution

When the problem is fixed, you should make a notation in your engineering notebook that describes how you fixed the problem. I like to describe what I did and how it affected the problem. It is sometimes the case that making a change reduces the problem but may not completely fix it. In this case, you would try the repair again until the problem is fixed. For example, if you need to increase the temperature of the hot end, and changing it by 5 degrees helps, increase it another 5 degrees and repeat until the problem is fixed.

Listing 6-3 shows the completed entry for the layer shift example. Notice that I tried several causes before I found the source.

Listing 6-3. Layer Shift Problem: Solution Added

```
Problem:  Layer shifted several times.
Date: 24 April 2015

Observations:
- Occurred on Y-axis
- Stepper motors are warm but not more than expected
- No heat, odor, noise, or smoke from electronics
- Axis movement is normal, no binding
- Belt on Z axis was much looser than the other two

Potential Causes:
- Loose belt on Z axis - YES
- Stepper motor failure - NO
- Stepper driver failure - NO
- Loose drive gear - NO
- Obstruction in axis mechanism - NO
```

---

[4]This only works for old 4x4 trucks and sewing machines.

Solution:
This problem was caused by a loose belt on the Z axis.

Notes:
I was able to repeat the problem but it occurs on some objects but not others. While not completely random, it does vary in intensity. I checked the belt tension and it was very loose with almost 40mm of flex. All clamps, bolts, and other mechanical items are working correctly.

Notice that in this example the problem was a loose belt. That is not unusual for delta printers. New printers are especially susceptible to belts coming loose. This can also be a symptom of loose clamps, loose or broken frame vertices, or a poor-quality (or worn-out) belt.

Another source for this problem is a slipping drive gear. Had I not considered it and focused only on belt tension, I may have spent a lot more time and not found the source of the problem. Be sure to consider all parts of the axis mechanism in your analysis.

SOLUTIONS VS. MAGICAL CURES

There is something I learned early on when troubleshooting problems with my 3D printers. It seems there is no end to differing ideas on how to solve some problems. For example, it doesn't take too many web searches to find dozens of solutions for lifting. Some offer some very good advice and a few may actually work well for most. However, there are others that resemble voodoo or magic. While it is possible some of these might work for you, I present only those techniques that others and I have found to work well. This does not mean that there are no other techniques; only that the ones listed here are the most tried and true.

Now that you have a good understanding of good practices for diagnosing and repairing problems, let's look at some specific hardware problems that you could encounter with your 3D printer.

Hardware Problems

There are a number of hardware-related problems that can occur. In this section, I present discussions of the most common hardware failures that can induce a number of problems that affect print quality. These include those related to the filament and its feeding to/through the extruder; adhesion of the heated filament to the print surface; and failures in the axes, chassis, and electronics.

I discuss each of these areas in the following sections. I include environmental influences because they affect how the filament bonds. Consider the fact that the hot end must heat to a specific temperature and that the filament extruded must cool in a controlled manner. If there are environmental factors that affect that balance, such as air currents, they can cause the filament to cool too quickly, or in extreme cases, they can cause the hot end temperature to fluctuate.

Filament

You may think filament-related issues are software related. That is, how the software (slicer) builds the objects from settings concerning the filament. However, there are a number of things that can go wrong with filament that is hardware related. Filament is also very sensitive to environmental factors. The following sections describe some of the problems you could encounter, along with recommended remedies.

Quality

The most common issue concerns the quality of the filament. Poor-quality filament can vary in diameter. Some variation is normal, but in this case you are talking about variances of more than a few tenths of a millimeter. This can cause the extruder to extrude too much or too little filament during printing. This manifests in a number of ways, including globs of filament deposited in corners (over extrusion) or small curved parts of the object becoming malformed (curling), as well as poor layer adhesion (under extrusion). In extreme cases it can also cause extrusion failures.

Another issue with poor-quality filament is the possibility of weak areas or portions of the filament that are hollow—or worse, portions that have contaminants embedded in the filament. Contaminants, in particular, can block the nozzle, resulting in extrusion failure.

Clearly, the best way to avoid these problems is to use a higher quality of filament. I have found the filament sold by major online retailers such as MatterHackers (`matterhackers.com/store`), Maker Shed (`makershed.com`), and MakerBot (`makerbot.com`) are very high quality.[5] I have switched to using their filaments exclusively.

Filament Spool Tension

When you buy filament, it is usually delivered on a spool. Most delta printers have accommodations for filament spools to ensure that the extruder can pull the filament with as little tension as possible. If your printer does not have a spool holder, you should consider getting (or printing) one. Choose a design that incorporates bearings or rollers that allow the spool to unroll filament easily. Figure 6-2 shows an adaptation of the stock spool holder on a Rostock Max v2 to accept 50mm spools (`thingiverse.com/thing:824442`).

Figure 6-2. *Spool holder adapter for SeeMeCNC Rostock Max v2*

When the spool has too much tension, the extruder can strip the filament and stop extruding. When this happens, you will likely not catch it right away (unless you stare into your printer while it prints). The result is called an *air print*, where the printer happily continues to move the axes as if the filament were extruding. There really isn't any way to detect this problem other than by observing it.

---

[5]The fact that they all start with M is a coincidence.

Filament sold in bundles or coils are susceptible to tangles—where one or more loops are intertwined so that the filament cannot be uncoiled. When this occurs, it will have the same effect as having a spool holder that has too much tension. Extreme cases can result in having to untangle the filament by unraveling the entire coil. If you buy coiled filament, I recommend rolling onto a used spool and using a spool holder. This will reduce the possibility of the filament tangling. But be careful and do not allow the filament to come into contact with dirty surfaces, such as your shop floor. Also, avoid handling the filament too much because oils (and dirt) from your hands can transfer to the filament. This will introduce contaminants that can cause extrusion failures. Cotton examination gloves can help avoid these problems.

Contaminants

You should store your filament in a clean, dry storage bag or plastic container. Make sure that your filament is not in a position to have dust or other debris fall onto it. Dust and other debris can stick to the filament and be fed into the hot end. If the particles are large enough, they can block the nozzle and cause extrusion failures.

When this occurs, it usually isn't obvious that there is any contamination. That is, you normally clean the extruder and test extrusion. Typically, filament will seem to feed normally, but when you start your print again, you may have another extrusion failure a short time later. If you get several extrusion failures and cannot find any reason for it, you probably have dust and debris on your filament, in your extruder, or partially blocking the nozzle.

STORING FILAMENT

Always store filament spools (that are not in use) in a clean, dry plastic bag with a small amount of drying agent (desiccant). I always save those little white packets you get in many products these days. I drop a few in the bag with each spool of filament. Since I started storing my filament this way, I haven't encountered a problem with humidity. Also, do not store the desiccant in the open air because this can reduce its effectiveness. You should keep it in a sealed bag when not in use.

The best way to eliminate external contaminants is to use a foam filament filter (sometimes called a *filament cleaner*) that mounts on the filament. The foam or sponge wipes off external contaminants as the filament slides through the filter. Like spool holders, filament filter/cleaner designs are plentiful. Figure 6-3 shows the filament filter (in white) that I've found works best for me. It mounts on the filament above the Bowden tube I used to route the filament through the frame. In this case, the cleaner is held in place by the Bowden tube. I use a dense sponge in my filters. I find I need to clean or replace the foam filter monthly when using the printer regularly. It is always amazing to see how much dust and debris that these filters catch.

Figure 6-3. *Filament filter/cleaner*

Environmental Factors

Another thing that can cause filament problems is moisture. Filament can absorb a certain amount of moisture if exposed to high humidity. The result can be popping or hissing sounds, steam, and even moments where the filament spurts from the nozzle (rather than flowing evenly). Should these problems occur, you must stop your printer and remove the filament. Continued use of filament with a high level of moisture is likely to produce poor-quality objects. It also isn't good for your hot end.

If you are thinking you will have to throw the filament away, you can relax because that isn't necessary. You need only place the filament in a plastic bag with a drying agent for a day or so. For severe cases, you can use a food dehydrator or heat the filament on lower temperatures in an oven.[6] Once it dries, you can resume printing with it.

I have referred to clogged nozzles and extrusion failures, but I have not explained them or how to fix them. The next sections will do exactly that—describe the types of problems you could encounter with your extruder and hot end.

Extruder and Hot End

The extruder and hot end can be a source of problems and frustration for new delta printer enthusiasts, including those who may have used Cartesian printers. This is because the Bowden setup most delta printers use can be a bit tricky compared to the extruder and hot end combinations of Cartesian printers. In this section, I list the most common problems and offer some suggestions on how to fix or avoid them. I limit the discussion to Bowden configurations.

Extruder Mechanism

Recall that the extruder is responsible for feeding filament to the hot end. Although very rare, the drive pulley (sometimes a hobbed bolt) can work loose and cause under extrusion, but the more likely scenarios are a clogged drive pulley, or too little or too much tension on the drive pulley.

---

[6]Do not use devices in which food will be prepared.

For example, if you use an extruder with a door, lever, clamp, or arm that you have to tighten to apply tension to the drive pulley, you could encounter problems if the door is tightened too much or too little—either of which can result in extrusion failures. Too much tension can result in the filament pressing into the drive pulley and eventually clogging it. Or worse, it can cause the filament to be squished, increasing tension in the Bowden tube. Too little tension can cause the drive pulley to strip the filament, also clogging it. If your drive pulley gets clogged often and there are no spool holder issues (no tension, tangles, etc.) and the hot end is operating correctly, you may want to check the tension on the extruder door, lever, clamp, or arm.

It is extremely rare for a stepper motor to fail, but I have had this happen once. It was on a printer that had several thousands of printing hours. The average enthusiast probably won't use their printer that much.

Bowden Tube Woes

Some people point to the Bowden tube as the source of extruder problems. However, in most cases, issues with the Bowden tube are consequences of other problems. For example, if your Bowden tube comes loose during a print, it is not normally due to the tube or the press-fit fittings, rather the problem is most likely related to the filament not flowing through the hot end (extruding)—either due to underheating or nozzle obstructions.

Another issue that I have read from enthusiasts is about filament getting stuck or binding in the Bowden tube, therefore causing the extruder to strip the filament. The problem here is most likely with the extruder, not the Bowden tube. That is, if the tension on the drive pulley is too high, it can dig into the filament, making small cuts that expand the diameter of the filament, and therefore it doesn't feed well (or at all) through the Bowden tube.

Another possibility is that the filament is of poor quality and significantly larger than the normal size. For example, if your filament measures greater than 1.85mm, it may bind in the Bowden tube.

Finally, make sure your Bowden tube is long enough so that the Bowden tube is not forced to make a tight spiral or curve (arc). Filament may bind when passing through the tube if the arc of the bend is too tight.

Nozzle Obstructions

There are several problems that can occur with the nozzle. Obstructions are normally the cause for filament extrusion failure in cases where the hot end is heating properly. You've seen this in the section that discussed filament contamination. However, there is a possibility that you could encounter other forms of obstruction.

For example, if the nozzle drags on the print surface, it can damage the small opening or the nozzle can pick up some debris. In these cases, you may see the filament curl when exiting the nozzle. When this occurs, you should remove the filament and let the hot end cool. Once cool, remove the nozzle and use a wire brush (brass or aluminum bristles) to clean the nozzle, and a micro drill bit to reshape the opening. You can also use a piece of emery cloth to lightly sand the nozzle tip, but be careful not to get any shavings in the nozzle itself. Use compressed air to blow out any such contaminants.

■ **Caution** Some hot ends are easier to disassemble than others. For instance, a J-head or E3D hot end are easy to disassemble, but a Buko-style hot end is not. Disassembly of complex hot end designs should be a last resort for clearing nozzle jams. Be sure to check with your vendor for recommendations on how best to service your hot end.

An alternative to removing the nozzle is to use the cold pull method, where you heat the hot end to a temperature slightly below glassing and pull the filament out by hand. This removes the majority of the filament stuck in the hot end, and often the obstruction as well. Temperatures for this technique are 160 to 180 degrees Celsius for ABS and 140 degrees Celsius for PLA (see `http://bukobot.com/nozzle-cleaning` for a complete analysis of this technique). Of course, you cut off the end of the filament and discard it before reloading.

Hot End Effector Mount

If your effector or the hot end mount to the effector becomes loose, extrusion can become inconsistent. This can manifest in a number of ways, including seemingly random variations in outer perimeters or artifacts (blobs, strings, warts, etc.). A loose nozzle can exhibit similar symptoms. If you encounter strange print artifacts, wait until your hot end is cool and check the nozzle, the hot end assembly, and the mounting hardware to the effector. Make sure that everything is tight, and if not, gently tighten the loose parts.

Fixing Filament Feed Failures

When your drive gear gets clogged with filament, it can no longer grip the filament to pull it from the spool and feed it to the hot end. The following presents a process you can use to clean out the extruder.

1. Loosen or remove the filament tension idler door (or simply the idler).

2. Disconnect the Bowden tube at the hot end and pull the tube back about 100mm.

3. Bring the hot end to temperature.

4. Remove the filament manually (watch out—it's hot!).

5. Turn off the heater and allow the hot end to cool, and then turn off the printer.

6. Unload the filament.

7. Use a pointed object to scrape out the filament from the drive pulley, turning the pulley to get to all areas.

8. Use a vacuum to remove all the filament shards.

9. Reload the filament and resume printing.

Figure 6-4 shows an extruder that has stripped filament, clogging the drive pulley. Notice how there is excessive buildup of filament on the pulley. This prevents the grooves from gripping the filament, and thus no filament is extruded.

Figure 6-4. *Clogged extruder*

Also shown is the use of a sharp pair of tweezers to clean out the grooves. A hobby knife works well too. Depending on how accessible your drive gear is, you may be able to use a brush to clean out the filament. Be sure to vacuum away the debris.

Now that you have seen what can go wrong with the extruder and hot end, the next section presents hardware-related problems that can cause adhesion problems.

Adhesion

Adhesion is the number-one bane of 3D printer enthusiasts. This is especially true for those printing with ABS. Adhesion problems are manifested as portions of the object that have started to curl and pull away from the print surface (hence, it appears to have "lifted" off the print bed). Figure 6-5 shows a large gear that has suffered significant lifting. In this case, the resulting part was unusable.

Figure 6-5. *Lifting example*

■ **Tip** Lifting may be worse for larger objects or objects with a small surface area that contacts the print surface. Increase the surface area by using a brim (set in the software) to print several loops of filament to extend the outer layer of the object. You can peel or cut away the brim once the object is removed from the print surface.

Conquering this problem involves tackling the three most common causes for lifting: proper calibration of the delta mechanics, ensuring that the print surface is prepared correctly, and eliminating environmental factors. I describe each of these in the following sections.

LIVING WITH LIFT

If you have followed the advice here (and elsewhere) to combat lifting, you should have reduced your lifting problem significantly. However, it is possible that you may not completely eliminate the problem. This is especially true for ABS, which requires more effort to perfect. For example, a small amount of lifting—such as a small corner or other part that lifts slightly off the print bed but does not ruin the part—may be acceptable. If you examine Thingiverse carefully, you may find signs of lifting on many things posted to the site. If you have treated your lifting problem by attempting as many techniques as you possible, but you still have an occasional small amount of lifting, you may want to declare success.

Delta Mechanics

If your parts are lifting in such a way that the lifting occurs more toward one edge, it is possible that either your print surface is not uniform, your towers are not calibrated, or your delta measurements are incorrect.

You may not notice this if you are printing small parts on a common area (like the center of the print bed). However, the larger the parts you print (particularly near one side of the print surface) or the more parts that you have positioned toward the side that is problematic, the more lifting can occur. Lifting occurs because the Z-height is too high and the first layer of filament is not being pressed onto the print surface. Conversely, having the nozzle too close to the print surface and compressing the filament can sometimes cause warping.

If your print surface is not a uniform thickness near one or more edges, it can cause lifting. This can manifest if you rotated the print surface at some time since you calibrated the towers, and your printer does not have a Z-probe (or you did not use it). This changes the Z-height at the thinner and thicker areas, which can cause the nozzle to be either too high or too low on one area of the print bed. If you find that your print surface (the glass plate) is not uniform, you may want to use a permanent marker to mark the edge and then always align the print surface at the same place so that you don't have to recalibrate.

If your Z-height is correct in the center, but it is uniformly too high or too low on the outer edges, you may have a convex or concave build plate, which can be corrected by adjusting the DELTA_RADIUS variable (see Chapter 5). However, if the Z-height is incorrect in only one area of the print bed, you most likely have one or more towers that are not calibrated. That is, the endstops are not at the same position (distance above the print bed). If your printer does not track evenly (a straight line) along the X or Y axes, your delta measurements may be incorrect. To correct these issues, you need to recheck your delta measurements and your software, and then perform tower calibration (as described in Chapter 5).

■ **Tip**   Filament jams are common symptoms of a poorly calibrated delta printer.

Another related problem that some delta printers encounter is a minor change in the Z-probe. That is, if your printer has a Z-probe, it is possible that the mechanism (probe arm or plunger) shifted or that the endstop became less sensitive, or perhaps the springs have relaxed or its mount has come loose. Any change to the Z-probe, especially with height or sensitivity, can cause your Z-height to be off. This is most likely going to result in Z-height that is too low, but sometimes can be too high, which is what contributes to lifting.

■ **Tip** If you find your Z-probe changes or requires adjustment, you may want to consider using the force-sensitive resistors mounted under the print bed (supported by Marlin). This solution works by the hot end pressing on the print surface, which activates the sensor, thereby detecting the correct Z-height.

Thus, when you experience lifting, especially if it occurs in one spot, you want to examine your towers, delta measurements, print surface, and even the Z-probe for damage or wear. Once you have fixed the problem either by recalibrating or adjusting the print surface or DELTA_RADIUS, I recommend reprinting the part to ensure that you have cured the lifting problem. There are other possible causes, as you will see in the next sections.

Print Surface

Another common problem that can cause lifting is a print surface that is worn or dirty. If you have touched your print surface with your fingers or other body parts, you could have transferred oils from your skin to the print surface, which will reduce adhesion. Similarly, a printer that has not been used for some time may have a layer of dust built up on the print surface. Or, the print surface could have been used enough to need replacing.

You can improve adhesion when printing ABS on Kapton film by cleaning the film with acetone. This removes oils and other contaminants, and renews the surface for better adhesion. If cleaning the surface does not improve adhesion, you should replace the Kapton film. I find that Kapton tape has a very long life when compared with other print surface treatments. Indeed, I usually have to replace Kapton tape when I've accidentally damaged it by removing parts.

■ **Tip** You can also use ABS slurry to increase adhesion on Kapton tape. In fact, if the Z-height is set properly, ABS slurry can almost completely cure lifting on ABS prints.

Blue painter's tape with PLA can lose its adhesive properties much sooner than Kapton film. Fortunately, blue painter's tape is easier and cheaper to replace. I recommend replacing blue painter's tape after five to ten prints,[7] or when parts show any signs of lifting.

Another strategy that works very well for PLA is to use a raft, which improves first-layer adhesion. A *raft* is a series of layers printed on the print bed and the object is printed on top. Most printer software includes settings to generate a raft. However, some software is better at printing rafts than others. You should experiment with rafts to be sure that your slicer will generate rafts that are easy to remove.

Environmental Factors

The effects of environmental factors that can cause lifting include unstable room temperature and air currents or simple drafts. If the room temperature is too low, it can cause parts to cool unevenly and to lift off the print surface. Likewise, air moving across the print bed can cause the filament on some layers to cool faster than others. This causes the part to curl, and the curling can cause the part to pull away from the print surface. Furthermore, it is possible for upper layers on larger objects to lose layer adhesion, which causes cracks because some areas cool faster than others.

---

[7]Some enthusiasts can get upward of 20 to 30 prints before the tape needs replacing.

You should always ensure that your room temperature is stable. The exact temperature isn't that important (as long as it's comfortable for carbon-based life forms), but it should remain the same for the duration of your prints. For example, do not use your printer near air conditioners or space heaters. If your room needs to be cooled or heated, allow time for the temperature to stabilize before printing.

You may think "drafts" mean any air driven by a fan or a breeze from an open window, but it doesn't take that much air movement to cause lifting. In fact, you may not even notice the draft. Fans and open windows should be turned off and closed. However, detecting or eliminating all drafts may not be possible. Thus, you need to try to reduce their effects.

The best way to reduce the effects of drafts is to eliminate the sources. You can move the printer away from open windows (or close them), close HVAC vents, and turn off any other source of drafts. However, if you cannot eliminate the source, there are several ways to reduce the effect, including the following (I describe each in more detail in the upcoming sections):

- Print skirts or walls around the object

- Place removable walls around the object

- Place the printer in an enclosure

Some printer software allows you to add a wall of filament, called a *skirt*, around your object. The skirt is printed as a single row to a specific layer height, forming a wall around the object. However, not all software offers this option, and some of those that do offer it have no option to increase the height. For example, the default slicer setting in MatterControl does not allow you to set the skirt height, but if you turn on the Slic3r option, you can set the height.

The effect of the skirt is to reduce effects of drafts from cooling the object. In fact, it helps keep more heat in the object. I find a skirt to work best for ABS prints, but I have used it for PLA prints with similar effect. Figure 6-6 shows the skirt settings for MatterControl (with the Slic3r option). It also shows the brim settings, which can be used to increase the surface area, making contact with the print surface. Using a skirt and brim together can help reduce the effects of drafts.

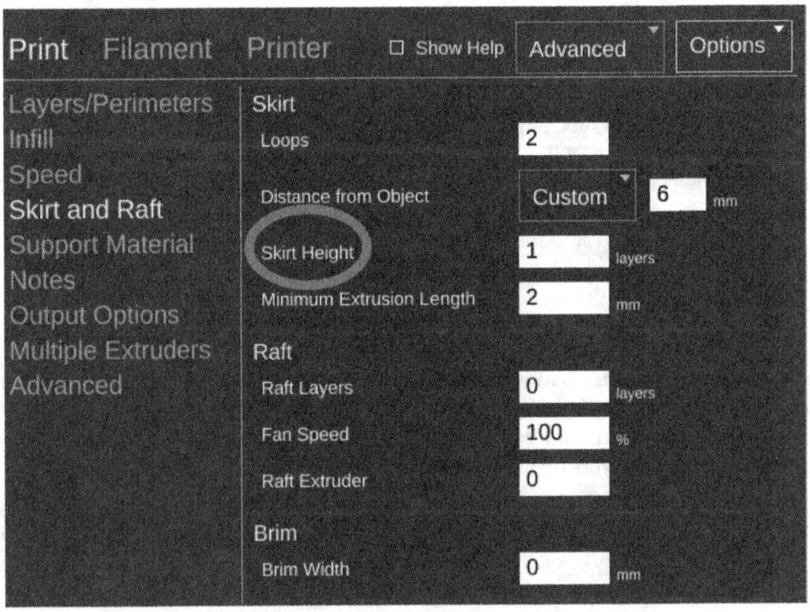

Figure 6-6. Skirt settings in MatterControl

Notice that you can set the distance from the object, as well as thickness in the number of loops around the object. Thus, if you want a thin skirt 20mm high, you can set Loops to 2 and Skirt Height to 20 divided by your layer height. For example, if your layer height is 0.25mm and you want to print a skirt 20mm high, you need 80 layers (20.0 ÷ 0.25 = 80.0).

If you don't want to use the skirt feature, you can use removable walls made by taping cardboard or paper walls to the frame. The shape of the delta printer makes this very easy to do. This may sound low-tech (and it is), but you'll be surprised how well it works. In fact, I find it a better treatment than printing a skirt.

Simply cut a length of paper to fit from one vertical frame segment to another and affix it to the frame with tape. Make the "walls" only about 100mm tall. Any taller and you could obstruct the axis movement. Apply the walls all the way around the printer.

If your printer uses axis movement outside of the frame for deploying or retracting the Z-probe, you may have to wait until printing has begun to mount the paper walls.

The best way to combat lifting caused by drafts that cannot be eliminated is to place the printer in an enclosure. However, there are few enclosures for delta printers. Indeed, the design and axis mechanisms make it difficult to add panels to the printer to enclose it. That does not mean you cannot create an enclosure for a delta printer, but it would most likely have to be quite a bit bigger than the printer itself to give everything room to move.

I have seen some early examples of enclosures (thingiverse.com/thing:711243), but none that I would recommend. It is only a matter of time before someone designs a universal solution. I recommend that you control the environment as much as possible before resorting to buying huge sheets of wood or acrylic for your own homemade enclosure.

Remember, the purpose of an enclosure is to block all stray air currents, not to retain heat; although there are enclosures for Cartesian printers that are designed to create a heated build chamber as an alternative to a heated build plate.

Another use for a full enclosure is fume extraction. You can use a low-power fan connected via a duct to a charcoal filter to remove a lot of the fumes caused by heating some filaments. For example, if you are sensitive to the odor of printing ABS, an enclosure with a fume extractor can greatly reduce the irritants.

Now let's turn to the axes and chassis as the source of print failures or quality issues.

Axes and Chassis

When diagnosing print quality problems, you often don't consider the possibilities that the mechanical components of your printer can fail or come out of adjustment. Sometimes this is because of normal wear or part failure; other times it is from accidental events or changes, and still other times from neglect. I discuss each of these in the following sections.

Obstructions

The most obvious hardware problems are those things that cause the axes to fail to operate properly or move from its minimum to maximum positions.

Sometimes the obstruction is accidental, but other times it can happen that a part of your printer comes loose or an object is knocked off the print bed, only to obstruct one or more axes. When an obstruction falls into the axis mechanism, you are likely to hear chattering, bumps, and other undesirable sounds. Should this occur, you should stop your printer as soon as you can. Use the reset button or simply turn it off. The print will be incomplete and therefore useless, but it is better than your printer breaking a component, belt, or bending some vital part of the printer.

■ **Caution**　You should treat your delta printer the same as you would any piece of equipment that has the capability to burn, pinch, and injure. Always keep your fingers, hands, small pets, clowns, and clothing away from the printer when it is operating.

Delta printers that use roller carriages or rollers in tracks are susceptible to small pieces of debris in the channel. This can cause slight layer shifting like I described previously. If your roller carriages are loose, even a small piece of tape can cause odd print quality issues.

To correct the problem, clear the obstruction and make sure your printer is not damaged and adjust any parts of the axis that you can (e.g., the roller carriages). Ensure all axes can be moved freely for their full range. In some cases, the obstruction can bend or dislodge endstops or cause minor changes in the axis adjustments. Be sure to check all components in the area. Power on the printer and home all axes then resume your print.

■ **Tip**　If your endstops have moved, you will have to recalibrate your towers.

Adjustments

Every printer differs, but most have several components that can be adjusted to accommodate changes or wear. These often include tension adjustments for belts, carriages, and delta arms. For example, the towers must be calibrated, and the carriage and the delta arm hardware tensioned properly to ensure that the nozzle moves across the print bed at the same height.

■ **Caution**　Never attempt to adjust your printer while it is printing. Likewise, never attempt to access your objects on the print bed while the printer is printing. The delta mechanism is fragile. If it strikes something like your body, it can damage the delta mechanism—and it probably isn't good for your body either. Plus, the nozzle can burn you. Quickly.

Certain events—such as obstructions, mechanical or electrical failure, or major overhaul or upgrades—can cause changes that foil your adjustments. You have already seen the effects of an uncalibrated or misaligned tower. This causes adhesion problems, which can lead to lifting. However, if the towers get too far out of adjustment, it can cause the nozzle to come in contact with the print surface. Recall that this can cause extrusion failure, as the print surface obstructs the nozzle.

Likewise, loose belts can cause layer shifts. This can be a major shift if the belt skips a cog on the drive pulley. If the belt is moderately loose, some backlash may be noticeable. As the belt becomes looser, it begins to introduce a delay—much like a stripped or worn gear—and can cause all manner of wacky print quality problems. You can tell a belt needs tension by simply moving the belt perpendicular to its travel (left and right). If you can move it more than about 20mm to 40mm, it is too loose. As I mentioned, if the belt becomes very loose, it can slip over a notch (or more). This will introduce an immediate and extreme layer shift.

Part Failure or Wear

While it is rare for parts to fail on a delta printer, it is still possible. I mention it here for completeness, as I have yet to see any of the parts on my delta printers fail from wear or breakage. However, Mini Kossel printers can suffer broken parts when transported or left in a hot area for a long time. In this case, the materials expand or are flexed so that too much stress is placed on the plastic parts. Some RepRap Cartesian designs are very susceptible to part failures with endstops and vertices. Fortunately, this is not the case for most delta printers.

■ **Tip**   Always take care to prepare your printer for transport by loosening belts and securing the effector and other moving parts.

When parts of your printer fail, you often notice the problem immediately and it is usually clear what failed. For example, if a belt or other vital component of the axis movement breaks, that axis also fails to operate properly and the print fails. In fact, if one of the axes stops operating, the effector will fall down and can make contact with the print bed or the part being printed. Again, this is very rare and not a likely possibility.

Whenever I encounter a print quality issue or print failure, I check the parts of the affected axes to ensure that there are no broken parts. I also check all the parts when I perform maintenance on the printer.

A problem common to delta printers is called by several names, but most commonly referred to as the "delta arm blues." This is when the joints on the delta arms become loose, allowing the arms to move slightly. It doesn't take much to cause minor imperfections on your prints in the form of artifacts or uneven outer perimeters. Some people have solved the problem by using springs, rubber bands, or flexible hose to hold the arms tight against the joints. Although this technique works, a more permanent solution is to replace the delta arm joints with new or more sturdy hardware.

Lack of Maintenance

Keeping your printer running well can be achieved through proper and regular maintenance. I discuss routine and periodic maintenance tasks in the next chapter. However, sometimes your printer needs maintenance (or even repair) more often. This can manifest as noises from your printer axes movement, including squeaks, clunks, or metallic sounds; all of these are early-warning alarms.[8]

The most common cause of these issues is lack of lubrication. For example, when bearings become dry or the smooth rods or roller channels become dirty, it is possible for friction to increase. Too much friction may cause stepping errors from too much stress on the stepper motors. If your object seems to have inconsistent layer alignment, you should ensure that all axes move freely and that your stepper motors are not overheating. Lubricating the axes, or more specifically, performing maintenance on the axes should return the printer to proper operation.

■ **Tip**   If your bearings start making noise, you've waited too long to lubricate them. If they squeak, groan, rattle, or otherwise make unfriendly metal-on-metal sounds, replace them. See Chapter 7 for more information about maintaining your bearings.

---

[8]Ignore them and you will be sorry. In fact, the sounds will say, "I told you so!" right before they fail.

You can also experience problems if you do not maintain your printer properly. More specifically, if parts wear down or become loose, your printer may start to lose some quality. I have already mentioned loose belts. If you do not adjust your belt-driven mechanisms regularly, they could become loose enough to cause axis shifts.

Another example is loose frame components or loose carriages. A loose frame can cause the entire frame to shift, causing slight shifts in the layers, as viewed vertically. Similarly, a loose carriage can cause minor shifts that manifest as horizontal layer shifts or even vertical layer shifts (uneven layers). This is similar to the Z-wobble problem for Prusa-style printers. If you notice slight variations in how layers are aligned, and the vertical walls are not even, check your frame components for tightness. However, if you add checking the frame for loose components to your maintenance routine, you are not likely to encounter this problem.

In fact, if you follow good maintenance practices, you can normally eliminate maintenance as a cause for a problem. For example, if you adjust and tighten your belts before printing the first print (that day or even that week), you do not have to consider lack of maintenance as a cause for print quality problems. Proper maintenance also permits you to detect and correct potential problems. For example, if you discover a part has cracked or is worn, you can replace it, even if it has yet to cause any print quality issues. Clearly, the importance of proper maintenance has significant benefits, which is why I devote the next chapter to the subject.

Now that you have explored problems related to filament, extrusion, adhesion, and the mechanics of the printer, let's look at the electrical components as sources of printing problems.

Electrical

Should an electrical component fail, it is the same as when a physical part breaks. That is, the mechanism fails to perform properly. For example, if a stepper motor stops turning, the axis will not move. However, electronic components can fail intermittently, which can be much harder to diagnose. An electronics failure, even an intermittent one, does not always manifest as a print quality issue. For example, when an LCD fails, your printer may continue to print.

Before testing any electrical component, you must ensure that you are properly grounded and follow all safety procedures for working with electricity. Most importantly, know where the mains and high power connections are and take care to avoid touching anything when the printer is powered on.

One thing that novices usually forget (and even some of us "mature" enthusiasts) is to check that the power supply is plugged in, the unit is powered on, and the USB cable is attached to both the printer and the computer (if that is how you print). I learned this lesson very early on and always check the cables when diagnosing a problem. If your printer is in a lab or another open area where others can interact with it, someone could have simply turned the thing off or unplugged it.[9] A properly seated plug and a firm click of the switch can fix a host of "dead printer" problems.

I explore a few of the more common problems related to electronics in the following sections. As you will see, there are several categories of problems: stepper motors, wiring, the main electronics board, and other components, such as switches and fans. I also give suggestions on how to diagnose intermittent problems.

---

[9]I once encountered a strange intermittent power problem in a lab. It turns out one of the wall switches also controlled a certain number of power outlets. And, yes, to this day the wall switch has tape over it that says, "Do not turn off!"

Stepper Motors

Stepper motors do most of the work for the printer. When one fails or begins to operate erratically, it has an immediate effect on the print. It can manifest as layer shifts, missed steps, and even complete failure.

There are two things to consider when focusing on the stepper motors as a source of print problems: the stepper motor itself and the stepper motor driver. If the stepper motor driver fails, it normally fails completely and the stepper motor will not turn. In some cases, it may fail so that insufficient voltage is sent to the stepper motor. This can be detected by excessive noise when the motor is turning, or even stuttering of the motor. If you correct the problem by adjusting the voltage, but it occurs again, you should replace the stepper motor driver.

■ **Tip** If your axis is traveling exactly half or perhaps twice the distance it should, you could have incorrectly set the stepper driver jumpers that control microstep settings.

Another symptom of an incorrectly set current is excessive heat. If the motors are getting really warm and the current is set correctly, you could have a stepper motor problem. If the stepper motor is too small, meaning it doesn't have sufficient power to move the mechanism, installing a larger motor can solve the problem. However, if the printer was working correctly, with no or little heat in the motors, it is possible that you need to replace the motor.

GOT FINS?

Resist the temptation to add a fan or heat sink to your stepper motors. Improperly configured stepper drivers (incorrect voltage, settings, or wiring) can cause stepper motors to overheat. Adding a cooling mechanism only delays the inevitable. Stepper motors that run too hot, like most electronics, will eventually fail. By too hot, I mean beyond the specifications of the motor itself. More importantly, you don't want the motor so hot that it weakens the plastic mounting materials.

I once encountered an extruder problem with a failed stepper motor. It was such a unique experience (I thought they would run forever, pending no abuse like too much voltage) that I was able to observe something interesting. The failing stepper motor on the extruder had very little torque. In fact, I could hold the shaft and turn it even when power was applied. From experience, if your stepper motor is very easy to turn and you are seeing skipped steps or layer shift, replace the stepper motor.

In rare cases, you could also notice problems with filament extrusion, where the filament seems to feed at different rates. That is, the filament extrudes sluggishly for short periods, freezes, or even stutters. In this case, you could have a stepper motor that is failing from overheating, or a simple electrical failure. If the stepper motor is overheating, you should check your stepper driver's current settings to make sure it matches the stepper motor.

There is a nifty new tool available from RepRap.me called the Easy Stepper (http://reprap.me/electronic/easy-stepper.html). It's a module designed to allow you to test your stepper motor and stepper driver. Simply plug in your stepper driver and plug in your stepper motor, and then attach a 9V or 12V power supply. Once powered on, you can use the rotary knob to turn the stepper motor. Turning it slowly moves it in a small number of steps; moving it quickly moves the stepper motor by many steps. Figure 6-7 shows the Easy Stepper module. I recommend this tool to anyone with a printer that gets many hours of use.

Figure 6-7. *Easy Stepper*

■ **Caution**   Never disconnect a stepper motor when the printer is powered on. Some stepper drivers can fail when the motor is unplugged while powered on.

Not only can you test your stepper motors and stepper driver, you can also use the Easy Stepper to set the voltage on your stepper driver. Having easy access to the small potentiometer on the stepper driver module is much more convenient than trying to locate the proper pin among your RAMPS and wiring.

If you really want to test your stepper motors, you can use the Easy Stepper to measure the holding torque and strength of each stepper motor. I leave this exercise for your exploration, but I will give you a hint via this web site: http://romanblack.com/stepper.htm.

Wiring

You do not think of wiring as being a part that can fail. However, consider the way the effector on your printer moves. Any mechanism that has wired electronic components that move with the mechanism has one thing in common: a potential stress point for the wiring that powers those components. For delta printers, this includes the hot end, Z-probe, and fans.

Wiring can break in two ways. It can simply break away from its solder or clamp, and it can break internally from stress. A broken wire that has come loose is easy to find and fix. Simply reattach the wiring by removing any bits of broken wiring, and then solder it back into place. If it is a clamped connection, try adding a stress relief to keep the wiring from flexing at the joint.

When building a printer, you should consider the wiring stress points. Failure to ensure that the wire can move freely and not bind or bend in only one area can result in broken wires. More specifically, as the effector moves, the wire is bent back and forth in a small area (the stress point). Over time, this will cause the copper filaments to break. If the flex continues and enough (as in *all*) filaments break,[10] the component will stop working.

---

[10]Always use stranded wire for wiring that needs to flex. Solid core wiring can fail when flexed.

If you encounter a situation where a fan stops, the Z-probe stops working, or the hot endstops heating, it is possible that your wiring is damaged.

Unfortunately, the break in the wire isn't so easy to see, and in some cases you won't be able to see it, but a quick continuity check will tell you if there is a break in the wire. When looking for broken wiring from stress, look at the stress points. You can locate the break by flexing the wire slightly. The place that flexes more easily than others is the location of the break. You may also see some discoloration of the outer insulation or even a slight bulge.

When you find the break, do two things. First, replace the wire, and second, use a stress relief to prevent future breaks. I like to use flexible plastic wire wrap to wrap all wiring that must flex. The wrap gives the wire more strength and is designed to distribute the flex over a larger segment of wire. I also secure both ends of the wrap to ensure that it can flex along the length and not at the attachment points.

Electronics Board

When your electronics board fails, it is normally an all-or-nothing affair. That is, your printer will go dark and you won't be able to communicate with it via USB (or over the network). In some cases, the host board (the Arduino) may still be functioning properly, but the rest of the devices—the hot end, stepper motors, and so forth—do not. In this case, I like to always check the power supply first before considering an electronics board as the source of failure, because sometimes it is a question of power.[11]

For those printers that use a RAMPS or similar setup, you have two boards to test: the Arduino and the RAMPS. If the Arduino board fails, you are likely to encounter a dead printer. However, if the RAMPS fails, you may still be able to communicate with the printer via USB. I had the RAMPS board fail once, and in that case, even the LCD panel, lights, fans, and so forth, all worked; just no motors and no heaters. I originally thought this was a power problem, but as it turns out, my RAMPS board failed (a blown polyfuse).

I have also seen where the electronics board can fail intermittently. This has many possible manifestations—all of them not good. If it is truly random, it may be very inconvenient and fail at the most inopportune times, like in the middle of a print. Or more frustratingly, only with taller or larger objects (most likely related to heat). If you suspect an intermittent problem with your electronics board, try replacing it with a new or known-good component.

Fans

One of my most favorite failures to hate is when a fan fails. Too often I find fans fail with far fewer hours than one would expect. Most fans fail gradually by making a noise: a hum, a buzz, or perhaps a rattle that gets progressively worse. Other times the fan doesn't start immediately or is very slow to get moving.

When fans fail, they can cause cascading problems. For example, if the fan on your electronics fails, the electronics can overheat. Worse is when the always-on fan for the hot end fails. In this case, the hot end will not heat properly and can even overheat, damaging the hot end or its internal components. For this reason, you should always check your fans for proper operation.

■ **Tip** Always check your always-on fans for correct operation before printing.

Whenever you hear a fan begin to make noise, order a replacement and replace it as soon as you can. Fans are relatively inexpensive. I recommend having spares on hand if you use your printer for work or time-sensitive projects.

---

[11]It is plugged in, isn't it?

Another fan-related problem concerns part-cooling fans. Some fans are not capable of running at lower speeds. That is, they do not respond to the pulse-width modulation (PWM) rate. This is normally seen where the fan will not turn at lower percentages in the software. For example, you may not be able to set it below 75%.

This is not good because it means your fan needs to run nearly full speed, which could lead to too much cooling and cause warping and cracking. So what do you do? Figure 6-8 shows a circuit I use to help PWM fans operate more smoothly.

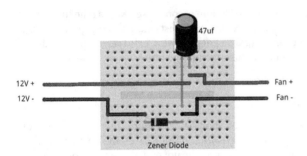

Figure 6-8. *Fan power smoothing circuit*

Notice that I use a 47uF capacitor wired across the positive and negative (the side with the white stripe) and a Zener Diode on the negative side to prevent backflow of current. I have seen similar circuits that use slightly different components, but they work the same way. I normally build this circuit on a generic printed circuit board using the legs of the components for the runs. Figure 6-9 shows a completed example.

Figure 6-9. *Fan power smoothing module*

Notice that the power from the Arduino (RAMPS) is on the left and the leads for the fan are on the right. I mount this in an electronics box and attach it to my frame (`thingiverse.com/thing:708932`). Now I can run my print-cooling fan from 8% to 100%.

Other Components

SD cards are not as robust as other media and can fail. They are also susceptible to corruption from electrostatic discharge (ESD). When an SD card fails, your printer will likely present an error message stating it cannot read the card. Reformatting the card usually fixes the problem, but requires you to reload the card with all the files you want to print.

In rare cases, the print file itself can become corrupt. This normally manifests as a print that fails in some bizarre manner, such as suddenly printing out in limbo land (away from the part), dropping the temperature unexpectedly, or just halting. If this occurs, and you've checked all other potential causes, try using a new SD card to see if it is the card or the file on the card.

In rare cases it is possible for your heating element to fail. In this case, your printer may never reach its target heat and therefore never start printing. Or in the case of the hot end, the print could fail in the middle. If you suspect your printer is not heating properly, use an infrared temperature sensor or a contact sensor to measure the temperature of your heater. If it is not heating properly, replace the heater. If that does not correct the problem, you need to consider that there is either a software issue or an electronics board failure.

Another possible reason for not reaching the correct temperature is that you are using a power supply set to 220VAC when plugged into a 110VAC outlet. This can cause the output of the power supply to be too low (around 10V), and therefore not enough to heat the hot end.

■ **Caution**   Never attempt to use your fingers, palms, or any appendage to test heaters. Some heaters can heat up very quickly to temperatures that can cause severe burns. Always use a sensor to measure heaters.

Software Problems

Fortunately, diagnosing software problems is a lot easier than diagnosing hardware problems.[12] Most times software problems are merely a circumstance of choosing the right values and adjusting them to improve print quality. However, as you will see, you can use software settings to solve or at least reduce the effects of some hardware problems.

In some cases, the software or its settings are not the actual cause of the problem. Thus, I recommend you explore all hardware causes before jumping directly into changing the software settings. For example, if your towers are not calibrated, objects could lift toward one corner of the print bed but not others. Changing the temperature or filament cooling settings via the printer software is not going to fix this hardware problem (but could improve it to a point).

However, there are situations where software settings can be changed to help correct a printing problem. For example, increasing the temperature of the hot end can improve layer adhesion. In other cases, the software can be the cause of the problem. For example, incorrectly specifying the diameter of the filament can cause very poor prints, including extrusion failures.

Like the hardware problems discussed in the last sections, knowing the software settings that can be used to treat and cure print quality issues can help you fine-tune your software so that you can get the most out of your printer.

Remember that the software you use to prepare objects for printing is CAM software and the software you use to control your printer is the printer controller. In this section, I discuss the more modern implementation of 3D printing software that includes CAM, the printer controller, and other features. Such examples include MatterControl and Simplify3D. For brevity, I simply refer to this as printer software.

---

[12]But can be just as frustrating if you get it wrong.

The CAM feature is responsible for taking input in the form of printer configuration settings such as filament size, temperature settings, and so forth, and an object file (.stl) to form a file that contains commands to direct the printer. This file is a .gcode file that is either read from an SD card or sent to the printer directly via the printer software from the computer or MatterControl Touch tablet.

Clearly, if there are any printer settings in the software (e.g., the slicer settings) that do not match your printer hardware, the resulting file will not match your printer. Printing a file with incorrect printer or slicing settings results in improperly printed objects. In the most extreme case, this means the printing fails. At the least, it means one of several print quality issues.

Even if the settings are valid and match your printer hardware, you can use the software to change certain parameters to help combat some of the more common printing problems. That is, objects that print poorly can sometimes be improved with certain changes. In similar fashion, you can use the slicer settings to help combat problems such as adhesion.

I discuss each of these areas in the following sections, with examples of how the software can be changed and screenshots of some of the more obscure settings. Let's begin with the settings that you can change in the software to correct printing problems.

First-Layer Adhesion

Adhesion problems most often occur between the first layer and the print surface. When the print pulls away from the print surface, it is called *lifting*. Adhesion problems can also occur between other layers of the object. Poor layer adhesion at higher layers is sometimes called *cracking* or *warping*.

Lifting can be controlled in a number of ways. The last section presented several possible causes of lifting related to hardware. You also saw how the print surface treatment can affect lifting. However, there is another element to consider: controlling the temperature of the heated print bed.

If your printer has a heated print bed, you should consider using it when you are printing objects. While a heated print bed is required for ABS, it is often considered optional for PLA and other filaments. The generally accepted heated print temperature for ABS is around 110 degrees Celsius and PLA is around 60 degrees Celsius.

Remember, the temperature settings are stored in the print file. Setting these values on your printer or through a printer controller application is possible, but most printers will override these settings as soon as the codes are read from the file. The following is a sample command (or code) to set the temperature:

```
M190 S60 ; wait for bed temperature to be reached
```

SOME SOFTWARE SETTINGS ARE PRINTER AND FILAMENT SPECIFIC

One of the common mistakes for those who print with both ABS and PLA is to attempt to print a file that was generated for PLA with ABS. In this case, the heated bed is too cold and lifting is much more likely to occur. The temperature for the hot end is also likely to be wrong, so you can also risk extrusion problems. On the other hand, if you attempt to print a file sliced for ABS with PLA, the print bed will be too high, which can cause the print to sag and print very poorly. Since the hot end temperature for ABS is normally higher, you could also encounter burning smells from the extruder.

If the print bed is too cold, the first few layers could cool too quickly, causing the layers to contract and pull the object away from the print bed, which happens more often with ABS. In this case, it isn't a matter of having a properly prepared print surface; rather it is a case of not enough heat stored in the layers to ensure a slower and more even cooling of the object layers.

If lifting is severe enough, it can even cause the object to come into contact with the hot end. This can cause the entire object to get knocked off the print bed, ruining the print. However, if it has lifted that much already, it is likely to get worse. Sadly, if you are not watching your printer, this can result in a partially printed object and a nesting of filament as the printer happily continues to extrude filament into the air. If the loose filament comes into contact with the hot end, it can melt and stick to places you don't want it to. Not only does this result in a big mess, it also wastes a lot of filament.

If you are experiencing lifting, check the temperature of your heated print bed. If it is lower than the preceding estimates, try raising it 5 degrees, and then check the results on your next print. In rare cases, I've found that lowering the temperature 5 degrees can help print quality in other ways. For example, having the print bed too hot can cause the object to retain too much heat, making it harder to print extreme overhangs. In this case, the overhang layers curl at the end, giving the overhand a stair-step look rather than a smooth transition. If you are printing with your print bed in excess of 110 degrees, consider lowering it 5 degrees at a time until you have the lowest setting possible that does not cause (or make worse) lifting.

So how do you set or change the heated print bed temperature? Recall from earlier chapters that the bed temperature can be set in the software in the filament settings. An example from MatterControl is shown in Figure 6-10. Notice in these figures that you can also set the hot-end (extruder) temperature as well as retraction settings (which can help eliminate blobs) on these screens.

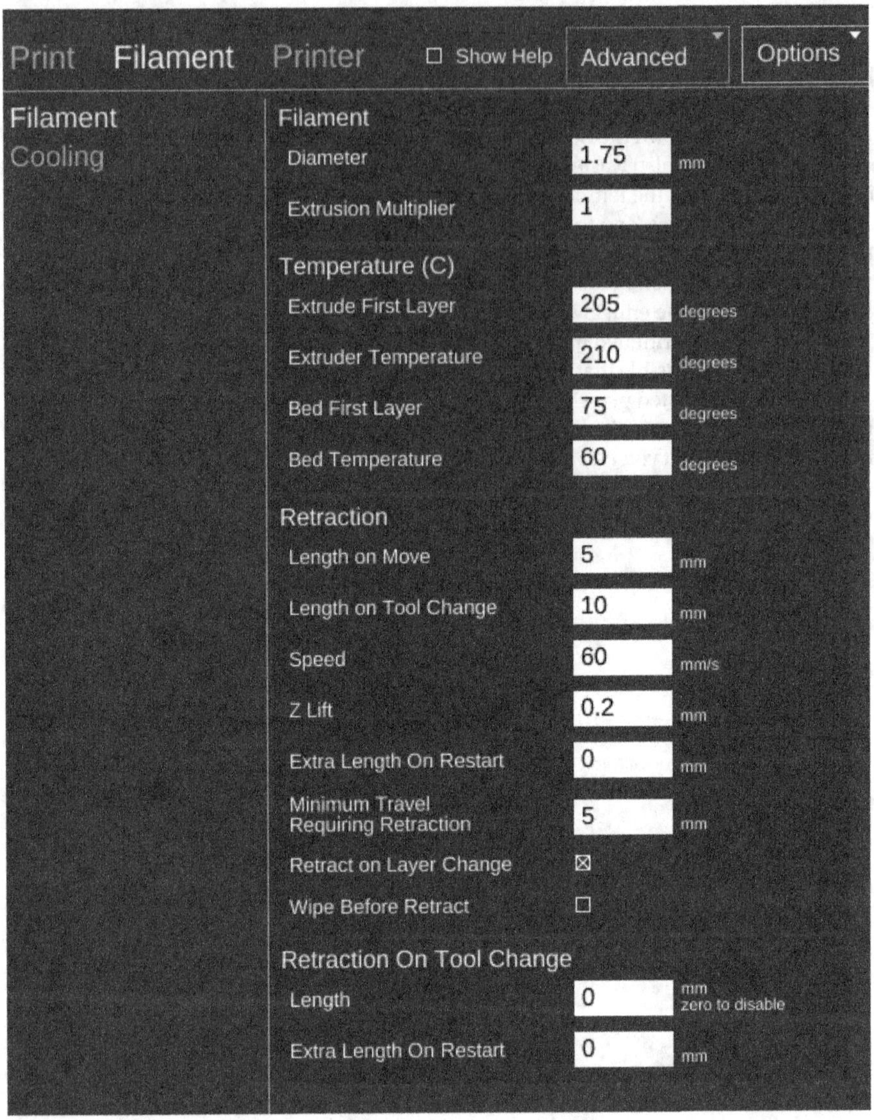

Figure 6-10. *Temperature settings in MatterControl (Slic3r engine)*

Another contributor to lifting is when the object has too small a surface area making contact with the print surface. If the object has small protrusion or thin areas, you may not have enough filament in the first layer to make a strong bond with the print surface.

The best way to treat this problem is to enhance the object with a brim. Recall that a brim is additional loops of filament laid down around the perimeter of the object, which increases the surface area. Figure 6-11 shows the brim settings on the Skirt and Raft dialog in MatterControl (with the Slic3r engine selected).

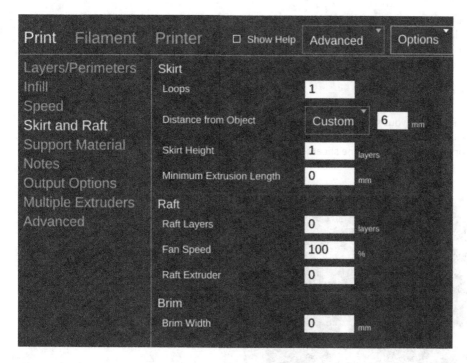

Figure 6-11. *Setting a brim in MatterControl (Slic3r engine)*

Another software-based tool allows you to print your object on a raft. Recall that a raft is several layers of filament laid down on the print surface to form a platform (raft) for the object to rest on. The raft has a larger surface area and can help prevent lifting on small objects and objects with thin areas. You can also turn on the raft in MatterControl on the Skirt and Raft screen (see Figure 6-11). If you turn on the raft, the raft appears as a platform in the preview.

A less frequently used heated print bed technique to combat first-layer adhesion is to set the first layer temperature higher than upper layers. If you use the Slic3r option, you set this in the filament settings (Extrude First Layer), as shown in Figure 6-10 . This setting allows you to set the first-layer temperature high enough to treat your lifting problem, and to set the other layers lower to retain heat in the object and to control cooling (and prevent warping and cracking).

Aside from heated print bed temperature, you can also treat lifting problems by slowing the print speed for the first layer. You can control this easily in MatterControl using the First Layer Speed setting in the Speed section on the Print Settings dialog. You can use a speed in millimeters per second or a percentage of the default speed (enter the value with a percent sign). For example, the value 25% sets the first layer speed to 25 percent of the default speed.

Slowing the print speed can improve first-layer adhesion by allowing the filament more time to bond to the print surface. If you notice filament peeling away from the print surface, or small perimeters not sticking well, slowing the print speed of the first layer can help you avoid these problems.

Another way to combat lifting is to use anchors (also called *mouse ears* or *lily pads*). These are normally small round discs placed on each corner or protrusion of the object to increase the surface area around the corner without increasing it everywhere, like a brim would do. You can create anchors however you like and add them to your slicer platter when slicing. The downside is that these anchors must be cut away from the final part.

Creating anchors is easy. Just use OpenSCAD to create a disc about 0.5mm thick (or two layers, depending on your layer thickness). Some prefer to make their anchors three or four layers thick for really strong bonds. However, the thicker the anchor, the harder it is to cut away. The following is the code for creating a disc-shaped anchor:

```
cylinder(h=0.5,r=5);
```

To use the anchors, open your slicer and place the object on the platter. Then add as many anchors as you need and place them on the corners, as shown in Figure 6-12 (see arrows). Notice that I placed the anchors on each corner of the object. Some slicers allow you to combine the anchors and your object into a single part.

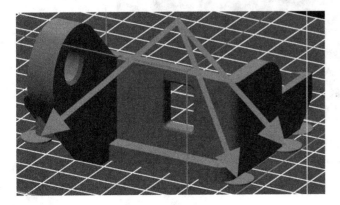

Figure 6-12. *Use anchors to combat lifting*

Layer Adhesion

Closely related to first-layer adhesion are print quality issues that occur at higher layers. These are often layer adhesion problems that are treated in similar fashion as lifting. The layer adhesion problems discussed here include warping, splitting, and sagging.

All of these problems can be treated by changing the temperature of the print bed and hot end. However, they are caused by filament cooling unevenly. Thus, like adhesion, you should fix any hardware problems before experimenting with temperature as a means to fix these print quality issues.

■ **Caution**   Never set the temperature higher than the maximum safe settings of your filament and hot end. High temperature can damage the internal parts of your hot end.

In most cases, you will raise the temperature of the hot end 5 degrees at a time, and then check the results. In rare cases, you could lower the temperature of the hot end 5 degrees at a time. Before changing your hot end temperature, be sure that you are familiar with the hot end features and capabilities. Never set the hot end higher than its maximum setting.

FILAMENT TEMPERATURE LIMITATIONS

When the temperature is too low, extrusion failure is likely. However, raising the temperature of the hot end can improve adhesion and extrusion. But you can go too far. If the temperature is too high, you will see the filament oozing from the hot end, or worse, it could burn.[13] Some ooze is OK, but the filament should not ooze more than a slight seeping over a few minutes. If it continues to ooze from the nozzle, you may want to lower the temperature.

Warping

Warping is when the higher layers of an object cool more quickly than the lower layers. When this happens, there may be too high a temperature in the object. Lowering the temperature of the print bed can help combat warping. If you are printing with PLA and using a fan, you may want to slow the fan speed to force less air over the object. Too much air can cause the higher layers to cool more quickly than the lower layers.

Warping can also occur on areas with overhang, which is a portion of the object that protrudes from the base at a low angle. Overhangs can be hard to print because they tend to cool much more quickly and can warp at the ends of each layer. When this occurs, you cannot do much about it while the object is printing. Most times the object is still usable because the hot end tends to push out the thin layers on the next pass. However, the quality of that portion of the object will suffer.

The best way to treat overhangs is to use *supports*. Supports are thin layers of filament extruded to form a scaffold to support the object during printing. You can turn on supports in the software, as shown in Figure 6-13.

---

[13]Burning smells from the hot end are always bad. Turn off the heaters and allow the hot end to cool before retrying your print.

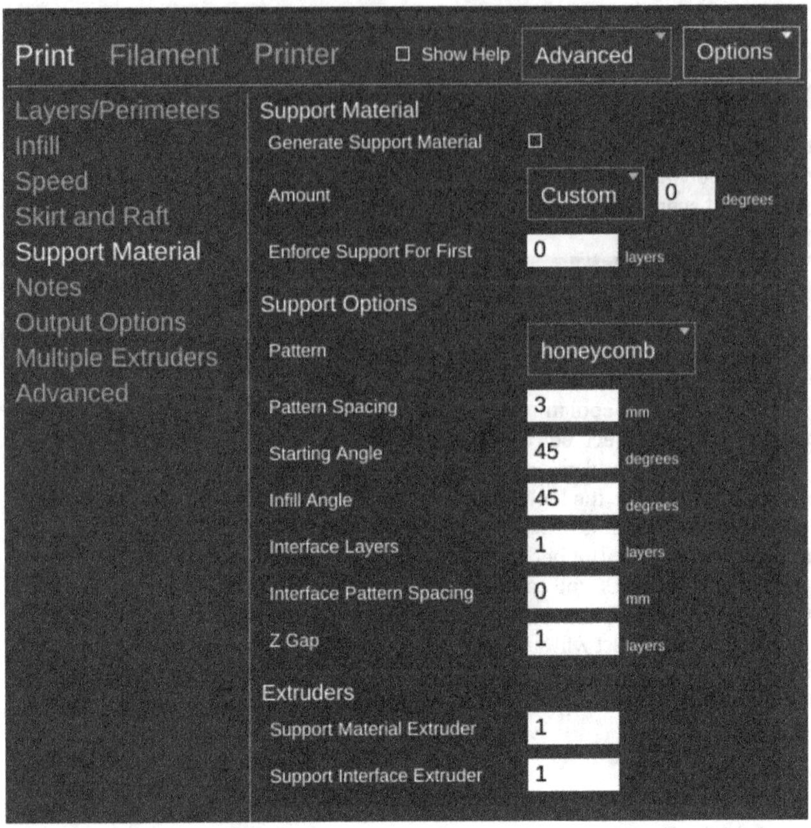

Figure 6-13. *Enabling supports in MatterControl*

Notice that there are a lot of settings here that you can use. To turn on support, click the Generate Support Material checkbox. You can change the orientation of the support material (great for round objects), change the space, and more.

Using supports effectively creates a false portion of the object that allows thin layers to be printed with greatly reduced warping. These supports are very thin and can be easily removed from the printed object by breaking them away, and then trimming with a hobby knife. Simplify3D allows you to create custom supports, which can help greatly by allowing you to target only a few areas instead of every area.

■ **Tip**   Be sure that you are not accidentally turning off the print bed at higher levels. If you neglected to turn on the heated print bed for higher levels, this could cause warping, as described here.

Splitting

Splitting (sometimes called *cracking*) is similar to warping; however, splitting occurs when the lower layers of the object cool faster than the upper layers. This can cause one or more layers of the object to lose adhesion, and, well, split the object. Figure 6-14 shows an object that has split (see arrows).

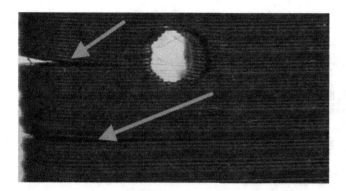

Figure 6-14. *Splitting example*

Splitting is often caused by drafts. Eliminating drafts can help considerably. However, you can also treat splitting by ensuring that your heated print bed is at the proper temperature and that the hot end temperature is set correctly. In some cases, slowing the print speed can also treat splitting. Slower speeds tend to improve the layer bonds. Again, the problem occurs when the object cools much faster than the newest layers. Raising the heated print bed by 5 degrees may help.

Poor layer adhesion may also be caused by insufficient extrusion width compared to layer height. For example, when using a layer height of 0.2mm, the extrusion width should be at least 0.35mm or more (but no more than 0.4mm). Some 3D printing software sets extrusion width automatically, and most allow you to set the value manually.

When objects split like the one shown in Figure 6-14, chances are the split or crack isn't isolated to those areas where the split is visible. I have seen objects that have had a small split in one area fail from layer-shearing forces (stress placed on the object parallel to the layers). This revealed that the object had poor layer adhesion throughout. In fact, when I removed the object and applied layer-shearing force, it broke in other places. Thus, when you encounter splitting or cracks in your prints, treat the problem and reprint the object.

There is a way to fix parts that split if the split is not too deep or long and only if the part is still usable. In this case, it is normally a spilt along the outer layers and not through the entire part. The best way I've found to repair splits in ABS is to use those discarded wipes and perimeter sweeps (skirts and brims). Simply soak them in a bit of acetone and lay them in the split, and then brush acetone over that. After the acetone evaporates, the part surface is solid again. It takes a bit of practice, but it is worth it. You can even sand the part and brush on some more acetone to hide the sanding.

However, you can also use a technique called *plastic welding* to repair splits. You can use this method for splits in ABS or PLA. Just take a bit of filament and insert it into a Dremel (rotary hobby) tool, as shown in Figure 6-15. Be sure to straighten the filament as much as possible.

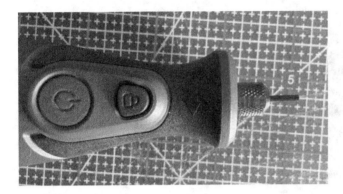

Figure 6-15. *Preparing Dremel for plastic welding*

Notice that I leave only about 15mm of filament extending from the tool. Next, run the tool on medium speed and press the spinning filament into the split. Move along at a steady pace and you will see the plastic melt in place—like a weld! Figure 6-16 shows an example of two splits repaired with this technique. It takes a bit of practice, but it can fix an otherwise ruined part quickly without toxic fumes.

Figure 6-16. *Plastic welding example*

Sagging

Sagging occurs in one of two ways: when bridging large gaps and when the object is too hot. Bridging small gaps is not usually a problem. Indeed, the slicer has accommodations for that. For example, a small hole or nut trap can be covered with a layer of filament without too much of a problem. However, large areas or areas without any form of support can be a problem for some printers.

If the gap is really big—more than a few centimeters—the slicer may not be able to compensate; the only solutions are to use supports in the form of the slicer option or to use artificial supports (parts designed into the object itself).

If the sagging is limited to a single layer under the gap or bridge, you can repair the sag. For PLA, simply use a hot air gun to heat the sagging filament and press it into the object. Be careful not to get it too hot because it can warp the object. You will not be able to get the filament hot enough to reform the layer bonds, but at least you won't have to cut away the filament or toss the object.

For ABS, use a lint-free rag soaked with acetone and rub it on the sagging filaments until they become soft, and then press them into the object. Within a few moments the acetone will evaporate, and the object will be repaired and likely just as strong as if it had not sagged.

I often combat sagging for large areas by incorporating support into the design. This is something you will have to do in the CAD software (OpenSCAD). You cannot use supports because supports are printed the entire length of the object, making it a pain to clean and wasting a lot of filament. Figure 6-17 shows a rendering of an air dam I use to redirect air away from the printer.

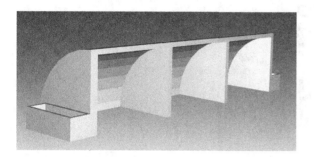

Figure 6-17. *Designing supports into your models*

If your heated print bed is too hot, it can cause the object to remain soft and sag. That is, the filament does not cool enough to become firm enough to support the weight of the layers above. When this occurs, lower the heated print bed temperature by 5 degrees and try the print again. If the sagging is severe, you may want to lower the temperature by 10 degrees at a time.

When printing with PLA, sagging can also be treated by increasing the fan speed on higher layers. This will ensure that the filament that is used to bridge the gap is cooled faster, and thus can keep its shape. You can also increase the number of shells, or in some slicing applications, increase the number of top layers. But these techniques only work if the gap is at the top of the object.

It can help to change the print speed for printing gaps (bridges). If the print speed is increased, it will reduce the chances of the bridge drooping, but may increase the likelihood that it will break.

Lastly, printing supports is the best way to avoid sagging in bridges and gaps.

Scaling

If your object prints well but it isn't the right size (it's too big or too small), you may be able to solve the problem by using a slicing feature called *scaling*. Scaling allows you to shrink or enlarge the object by a certain percentage. Normally scaling is uniform. That is, you can change the size of one axis and the other two will scale accordingly. This can be very helpful if the object is just slightly off on one axis or if you want to print interesting distortions of objects.

Orientation

Recall from the discussion about first-layer adhesion that I mentioned surface area as a potential cause of lifting. If your object has a larger surface area on another plane (side), you can use the slicer feature called *orientation* (sometimes called *rotation*) to reorient the object on the print bed.

■ **Tip**   If you design the object yourself, it is best to set the orientation before you export the file.

For example, suppose you have designed the dollhouse table shown in Figure 6-18. It is a simple design and presented in the orientation that you envisioned it—right-side up.

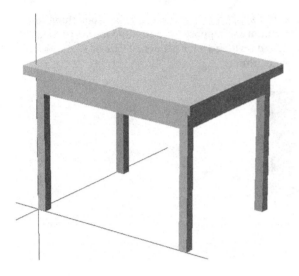

Figure 6-18. *Dollhouse table*

Notice the legs of the table. They're small and only a fraction of the object touches the print surface. Not only that, but there is a large area that will have to be bridged (the table top). You could add supports to ensure that the gap doesn't sag; however, if you flip the object over, you have a much larger surface area and the small bits (legs) are pointing up. Figure 6-19 shows the reoriented object.

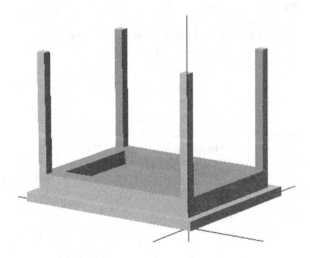

Figure 6-19. *Dollhouse table reoriented*

Most printer software allows you to rotate objects on the build plate. For example, in MatterControl, you select the object, click Edit, and use the menu on the right to change rotation, scaling, and more. Figure 6-20 shows the options available.

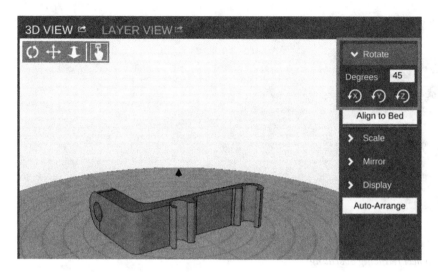

Figure 6-20. *Rotating objects in MatterControl*

Orientation can also be used to eliminate bridging and to help prevent warping. Figure 6-21 shows an object that can be printed easily, and in most cases, well. However, you may experience some sagging and even warping on the overhang (the rounded portion). If you reorient the object as shown in Figure 6-22, you not only increase the surface area but also eliminate the overhang and its possible issues.

Figure 6-21. *Object with overhang*

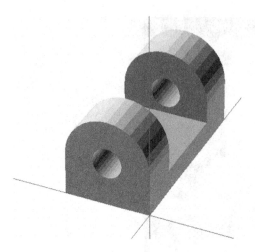

Figure 6-22. *Reoriented object reducing overhang*

Another example of how orientation can help is with printing supports. Consider the object in Figure 6-21. Sometimes designers want to orient curved sides in the Z axis because they can print slightly better that way. In this case, the object would appear as shown in Figure 6-23. To print this object in this orientation, you have to use supports because there is no way to print an overhang that is parallel to the print bed without them.

Figure 6-23. *Reoriented object with overhang requiring support*

However, you should still consider this option if you need to use it. In fact, one reason you might want to reorient an object in this manner is for shearing. The layers in the object in Figure 6-23 run perpendicular to the layers of the object in Figure 6-22. If you need to consider shearing forces, you may want to reorient your object to ensure that the layers run perpendicular to the shearing force.

For example, if the object in Figure 6-22 is going to be used as an anchor for supporting a pulley or as an idler bearing for a belt-driven mechanism, and thus the forces will be pulling away from the base, this orientation could be slightly stronger than the orientation of the object in Figure 6-22. This is because the layers run perpendicular to the shearing force in Figure 6-23, but parallel in Figure 6-22. Think of it this way: it is easier to break layer bonds than it is to break filament.

When creating your own objects, or printing objects made by others, check the orientation of the object before printing it. Consider not only how much surface area is needed for a strong first-layer bond, but also for reducing overhangs and gaps (bridges). In some cases, shearing force may determine how you orient the object. Better still, you can avoid using supports—and thereby reduce sagging!

Filament and Extrusion

In general, problems with filament and extrusion can be difficult to diagnose. This is because of the slight variations that exist among filament. Recall our discussion about filament and how it can vary in size and temperature settings. PLA does not have the same properties as ABS. In some cases, even the same type filament, but of different colors, can have different heating properties.

The most common problems are poor extrusion, oozing of the filament from the nozzle, and layer inconsistencies. All of these can be controlled, or at least reduced, with key settings in the slicer. I discuss each in more detail in the following sections.

Poor Extrusion

If your slicer is set up to match the settings of your printer and the filament you are using, extrusion should occur normally without much issue. Hardware-related issues are still a concern (obstructions, blocked nozzle, etc.), but once those issues are solved or eliminated, you should be fine. However, if your slicer settings do not match your filament, you can encounter poor extrusion.

The most common issue is filament that extrudes too much or too little. This is caused by using the incorrect filament diameter in your software (slicer). Figure 6-24 shows the filament settings in MatterControl.

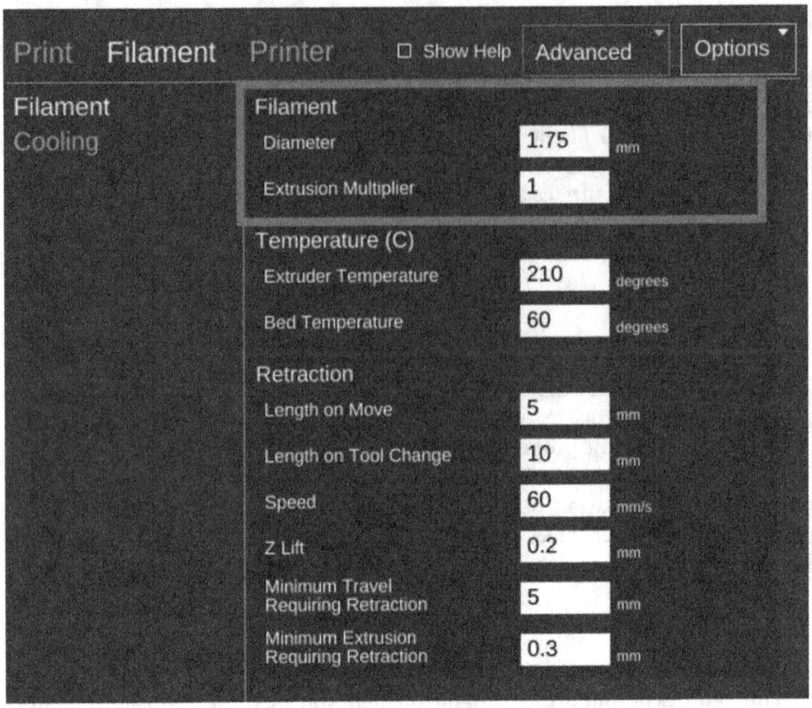

Figure 6-24. *Filament settings in MatterControl*

■ **Tip** Be sure to measure your filament each time you prepare an object for printing or change filament.

If you enter a value that is too large, the extruder may not extrude enough filament. In this case, the layer adhesion may suffer and the part may be easier to break with shearing force. In the case where you use a setting that is too low, the filament may clump, or strings (sometimes called *threads*) may appear as the hot end moves from one place to another. If you see a lot of stringing, check your slicer for the proper setting for the filament diameter.

Another cause of poor extrusion is using the wrong settings for your hot end temperature. Too high a setting can cause the filament to extrude more easily, which also causes clumping and stringing. Too low and the filament may not extrude properly. Signs of the wrong temperature can manifest as a slipping or chattering extruder drive pulley. You may also see cases where the filament comes out in spurts or with short sections of thinner filament. In other cases, you may see the filament appearing as dots. If the filament is not extruding in a clean line, you likely are experiencing problems with hot end temperature.

In the extreme, this problem can cause the filament to strip and extrusion to stop. I upgraded one of my printers recently with a really nice set of milled aluminum extruder hardware, only to discover that the spring I used was just a wee bit too stiff. This caused the stepper motor to strip on only one of several spools of filament. The filament was a bit softer than the other spools. I fixed the problem temporarily by increasing the hot end temperature. The correct resolution was to replace the spring.

If your filament seems to clump or string among the part, reduce the hot end temperature by 5 degrees and try the print again. If it gets better, try another 5 degrees until you find the correct setting for that filament. Similarly, if your filament does not extrude well and there are no obstructions or blockages in the hot end or nozzle, increase the hot end temperature by 5 degrees at a time until the filament extrudes well.

When I encounter situations where I know it is a slicer setting, especially with hot end temperatures, I use a printer controller application to test extrusion by heating the hot end to the new value and extruding between 30mm and 100mm of filament. You can tell everything is going well by observing the extruder and the filament as it exits the nozzle. If it flows well and the extruder turns without stopping, stuttering, or any noise of stripping, I then retry my print. This saves me a lot of filament and doesn't ruin as many parts. Fortunately, you only have to do this when you use new filament or filament from a different vendor.

Oozing

One of the side effects of having the hot end set to the optimal temperature for extrusion is oozing. If the printer sits idle with the hot end heated to temperature, you can observe a small amount of filament oozing from the nozzle. This is normal, so long as it isn't more than a few millimeters. And depending on how long your printer will be idle, this should not be a problem. The filament that oozed out will be expelled when the printer does its purge around the object.[14]

■ **Tip**   You can also treat oozing by doing a manual purge prior to starting the print. Just bring your hot end to temperature and extrude about 10mm–30mm of filament using ESD tweezers to remove it.

However, if you are experiencing a lot of ooze, you may have your hot end set too high. Too much oozing can transfer to the object in the form of extraneous bits of filament, rounded corners that should be sharper, and odd deposits of filament in places where the hot end has moved from one location to another. This is normally not the thin strands, strings, or threads like you see with a hot end that is a little too hot. In this case, the hot end is much hotter than necessary. If this happens, reduce the hot end temperature by 5 degrees at a time until the oozing slows to only a small amount. If your filament is oozing more than 5mm to 10mm in a few seconds, your hot end is too hot.

It should be noted that some hot ends have a larger heat chamber or are designed in such a way that oozing is more prevalent. For hot ends like this, the slicer application can be helpful in controlling the effects of oozing. MatterControl has a feature that can help: retraction. Figure 6-25 shows the retraction settings in MatterControl. This is the same location that you enter the nozzle size to match your printer.

---

[14]Sometimes called a *skirt*.

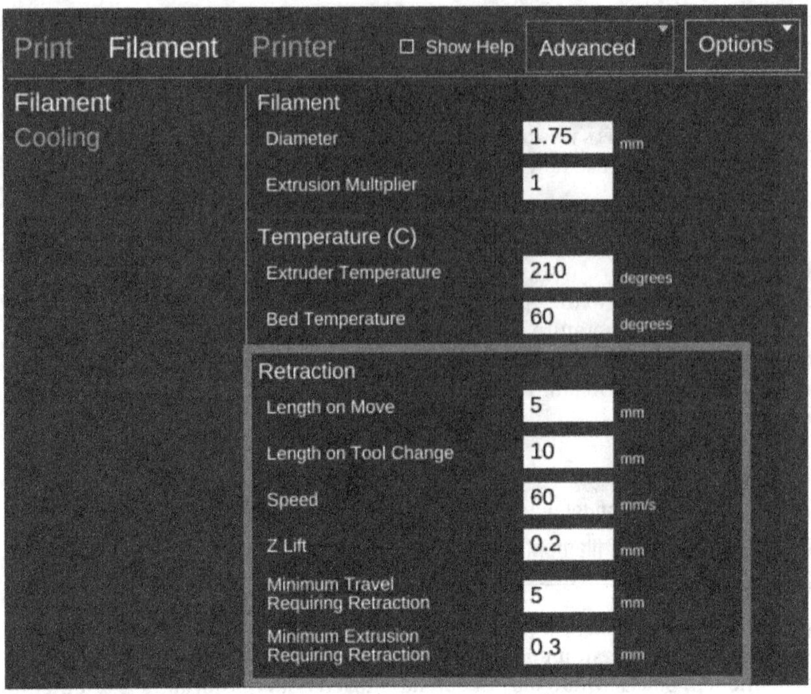

Figure 6-25. *Treating oozing with retraction in MatterControl*

Notice the Retraction section. Here you can use settings to retract a certain amount of filament, for lifting of the Z axis, to set speed, and more. The two most common options to set are lift and retraction length. As you can see in the example, I have set retraction to 5mm and a lift of 0.2mm. This will cause the extruder to turn backward for 5mm, sucking in the filament.

The lift is primarily used to prevent the nozzle from striking areas of the print that may be higher than the current Z position. Lifting also gives the filament a chance to break away from the layer, and thereby reduce stringing from the retraction. Use retraction if your hot end oozes a bit more than you'd like or if there is significant stringing (small threads stretching across movements without extrusion) but your hot end temperature settings are correct.

NOT ALL FILAMENT IS CREATED EQUAL

As I mentioned in earlier discussions about filament types and heat characteristics, filament can vary. In fact, different colors and even different vendors of the same type (PLA, ABS, etc.) can have different heating properties and even vary in diameter. Once you zero in the hot end settings that work best for the filament, make a note of these settings and the diameter on the spool itself. I like to use a sticky label to write down the optimal values. This can help you remember the finer details if you have more than a couple of spools or you do not use a spool for some time. You really don't want to go through all the experimentation again, do you?

PLA Layer Inconsistencies

One of the hardest things to diagnose are inconsistencies that appear among the layers of the print. These can manifest as missing portions of a layer or filament run, gaps in the print layer, extra filament deposited in holes, and poorly formed objects.

The most common cause for some of these inconsistencies is insufficient cooling on PLA prints. You should always use a cooling fan that directs air onto the top layers of the object. This will ensure that the layer cools fast enough to make a good bond and a firm and consistent layer. Having too much air flowing over the layer can cause the layer to deform, portions of the filament run to come loose, and poor layer adhesion in general. If this occurs, check the speed of your fan in the slicer and use the automatic settings. These are generally acceptable and optimized for properly cooling PLA. Figure 6-26 shows the cooling settings in MatterControl.

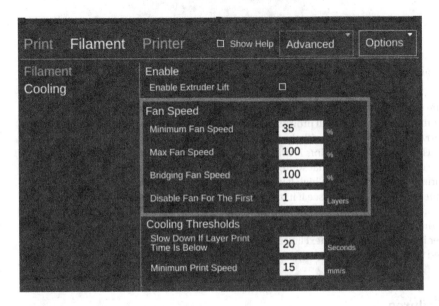

Figure 6-26. *Cooling settings in MatterControl*

Notice that you can choose to turn the fan on at higher layers. I recommend leaving the fan off for at least the first couple of layers. Some software, like Simplify3D allows you to set the fan speed for different layers. That is, you can set a different speed for any layer you want. Figure 6-27 shows an example of setting fan speed for different layers in Simplify3D.

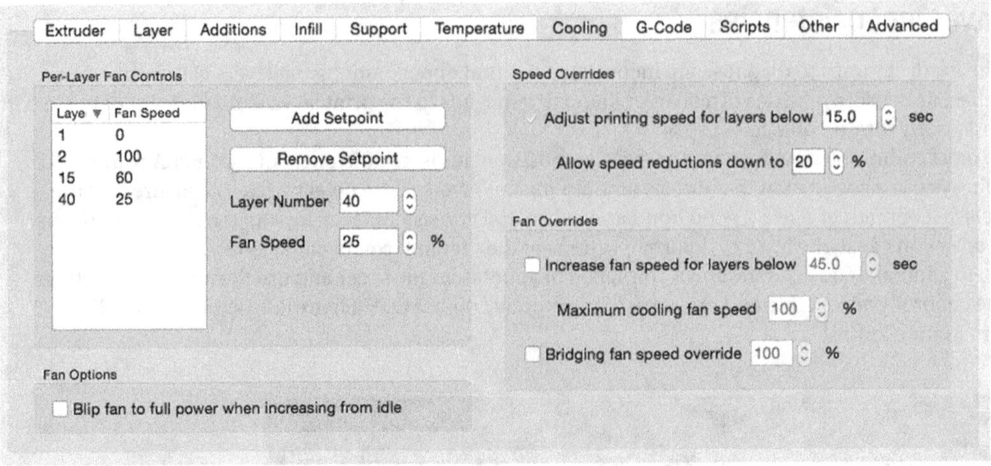

Figure 6-27. Setting fan speeds per layer segments in Simplify3D

For some objects, the print speed may contribute to inconsistent prints. I have seen this in tall objects with intricate portions at the higher levels (small protrusions, small holes, tall, thin columns, etc.). Slowing the print speed can improve quality for objects with these features.

Another possible cause for inconsistent prints is using a layer height that is too coarse for your hardware. Recall from the calibration chapter that some layer heights can introduce errors in the layer calculations. If you are printing an object with a high layer height, try using a lower value and set your extrusion width to 1.5 times normal or more to see if it improves consistency. Do not exceed 2 times the size of your nozzle for extrusion width values.

Lastly, it is possible that when printing large objects (particularly those printed with PLA) can cool too much before the layer is complete and the next layer is applied. To combat this issue, increase the temperature of the heated print bed, slow the fan, or use an enclosure to ensure that more heat remains in the object at lower levels.

Communication Failures

If you are printing from your computer, you can sometimes encounter problems when your computer goes to sleep. In fact, depending on your computer's energy settings, your computer could go to sleep and suspend all applications.

When that happens, your print will most likely be ruined. This is because the printer will be waiting for the computer to send more data. If the printer waits too long, the heat built up in the object could dissipate, increasing the risk of warping and splitting. Sometimes awakening your printer will not harm the print. Regardless, if you have a large file to print, you should either transfer it to SD and print it directly from the printer, or turn off your energy-saving settings while you print (screen savers are generally OK).

It is also possible that a USB cable could be bad or its connector loose or faulty. Unshielded cables are susceptible to EMI, which can cause intermittent communication failures. A new cable may fix the problem, but printing from the SD card will avoid risks of using a bad cable.

In the rare event your printer controller software freezes or goes wonky,[15] you may have little choice but to terminate the application and restart your print. Once again, if you want to print from your computer, be sure that you are using the latest and most stable release of your printer controller software.

Axis Crashes

Some very common, accidental problems for those new to delta printers concerns crashing the hot end into the print bed, or attempting to position the effector and either it or the delta arms collide with the frame or axis mechanical bits.[16] These types of accidents can occur when you have started your printer for the first time but have not homed the printer. When this happens, you then use the printer controller software (or the LCD panel) to move the axis until the crash occurs.

Failing to home the axes means the printer can consider its current location as (0,0,0). Moving the effector in one direction could mean it attempts to travel farther than physically possible, resulting in the delta mechanical bits coming into contact with the frame or other parts of the printer. This is bad, and you should avoid it by always ensuring that you home all axes before trying to move (jog) any axis. You can cover the print surface with a piece of cardboard or similar material to protect it from head crashes.

Also consider that if you reset your printer (for whatever reason) while it is printing, it can also lose its home orientation, and then it must be rehomed before resuming printing or printing another object.

Firmware Problems

The firmware isn't normally something that has issues. This is most fortunate because you rely on the firmware working correctly. If it were to fail, so too would almost every feature of the printer! However, there are some cases where the firmware can be a source of problems.

First and foremost is when you upgrade your printer. If you modify your printer with a new LCD panel, hot end, or extruder, you need to change the firmware. In each case, you may have to enable some feature, change the values for offsets or Z-height, or change the characteristics of the steps per millimeter. In most cases, upgrades that change or add hardware that is different from your original configuration may require changes to the firmware. You should always modify the firmware settings to correspond to the exact hardware.

Another possibility concerns problems encountered after repairs. If you changed the electronics or repaired them in some way, you may inadvertently erase the firmware settings in nonvolatile memory. If you made any changes by way of a G-code, you could lose those settings when the nonvolatile memory is erased. If you repair your printer and it suddenly acts strangely, especially components you did not modify, try reloading the firmware with the correct settings.

Finally, and I've only seen this a couple of times, it is possible for the firmware to become corrupt. This can occur from an ESD, corrupt EEPROM (the location where the firmware is stored), or a failed firmware upgrade. If this happens, your printer will either not work at all or work very strangely (e.g., errors on the LCD or no axis movement). If you suspect your firmware is corrupt, however unlikely, you can always reload—but only do this as a last resort. That is, if you made changes to your firmware by modifying EEPROM settings, and you did not make the same changes in your firmware code, reloading the firmware will erase (reset) all of these settings.

---

[15]Not to be confused with *hinky*, which is more serious.
[16]You should strive to avoid this. Even a mild collision can damage the delta mechanical parts; colliding with the print surface can damage nozzles made from softer metal like brass.

Summary

Hardware problems can cause a host of print quality issues. As you have seen, finding the cause of the problem requires you to consider several possibilities, because most problems can be caused by several different sources.

Similarly, software changes can help you solve a number of problems—from controlling the temperature of the hot end or print bed to changing the size of the object (scaling). Make sure that your printer controller software is stable, or in the case of upgrades, make sure that your firmware settings are changed to match the new hardware; this can solve more specific problems.

In this chapter, I presented some basic best practices for troubleshooting problems. I also discussed a host of hardware and software problems that you could encounter. While it is my hope that you never encounter any of these problems, knowing what could fail is a key to being able to detect and repair the problem.

Furthermore, knowing what can cause problems and how to fix them helps you get your printer going again when it breaks or when your print quality suffers. You can prevent some problems from occurring by keeping your printer adjusted, cleaned, and lubricated.

In the next chapter, you explore another seldom practiced task and skill: maintenance. Failing to keep your printer maintained eventually results in print quality issues, and if neglected long enough, complete failure of your printer. It is not unusual for me to find a used printer that the owner has chosen to sell because it started printing poorly; but most problems can be solved with simple maintenance and adjustments.

CHAPTER 7

■ ■ ■

Delta Printer Maintenance

Owning a delta printer can be a lot of fun. You should take pride when using your printer to create things for your household, family, and friends. Whether you are creating new gadgets or gifts, making parts to fix things around the house, the enjoyment factor is quite high. However, the enjoyment will fade a bit if your printer starts underperforming or breaking. Fortunately, many common failures and problems can be reduced, and in some cases eliminated if you perform a few key maintenance tasks.

Delta printers are a bit more robust than some of the older RepRap Cartesian designs due, in part, to the frame design and axes orientation. In fact, I've found I have to maintain my delta printers far less than my Cartesian printers, some of which are professional-grade, popular brands.

It also helps that, in general, delta printers have fewer parts that need attention. For example, most delta printers do not have to be trammed periodically (also called *leveling the print bed*). This is because Cartesian printers often have an axis that uses multiple lifting mechanisms that can become askew (not parallel with another axis), whereas delta printers use a bed that is fixed to the frame. To tram the print bed on a Cartesian printer, one has to use a set of adjustment screws to make the print bed level with the axes—an often-neglected task that can make lifting a nightmare.

While delta printers do not have to have their print beds trammed,[1] there are a number of other maintenance tasks that you should be prepared to execute over time. That is, keeping your printer running well requires vigilance and the judicious application of proper maintenance. You have to learn to pay attention to the printer mechanicals (sights and sounds) and understand the tasks needed to keep things running properly. Even the best-calibrated printer will eventually have problems if you never adjust or repair it when things go a little wrong (or worse, break).

I like to categorize maintenance tasks into three groups: tasks that you should perform before each print, once each day that you use your printer, or as needed (*basic maintenance*); tasks that should be performed at certain milestones (*periodic maintenance*); and tasks that you must perform whenever the printer has a problem or as part wears out (*corrective maintenance*). The frequency of these depends largely on how much you use your printer, as well as the general reliability of your printer design.

I recommend your reading this chapter before you start using your printer for a long period of time. If you have used your printer for more than 25 hours, take some time to read through this chapter and implement the recommendations for observing, adjusting, and repairing.

Let's begin by looking at some best practices and advice for maintaining a delta printer.

---

[1]Loosely equivalent is calibrating the towers, but this only needs to be done when something changes, like moving or upgrading the printer.

Getting Started

Maintenance of delta printers involves a lot more than some may think, and yet not nearly as much as others fear. That is, there are certain things you should do every time you use your printer, or as needed, things you need to do regularly (e.g., every 50 hours), and things you need to do after significant use (e.g., every 250 hours). However, none of the maintenance tasks are very difficult or require any extensive skills or familiarity with complex procedures.

Your best tool is the desire to maintain your printer to keep it printing well. Beyond that, you should be aware of certain best practices for maintenance in general. The following sections outline some of the common practices for performing maintenance. These apply to almost any type of maintenance, from automobiles to Zamboni machines.

Keep Your Area Clean and Free of Clutter

Let's face it: things tend to pile up after a while. This is especially true for hobbies like 3D printers. As you have learned from a previous chapter, there are all manner of tools needed to use and maintain your printer. And it isn't just the tools that can clutter your work area.

Indeed, it doesn't take long for printed parts (prototypes or otherwise) and little bits of filament to litter the area around your printer. Be it from discarded rafting, shavings from finishing your pieces, or simply trimmings for cases when things need a little adjustment to fit properly.

Let's not discount the possibility of personal detritus. I've seen some work areas that have more discarded food and drink containers than anything else. Whatever the source, you should avoid the temptation to let things pile up to the point where you are spending time looking for things, or pushing things around from one pile to another.[2]

Not only does the clutter make it harder to work around your printer, but it can also interfere with the normal operation of your printer. I once forgot to remove a piece of tape I placed on one of the axes that I used to hold a bolt in place. I don't recall having done so, but I was clearly in a hurry at some point and forgot to remove it. Suffice it to say, it became very obvious when I started the print and heard the roller carriage bump and click as it rode over the tape. Fortunately, no harm was done (other than a slightly lower-quality print), but I learned a valuable lesson: even if you don't put your tools away, take inventory and survey your printer to make sure that everything is cleared away from the printer.

Consequently, I've formed the habit to make sure that the area around my printers is cleaned once per day. That is, I discard unwanted filament and parts, use a vacuum to remove the little bits of filament, and put my tools away. If you do this once per day, you can avoid unexpected surprises and always know where things are stored.

Organize Your Tools for Quick Access

If you have friends and family that are mechanically inclined, you may have encountered a variety of garage and tool organizational styles or methods. There are the compulsive types that like to keep everything in its place—with a place for everything, those that group things in similar yet somewhat disjointed containers, the free spirits who let things fall where they may,[3] and of course, everyone in between.

---

[2]Else you could earn your own PhD—piled higher and deeper.
[3]Which means you can always tell what they worked on last.

No matter which style you subscribe to, you can make maintenance tasks easier by gathering the tools you need ahead of time and placing them nearby. Not only will this save you time, you won't have to drop everything—sometimes literally—to find the tool you need. Experience and familiarity with your printer will teach you which tools you need for certain tasks.

You don't have to lay your tools out like a dental hygienist's tray,[4] but placing them in a shallow basket, or even on the table near the printer, is a good plan. When maintaining or repairing my printers, I like to gather my tools and lay them in front of the printer so that I can reach them easily and quickly.

In fact, as I mentioned in a previous chapter, I keep a complete set of tools to perform all maintenance and repair tasks on my printers in my workshop. I keep them organized into several groups to make it easier for me to select a subset for whatever I want to do. It takes only a small amount of discipline to return the tools to their proper places when the task is complete.

Unplug Your Printer

Most maintenance tasks should be performed while your printer is turned off and unplugged from mains power. This may seem like a very prudent thing to do (and it is), but you would be surprised at how tempting and easy it is to think your off switch can save you from a nasty electrical surprise. In most cases, this simply isn't true. Even if the switch was designed to interrupt power completely, the fact remains that power is still live on the mains side of the switch.

The best practice is to simply unplug the printer when working on it. For those cases where you need power to manipulate the axes, you should take care to avoid areas of your printer that contain electronics and power connections. If you must come into contact with the electronics, use a grounding strap to avoid ESD damage.

■ **Tip** Use an electronics enclosure to help protect against accidental damage to your electronics from foreign objects such as small animals and insects, liquids, solder, stray wire strands, fingers, arms, and other miscellaneous human tissue. Although most of the printer uses 5V and 12V systems, even 5V power should be treated with a degree of caution. Don't assume low DC voltage is harmless.

Take Your Time

With the risk of sounding like your grandmother, you should not rush yourself when working on your printer. A rushed task will lead to mistakes and, often, rework. Rushing can also result in misplaced tools, added clutter—or worse, mistakes. While very easy to say (write), this is one area many of us struggle to overcome. I can say with few exceptions that every time I've rushed through a procedure, I didn't do quite as good of a job as I preferred.

The best way to avoid rushing is to give yourself plenty of time to complete your work. For example, if you are planning to do some maintenance on your printer before a print job, plan to set aside an hour so that you can be sure to get your printer going in time to complete whatever print you need. If you find yourself rushing because you have other things to do (be it with family, your job, etc.), take a break and take care of the more important tasks first, and then return to your printer when you are done and can take the time you need to do the task properly.

---

[4]But there's nothing wrong with that. I do it occasionally when no one is watching.

Record Your Observations

In the last chapter, I encouraged you to record observations about your printer to help you diagnose and repair something that has broken or become misaligned. The same philosophy applies to performing maintenance on your printer.

Actually, you should make observations about your printer each time you use it. Visually inspect things to make sure that nothing has become unfastened, broken, or loose. As with the diagnostic tasks, I recommend keeping a journal and recording anything you observe about your printer. For example, you may notice a belt starting to get a little loose, or even some buildup of filament on the nozzle. Neither of these things are necessarily things that need to be fixed immediately, but entering the observation in your journal will help you stay aware of what your printer is doing. Not only that, it can also help you spot trouble before it becomes imperative.

For example, if you observe that one of the belts is a little loose one day, and looser still the next day, and then tight the third day, you should stop and check the axis mechanism for loose or broken parts. That is, a gradual decrease in tension may be normal, but a sudden shift from loose to tight or tight to loose means something is wrong.

Visual inspection isn't the only observation technique you can employ. You can observe your printer by listening for odd sounds, and being aware of odd smells or any strange movements. Sometimes a strange sound is fine, but it can also be a precursor to failure or something that will affect your print quality.

For example, if you hear a clunk, or a knock, or a similar collision sound, it could mean a portion of one of your axes mechanisms has become loose or out of alignment. Checking for this when you observe the behavior may permit you to fix the anomaly before it becomes an issue.

If your printer starts to move strangely, such as extra movement, it doesn't necessarily mean that the printer is at fault. It could be that the print file contains unusual commands. It can also be caused by intermittent errors in your electronics. The bottom line is: if your printer does something strange, pay close attention to what it is doing, stop your print, and diagnose the problem.

Basic Tasks

Once again, basic maintenance tasks are those that you should do every time you use your printer and things you should do before each printing session (each day that you use your printer). There are two types of basic maintenance tasks. First, you should inspect your printer for potential problems (loose or broken parts, etc.), and second, there are a few minor adjustments you should perform each time you use your printer, or as needed. I say "as needed" because some of these tasks apply to new or newly built (or upgraded) printers and may not be required each and every time you print on delta printers that have proven to be reliable. I describe each of these types in more detail in the following sections.

Inspection Tasks

The first type of basic maintenance task involves observing the printer: its mechanisms, wiring, frame, filament, and so forth. More specifically, you need to check your printer for anything that looks out of place, and then take action to correct the problem before you start a print. For example, if you observe that one of the belts is loose, you can adjust it so that print quality is not affected. Inspection tasks include the following.

- *Frame*: Checking for loose bolts and alignment

- *Axes*: Checking for loose or misaligned mechanisms

- *Filament*: Measuring the filament to ensure that your slicer options are set correctly

- *Extruder*: Checking for broken, worn, or loose parts

- *Belts*: Checking tension

- *Wiring*: Checking for loose connections or broken wires

- *Print surface*: Checking the print surface for damage or wear

For new printers, I recommend performing these tasks each time you print. If you have a new delta printer or one that you built yourself, it is important to perform these inspections before each print—at least for the first dozen or so prints. Doing so will help you make minor adjustments to get the printer broken in. Even if the vendor built your printer, inspecting it before each print gives you a better sense of its reliability.

As you become more familiar with your printer, you may be able to perform these tasks less frequently. However, even if you have printed many objects and your printer is reliable, such that adjustments or repairs are infrequent (more than every 50 hours of use), inspecting it can help detect when adjustments or repairs may be needed. For reliable printers, I recommend performing these tasks the first time you use it on a given day. For example, if you are going to print a series of objects, inspect the printer before printing the first object.

Table 7-1 will help you determine when you should perform each of the inspection tasks in the following sections. Notice that I have columns that apply to new printers, including those that are built from a kit (new); printers that are prebuilt or are not used much (low usage); and printers without issues after many hours of printing (reliable).

Table 7-1. *Frequency of Inspection Tasks*

Task	Description	New	Low Usage	Reliable
Frame	Check for loose bolts and alignment	Every print	Every 3 or 4 prints	Only when the printer is moved
Delta mechanisms	Check for loose belts, smooth operating carriages, loose delta arms	Every print	Once per month	Only when the printer is moved
Filament	Measure filament diameter	Every print	Every 3 or 4 prints	Depends on vendor quality
Extruder	Check for loose bolts, broken parts, clogged drive gear	Every print	Every print	Every print
Belts	Check for loose belts	Every print	Every first print of the day	Monthly
Wiring	Check for loose connections	Every print	Every first print of the day	Monthly
Print surface	Check the surface for wear or tears	Every print	Every print	Every print

Frame

Recall from the discussion about building a delta printer that the frame is the foundation upon which all other mechanisms are attached. If the frame (some use the term *chassis*) is loose or misaligned, these anomalies will translate to the effector, and therefore can affect print quality. For example, if the frame becomes misaligned or loose, it can cause poor print quality, or worse, axis travel failures and ruined prints.

Tighten Bolts

At a minimum, you should check the vertices for tightness. Most delta printer frames will not work loose, but I have seen it once, so it is worth a cursory check on a new printer, especially if you built it yourself. Make an inventory of the sizes of the wrenches, screwdrivers, or hex bits you need to tighten the fasteners, and enter that data in your journal so that the next time you need to do this, you will know what tools to gather.

Check each bolt to make sure that it is tight. Some people suggest using your fingers to loosen a nut or bolt. The idea is that if you can loosen it with your fingers, it isn't tight enough. I think this is a fine strategy, but it only works for those bolts and nuts that you can get to and grasp.

I prefer to use the appropriate tools to check tightness. Rather than try to loosen things (which is all too easy), I grip the tool lightly and try to turn each nut and bolt to ensure that it is tight. The idea here is that if you can move the bolt or nut with very little effort, it is too loose. When I encounter a bolt or nut like this, I give the tool a one-eighth to no more than a quarter turn to ensure that it is tight. Be sure to not overtighten.

■ **Caution**   Do not overtighten your frame fasteners. If your frame uses plastic components (printed or injection molded) or wooden parts, overtightening a bolt can compress or break the nut trap and ruin the part. Although it is not as easy to overtighten fasteners on all-metal frames, the consequences of doing so are the same.

Repeat the process until all the bolts and nuts are checked. It is not unusual for a new printer to have several bolts or nuts that need tightening. But you should not have to retighten them more than once or twice.

■ **Tip**   Use Nyloc fasteners where possible for all frame components.

Check Alignment

Aside from tightening the bolts, you should check the alignment of your frame. The frame on a delta printer should not lose alignment, so normally you should not have to do this task. However, if your printer was moved, accidentally bumped, or several parts of the frame have come loose (or you removed them intentionally for an upgrade), there is a chance the frame could have become misaligned or twisted. To check alignment, use a square to check that the vertical frame components are at right angles to the print surface. You should also make sure that all axes move smoothly without binding.

Check for Broken Parts

Finally, examine all the plastic parts to ensure that they are not cracked or show any signs of stress. The effects of stress can manifest in a number of ways. Most often, the part shows small cracks between the layers, but in the extreme case, you could see discolored sections—or worse, breaks in the plastic. Replace all parts that show any sign of damage. If the part is still functional and you do not have a spare, you should print a new part immediately to avoid down time while you wait for a friend or vendor to send you a new one.

Once you have performed this inspection to the point where there are no loose bolts and the frame components have not become unaligned, and no parts are broken or loose, you can consider changing the frequency of the inspection. That is, if you haven't tightened a bolt in three or four prints, try making the inspection once a week. If nothing comes loose or misaligned after several weeks, you can consider making the inspection only when the printer is physically moved.

Delta Mechanisms

Your printer's delta arms, effector, and carriages are often subjected to small, rapid movements, which can put a lot of stress on the components. New and recently modified printers should be checked frequently to ensure that the delta mechanisms are working properly. Not only should you check for loose parts, you should also check them for cracked or broken parts as well. While this is rare for a delta printer, it can happen if there has been an unusual event (e.g., a print surface crash), the printer has been moved, or you have partially disassembled and reassembled the mechanisms for an upgrade.

Like the frame, check each bolt to make sure that it is tight, that the delta arm joints are not loose, and that there is no excessive backlash in the joints (no free play). Inspect each of the plastic parts carefully to ensure that they are not damaged in any way. That is, if there has been any flexing of the frame, there is the possibility of plastic parts failure in the delta mechanisms.

You should also check the endstops for damage or loose mounts. An endstop that has moved or can move will make homing your printer difficult and could allow hard parts to collide. Endstop holders made from PLA may be more brittle than those made with ABS. Endstop holder breakage most often occurs as a result of a malfunction in axis movement that causes the axis to crash into the endstop on homing. For example, if you set the axis movement speed too high, it can cause the carriages to crash into the endstop, bending or breaking it or its holder.

You should check your delta mechanisms semifrequently (and always after moving the printer from one place to another). Once per each day that you print should be sufficient. On the other hand, if you find you have to adjust the frame, or even realign the axis from loose or worn parts, you should perform this inspection more frequently.

Filament

Filament is one of the areas often overlooked as a source for inspection or adjustment. The diameter of the filament can vary, often changing several times during the spool. Unless your filament vendor has very high standards, it is possible to experience variations that cause issues with printing.

Recall that you measure the diameter of filament with a caliper. If the measurement is more than a few hundredths of a millimeter larger or smaller than what you specified in your software (slicer settings), you may need to change your filament diameter setting, which normally requires reslicing (preparing the .stl file for printing). If you are printing an object you have already sliced, you should consider slicing your object again.

You need to do this to ensure that the correct amount of filament is extruded when laying down runs. If you use too much filament (the actual diameter is larger than your slicer settings), you risk bulges, stringing, and excess filament in smaller and narrower protrusions. If you use too little filament (the actual diameter is smaller than your slicer settings), you risk poor layer adhesion and weak parts.

I recommend changing your slicer settings if you encountered a change in the diameter greater than 0.05mm. Any more than that and you risk the problems stated previously. For example, if you measured your filament at the start of a spool at 1.77mm and find that it varies between 1.74mm and 1.80mm, a setting of 1.76 in your slicer filament settings should be fine.

While you should always check the diameter of the filament before slicing an object for printing, most people forget that the diameter of the filament is a variable in the sliced file. Thus, it is important to make sure that you check the filament diameter regularly and compare it to what is in the sliced file.

If you are working with spools of filament from a reliable vendor, you may only need to check it once every few prints, or even once each time you start a new spool. However, until you are comfortable with the variance of the filament from your vendor (it may require sampling a number of spools), you should check the diameter every time you print.

Extruder

The extruder is the workhorse of the printer. There are several parts to the extruder, all of which need to be checked for wear or damage. The parts of the extruder include the stepper motor, the extruder body, the idler bearing or pulley (if equipped), the drive and driven gears (if equipped), the filament drive gear, and wiring for the stepper motor.

The filament drive gear is one of the top areas that can cause you trouble. This is because it can become clogged with pieces of filament and start to slip. Furthermore, if the extruder uses a set of gears, they will wear over time; thus they should be checked for excessive wear, broken or missing teeth, or loose gears.

The stepper motors in axes are always turning, and therefore get more use than any other stepper motor. There really isn't any way to visibly observe problems with a stepper motor to tell if it needs replacement or has excessive wear (other than complete shutdown in one or both directions). I have seen stepper motors wear out; but the only symptoms were a loss of holding torque where the stepper could not hold its position, or a lack of torque when stepping, such that it missed steps. When this happens, the stepper motor is easier to turn by hand. However, unless the filament is unloaded, you cannot turn the stepper motor. Fortunately, you don't normally have to worry about this until your stepper motor has been used for hundreds of hours of printing.

The extruder body should be checked for breaks and wear. The pivot point on the idler can wear over time. The tension on the bolts that press the idler against the drive gear can put stress on the pivot point, eventually making the hole larger. I have seen this myself a couple of times. The telltale sign is a loose idler door. You can see this visibly whenever you change filament, but you can also see the door flex as the extruder moves. If you see any play in the idler door, you should consider replacing it.

Even if the extruder body does not have multiple parts, it is a good idea to check it for breakage. Look for changes to the way it mounts to the frame, loose bolts, or the extruder loosing from its mount. Any of these are warning signs that the extruder body may need replacing.

If your extruder uses a set of gears to drive the filament pulley, and if they are 3D-printed parts, you should check the gears for wear and damage. That is, if the gears wear long enough, it is possible that the teeth can become worn down to the point where there is play in the gears. In rare cases, the teeth could break off of the smaller of the two gears. The telltale sign of worn gears is a light dusting of plastic debris in the valleys of the teeth.

If your extruder uses an idler bearing (sometimes called the *idler pulley*), you should also check it for play. If the idler bearing uses a modern sealed bearing, you aren't likely to see it fail, but if the mounting point is a 3D-printed part or is mounted to the same, you should check the bolts for tightness and any play. Play in the idler bearing can cause filament extrusion problems if the play is enough to change the tension on the filament. I have seen a case where the play was no more than about 0.04mm, but that was enough to ease tension and cause an extrusion failure. I originally increased the tension to compensate (which does work temporarily), but that only made the problem worse, and eventually resulted in a cracked idler door.

■ **Tip**   Any play or loose bolts on the extruder should be corrected immediately.

As mentioned, the filament drive gear is the one spot on all delta printers that eventually requires service. If your extruder is constructed so that you can see the filament drive gear, check it for filament debris in the teeth. If you see any buildup, you should remove the debris from the teeth or grooves. I discuss this in more detail in the Adjustment Tasks section.

In summary, check the extruder's fixed parts for wear, the gears for play, the filament drive gear for buildup, and the wiring for any breaks.

Since the extruder does so much work, I recommend checking it before every print. At the very minimum, you should do a quick look at the extruder body, the stepper motor, the drive and driven gear (if equipped), and the filament drive gear to ensure that nothing is wrong. Remember, if something goes wrong in the extruder, your print will likely be ruined.

Belts

The belts on your delta printer can loosen over time. The slack or looseness is normally very little, and only after many hours of printing. What is more likely to cause loosening belts is slippage of the securing blocks or clamps. This is especially true for printer designs that use zip ties or press-fit parts on each end of the belt.

Loose belts are those that have more than about 10mm to 30mm[5] or more of play (perpendicular to the belt travel). Any more than this and the belt can slip on the drive gear. Not only that, but the extra length of the belt can cause minor layer shifts on that axis. The amount of play or slack in the belt depends on how long the belt is, as well as its type. Check your vendor's documentation for the correct threshold for your printer.

Checking the belts for tension is a very quick test: just press left and right (sideways) on the belt (or back and forth if you will). I recommend checking belt tension before each print for new printers and for printers that use clamps to secure the belts. If you don't notice any looseness in the belts, you can delay the check to once every day of printing, and if no looseness is detected then, delay the check to once a month.

Wiring

The wiring on your delta printer is another often overlooked source of problems. Printers built by vendors typically use electronics with connectors that are securely fastened and rarely come loose. However, kit-based printers are more susceptible because most wire connections are press-fit and not secured with tabs, screw terminals, or other forms of keeping the wire in place.

For printers that are assembled from kits, you should make it a priority to check all the wiring for loose connections for at least the first dozen or so prints. A visual inspection is enough to see a connector that is not seated properly. Check slip and press-fit connections to make sure that they have not become unplugged; screw terminals to ensure that wires are still tight; and look for worn insulation or bare or broken wires at any area where the wiring crosses a metal object. Wiring can loosen due to the normal vibrations of a printer, or it can loosen due to accidental stress on the wiring when performing maintenance.

■ **Caution**   Be sure to check the higher voltage wiring on the heaters. If they become loose, they can overheat and damage the connector.

But it isn't just the wiring connections that should be checked. I already mentioned the need to inspect the wiring on the effector for flexing and signs of breakage; but this is just one of the stress points. There is also the other end of that wiring bundle, where it meets or is secured to the frame. Check this end too.

■ **Note**   While you would rarely be concerned about soldered connections, if you soldered your own connections and have not had a lot of practice soldering, you may want to check these for the first few prints to make sure that the connections are strong.

At least once each day for a new, unproven printer, I recommend checking all wiring connections to make sure that they are securely fastened. Otherwise, check the wiring on reliable printers once every week until you feel comfortable that no connections are loose.

---

[5]Sometimes as much as 40mm can be OK. It mostly depends on how smoothly the carriages move and how much work the stepper motors must do to move them.

Print Surface

The print surface is another wear site. When you use blue painter's tape or Kapton tape without ABS juice, you only need to replace the print surface if there are adhesion problems (sudden lifting after many prints without lifting) or if you have torn or gouged the print surface treatment by removing parts. Figure 7-1 shows a print surface that is in need of replacement.

Figure 7-1. *Worn print surface (blue painter's tape)*

Notice here that there are small tears and some discoloring in the print surface. Normally, discoloring won't affect adhesion, but any tears will affect adhesion. If your print surface starts looking like this, I recommend changing it. On the other hand, you could just move the start of the print to another portion of the print bed. In Figure 7-1, the surface on either side of the wear is still good.

Recall from a previous chapter that if you use narrower strips of tape, you can replace only those strips that are affected. In Figure 7-1, I needed to replace only the centermost strips.

Even if you do not need to replace the print surface, it is a good idea to wipe it with a lint-free cloth to remove any oils caused by touching it with your hands, as well as any dust that may have accumulated. For Kapton tape, a cloth with a small spot of acetone will remove any filament residue, as well as oils and dust. For PLA printed on plain glass, use a good glass cleaner.

■ **Caution**   If you use a spray-on solution, be sure to cover the electronics to avoid getting them wet with overspray. It is best to first spray the solution on a lint-free cloth or paper towel, and then wipe the surface.

Checking the print surface is another easy thing you can do; and, in fact, you should do this before every print. Only a brief glance at the print surface is required to tell if it needs replacing.

Adjustment Tasks

The next type of basic maintenance task includes those things that require minor adjustments on a semiregular basis. I recommend checking to see if you need to do these tasks as your first step when using your printer on any given day. Adjustment tasks don't have to be done before every print (although they can), and printers that have proven to be reliable can have these tasks done on an as-needed basis.

Adjustment tasks are those that are typically needed to keep your printer running well. They are tasks you should perform more often. They include the following (I discuss each in more detail shortly).

- *Clean the filament drive gear*: Remove debris from the drive gear.

- *Clean the nozzle*: Remove melted filament and contaminants from the exterior of nozzle.

- *Adjust belts and carriages*: Ensure that the belts are tight and the carriages are adjusted.

- *Set the Z-height*: Adjust the height of the first layer with respect to the print surface.

- *Calibrate the towers*: Keep the print bed adjusted properly to ensure accurate tracking over the print surface.

In the following sections, I provide example procedures for performing these tasks. I have tried to keep them generic enough to be applicable to most delta printers. That said, you may find that slightly different steps are needed for your particular printer. You should still be able to adapt the example to your printer by manually jogging the axes.

Table 7-2 will help you determine when you should perform each of the inspection tasks in the following sections. Notice that I provide columns that apply to new printers, including printers that are built from a kit (new); printers that are prebuilt or not used much (low usage); and printers without issues after many hours of printing (reliable).

Table 7-2. *Frequency of Adjustment Tasks*

Task	Description	New	Low Usage	Reliable
Clean the filament drive gear	Remove debris from the gear.	Daily	When you change filament	As needed
Clean the nozzle	Remove extra plastic from the nozzle.	Daily	Weekly	As needed
Adjust belts and carriages	Tighten belts and adjust tension on carriages.	Daily	Weekly	As needed (50-100 hours)
Set the Z-height	Adjust the nozzle height over the print bed. Sets first layer height.	Daily	Weekly	When you change the print surface or print bed
Calibrate the towers	Adjust the print bed so that it is parallel (trammed) with the X and Y axes.	Weekly	Monthly	When you change the print surface bed

Clean the Filament Drive Gear

Cleaning the filament drive gear is the first line of defense in correcting extrusion failure, because most extrusion failures are related to either slipping filament caused by a dirty drive gear, or a blocked nozzle (or similar filament obstruction). Any time you have an extrusion failure, you should clean the filament drive gear.

The process for cleaning the filament drive gear varies from one printer (extruder) design to another. You saw how to do this in Chapter 6. Most extruders on delta printers have a similar process.

■ **Tip**   If you are using PLA, check the flexibility of the filament near the end that you removed. You may find that the filament is a bit more flexible than normal. I like to move up the filament (toward the spool) until I find a more brittle place, and then I snap off the filament there, removing the previously heated portion. I've found that filament loads a bit easier if it has not been heated and cooled.

I recommend checking the filament drive gear once each day that you use the printer. If you do not notice any buildup, you can check it every time you change filament, and clean it when needed. In fact, I always clean the filament drive gear when I encounter an extrusion problem.

Clean the Nozzle

The hot end nozzle is one area that many people neglect. Although there isn't anything that needs to be adjusted, it is possible for the nozzle to become dirty over many prints—that is, bits of filament can stick to the outside of the nozzle. This can happen whenever there is stringing from the end of a print, oozing from the nozzle due to higher temperatures, or collisions with objects on the print bed. Figure 7-2 shows a Rostock Max v2 hot end with a brass nozzle. While this specimen is reasonably free of debris, there are some small pieces on the side.

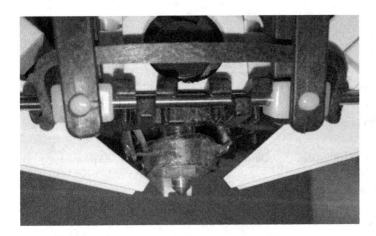

Figure 7-2. *Hot end nozzle (Rostock Max v2)*

■ **Caution**   You will be working with a hot end that has been brought up to temperature. When moving around inside the printer, be careful to avoid touching the hot end or nozzle. It will burn you. Also, make sure that the printer is off before using any tools near the nozzle.

Over time, these bits of filament can harden and turn dark—encrusting the nozzle. Although some users may say that this isn't a big deal (I suppose I must admit that it could be OK), I don't like my tools or equipment to get so dirty. And it turns out that if you switch filament often, especially from PLA to ABS and back, some of the extra bits of filament can melt off and fall onto your prints. This is most noticeable when printing with light-colored filament.

I've seen it happen on occasion; one particularly gnarly nozzle would leave dark spots on the prints. I observed a very good white-colored print with four or five tiny black spots that despite their small size, made the part look bad.

You can avoid this problem by simply cleaning the outside of your nozzle whenever it gets dirty (filament buildup). Best of all, it does not require you to remove the nozzle. Although it may be easy with some printers, with others it is a very involved process. The process to clean the nozzle in place is as follows. As you will see, it is very straightforward and not difficult. I describe the more involved steps in more detail.

1. Home your printer to give yourself room to work.

2. Heat the hot end to the temperature for the filament used.

3. Turn off the printer and unplug it.

4. While the hot end is still hot, use tweezers (ESD-safe) to remove the larger pieces of filament.

5. If your nozzle is oozing, wait for it to cool until it no longer oozes.

6. Use a soft wire brush to remove loose filament while the nozzle is still warm.

7. Vacuum away the loose debris.

8. Soak a small portion of a paper towel with acetone and then wipe the nozzle once it has cooled.

I use ESD-safe tweezers to remove hot filament. It removes the majority of the loose filament from the nozzle. Figure 7-3 illustrates this process with a typical J-head hot end, which is very common on Mini Kossel and similar delta printers.

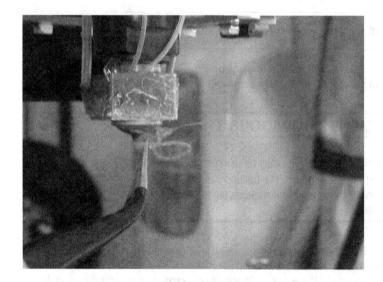

Figure 7-3. *Remove loose filament from the nozzle with tweezers*

While the hot end is still warm, remove any remaining filament residue with a soft wire brush. Figure 7-4 shows this step in progress.

Figure 7-4. *Cleaning the outside of the nozzle with a brush*

Be sure to use a metal brush with bristles of the same or softer metal than the nozzle. A wooden or metal handle is a must. In the photos, for example, I used a brash brush to clean a brass nozzle. You can also use a metal scouring pad, but be sure to use the kind without soap! I do not recommend the use of steel wool because it can deposit several small bits of steel into your printer.

■ **Caution**   Never use a plastic-handled brush or one with plastic bristles.

You can scrub the burned-on parts harder, but be sure to not put too much pressure on your hot end. Don't worry about any filament sticking to the brush. You can remove it easily once it has completely cooled.

BURNED FILAMENT? HOW DOES THAT HAPPEN?

If your nozzle has a lot of melted filament buildup, you may be using temperatures that are too high, and so you should consider lowering the temperature. The buildup can also occur when switching from filament that requires lower heat ranges to filament that requires higher heat ranges. Thus, always clean your nozzle before switching filament types.

To complete the cleaning process, use a towel soaked with a small spot of acetone. Fold the towel a couple of times to help absorb the acetone, as well as help protect your fingers if the hot end is still warm. By now, the nozzle should be cool enough to touch. If it is not, wait until it cools some more, and then use the acetone cloth. I use a paper towel to help reduce the temptation to scrub the nozzle. Putting too much force on the nozzle could damage the hot end, its mount, any accessory lighting—or worse, the wiring for the heater core and thermistor. Figure 7-5 shows the use of the towel to clean the nozzle. Notice how close the wiring is to the cloth. Be careful not to damage the wiring.

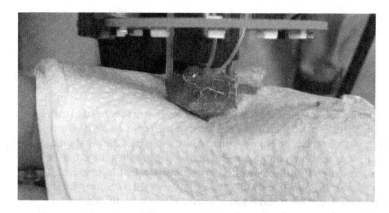

Figure 7-5. *Cleaning the outside of the nozzle with acetone*

Once you are done, be sure to vacuum any bits of debris—filament, unidentifiable black flakes (burnt filament), bristles, and so forth, before using the printer. Be sure to cover the electronics with a cloth (or similar covering) to protect them from falling brush bristles.

■ **Tip**   The nozzle should not be heated to temperature without extruding for extended periods. This is because filament in the nozzle will ooze out and be replaced with an air pocket. This can cause plastic to oxidize inside the nozzle, which can blacken, and in some cases clog the nozzle.

I recommend cleaning the outside of the nozzle once each day that you use the printer, or as needed. If you are using the proper temperature for your filament and you haven't had any extrusion or build failures, you may not need to do this procedure very often. Regardless, buildup is very easy to spot, and except for waiting for the heating and cooling cycles, it is very easy to correct.

Adjust the Belts and Carriages

If your delta printer uses belts to move the carriages, you must ensure that the belts are properly tensioned. Most delta printers have some form of belt tensioner that you can use to tighten the belts. For example, the Mini Kossel design uses a bolt on top of each axis to raise the top frame vertex and therefore tighten the belt. Just loosen the top frame vertex outer bolt and tighten the belt adjustment bolt until the belt has no more than 20mm to 30mm of play.

For newly assembled printers, I like to check the tension for the first three to six prints to ensure that everything is tight. For printers that have proven to be reliable, I check and adjust the belts every 50 to 100 hours of printing.

If your delta printer uses roller carriages or similar carriages that have an adjuster, check the play in the carriages and adjust accordingly. If your roller carriage has four or more rollers, this task can be a bit of a challenge. For example, the roller carriages on the Rostock Max v2 require using two box wrenches to move the two concentric spacers together.

The carriages need to move freely without any play. That is, you should not be able to move the carriage other than up and down. The carriage should float freely so that when you move it up, it immediately falls down (but don't let it crash into the frame). Carriages that stick or move slowly are too tight. Fortunately, the roller carriages need very little adjustment, and then only occasionally. So far, I've only had to do this once.

Thus, you should check the carriages every 50 to 100 hours of printing and adjust them when there is significant play in the carriages. Refer to your vendor's documentation for the exact procedures for adjusting your printer's carriages.

Set the Z-Height

The Z-height is another area that normally doesn't need to be adjusted. However, you may need to make small adjustments if your environment changes or your change the print surface. For example if your work area changes from hot, dry conditions to cool, moist conditions. You may want to adjust the Z-height if you encounter lifting or you want a lower first layer. Wear is another factor in needing to adjust the Z-height.

Recall from Chapter 5 that the purpose of setting the Z-height is to establish the first-layer height. This should be slightly less than your chosen layer height. For example, if your layer height is 0.3mm, you should consider making your first-layer height between 0.1mm and 0.2mm. A good gauge is the thickness of a piece of paper. The paper should be able to slide under the nozzle with only a small amount of friction. The smaller the value, the more pressed or squished the first layer is against the print surface. Generally, a lower Z-height can improve adhesion and reduce lifting.

■ **Tip**   You can also use a Post-it note. The sticky portion makes holding the paper a bit easier.

Some printers, like the Rostock Max v2, have a nifty process for setting the Z-height built into the firmware. As you saw in Chapter 5, all you need to do is preheat the nozzle to about 180 to 190 degrees, and the print bed to about 50 to 60 degrees. You also need to ensure that the proper print surface treatment is applied. That is, if you plan to use blue painter's tape, you must apply it before heating the print bed.

When ready, select Advanced Settings from the menu, and then select Calibrate Z Height. On this menu, you first home the axis with the Home Towers selection. Next, select Z-Position, and then use the rotary knob to lower the effector until the nozzle is close to the print surface. Use a piece of paper to check the gap. When you feel a slight friction from the nozzle touching the paper, press in the knob to return to the previous menu, and then choose Set new Z=0.00.

Printers without this nifty procedure require calculating the Z-height by homing the axes, and then slowly lowering the nozzle to the print surface. If you reach 0 before the nozzle touches the print bed, you may need to increase the Z_MAX_POS or MANUAL_Z_HOME_POS in the firmware, and then try the procedure again. Once you find the position, update the value in the firmware (or EEPROM settings) to set the Z-height.

If your printer has a Z-probe, you can set the Z-height very easily by setting the Z_PROBE_OFFSET_FROM_EXTRUDER value in the firmware. For example, if the Z-height needs to be lower and you have a value of –5.1 for Z_PROBE_OFFSET_FROM_EXTRUDER, you can use –5.15 or –5.20 to lower the nozzle. Some printers save this value in EEPROM so that you can make the change without reloading the firmware.

■ **Note**   Johann Rocholl's version of the Marlin G29 autolevel command also accepts an optional Z adjustment. For example, G29 Z-0.15.

Although you may have to make an adjustment to your Z-height more frequently than you have to calibrate the towers, this task is on an as-needed basis.

Calibrate the Towers

The towers are normally not an area that needs regular adjustment. That is, once the towers are calibrated, you should never have to calibrate them again. Well, almost. If you move your printer, bump into it, or upgrade, you may need to recalibrate the towers. I recommend doing the recalibration if you move your printer or if you encounter any significant lifting in one or more areas along the perimeter of the print bed.

Recall from Chapter 5 that the purpose of calibrating the towers is to ensure that each axis is the same height over the print bed. If anything interferes with the end stops or changes the alignment of the frame (like moving or bumping into the printer), the tower calibration may have been affected.

The process for calibrating the towers is described in detail in Chapter 5. In brief, you will need to home all axes, and then check each tower by lowering the effector to Z=0 positioned at the base of the tower and checking the gap between the nozzle and the print surface.

If you meet any of the criteria listed here, you should perform the calibration. Unlike other adjustment tasks, calibrating the towers is required only as needed.

Now that you have explored the inspection and adjustment tasks, let's now explore those tasks you can perform to prevent failures and poor print quality.

Preventive Tasks

The goal of preventive maintenance is to execute small tasks frequently to reduce the risk and downtime of equipment failure. More specifically, you take steps to keep your equipment in a condition where it is operating at the highest degree of efficiency possible. This includes making sure that the equipment remains free of debris and dust, that the parts that require lubrication are lubricated properly, and that worn parts are replaced before they fail. Normally these tasks are not time-consuming, but should be performed on a regular basis.

Fortunately, there aren't many preventive tasks required for maintaining your delta printer. The following sections describe the preventive tasks you should perform on your printer on a regular basis. As you will see, the frequency will vary from one task to another, but they are based on hours of use, and in some cases, influenced by the environment. I begin with the simplest preventive task: keeping the printer clean.

Cleaning the Printer

Keeping your printer clean may not sound like a preventive task. However, dust and dirt can accumulate on your oiled parts, fouling the lubrication to the point of increasing friction and wear on the bearings, wheels, or linear rails. I should note that printers with partial or full enclosures are not immune to these effects. It just means the accumulation will be slower.

■ **Tip** You can reduce dust buildup on your print surface if you attach a cover on top of your delta printer. I've found that a piece of acrylic or thin plywood works well. If you don't want to calculate the shape of the panel, you can use a piece of cardboard cut to shape. Remember to leave room for any accessories and the belt tensioners, which are typically on top of each axis.

A bigger concern for delta printers is the accumulation of small bits of plastic falling into the build area (the area around the build platform). This can include brim material, run-off filament from a print, oozing filament from the hot end, and so forth. While it may require a lot of plastic bits accumulating in your build area to cause major problems, you should still take the time to clean your build area periodically. However, even a small amount of debris in the belt channel or on the drive pulley can cause issues. Be sure to keep debris away from the axis mechanisms.

More importantly, you mustn't allow plastic to accumulate on your build platform. Even a small amount of plastic debris on your print surface can cause problems such as uneven first layers and nozzle blockages, leading to extrusion failure.

So how do you clean a delta printer? Resist the temptation to commandeer the household vacuum. Vacuums must be used carefully because they can generate a lot of static electricity and can harm your electronics. Also, you should never use any cleansers whatsoever. The only possible exception would be cleaning the outside of your frame. Even then, you should use a mild cleanser designed for the material of your frame, and do so sparingly. Check your owner's manual for recommended cleaning procedures and cleansers.

The specific procedure will vary from one printer to another, but there are several areas or subtasks you should do to thoroughly clean your printer. These tasks include the following:

- Dust and clean the frame.

- Remove dust from the electronics.

- Remove plastic debris from the build area.

- Clean vertical frame components and rails.

How frequently you need to clean your printer and which areas you need to clean depends on how dusty and debris-filled your print environment is. I recommend checking for things that need cleaning after every 25 hours of use. At the very least, clean your printer every 50 to 100 hours of printing.

Frame

The frame of the printer is one area that some enthusiasts neglect. That is, the frame isn't something you think about. Regardless, you should remove any accumulation of dust on your printer. If your delta printer has an enclosed top or bottom section, you can use a simple dry duster to wipe away any accumulation. I find a household-dusting wand or dusting glove works best for most surfaces. If your printer has a skeletal frame, like the Mini Kossel, use a vacuum to remove dust, or use canned air or an air compressor to blow off the dust from the components inside the frame.

■ **Caution** If you use a duster, stay away from the electronics! Some dusters can generate electrostatic discharge (ESD), which may damage electronics.

If your vacuum has a dusting brush, you can use it, but be careful using it around any exposed electronics or ports. While cleaning, you should also avoid removing the oil or grease from any of the axis movements. Remember, the goal is to remove accumulation of dust, not to sanitize it for food consumption.

Electronics

The electronics on your printer must also be free of dust and debris. If you allow it to accumulate on your electronics, you risk overheating because dust can act as insulation. If there is too much heat, the electronics can fail. Admittedly, it would take a lot of dust to become a danger to some components, but that is no excuse to ignore the danger altogether.

However, cleaning electronics is not as easy as cleaning the frame. Electronics are very sensitive and most dusting devices use static to attract dust. Thus, you should never use anything other than compressed air to blow off the dust.

I like to use a can of compressed air known as *canned air*. It emits a concentrated blast of air that is very effective at removing dust and small debris. However, you should be aware that some canned air suppliers use chemicals in their products. Those that contain chemicals are not generally harmful to electronics, but always check the label for applicability before using. Be sure to purchase canned air that is designed for electronics.

You should also remove any debris that falls into your electronics. Use a pair of ESD-safe tweezers to remove the larger pieces that cannot be removed by using canned or compressed air.

■ **Tip**   An electronics enclosure can help prevent dust build-up. If you choose to use an enclosure for your electronics, be sure to use one with sufficient documentation or a fan to circulate air over the electronics.

Build Area

One area that can become littered with debris over time (as well as dust) is the build area. This is the area around your print bed. On some delta printers, the print bed is on top of the frame, so debris can fall into the frame but generally cannot accumulate enough to be a problem—but you should still clean it out. Debris can litter the area around delta printers with a print surface on top of an enclosed frame section, such as the SeeMeCNC Orion or Rostock Max v2. This can become a problem. As you use your printer, small pieces of filament are discarded from excess extrusion (before and after a print), which can fall into the build area. If you print with a raft, brim, skirt, or even ABS juice, it is possible for small fragments to break off and fall into the build area.

While none of these situations pose an immediate threat to your printer, you should take the time to periodically clean out the build area. I like to vacuum after each day I use the printer. If you use your printer only occasionally, you may not need to vacuum as often. I recommend cleaning the build area at least once every time you change or clean the print surface. That is, do it weekly.

The best way to do this is to use a small vacuum to remove the debris. I use a long, flat attachment that can reach under the build platform. Be sure to home your printer before turning it off so that you can vacuum underneath it.

■ **Caution**   Take care when vacuuming your build area. Some vacuums can cause ESD, which can damage electronics.

You should also take the time to vacuum the area around your printer and the floor underneath your desk or workbench. Small pieces of plastic and similar small particles can pose a threat to children and small animals.

Vertical Frame Members

Your delta printer's vertical frame members host the axis mechanisms. As you saw in Chapter 2, this can be a set of roller carriages or similar rollers that travel up and down using a channel in the frame. Other mechanisms include linear rails or smooth rods.

■ **Tip** If you have an older delta printer design that uses smooth rods, see Chapter 10 in my book *Maintaining and Troubleshooting Your 3D Printer* (Apress, 2014) for a complete description and process for cleaning and lubricating smooth rods.

If your printer uses roller carriages, you need to keep the channels completely free of debris. Unlike bearings that have seals that can push dust away, channels and tracks generally do not have anything to push away debris. Given that the axes are mounted vertically, dust may not be a problem, but other obstructions can be.

That is, if a piece of plastic falls into the channel or track, it can cause the carriage to bounce over the obstacle, thereby shifting the axis momentarily. If the piece is large enough, it can cause the axis to stop—or worse, derail. Thus, you should keep your frame channels and tracks clean, checking them before each print and cleaning them whenever you find any debris.

However, debris isn't the only hazard. I've found that delta printers with roller carriages can wear eventually, leaving a small amount of debris from the wheels in the channel. So far, this hasn't proven to be a problem, but I recommend cleaning the channels or tracks periodically to remove this debris.

To clean the linear rail, position your axes at the top (by homing the printer), and then use a lint-free cloth dappled with a bit of light machine oil, as shown in Figure 7-6. Wipe the linear rail from top to bottom with the oiled cloth. Turn the cloth a few times to ensure that you wipe away all the dirt. Position your axes a bit lower to ensure that you clean the top part of the linear rail.

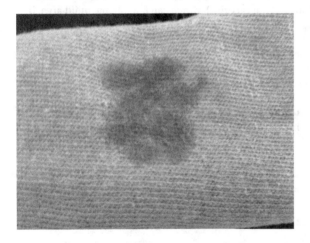

Figure 7-6. *Oiled cloth for cleaning linear rails*

Be sure to not use too much oil on the cloth, as this will make the situation worse. You only need a small amount of oil to clean the linear rail. You will see how to properly lubricate the linear rail carriage in the next section.

In summary, you should clean your vertical frame members every 50 hours of printing, or sooner if you notice dust and dirt buildup in the channels, tracks, or linear rails.

Lubricating Moving Parts

All delta printers have metal and other parts that need lubrication. Some are designed to use light oil, and others are constructed so that they contain some form of lubrication. For example, linear rails require light oil, some bearings without seals require light oil, and sealed bearings have lubrication inside the seals.

If your printer uses tracks or grooved channels, the wheels or rollers that ride in them may need lubrication. If sealed bearings are used, you may not need to lubricate at all. It is best to check your documentation to make sure.

Linear rails are one form of axis mechanism that needs special mention. Some people believe the linear rails do not need lubrication. This is misleading. While it is true you do not need to oil the linear rail other than cleaning it with a lightly oiled cloth, the carriages need lubrication. Some people use grease and pack it into the carriage, but I prefer light machine oil added very judiciously.

I like to use small paint dabbers (also called *micro dabbers*), which you can get from most automotive supply stores. These dabbers have a short wand, tipped with a small, round brush or bristles. I like to use the ones from Automotive Touchup (automotivetouchup.com/store/accessories/micro_dabbers.aspx), but any that are designed for small paint application work well. Figure 7-7 shows an example of these dabbers.

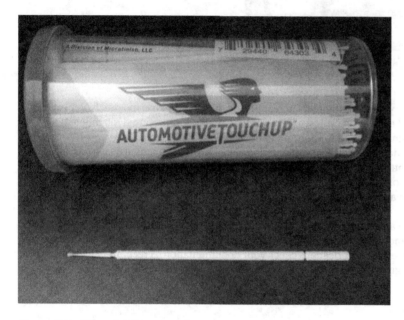

Figure 7-7. *Micro dabbers*

To lubricate the linear rails, first clean them with an oiled cloth, as described in the previous section. Then use the paint dabber to absorb some of the same light machine oil. Place the dabber into the carriage mechanism and slowly move the carriage while holding the dabber in place. Figure 7-8 shows the position of the dabber on a typical linear rail.

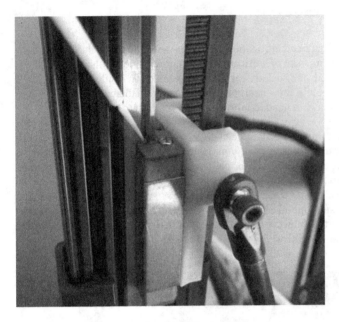

Figure 7-8. *Lubricating a linear rail*

You may want to pause every 1 or 2 centimeters to reapply the oil, but don't use too much. Repeat this for each side of the carriage and each axis. If you see oil running or pooling, you've used too much. If this happens, just use a clean, dry, lint-free cloth to wipe away the excess oil.

If you do not want to use a dabber or do not have one, you can apply light machine oil with an oil dispenser that has a long tip. Bottles of 3-IN-ONE lubricant are available with long applicator tubes. You can use this, but be careful to apply only a small drop at a time. Be sure to wipe away the excess if you apply too much oil. Remember, you just want to keep the carriage lightly oiled. It does not need to be bathed in oil. That would be a mess.

There is one other possible area where you may need lubrication. Delta printers use belts, cables, and sometimes chains with one or more idler pulleys in the axis mechanism. These idler pulleys may need lubrication. If your idler pulley requires lubrication (check your documentation), I recommend cleaning the idler pulley and reapplying the grease or oil at the same interval you clean them, every 100 hours.

Replacing Worn Parts

You should replace any worn part when you discover the problem. As I discussed in an earlier section, periodic inspections can help you find parts that are worn. Whenever you discover a worn part, you should replace it as soon as you can. Continuing to use your printer with worn parts can risk problems with print quality. Some of the most common wear parts include the following:

- Print surface treatments

- Fans

- Belts

- Bearings

Of course, print surface treatments wear most of these things. I have already discussed the specifics of inspecting and replacing the print surface. Recall that the print surface treatment (blue painter's tape, glue stick, or Kapton tape) should be replaced any time you see breaks or damage (like those caused by removing parts). You should also replace or reapply the print surface treatment when you begin to see more lifting than normal.

■ **Tip**   Lifting may also be caused by incorrect Z-height or environmental factors; it may not necessarily be related to the print surface treatment. Some people replace the print surface treatment as soon as they see any lift. If you replace the treatment and the lifting issue doesn't get any better, check the Z-height.

Fans are one of my pet peeves. I've had numerous electronics projects and a good number of manufactured gear (some very expensive) fail because a small, insignificant fan stopped working. Fans typically broadcast potential trouble in the form of slow startup or excessive noises, such as high-pitched squeals or rattling. When you encounter these symptoms, replace the fan as soon as you can. Fortunately, most delta printer fans are used in only three areas: the hot end, part cooling, and the electronics. Thus, they are easy to get to and normally easy to replace.

Belts are also wear items that may need replacing, but they wear after many hours of printing. Indeed, I have printers with hundreds of hours of printing and the belts look like new. Some of my Cartesian printers seem to need the belts replaced every 500 hours.

However, the wear isn't normally from friction (but can be if your drive gear is misaligned), but rather because belts can stretch—eventually fouling the mating of the teeth and the drive gear. In rare cases, belts can lose teeth or break. However, these are very unlikely events. In fact, unless you use your printer for hundreds to thousands of hours, you may never encounter a problem with worn belts. However, I have seen it happen at least once.

Bearings wear down as well, but like belts, they are unlikely to need replacing. However, when bearings wear, they can start making noises (from lack of lubrication), have excessive play, or even bind or break apart. These events are even less likely than worn belts; but again, if you use your printer a lot or if you fail to keep the bearings lubricated (or they fail from a manufacturing defect), they can fail. Check the bearings at least every 100 hours to ensure that they are in good order.

Now that you know some of the maintenance tasks that you should perform regularly, and before I describe the common corrective tasks, I want to discuss the spare parts that you should have on hand for things that wear or break.

Gather Spare Parts

Having a store of spare parts is key to keeping your printer running in the long term. Indeed, having spare parts on hand means you won't suffer extended downtime should a part wear or fail.

Sadly, some vendors do not mention spare parts at all. That is unfortunate because there are a small number of spares you may want to have on hand if you plan to use your printer for many hundreds of hours. Fortunately, some vendors offer spare parts for sale. Two such examples are SeeMeCNC and TriDPrinting.

SeeMeCNC (`http://seemecnc.com/collections/parts-accesories`) offers a long list of spare parts that you can buy, including fans, belts, frame extrusions, and extruder parts—everything you need to keep your printer in top shape. In fact, they also offer parts for repairing the roller carriages, which is a wear item. (As you will see in the next section, there are must-have spares to keep on hand.) SeeMeCNC even has those dastardly fans that fail far too often. Pick up a couple the next time you visit the site.

TriDPrinting (`tridprinting.com/BOM/Kossel-Mini/`) is actually a Mini Kossel (and other designs) parts vendor. They offer a complete list of replacement parts, such as the printed parts, wiring, and more.

Don't assume that just because your vendor doesn't offer spares that you will never need to repair your printer. Even if you print only a few hours a week, you will eventually need a spare part. A lot depends on how well the components in your printer were made, how often you perform the required preventive maintenance, and whether events occur that can damage a component.

I suggest certain spares in the following sections. The lists are based on my experiences with a wide variety of printers. The lists for your specific printer may vary from what is presented here. However, you should be able to use the lists to construct your own spares inventory.

But take care to think through what you need. Taken to the extreme, you could end up with enough parts to build a second printer.[6] Of course, once a part has failed, I tend to keep a second one on hand—just in case it fails again.

■ **Tip**   I suggest setting a budget for buying spares. Sometimes a spare part may be too expensive to keep on hand. For example, the electronics board is one of the more expensive parts and it (fortunately) rarely fails. On the other hand, if you rely on your printer for your business, you may want to have one on hand so that you don't encounter significant downtime.

Recommended List of Spares

In this section, I present a set of spares you should consider having on hand. If you have the budget to buy a complete set of spares, you should do so. However, if you are budget conscious, you may want to consider finding a source for the spares and saving that information so that when you do need the spares, you can get them quickly. On the other hand, if you are using your printer for a business or cannot afford the downtime to wait for a spare, you should consider investing in a set of spares as soon as your budget permits.

Printed Parts

Delta printers generally do not wear or break their printed parts unlike some early Cartesian designs. However, there are some parts that are known to fail occasionally. The following lists the printable spare parts that you should keep on hand. This list is based on the Mini Kossel RepRap delta printer, but other RepRap variants are similar. Take some time to examine your printer and locate any similar part to determine whether you can print it or must buy it from your vendor. (If your printer does not use printed parts, you may not need any of these.)

- *Endstop holders*: Endstop holders can take some abuse. Most are rather flimsy, which doesn't help. If your printer uses the same holder for all axes, just print one; otherwise, print a set.

- *Belt clamps*: Some older designs use belt clamps that can slip. The natural treatment is to tighten them down, but this act has a tendency to damage the clamps. If you have had to tighten your belt clamps more than once, I recommend that you print an extra set or look for an improved version to replace the existing clamps.

- *Other*: I would print a spare of any part that breaks. That is, if a part breaks, print two new ones so that you have a spare.

---

[6]An event that seems to occur more often than you think. I've built another Mini Kossel from my set of spares and I think I have enough to build another. All I need are the frame members. Will the circle ever be broken?

Replacement Parts

The following is a list of the spares that you should consider buying if you want to keep your printer running over the long term. Once again, these spares may not apply to all delta printers; you should buy those parts that do apply to your printer.

- *Fans*: As mentioned, fans can wear out surprisingly early with little warning. Unless your printer is built with exceptionally high-quality fans, you will eventually need a new one.

- *Belts*: Belts are long-wear items. I recommend buying a new set once you have had to adjust them a couple of times since the initial calibration. That is, if you were able to print for 100 or more hours without having to adjust the belts, and then suddenly you had to adjust them, you should obtain a spare. Replace the belt once it begins to need adjustment every few prints.

- *Rollers or roller covers for roller carriages*: These are long-wear items, but when they begin to fail, they may fail quickly. Get a complete set if your budget allows. Replacing them can take time and require recalibrating the towers, so be prepared for an extended service time.

- *Nozzle*: The hot-end nozzle is an item that many people have as a spare so that they can change it when it gets clogged. As you will see in the next section, you can clean even the most stubborn clogs. Regardless, having at least one spare nozzle will help you keep your printer running should you encounter a clog that cannot be cleared with the cold pull method.

- *Stepper motor*: This is another long-wear item. If you want a complete spare parts supply, I recommend having one of these on hand. You should not need a complete set unless your printer uses different sizes for each axis (not likely, but I have seen it at least once).

- *Stepper driver*: The stepper driver boards are susceptible to ESD and have been known to fail on occasion. I've had three fail over several hundred hours among different printers. If you have a RepRap delta printer or a printer that has separate stepper drivers, I recommend having at least one spare.

- *Endstop*: Endstops are simple switches and generally have a very long life. However, if the endstop is subjected to axis crashes (where the axis runs into the endstop violently), you could damage the endstop. Given its role, I recommend having at least one spare.

- *Electronics board*: Commercial- and professional-grade printers generally have proprietary electronics boards that are usually very expensive. If your printer uses one of the more popular general options (RAMPS, Rambo, etc.), and you must rely on your printer, you should have a spare to avoid a lengthy downtime.

If you cannot buy the part from your vendor directly, you want to ensure that you are getting the correct part for your printer. If you have any concern, be sure to compare the new spare part to the matching existing part. In those cases where the new spare is somewhat different (e.g., not the same supplier), I install the new part and test it, and then put the original part back in when I confirm the replacement is compatible.

Another factor is the cost of the spare part. Some spare parts can be expensive. To decide if you should buy one, you need to balance the cost of the spare with the availability and time to get the part.

Now that I have discussed the spare parts needed for long-term use, in the next section I discuss some common and not-so-common repair tasks.

Corrective Tasks

This section describes a number of corrective maintenance tasks (repairs) that you may need to do to keep your printer in good working order. I have tried to keep this discussion general, but some of the examples may feature specific printers or components. However, you should be able to draw parallels and knowledge from the examples should you need to fix a similar problem.

■ **Caution**   When repairing your printer, be sure to turn it off and disconnect the power and the USB cable. Unless you are diagnosing a problem, you should not need power to repair your printer.

Also, I recommend removing any access panels, enclosure panels, hoods, fans, and so forth, so that you can access the area for the repair. It is also a good idea to remove the build plate if it can be detached—especially if it is made of glass or other materials that are easily scratched or broken. It is all too easy to accidentally drop a sharp tool or part onto the print surface. LCD panels are another fragile item that should be removed if possible. Most panels have a clear plastic or glass cover, which can scratch easily.[7] Even if you aren't concerned about the print surface treatment, the build plate itself may be fragile.

As I mentioned in Chapter 4, it is also a good idea to gather the tools you need and place them nearby. If your printer is positioned where access to the repair area requires you to lean over the printer or reach behind it, move the printer to a place where you can access the area more easily. I use a small vintage typewriter stand with a piece of plywood on top as a workstation. Not only does this allow me to move the printer around, it also means I can push the stand out of the way if I don't finish the repair in one sitting.

Corrective tasks—hence, repairs—can take many forms: removing obstructions from the axis movement, cleaning out a hot end, replacing a worn or broken part, or replacing consumables like print surfaces and filters. I discuss some common corrective tasks (repairs) in the following sections.

Clearing a Clogged Nozzle

One of the most frustrating experiences I've encountered is a series of extrusion failures over a short period of time. For example, not being able to complete a print without having an extrusion failure. I discussed the causes of this problem in an earlier chapter. Recall that most of these problems are caused by obstructions in some form: the filament cannot exit the nozzle, the filament tension is too high, or a foreign object has found its way into the hot end. In the last case, the object is larger than the opening in the nozzle, and hence clogs it from within.

If you encounter this problem but the cold pull method does not work, you may have to remove the nozzle and clean it out. There are several techniques for doing this. What I present here is the most reliable procedure, but it requires care to execute it safely.

You will need a pair of heat-resistant gloves, the proper tools to remove the nozzle, metal tongs or pliers to hold the nozzle, canned air, a butane torch, a metal trivet or heat-safe area to place the heated nozzle during the procedure, and two drill bits—one that is the exact size of your nozzle opening and another that is the same size as the filament chamber (1.75mm or 3mm).

I recommend purchasing a set of small drills like those shown in Figure 7-9. You should buy several of each size because they are very easy to break.

---

[7]Can you guess how I know this?

Figure 7-9. *Micro drills*

These kits often come in several sizes. If you have multiple printers with differing nozzle sizes, or want to try different nozzle sizes, get a variety pack. I use drills in the 0.3mm–0.5mm range to match the nozzles I use. On the other hand, if you only have one nozzle size (or printer), get several of the correct size. The best are the ones packaged in a protective case with a large plastic ring to aid in identifying the size and holding the drill.

If you do not have any heat-resistant gloves, a good option is the Tuff Glove, which is found in most kitchen supplies stores. They come in a variety of colors and prove handy when you need to pick up or move a hot piece of metal. They can resist temperatures up to 500 degrees Fahrenheit (260 degrees Celsius) for short periods. Figure 7-10 shows my Tuff Glove.

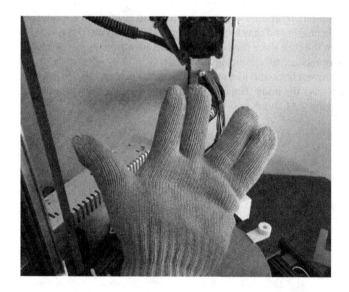

Figure 7-10. *Heat-resistant glove[8]*

---

[8]Rest in peace, Mr. Nimoy. May your Katra endure forever.

■ **Caution** Never, ever use a powered drill to drive the drill bit. You are only using the bit to grab the plastic, not change the internal structure of the nozzle. You only want to grip plastic; do not remove any metal. You should practice on a nozzle that you have considered a lost cause before trying it on your only nozzle.

The procedure is as follows. I explain each step in more detail afterward.

1. Remove the nozzle.

2. Place the torch on a workbench in an area where there are no combustible liquids or flammable material.

3. Pick up the nozzle with a pair of metal tongs or pliers.

4. Turn on the torch and turn it up to about a medium setting.

5. Place the nozzle in the flame. Do not heat the nozzle more than a few seconds. You do not want to use so high a flame that you burn the plastic.

6. After 10 to 20 seconds, remove the nozzle from the heat and use the larger drill bit to pull out melted plastic. Let the drill bit and nozzle cool.

7. Reheat the nozzle and repeat step 6 until you cannot get any more plastic.

8. Let the nozzle cool, and then use the small drill bit to clear the nozzle opening.

9. Reheat the nozzle and use canned air to blow out any remaining filament.

10. If you printed with ABS, soak the nozzle in acetone to remove any traces of filament.

You may need to disconnect the heater element, temperature sensor, wiring, and so forth, to remove the nozzle. Some hot ends do not have a removable nozzle and may require removal of the hot end. Others may require you to disassemble the hot end to get to the core since the nozzle and core are all one piece. Consult your hot end's documentation for the precise procedure for removing the nozzle.

When you place the nozzle in the flame, move it back and forth to heat the entire nozzle. I like to grip the nozzle by the bottom and let the flame flow over the body. The filament melts quickly. Some filament may ooze from the opening. This is normal. Figure 7-11 shows how to position the nozzle.

Figure 7-11. *Place the nozzle in the flame*

■ **Caution** You must wear protective gloves while using the torch. Proper eye protection is also prudent, as is having a fire extinguisher nearby in case something goes awry.

Next, use a drill bit that is the same size as the chamber and press it into the melted filament, and then pull it out. Don't use a drill or electric driver for this step. This mimics the cold pull procedure, but in this case you're using the cold drill bit to help grip the plastic and remove it. Figure 7-12 shows the proper size and position of the drill bit. You want to use the drill bit with one hand while holding the heated nozzle with the tongs or pliers.

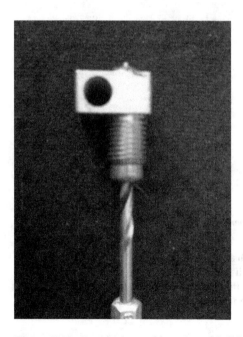

Figure 7-12. *Proper size and location of drill bit for removing plastic*

You can also use a piece of higher-temperature filament such as nylon or similar to press into the heated nozzle and pull out quickly. You can use this technique as an alternative to using a drill bit, but it may not remove all the plastic. Another alternative is to turn the nozzle upside down and let the heated plastic drip from the nozzle. Be sure to direct the flame away from the plastic so that it doesn't burn on exit.

■ **Caution** Be very careful when handling the heated nozzle. The nozzle—as well as the tool you use to hold it in the flame—gets very hot. Also, never use any form of electric driver or drill in this step. Use your hands to manipulate the drill bit.

Remember, you hold the heated nozzle with one hand while your other hand manipulates the drill bit. Once you have removed some plastic, place the nozzle on a safe surface (e.g., a metal trivet), allow the drill bit to cool, and then remove the plastic from the drill bit. Reheat the nozzle and try removing more plastic. Do this a few times until no more plastic can be removed.

■ **Caution** The goal is to remove plastic, not reshape the interior of the nozzle. Thus, you should apply only enough pressure to grasp the filament. If you see metal shavings, you've gone too far.

Once you can no longer get any plastic from inside the chamber, use the small drill bit to gently drill out any plastic from the opening. This step requires a bit of patience and the proper drill size. Be sure to get the properly sized micro drill that matches your nozzle. Figure 7-13 shows the properly sized drill bit and orientation for cleaning the opening.

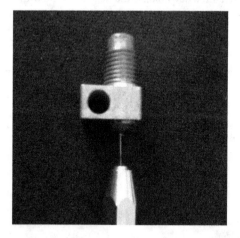

Figure 7-13. *Proper size and location of drill bit for cleaning opening*

Don't apply a lot of pressure here. The drill bit is very small and can break easily. You want to drill out the plastic, not reshape the opening (although you can do that if the opening has been damaged from a crash into the build plate). If this step makes you a bit nervous, that's OK. In that case, try using a drill bit that is slightly smaller than the opening to remove the plastic, and then switch to the correct size once the opening is clear.

At this point, the foreign object should be removed. You should also be able to hold the nozzle up to the light and see a pinpoint of light coming through the opening. If you do not, repeat both drill bit steps until you see light through the opening.

Return the nozzle to the heat again. Let it heat up for about 20 to 30 seconds, and then position the nozzle so that the opening is facing you and the chamber is facing the workbench (cement or metal floor, metal trash can, etc.) or some area that is safe for melted plastic. Use canned air to blow through the opening. Direct the air through the opening (reverse of the extrusion direction). This will remove the larger of the remaining bits of plastic, such as shavings from the drill bit.

At this point, your nozzle should be completely unclogged. You should clean the nozzle thoroughly with a wire brush before reinstalling it.

If you print with ABS, and ABS was indeed the filament used last, you should consider soaking the nozzle in acetone for about an hour. This will completely remove any stray bits of plastic that the previous steps missed. Figure 7-14 demonstrates this step. Notice there is enough acetone to completely submerge the nozzle. Also, the acetone is placed in a glass jar. Any acetone-safe container will work.

Figure 7-14. *Soaking the nozzle in acetone (ABS only)*

Now that wasn't so bad, was it? As you can see, this procedure is not for the faint of heart. Indeed, if you have any concerns about performing the procedure, you can always take the easier route and simply replace the nozzle. Replacement nozzles are generally less expensive than an entire hot end (if it is a separate part, like the J-head or E3D hot ends), but they are not cheap by any measure.

I recommend buying a replacement nozzle first and then trying this procedure on the original. If you dig too deeply with the drill bit or experience some similar mishap, you will gain practice without so much risk.

■ **Tip**   Until you perfect the procedure, don't try this procedure on your only nozzle!

Replacing Belts

Recall that the belts used in your printer are designed to have teeth or grooves that allow the drive gear to move the belt consistently. If the belt is worn or there are teeth missing, the belt can slip and cause problems with axis shift. If you have monitored your printer over time and notice that the belts become worn (or worse, break), you should replace the belts.

Some printers use a length of belt with the ends secured to the carriage; whereas others use continuous or closed belts (they have no break). Open belts are much more common but some Mini Kossel printer kits come with closed belts. Check your printer's manual or the vendor's web site for the specifics on replacing your belts.

Belts are typically a long-wear item. Depending on how much you use your printer, you may never have to replace the belts. You may have to adjust the tension periodically, but replacing belts is normally for those who use their printers for hundreds of hours per month. I include the procedures in this chapter for completeness.

Replacing Open Belts

Open belts are easier to fix. I like to clamp the carriage in position so that the effector isn't allowed to flop around. That is, once you disconnect the belt, the carriage drops to the bottom of the frame. It is best to secure the carriage in position by placing a small clamp under it. Don't grip the frame tightly. Use only enough tension to hold the carriage in place.

Once the carriage is secured, you need only to loosen the belt tensioner, disconnect the belt at both ends, and then pull it out. To install the new belt, thread it over the drive gear and idler, and then attach the ends with the existing clamps. You should pull the belt as tight as possible before securing the second end. If you find there is too much slack in the belt—your tension adjustment is at its maximum position—you should remove one end and pull it tighter before securing it.

Replacing Closed Belts

Closed belts can be a bit more difficult to replace. This is because the belt must be removed from the axis mechanism by partially (or completely) disassembling the axis. Depending on the delta printer design, you may not need to do this. For example, Mini Kossel printers with closed belts have enough room to remove the belt from the drive pulley, but you must remove the idler pulley to remove the belt completely.

If the axis mechanism can be disassembled without removing it from the printer, things aren't so difficult; but if you must remove the axis mechanism, be prepared for a potentially lengthy repair. I recommend taking your time and making notes (assuming your documentation doesn't cover this procedure) so that you can reassemble the mechanism properly. If you must disconnect the axis or frame members, you will have to recalibrate the towers (as described in Chapter 5).

Delta Arms and Joints

The delta arms—or more precisely, the delta joints—are another area that can wear on a delta printer. If your delta printer uses typical metal rod ends, these rod ends can wear over time and eventually become loose. This can lead to backlash, or more commonly, the delta arm blues. It can be treated with tension mechanisms such as springs or rubber and elastic bands.

One telltale sign of wear is a buildup of debris on the metal parts of the joint. For example, the swivel part of the rod end will accumulate dirt and dust. This can form a dark sludge-like residue on the perimeter, which can occur more frequently if you have been lubricating them more than necessary. Another common symptom is irregularities or artifacts appearing on the surface of your prints. If bad enough, you could see small layer inconsistencies.

You may need to tighten the delta joint bolts on newly assembled printers. Thus, you should check them for the first few prints to ensure that they are not working loose.

If you find that the delta arm joints are getting worn, you should replace them to ensure good print quality. Be sure to measure your existing delta rods to ensure that you get the same length rods. Replacing your delta arms with slightly smaller or larger arms will require recalibration, or at a minimum, firmware changes to compensate.

Fortunately, delta joint wear occurs infrequently and can vary from one solution to another. I've found that the Traxxas rod ends tend to need replacing after about 250 to 500 hours of printing. Unless you do a lot of printing, you may not encounter this problem; and even if you do, it is after many hours of printing. Thus, noticing wear is likely to be a result of print quality rather than measuring or noticing any play in the arms.

That said, I recommend checking the play in your delta joints after every 50 hours of printing.

Bearings, Bushings, and Rods

Bearings and bushings are typically made of metal and can withstand many hours of use. There are many forms of bearings and bushings. Most printers use several types. Bearings are typically designed for use on a shaft and have internal parts designed to rotate freely. Bushings are typically a solid part designed to slide over a rod or similar uniform rail. Figure 7-15 shows a number of the bearings and bushings that you may find in your printer. There are also many types of plastic bearings and bushings with similar designs and applications.

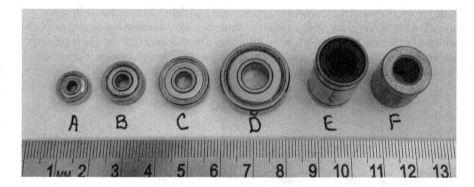

Figure 7-15. *Bearings and bushings*

Each of these bearings has a standard size that equates to its number, including bore (inner diameter), outer diameter, and length (perpendicular to the shaft or bore). For round bearings, the width is the outer diameter; and for linear bearings and bushings, it is the length. Table 7-3 describes each of the bearings shown. Note that Item F is an oil-infused brass bushing.

Table 7-3. *Some Common Bearings Found in Delta Printers*

Item	Type	Bore	Outer Diameter	Length	Sealed?
A	623ZZ	3mm	10mm	4mm	Yes
B	624ZZ	4mm	13mm	5mm	Yes
C	625ZZ	5mm	16mm	5mm	Yes
D	608ZZ	7mm	22mm	17mm	Yes
E	LM8UU	8mm	15mm	24mm	Yes
F	Common bushing	8mm	17mm	15mm	No

■ **Note** Some manufacturers specify "width" as the outer diameter and "thickness" for length.

The bearings in your printer are typically of high quality and more than capable of handling the task. Unless you encounter a defective bearing or the bearing is subjected to lack of lubrication, you should not need to replace bearings very often. However, if your printer starts making squeaks, grinding, or other metal-on-metal noises, you may have a bad bearing.

Replacing the bearings or bushings can take time. Most bearings are located in the belt idler pulley; roller carriages typically use bearings in the rollers; and some extruders use a bearing in the idler door. Also, most delta printers use sealed bearings that do not need lubrication. Bearing failure is rare but it can happen. Always pay attention to any strange sounds that your printer makes and try to isolate the noise. If it is coming from any of the bearings, replace them as soon as you can.

Replacing Filament Cleaner

There is a device designed to wrap around the filament to remove dust and debris from it. These cleaners (sometimes incorrectly called filters) are made from a variety of materials. After filament has passed through the foam, it can be damaged by friction. However, it is more likely that if the filament is dusty, the foam will become dirty, and since there is relatively little surface area, it may require frequent replacement. Figure 7-16 shows an example of a filament cleaner that needs replacing. The foam in the cleaner was used for more than 30 hours.

Figure 7-16. *Dirty filament cleaner foam*

This filament cleaner is made from a kitchen sponge and placed inside a printed cylinder casing (thingiverse.com/thing:16483). The sponge is cut half way through longitudinally, and then wrapped around the filament and inserted into the casing. I like this version because it fits just about any printer.

Notice in Figure 7-16 that there is a bit of debris inside the foam. This is mostly trapped dust and small particles. Had I not used the cleaner, all of this would have been sent through my hot end. Any one of the small particles in the foam could have easily caused an extrusion failure. This is clear evidence that filament cleaners really do work. If you don't have one, I suggest that you make it a top priority to add one as soon as you can print it.

If your printer has a filament cleaner, I recommend checking it after every 10 hours of printing, and replacing it every time you change the filament, or every 25 hours, whichever comes first.

Firmware Updates

There is one other corrective task you may want to consider—upgrading the firmware. Sometimes printer manufacturers release a new version of the firmware that has fixes or enhancements for the printing process or quality. However, most vendors do not release new versions very often. Firmware changes were common a few years ago, but not so much now.

It is generally a good idea to keep your firmware current, but I would not do it unless I encountered a need for the changes. Check your vendor's support web site for any changes to the firmware, and read the change notes carefully before deciding to upgrade.

If you own a RepRap delta printer, the firmware is really up to you since it is very much a DIY affair. The same philosophy applies: don't upgrade unless you find changes that you need. If you find that the latest variant of your firmware supports some nifty feature that you want, then upgrade; otherwise, wait. For example, if you want to add Z-probing or a new hot end or extruder, you will likely need to upgrade the firmware.

Summary

Keeping your delta printer running well requires some patience and discipline to perform some simple routine tasks. Whereas some tasks make sense and are quite clearly needed, like setting the Z-height or keeping the belts tight, other tasks—like tightening the frame—may seem mundane; and tasks like keeping the print bed clean and free from debris may not seem to have a lot of benefit. The periodic tasks that reduce the chance of failures and degradation of print quality may also seem mundane.

However, failure to do any of these tasks can have a cumulative effect on your printer, and you will eventually see some degradation of print quality. That is, if it doesn't break first! Ultimately, you save a lot of time by keeping up with the needs of your printer through inspection and adjustment.

In this chapter, you saw the more common inspection tasks that help you determine when things need adjustment or repair. This chapter also covered preventive and corrective tasks associated with delta printers. Preventive tasks keep parts from wearing and eventually failing; these tasks include keeping the printer clean, and the metal parts lubricated and adjusted correctly. Corrective tasks are repairs to fix the printer when it fails.

The next chapter covers one of my favorite things to do with my delta printers: upgrading to improve usability and quality. I present a number of useful upgrades, as well as some must-have items.

CHAPTER 8

■ ■ ■

Delta Printer Enhancements

One of the things that I find really fun to do with 3D printers, besides making amazing objects for gifts or solving problems around the house, is upgrading my printers. I have a number of printers, each in a perpetual state of refinement. Indeed, if you look closely at some of the photographs in this book you will see slight differences as I've continued to upgrade some of my delta printers. I am always looking for a better mount, clamp, or mechanism to improve my printers.

I think this is a lot of fun because it allows you to customize your printer to meet your needs, and if your needs change, you can change the printer accordingly. If you plan the upgrade carefully, you can even revert back to the original solution.

For instance, if you've built a Mini Kossel from a kit, it is likely the kit did not include a heated print bed. If you find you need to print with ABS, and you don't have another printer set up for ABS, you can simply add a heated print bed. I discuss this particular upgrade in this chapter, as well as some ideas for other upgrades and enhancements specific to delta printers, including some helpful tips on how to go about planning and implementing those enhancements.

The most important thing to consider before you embark on any enhancement or upgrade is to complete a comprehensive set of calibration tasks like those described in Chapter 5. I cannot stress that enough. You really should complete the calibration process before making any changes to your printer. This is because while some upgrades are designed to improve quality (or known to do so), most are not solutions to calibration problems and can make a small problem a larger one.

■ **Tip** Be sure to complete calibration before embarking on upgrades that are designed to improve print quality. Failure to do so may end in frustration.

Enhancements fall into three categories: features that add some minor function (farkles), enhancements to existing features that improve quality (enhancements), and upgrades that add completely new features that improve quality as well as usability, maintainability, and in some cases reliability (upgrades). I discuss each of these categories, along with examples of some common delta printer enhancements and upgrades. But before that, let's look at some best practices for making upgrades.

Getting Started with Upgrades and Enhancements

I hope that you are excited about the many possibilities and ideas for upgrading your delta printer. I know I've really enjoyed working on my printers and making them better.[1] However, you should probably hold off downloading and printing a bunch of parts or ordering any expensive machined parts until you figure out what you want to achieve and how to get there. In other words, you need a plan.

Failure to do this could lead to less-than-expected results, wasted time and money, and a great deal more frustration than you ever wanted. For example, resist the temptation to buy the latest and greatest hot end on the market until someone has reviewed it or at least used it for some time. If you fall into this temptation, you could end up with a very nice-looking knickknack shaped like a hot end. Yep, I've got one. I suppose several of us do.

Do Your Research: Finding Upgrades

You can search Thingiverse for ideas and objects to perform upgrades and enhancements to your printer. Depending on how long your printer design has been used, you should be able to find solutions that other enthusiasts have created. I recommend starting with those before attempting to develop your own. It will save you a lot of time (and frustration) and could give you ideas for design improvements that you can publish for others to use.

Since professional- and consumer-grade delta printers are not quite as numerous as Cartesian printers (at least not yet), you may not find too many updates for your delta printer. However, if you choose to build, or you own a RepRap delta printer like a Mini Kossel, Rostock, or similar, you may find a lot of ideas for upgrades. If you have one of the newest printers from SeeMeCNC[2] or OpenBeam,[3] you may find some upgrades, but not nearly as many as the RepRap designs. This isn't a bad thing because those printers come with nearly all the features you could want anyway.

Once you find the thing you want to use, check the object page and read all the information. Pay particular attention to the instructions and any installation tips or requirements for hardware. I typically avoid using things that have little or no information—especially if they are complex, multipart things. For example, I once found a nifty dual extruder, but it was made from at least a dozen parts, there were no instructions, and no parts list. Don't make your experience worse by trying to figure out someone else's half-baked idea.

Before you use any object you find online, be sure to check the license associated with the object to make sure that you are permitted to use it the way you plan to. Fortunately, most things on Thingiverse have few restrictions.

CHECK THE LICENSE

Make sure that the way that you plan to use the object is permitted by the license. Under most licenses, you are typically free to download and print the object, and can even make minor changes to it, but you are not allowed to claim the derivative as your own. See http://creativecommons.org/licenses/by-sa/3.0/ for an example of a popular license for objects on Thingiverse.

---

[1]Well, for the most part. I have a small collection of parts that didn't quite meet my expectations or made quality worse.
[2]See seemecnc.com.
[3]See openbeamusa.com.

More importantly, always check with the creator before downloading an object with the intent to monetarily profit on the design. The object creator generally owns a design. In most cases, a design is free for you to use, but may have severe restrictions on what you can do with the result. That is, some creators prohibit anyone from selling the printed objects that they designed. It is best to check the fine print before downloading an object and trying to profit from it.

Set Your Goals and Expectations

Once you find an upgrade (or several) that you want to perform on your printer, you need to set your goals and expectations. You should have a clear idea of what you want to upgrade and why. Unless the upgrade is minor, or even trivial (a farkle), you should understand how the upgrade should affect your printer. With this knowledge you should be able to set your expectations accordingly.

This most appropriately applies to upgrades found online. Prepackaged upgrade kits from vendors are typically well-sorted out and should work as expected, but things created by the community may or may not be as reliable (though many are). What you do not want to do is find some gee-whiz upgrade, download and print it, and then install it, only to discover it doesn't work, lowers the print quality, or even makes the printer unusable.

Thus, you should research the upgrade carefully. Pay particular attention to the people who have commented on the upgrade. One indication of the quality or applicability of the upgrade is how many times it has been downloaded and printed.

Once you have this information, compile it so that you understand what the upgrade will do for you. If the upgrade is designed to improve quality, try to determine how much it will improve quality. I recommend tempering your expectations and avoiding the trap of thinking an upgrade will solve all of your problems. Simply put, very few upgrades fall into this category.

Check Your Calibration

Once you perform an upgrade, always check your printer for proper calibration. Most times this is simply making sure that things are still aligned like they are supposed to be. If you have to partially disassemble the frame to install some upgrade, make sure that the frame is square and true during reassembly.

For example, if you replace the endstop mounts on your delta printer for a variety that makes adjustment (and hence calibration) easier, you will have to run the full recalibration process (see Chapter 5). This is because the endstop is a critical component of the printer geometry.

Before declaring victory, you should do at least one test print of both an easy object and a more difficult object. Sometimes minor changes that impact print quality can be incurred during the upgrade. These changes may not have anything to do with the upgrade itself, but something may have been changed unintentionally that can cause a problem.

■ **Tip** If you change any axis mechanism, endstop, or frame component, keep your hand on the power button the first time you home the printer. At the first sign of trouble—noises, the axis not stopping, and so forth—power it off and check your adjustments. You can also trigger the endstops manually and use the M119 command to make sure that everything is in working order.

One Upgrade at a Time

This may sound like a given, but you should resist the temptation to perform multiple upgrades at the same time. This is one way you can make your life much more difficult than it already is. More specifically, if you attempt to upgrade multiple parts of your printer and something goes wrong, or worse needs recalibration, how do you know which upgrade introduced the problem or even what calibrations need revisiting? Thus, you should always stick to one upgrade at a time: perfect the installation and calibration, and use the printer for several prints of various difficulty and length before moving on to the next upgrade.

Types of Enhancements and Upgrades

Depending on the printer you have, you could encounter many types of upgrades and enhancements. I like to break them into categories based on their function and goals, which indirectly relates to their importance or value for the enthusiast (what you get out of having the upgrade or enhancement).

Of least value for print quality, usability, or maintainability are enhancements for aesthetics and minor functions. I call this category "farkles" because while they can add some value, most are for beautification or ambiance. The next category includes more useful additions because they are targeted at or indirectly equate to improving quality. I call these "quality upgrades." Lastly, anything else that adds a new feature that has some significant improvement for usability, maintainability, or reliability I call simply "feature upgrades."

The following sections discuss each category in more detail; I include a couple examples for each. Keep your own printer in mind while your read, as it may help you decide what you want to do next with your fully calibrated 3D printer!

WHAT IS A FARKLE?

"Farkle" is a term borrowed from motorcycling that is a mash-up of *function* and *sparkle*.[4] We call something a farkle if it has a specific function, but is nonessential to the mission of the device on which it is installed, or it adds more glitz and glamour than function. For example, consider a motorcycle festooned with three GPS devices, a compass, multiple cup holders, and more LED lights than a semitractor truck from those trucker movies from the 1980s. Excess is one of the side effects of farkling. However, some farkles are helpful in some way, even if they are not essential.

One of the most common farkles is an enhancement to the printer frame. Delta printers generally have metal frames, although the SeeMeCNC models use melamine frames and I have seen a few examples of maple and other hardwood frames.

For metal frames, such as the Mini Kossel, you can buy the OpenBeam extrusions in silver (clear coat) or black. I have seen some photos of other colors, but as of today you can only get the two.

Those who have printers with a wooden frame sometimes stain or paint the frame to add some décor to their printer. This often adds only aesthetics and no functionally to the printer other than your own taste for adventure and personalization. However, it should be noted that sealing a wooden frame could protect it from moisture.

If you decide to paint, stain, or otherwise apply decorative coatings to your wooden printer frame, take care to use a finish that will not warp, crack, or otherwise swell (or shrink) the wood. Any distortion in the wood can cause alignment problems that may not be corrected with recalibration. I once stained a small

---

[4]As much as I detest portmanteau words like "framily" (friends and family), I must admit defeat given I use the term "farkle."

wooden box made from the same thin plywood that some printers use. Once it dried, the lid never closed properly again. Why? The wood warped a tiny bit and caused the lid to deform. You definitely do not want your wooden printer frame to warp.

Some of the enhancements that fall into this category include the following:

- Frame color/covering

- LED lighting

- Ambient lighting (lights under the printer)

- Adjustable feet (for physical leveling)

- Beautification covers

GOT FARKLES?

So do you farkle your printer or not? That's entirely up to you. If you feel like your printer resembles a well-designed fine machine, then you probably won't care about adorning your printer with aesthetics and farkles. However, if you desire something more than a lump of humorless components, you just might be in the farkling state of mind. I say farkle at will!

Quality Upgrades

The category of improvement that has the most potential for delta printers (the Mini Kossel and Rostock variants) is quality upgrades. There is a seemingly endless array of improvements designed to bolster quality for these designs. You may immediately associate this (and rightly so) with how well objects are printed. However, there is more to this category.

This category also includes the quality of the printer and the quality of the print experience. In other words, not just how well the printer can print, but how effectively it operates, how well you enjoy using it, or how well it works with your software. Quality enhancements may include bracing to help wobbly frames, devices designed to reduce or remove vibration, improved electronics, heating, and so forth.

For delta printers, the biggest quality upgrade is a good working spool holder (also called a *filament management system*) that allows for as little tension on the extruder as possible. You need some tension to keep the spool from unraveling, but it should not be so much as to make the extruder work to pull the filament. Too much tension and the extruder can skip steps, or worse, strip the filament and fail to extrude, thereby ruining the print. If you are having issues with inconsistent filament feed, a smoothly rolling spool holder may help.

Another area that some delta printers benefit from is frame supports. Some delta designs are prone to twisting at higher Z-heights, particularly during rapid movement. Some people have reported this as slightly uneven layers in the print. When designing or using frame supports, ensure that the axis movement is not obstructed by the brace. That is, some braces are designed for printers with linear rails and will not fit those that use larger side roller carriages.

Some of the enhancements that fall into this category include the following:

- Spool holder

- Frame supports

- Enclosures or wind breaks

- Print cooling fans

Feature Upgrades

"Feature upgrades" is the improvement category that allows you to adapt your printer to changing requirements. More specifically, feature upgrades are those things that add capability to your delta printer. The upgrade may enable you to print with another type of filament ,print with a second (or third!) extruder, or enable remote print monitoring or printing over a network.

Most delta printer kits do not include a heated print bed. However, it is fairly easy to add one. There are some trade-offs, such as a slight decrease in max Z-height. Some kits may require upgrading your power supply, and in rare cases, the electronics too.

Some of the enhancements that fall into this category include the following:

- Heated print bed

- Multiple extruders

- Print controller or monitor

Example Upgrades and Enhancements

Now let's get to the good stuff. In this section, I present a number of the common upgrades and enhancements you may want to consider for your delta printer. I cover a great deal of information here to provide you with as much knowledge as possible.

While many of the examples are based on one printer or another, it is likely you will be able to find a similar upgrade or enhancement for your own printer. Most of them are for the Mini Kossel but can be used for similar designs, like the Rostock Mini. This is mainly due the superb job the professional- and consumer-grade delta printer manufacturers have done in delivering complete solutions. If nothing else, you should be inspired to design your own solution—and I encourage you to do so!

I discuss the upgrades and enhancements roughly in order of popularity, but this is by no means an exhaustive discussion. Depending on the delta printer you own, you may decide some of the items may be more important than others. As mentioned previously, let your own experience and needs guide which upgrades and enhancements you decide to implement and which to implement first.

Heated Print Bed

If you plan to print with ABS or some of the higher-temperature filaments, you need to upgrade to a heated print bed. ABS is far too tricky to print without a heated print bed.[5] As mentioned previously, you can also use a heated print bed to help reduce lift and assist in reducing the effects of rapidly cooling PLA prints, but you use a lower temperature when printing with PLA (see the discussion on filament types and their characteristics in Chapter 1).

There are two main prerequisites for adding a heated print bed. First, the power supply must be capable of powering the heater. Second, your electronics must be capable of driving the heater. Most delta printer electronics support a heater, but it is best to check first. If it does not support a heater, you could have a bit more work to do in replacing the electronics. Depending on your skill level, this may be a deal breaker. It's best to check first.

If your printer was prebuilt and did not include a heated print bed, or if you built your delta printer from a kit, you may have a power supply that isn't up to the task. Check with your vendor to see what they recommend, but I would suggest a 30A 12V LED power supply. This power supply is a very popular choice.

---

[5]I tried this once just to say I had. I found that smaller parts that printed quickly can survive, but not without the use of ABS juice (and a lot of it).

The power supply is rectangular and can be mounted on the delta frame in a variety of places (or made into an oversized brick-like power supply like the one at thingiverse.com/thing:383877). Figure 8-1 shows a modified LED power supply. You can use this to upgrade your power supply, should you need to.

Figure 8-1. *LED power supply*

You can also use a PC power supply (also called an *ATX[6] power supply*), but I've found these to be cubical in shape and a bit harder to mount on some delta designs. Also, you have to trick the power supply into powering on. See http://reprap.org/wiki/PC_Power_Supply for more information on converting a PC power supply for use with your printer.

One thing to consider when adding a heated print bed to a delta printer is that it will likely raise your print surface, and therefore you will have to recalibrate the Z axis. In short, this means reducing the maximum Z axis travel in the firmware, as described in Chapter 3.

Another thing to consider when using a heated print bed with a built-in or supplied thermistor is whether it is supported in the firmware. If you use the Marlin firmware, as described in Chapter 3, remember to check to see if the thermistor is supported. If it is not, you will have to either change the thermistor (sometimes this is not possible) or ask the vendor to provide a link to the thermistor value table and modify the thermistortables.h file accordingly. Listing 8-1 shows the code I added to the file of a thermistor that wasn't supported by Marlin.

Listing 8-1. New Thermistor Values for 3950 Thermistor (thermistortables.h)

```
#if (THERMISTORHEATER_0 == 81) || (THERMISTORHEATER_1 == 81) || (THERMISTORHEATER_2 == 81)
|| (THERMISTORBED == 81)
// QU-BD silicone bed QWG-104F-3950 thermistor
const short temptable_81[][2] PROGMEM = {
        {1*OVERSAMPLENR,        938},
        {31*OVERSAMPLENR,       314},
        {41*OVERSAMPLENR,       290},
        {51*OVERSAMPLENR,       272},
        {61*OVERSAMPLENR,       258},
```

---

[6]ATX is a form factor for motherboards. See https://en.wikipedia.org/wiki/ATX.

```
                {71*OVERSAMPLENR,          247},
                {81*OVERSAMPLENR,          237},
                {91*OVERSAMPLENR,          229},
                {101*OVERSAMPLENR,         221},
                {111*OVERSAMPLENR,         215},
                {121*OVERSAMPLENR,         209},
                {131*OVERSAMPLENR,         204},
                {141*OVERSAMPLENR,         199},
                {151*OVERSAMPLENR,         195},
                {161*OVERSAMPLENR,         190},
                {171*OVERSAMPLENR,         187},
                {181*OVERSAMPLENR,         183},
                {191*OVERSAMPLENR,         179},
                {201*OVERSAMPLENR,         176},
                {221*OVERSAMPLENR,         170},
                {241*OVERSAMPLENR,         165},
                {261*OVERSAMPLENR,         160},
                {281*OVERSAMPLENR,         155},
                {301*OVERSAMPLENR,         150},
                {331*OVERSAMPLENR,         144},
                {361*OVERSAMPLENR,         139},
                {391*OVERSAMPLENR,         133},
                {421*OVERSAMPLENR,         128},
                {451*OVERSAMPLENR,         123},
                {491*OVERSAMPLENR,         117},
                {531*OVERSAMPLENR,         111},
                {571*OVERSAMPLENR,         105},
                {611*OVERSAMPLENR,         100},
                {641*OVERSAMPLENR,          95},
                {681*OVERSAMPLENR,          90},
                {711*OVERSAMPLENR,          85},
                {751*OVERSAMPLENR,          79},
                {791*OVERSAMPLENR,          72},
                {811*OVERSAMPLENR,          69},
                {831*OVERSAMPLENR,          65},
                {871*OVERSAMPLENR,          57},
                {881*OVERSAMPLENR,          55},
                {901*OVERSAMPLENR,          51},
                {921*OVERSAMPLENR,          45},
                {941*OVERSAMPLENR,          39},
                {971*OVERSAMPLENR,          28},
                {981*OVERSAMPLENR,          23},
                {991*OVERSAMPLENR,          17},
                {1001*OVERSAMPLENR,          9},
                {1021*OVERSAMPLENR,        -27}
};

#endif
```

Be sure to check the firmware for your thermistor, as these tables tend to get updated frequently. Indeed, you may find the 3950 thermistor added in the near future.

■ **Tip**   Heated print beds come in a variety of shapes and sizes. You will need to consider the maximum build area for your printer before ordering a heated print bed. That is, assuming your vendor doesn't have an option for your printer.

You can choose a typical PCB-based heater in a square, circular, or hexagon shape. You can also find heaters made from aluminum, but these tend to be more expensive and a bit thicker. If you built your delta printer using a borosilicate glass build plate, you can use a Kapton heater (tridprinting.com/Electronics/#3D-Printer-Kapton-Heaters) that adheres to the bottom of the glass. Figure 8-2 shows a Kapton heater attached to a glass plate for a Mini Kossel.

Figure 8-2. *Kapton heater*

This option saved me from changing my Z axis travel settings. I also created a different bed mount that uses spring-loaded clasps. See thingiverse.com/thing:705910 for more information and to download and print a set for yourself. I printed mine in ABS on another printer, but PLA may work OK until you get your heater mounted (long enough to print new mounts in ABS), provided that the heater element does not come into contact with the mount and you keep the temperature low.

However, there is one drawback. The Kapton heater, once adhered to the glass, does not come off without risk of destroying it. Thus, you cannot completely remove the print surface from the printer. If you mount your electronics on or near the lower frame, you will have enough extra wire to allow you to remove the glass and service it next to the printer. Naturally, this arrangement also prohibits the use of multiple print surfaces for different print surface treatments. If Z travel is not an issue, it may be best to consider a PCB heated bed with a removable glass print surface.

Figure 8-3 shows a typical round heated print bed. It is designed to fit SeeMeCNC's printers but can be used in a number of larger delta printer designs.

Figure 8-3. *Heated print bed (courtesy of SeeMeCNC)*

You can find heated print beds for delta printers online from a variety of vendors. You can also find them on online auction sites, where I routinely see hexagon-shaped heated print beds for Rostock, Mini Kossel, and similar RepRap designs.

Print Cooling Fan

The next most important or popular upgrade is adding one or more fans to cool your prints. This is generally used for PLA printing but can be used for other types of filament. If your delta printer did not come with a print cooling fan and it is set up to print with PLA, you should seriously consider adding one as soon as you can.

■ **Note**   This type of fan is also called a "part cooling fan" and many people name it such. A perhaps more correct term is print cooling fan.

There are a number of print cooling fan solutions that you can use or draw upon to adapt to your printer. If you search Thingiverse, you are likely to find dozens or even hundreds of examples. I recommend using keywords that match your printer, such as names of your printer design (Kossel, Rostock, etc.) and one or more appropriate search terms, (fan, duct, cooling, etc.). I would also sort by number of makes or look for ones that a lot of people have liked. These are likely to be the ones that work the best.

However, depending on your printer, especially whether you built it yourself, you may not be able to use some of the solutions—even if they happen to be very popular. For instance, due to how I mounted my power supply on my Mini Kossel, I was not able to use a fan duct that extended beyond the effector. What I really wanted was to utilize the abundance of space above the effector to mount a squirrel cage fan for higher airflow (see the "Got Fans" sidebar later in this chapter for why I chose a squirrel cage fan).

My solution was to design my own fan mount and nozzle. I created a raised squirrel fan cage fan mount that mounts to the effector by using one of the existing bolts for the hot end. I also created a fan duct[7] that suspends from the same location. Since I wanted the ability to experiment with different nozzles and to keep the intervening connecting duct close to the effector, I used a short piece of flexible hose to connect the two. Figure 8-4 shows the end result. You can find this thing on Thingiverse (`thingiverse.com/thing:705864`).

Figure 8-4. *Print cooling fan for Mini Kossel*

I printed both parts using ABS, but since the fan mount is isolated from the heat of the nozzle, you can print the mount with PLA. However, you should print the nozzle with ABS because PLA may deform when placed close to the nozzle as shown.

---

[7]I also use *nozzle* to describe this part, but *duct* is a more appropriate name.

If you want to make this for your own Mini Kossel, or perhaps adapt it to your own delta printer, I encourage you to do so. If you use the parts as they are designed (you print the .stl files), you will need a short piece of 18mm inside diameter hose to connect the nozzle to the mount. I used a piece of a medical air hose, like those found on some CPAP masks. If you have a medical supply store nearby, you can check with them. It is possible they can sell you a hose or give you one (be sure to wash it really well because you don't know where it's been). You could also use a stiffer hose, like those for outdoor garden ponds.

Note that the nozzle is 63mm tall. It mounts to the top of the effector. If you are installing this on a Mini Kossel built from the original source files, and you are using an E3D hot end, you may not need to change the height of the fan duct. To check, measure the distance from the top of your effector to the bottom of the heater block on your nozzle. If it is 62mm to 64mm, you're good. Otherwise, open the .scad file and change the height as needed.

■ **Tip**   Recall that a .scad file is a script that you can use in OpenSCAD to generate a .stl file.

Listing 8-2 highlights in bold an excerpt of the code that changes the height (the default is 64). It simply changes the height of the mount point, not the fan duct itself.

Listing 8-2. Changing the Height of the Fan Duct

```
...
// To change the height of the fan duct, enter the height in the method call.
// Note that the minimum height is 44.
// Create a fan duct that extends 64mm down from the top of effector.
fan_duct(64);
translate([-30,35,0]) fan_connector();
```

To complete the build, you also need a longer M3 bolt of about 25mm and an M3 nut. To prepare the fan mount, insert the M3 nut into the mount. If it is loose, use a bit of super glue to hold it in place (you won't be able to get to it during installation), and then secure the fan to the mount using zip ties. Next, slide on the hose to connect the mount and nozzle.

To prepare the fan duct, remove the rearmost bolt from your effector, holding the hot end in place (or whichever point you want). Slide the longer bolt through the effector and the fan duct mount point. Connect the hose to the fan duct, and then slide the fan mount over the bolt and tighten.

Finally, wire the fan to your electronics board. Use the appropriate connection point. That is, do not attach it directly to 12V power because the fan will run at 100% speed all the time. You don't want that. What you want is to allow the printer electronics to alter the speed of the fan during the print.

Once everything is installed, use your printer controller software to connect to your printer and turn on the print cooling fan. Experiment with different speeds to ensure that the fan can be used at these speeds. If your fan only works at near 100% power, see Chapter 2 for information on how to build a circuit to fix this.

If you have a professional- or consumer-grade printer, you may be able to get a fan duct from your vendor. For example, SeeMeCNC provides a fan duct for its printers that can be downloaded and printed. Figure 8-5 shows a completed fan duct for a Rostock Max with the fan inserted.

Figure 8-5. *Print cooling fan for Rostock Pro (courtesy of SeeMeCNC)*

Like my solution for the Mini Kossel, the fan duct uses a squirrel cage fan mounted to the effector. In this case, it is a very small but effective fan that is included in the kit. However, unlike the Mini Kossel, where space is a premium, the minimal distance that the fan protrudes is not an issue. In fact, the documentation suggests that you can add as many as three fans to the effector.

GOT FANS?

You may think that all fans are created equal. This isn't the case. Indeed, the design of a fan—how it moves air—can influence its application. I won't go into all the fan designs available (there are many), but I will discuss those used on most 3D printers: axial[8] and centrifugal fans (sometimes incorrectly called radial fans).

Axial fans are oriented like the traditional house fan, where the blades are used to drive air through the fan at a 90-degree angle to the chassis (frame) or parallel with the axle (hence the name). Axial fans are good for moving a lot of air, but at reasonably low pressures. For this reason, they are excellent choices for general cooling, like for electronics.

Centrifugal fans, or squirrel cage fans, are designed with their blades aligned with the axle and shaped to draw air through the center of the fan, compress it, and force it out of a fixed opening. The most obvious characteristic is that they are shaped similar to a vintage hair drier with a very short nozzle. However, due to their design, they can move air at higher pressures per air volume, making them best suited for precision cooling. Centrifugal fans tend to be more expensive since they are used in far fewer applications than axial fans.

Sadly, most enthusiasts tend to use axial fans everywhere, thinking a fan is a fan is a fan. I know I used to think that until—well, I thought about it. While it is difficult to argue with success, a ducted axial fan (in general) cannot reach the same pressure and accuracy of a centrifugal fan. So where should you use each?

As it turns out, the only real issue is print cooling. Again, some people have had great success using ducted axial fans, but I have found the design of the centrifugal fan is much better for part cooling. You may still want to use a duct to direct the air, but a squirrel cage fan is the best choice for part cooling.

[8]See http://en.wikipedia.org/wiki/Mechanical_fan.

Another reason to upgrade your print cooling fan is if your printer came with an axial print cooling fan or you want to add some other accessory that obstructs movement of the delta arms. I recommend searching Thingiverse for ideas if you don't like your current fan arrangement or need to replace an axial fan with a squirrel cage fan. You may also want to wait to purchase a squirrel cage fan until you decide on which fan duct and mount to use.

For printers that have electronics that do not support print cooling fans, you can still install one (or replace your electronics, but that is a major endeavor). To use a print cooling fan without electronics support, wire the fan through a switch so that you can turn it on and off. You may also want to consider using the high/low circuit shown in Chapter 2 so that you can run the fan on low speed to start and perhaps at high speed later in the print. This isn't ideal because it means you must monitor the print and manually control the fan, but it is better than no fan at all.

Spool Holder

Adding a spool holder, sometimes called a *filament management system*, can help solve problems with extrusion. More specifically, if the filament cannot be drawn into the extruder easily, the tension can cause slow extrusion, and therefore too thin runs, or cause the filament drive gear to skip or strip the filament and thereby stop extrusion.

A well-designed spool holder should be capable of allowing the extruder to pull filament with very little tension. You need some tension in order to keep the spool from unraveling, but not so much that the extruder needs to work at it.

Like print cooling fans, there are many spool holders available. In fact, I've found there are hundreds to thousands of examples to choose from. They range from freestanding units to printer-specific solutions that mount to the printer itself. Figure 8-6 shows one example of a spool holder that I created for a Mini Kossel. It can easily be adapted to other delta printers.

Figure 8-6. *Spool holder for Mini Kossel*

This solution was inspired by another spool holder I found on Thingiverse. It is designed to use a really nifty roller from a spool holder for a MakerBot printer. Since all of my filament spools are the same internal size, I can use my store of filament on any of my printers. You can find my spool holder for the Mini Kossel on Thingiverse (thingiverse.com/thing:705838).

What you will find on that site is the mount that is designed for the 15×15 OpenBeam frame. If you have a differently sized frame, you can modify it to fit your frame because I include the .scad file. To complete the build, you will need the following vitamins:

- (3) M3×8 bolts
- (3) M3 nuts
- (3) 5/8-inch washers
- 5/8-inch Nyloc nut
- 5/8×5-inch bolt

You will also need to print out the roller from thingiverse.com/thing:119016.

The mount is designed to mount to the Z tower using three 8mm M3 bolts. You can drop all three nuts down the frame from the top, provided you made the modification described in Chapter 4. To hold the nuts in place while you thread the bolts, use a long-handled hex key to hold the topmost nut in place, and then slide the mount over the frame rail and align the hole over the nut. Thread in the nut until it is snug. Repeat the process with the next lowest nut and so on.

Next, mount the roller to the bracket using a 5-3/8″ bolt and Nyloc, placing washers between the roller and the mount, as well as between the Nyloc and the mount. Tighten the bolt so that the roller can spin, but not so loose that it has a lot of play. A small amount of tension is best.

There are a number of other spool holders that you may be interested in. I list of few of them next. Some of these mount on top of the delta printer, but I've found that the added weight can increase the flex some delta printers with smaller frame components can exhibit. Also, consider the location of your extruder (cold end) so that you don't have to relocate it to accommodate the spool holder. Although you can mount the spool holder on the top and the cold end on the bottom (it is just a matter of a longer Bowden tube properly routed), I find that locating them closer together a bit nicer and easier to work with. It is far easier to add a mechanical thing like a spool holder than to reroute and possibly rewire an electronic component.

- thingiverse.com/thing:454808
- thingiverse.com/thing:114717
- thingiverse.com/thing:508896
- thingiverse.com/thing:143424
- thingiverse.com/thing:60352
- thingiverse.com/thing:118330

Other considerations include your filament spool's inner diameter size, the width and diameter of the spool, and whether you need a spool holder that can be adapted to differently sized spools. Whichever spool holder you decide to use, you will find it to be a very convenient enhancement.

LCD Panels and Mounts

The first printers I built and used did not have any form of display. Sure, there were a few LEDs on the electronics, but that was about it. That is, until I wanted to add my own feedback mechanisms. I found several ideas using seven-segment displays (think of an old alarm clock) to show axes position and voltage, but they would have been a lot of work.

But feedback isn't really that helpful given you still must have a computer connected to print. This is because most printer controller software has the ability to display the current axes positions, temperatures, and more. A display panel provides much more than simply displaying information about the printer status. In fact, most add-on display panels are liquid crystal displays, which we simply call *LCD panels*.

These panels are enabled by the firmware to display feedback, as well as a host of printer-side controls that home axes, set the hot end temperature, turn on a fan, or print from files on an SD card. Figure 8-7 shows an LCD panel mounted on a Mini Kossel.

Figure 8-7. *LCD panel for Mini Kossel*

The panel shown is a typical text display capable of displaying four lines of twenty characters (called a 4×20 display). Notice that there are some special symbols that may appear as graphics, but they are simply special characters programmed in the firmware. The vast majority of LCD panels are text panels. This is a RepRapDiscount panel available from most 3D printer online stores and online auction sites.

There are also graphic LCD panels that allow more freedom for implementing more interesting displays. There are fewer choices for graphic LCD panels and most are more expensive. Check your firmware or with your vendor before adding a graphic LCD panel.

If you have a RepRap printer, you may be able to use one of several LCD panels—either text or graphic. Look for one that is designed to work with your electronics. For example, if you have a RAMPS setup, choose one that has an adapter made for the RAMPS shield. In order to activate the LCD panel, you have to modify the firmware by enabling the corresponding #define in the Configuration.h file. Listing 8-3 shows an excerpt of the Marlin firmware that lists the types of panels supported. Just uncomment the one that matches your panel, compile, and upload the firmware.

Listing 8-3. LCD Panel Support in Marlin

```
...
//LCD and SD support
//#define ULTRA_LCD  //general LCD support, also 16x2
//#define DOGLCD  // Support for SPI LCD 128x64 (Controller ST7565R graphic Display Family)
//#define SDSUPPORT // Enable SD Card Support in Hardware Console
//#define SDSLOW // Use slower SD transfer mode (not normally needed - uncomment if you're
getting volume init error)
//#define SD_CHECK_AND_RETRY // Use CRC checks and retries on the SD communication
//#define ENCODER_PULSES_PER_STEP 1 // Increase if you have a high resolution encoder
//#define ENCODER_STEPS_PER_MENU_ITEM 5 // Set according to ENCODER_PULSES_PER_STEP or your
liking
```

```
//#define ULTIMAKERCONTROLLER //as available from the Ultimaker online store.
//#define ULTIPANEL   //the UltiPanel as on Thingiverse
//#define LCD_FEEDBACK_FREQUENCY_HZ 1000          // this is the tone frequency the buzzer
plays when on UI feedback. ie Screen Click
//#define LCD_FEEDBACK_FREQUENCY_DURATION_MS 100 // the duration the buzzer plays the UI
feedback sound. ie Screen Click


// The MaKr3d Makr-Panel with graphic controller and SD support
// http://reprap.org/wiki/MaKr3d_MaKrPanel
//#define MAKRPANEL


// The RepRapDiscount Smart Controller (white PCB)
// http://reprap.org/wiki/RepRapDiscount_Smart_Controller
//#define REPRAP_DISCOUNT_SMART_CONTROLLER


// The GADGETS3D G3D LCD/SD Controller (blue PCB)
// http://reprap.org/wiki/RAMPS_1.3/1.4_GADGETS3D_Shield_with_Panel
//#define G3D_PANEL


// The RepRapDiscount FULL GRAPHIC Smart Controller (quadratic white PCB)
// http://reprap.org/wiki/RepRapDiscount_Full_Graphic_Smart_Controller
//
// ==> REMEMBER TO INSTALL U8glib to your ARDUINO library folder: http://code.google.com/p/
u8glib/wiki/u8glib
#define REPRAP_DISCOUNT_FULL_GRAPHIC_SMART_CONTROLLER


// The RepRapWorld REPRAPWORLD_KEYPAD v1.1
// http://reprapworld.com/?products_details&products_id=202&cPath=1591_1626
//#define REPRAPWORLD_KEYPAD
//#define REPRAPWORLD_KEYPAD_MOVE_STEP 10.0 // how much should be moved when a key is
pressed, eg 10.0 means 10mm per click


// The Elefu RA Board Control Panel
// http://www.elefu.com/index.php?route=product/product&product_id=53
// REMEMBER TO INSTALL LiquidCrystal_I2C.h in your ARUDINO library folder: https://github.
com/kiyoshigawa/LiquidCrystal_I2C
//#define RA_CONTROL_PANEL
...
```

■ **Tip**   If you made any changes to your firmware settings and saved them to memory with the M500 command, use the M503 command via your printer controller software and write down all the parameters. You may need to reset these once the firmware is updated.

More recent delta printers are being shipped with LCD panels as a standard feature. However, if your delta printer did not come with any form of a control, adding an LCD panel will make it easier to use.

Remote Printing Capabilities

If you have used a printer that has networking capabilities, especially remote control, you know how convenient such a feature can be. On the other hand, if you have never used such a feature, you may be wondering what all the fuss is about. I describe two such solutions in Chapter 3: the OctoPi and MatterControl Touch.

What I find most convenient about remote printing is the ability to send files to the printer without having to attach it to your computer or dedicate a computer for printing. This is especially bothersome when you have a really long print job and you need to use your computer. More than once I have shut down my printer software either accidentally or as a result of an inadvertent reboot.[9]

But it is not just the ability to send a print job to a printer over the network that I find convenient, it is also the ability to control the printer remotely. That is, to turn on preheating, initiate auto Z-probe (leveling), and other miscellaneous tasks. As I discussed in Chapter 3, either the OctoPi or MatterControl Touch can meet your remote printing needs for printers that do not have these features.

I also like the ability to check on a print job when I cannot be in the same room as the printer. Let's face it. There are too many things that can go wrong during a print. Having the ability to remotely monitor the print can allow you to stop the printer should something go wrong.

Lighting

Adding lighting to your printer can be an enhancement or a farkle, depending on what you are trying to illuminate. If you are adding lighting to make it easier to see your print (the build plate), then it is an enhancement and something you may want to consider. That's not to say ambient lighting isn't useful, it can be, but it's more of a farkle in that it isn't strictly necessary.

Some printers include a lighting feature that illuminates the build plate and can be quite handy for watching the printer lay down the first layers. It is during the first layers that adhesion problems can occur and if you detect it soon enough, you can avoid wasting a lot of filament on a print that has lifted too much.

Those printers that have enclosures (like some Cartesian printers) can be quite dark inside, and thus difficult to see clearly what is going on in there. Fortunately, most delta printers, by consequence of the design, have an open frame where room lighting can be sufficient. In cases where the frame isn't open, you can easily add 12V super-bright LEDs to your printer. Figure 8-8 shows one such example.

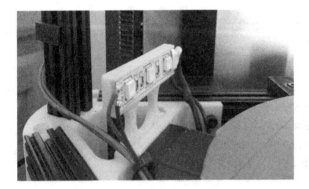

Figure 8-8. *Bed LEDs for Mini Kossel*

---

[9]Which is why I never use a laptop for a long print job unless connected to a charger, and depending on the operating system, I turn off automatic updates.

This light fixture was built from a mount I made myself (`thingiverse.com/thing:705814`); it secures to the lower frame using the two upper stepper motor bolts. I installed two of them: one on the X tower and one on the Y tower.

The LED is a self-adhesive LED strip I purchased from an electronics store. In this case, the strip could be cut into smaller, three-LED sections. Wiring LED lighting is best accomplished by wiring them through a switch so that you can turn them on and off at will.

Adding LED lighting is one upgrade that I recommend for anyone who wants to tinker with their printer, but doesn't want to risk changing the configuration or calibration. As long as you are confident (and careful) wiring the LEDs to your 12V main, you shouldn't have any problems. Plus, the reward can be illuminating.[10]

There are several lighting-upgrade examples on Thingiverse for a variety of delta printers. If my example doesn't inspire you, navigate to Thingiverse and do a quick search.

Alternative Effectors for Accessory Hot Ends

Your delta printer has a single effector that the vendor (or designer, in the case of a RepRap model) has designed to work with a specific hot end or class of hot ends, as well as the delta arms themselves. Since there are so many hot end choices, you may decide to change your hot end. You may even want to add a second extruder to your printer. If your effector isn't designed to be adapted to the new hot end, you will need to replace it.

If you want to change your hot end or use a different delta arm and carriage setup, you will have to change your effector to match. You can also use an alternative effector that permits you to mount part-cooling fans and other accessories. If maximum Z-height is an issue, you can find effectors that mount the hot end on a raised platform, thereby increasing maximum Z-height.

Fortunately, there are a number of people who have made alternative effectors for many of the delta printer designs, motivated by a variety of reasons. Whatever your need may be, it is likely you will find what you are looking for on Thingiverse, or at least get some inspiration for making your own alternative design. Here are just a few of the alternative effectors available on Thingiverse. I group them by delta design

- **Mini Kossel**: `thingiverse.com/thing:684434`, `thingiverse.com/thing:225718`

- **Rostock Max**: `thingiverse.com/thing:80616`, `thingiverse.com/thing:373772`

- **Rostock**: `thingiverse.com/thing:17175`, `thingiverse.com/thing:622082`

■ **Tip**   I prefer to use ABS for all parts that get near or touch the hot end body and mount.

Alternative Delta Arm Attachment

One of the bleeding-edge modifications to delta printers is the use of alternative joints or links for the delta arms. Although it is still an emerging feature, and not as popular as some of the other upgrades and enhancements, I include it as an example of what is possible for delta printers and how people are improving the design.

The purpose of using alternative arm joints is to reduce delta arm backlash and vibration, eliminate a common wear item, and make it really easy to remove, replace, and service the effector and hot end.

One design uses magnetic joints (sometimes called *magnetic effectors*). It replaces the normal joint on the delta arm with a spherical magnet and socket (or spherical steel ball and magnetic socket). There are various designs under way, some mount the magnet to the arm or effector, and others use a pair of steel sockets with the magnet in between (as well as a few other variations). Figure 8-9 shows one example of a magnetic effector.

---

[10]Sorry. Corny humor alert.

Figure 8-9. *Magnetic effector (courtesy of Andy Carter)*

You can find this on Thingiverse (thingiverse.com/thing:210028). As you can see in the photo, it also uses a specially raised hot end design to increase the maximum Z-height. Notice that both the arms and the effector use metal cups and the spherical magnet makes the connection. There is also an endstop mounted on top that is triggered when the hot end makes contact with the print surface; this is used for auto leveling.

The designer of this particular variant has improved upon the design by changing the magnets to steel ball bearings and cups, and then adding a spring and cable to keep tension on the joints. This retains the benefits of the magnetic joints while greatly reducing the chances of disconnection. You can find these parts on Thingiverse as well (thingiverse.com/thing:543303). You can also find more information about this modification at http://forums.reprap.org/read.php?178,361141. Scroll through to the post that is dated July 27, 2014 by Andy Carter. Figures 8-10 and 8-11 show an example of this implementation.

Figure 8-10. *Ball bearing, socket, and tension mechanism—effector (courtesy of Andy Carter)[11]*

---

[11]I like how he mounts the fan. This is an excellent example of using the correct fan type.

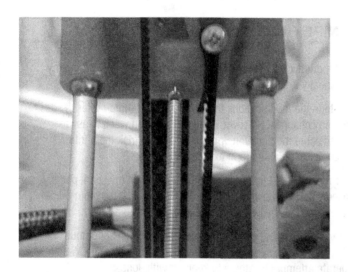

Figure 8-11. *Ball bearing, socket, and tension mechanism—carriage (courtesy of Andy Carter)*

There are some limitations to using experimental joints, especially those with magnets. Unless you use powerful rare earth magnets (recommended by many early adopters of this design), it is possible for one or more of the arms to become detached. This normally happens when some other problem occurs (like the hot end colliding with the print bed or some other obstruction), but has been reported to happen if there is significant lifting, resulting in the hot end diving into the part. Should this happen, you would have to stop the printer immediately to avoid any additional damage to the delta arms, effector, and hot end (your part will likely be toast at this point).

■ **Caution**   Magnets can be fatal if swallowed. Be sure to keep them away from small children and pets.

Another limitation is lubricating the magnetic joint. Some people have experimented with various materials, such as nylon fabric, Tyvek fabric, and even wax paper placed between the magnet and the socket. Of course, PTFE grease will also work, but you have to be careful not to use so much that the magnet detaches.

Although this is an experimental upgrade, you should not be deterred from trying out this feature and experimenting on your own. If you want to experiment with bleeding-edge upgrades, you should consider building a second printer so that you don't jeopardize your printing capabilities.

Delta Arm Vibration Dampers

When I first started experimenting with delta printers, I noticed photos of other people's delta printers showed a curious appendage to the delta arms, mounted about 3cm to 4cm from the effector. I saw that people had placed rubber bands, plastic clips, or elaborate spring tension mechanisms to link the arms together. I naturally looked at this as treatments for an imagined problem.

SNIPE HUNTING

Many years and many pounds ago, I raced motorcycles. I raced Motocross and Grand Prix.[12] During my long, albeit aborted, career, I discovered a sneaky practice.

Tuners would use all manner of trickery to hide the modifications they made to their motorcycles. If done right, no one could tell you had made any changes. However, if the modification wasn't easy to hide or if you wanted others to think you had some modification or other, you could trick them into applying some unproven and in some cases detrimental upgrade to their own bikes.

For example, one of my friends—a master mechanic—told me to put yellow boots on my spark plugs. He said there was a vendor with a supposedly better plug wire with, yes, yellow caps. It turns out these were worse than the stock unit and could even make the motor produce less horsepower.

Although I did not do this to my motorcycle, another friend did just to experiment. Within about four races, most of the other motorcycles on the grid had the very same yellow booted modification. We all had a good laugh when we saw the desperate attempts by others to keep up with Jones'.

Sometimes I wonder when I see some modification or other if it isn't yet another example of a snipe. My advice is to challenge the premise first by experimentation, and confirmation of results before adoption.

However, it turns out it can be a problem, depending on how your delta printer was constructed. Some delta printers can induce vibration in the delta arms. So much so that it has been known to cause the arms to make a lot of noise—more than even a noisy fan.

In rare cases, it can also affect print quality in the form of slightly uneven layers. That is, the arms vibrate enough to change the geometry, and therefore cause the effector to be out of place. Some call this phenomenon "ringing," which describes the effect on the part: it forms a wavy pattern that, if severe, can be easy to see.

Placing tension on the arms reduces the vibration (or chattering) and can reduce the ringing effects. This is called *backlash*. Backlash can manifest as loose joints, where the outer portion is slightly too large and allows the inner part to move back and forth. Adding the springs keeps the joints from moving, but the best cure is replacing the joint(s). As you saw in an earlier chapter, your delta arms should be inspected regularly for worn joints and repaired before the wear affects print quality. Figure 8-12 shows an example of spring dampers for delta arms (thingiverse.com/thing:777094). I used lightweight springs (7/32" × 1").

---

[12]Yes, I am one of those people.

Figure 8-12. *Delta arm spring dampers*

Although I have not seen the vibration of the delta arms affect print quality on my own delta printers, I concede it is possible that vibration can be a problem. If you encounter this problem, I recommend using soft-wound springs or a similar solution that does not put so much tension on the delta arms that it puts additional, side force on the joints. Or worse, limits the delta arms from freedom of movement.

■ **Tip**   Always use the lightest tension springs available. Do not put extra tension on the delta arms.

The vibration can be greatly reduced with light tension. One of the best designs for delta arm dampers can be found on Thingiverse (thingiverse.com/thing:78095). If your delta arms are noisy or vibrate a lot during rapid movement, a simple lightweight spring or rubber band may be a good treatment.

Nema 17 Dampers

Another enhancement for noise is the use of dampers on the stepper motors. I have used Nema 17 damper plates to reduce noise from loud stepper motors. These are specially designed plates with a thick, stiff rubber center (think automotive motor mount) that absorbs much of the vibration while limiting rotational movement. Figure 8-13 shows an example of a new mount.

Figure 8-13. *Nema 17 dampers*

The mount uses only two of the bolts in the stepper motor and the other two can be used to mount the unit to your frame. Note that there is ample clearance for using the existing mounting bolts.

If you find your delta printer makes a lot of noise when moving the axes, you can add a Nema 17 damper plate. It will help with the noise. It won't eliminate it, but it will make it more tolerable. However, be sure not to overtighten the belt so that it forces the stepper motor to flex on the damper plate. This can prevent the drive pulley from running parallel with the belt, and in extreme cases, it can cause belt wear or misalignment.

You can find these plates on popular online auction sites and in online 3D printer stores such as TriDPrinting (www.tridprinting.com/Electronics/#Stepper-Motor-Dampers). If you decide to install them, I recommend installing one on each axis. Do not install it on your extruder; although the mount is very stiff, it does permit the stepper motor to move, which can mean the difference between proper tension on the filament or not.

Electronics Enclosure

The last of the more popular enhancements is adding an enclosure for your printer's electronics. The main reasons you would want to consider an electronics enclosure is to reduce dust buildup (hence enhancing cooling), to keep the electronics safe from accidental touches and electrostatic discharge,[13] and of course, to keep the RAMPS board cool by directing a fan over the board.

Some delta printers (like those from SeeMeCNC) have their electronics mounted in an out-of-the-way location behind a panel in the lower frame section. Most RepRap delta designs and some consumer-grade printers and kits do not have any enclosure, instead leaving the electronics out in the open. A few vendors mount the electronics under the build plate, but if you add a heated print bed, you may need to move it.

Such was the case for one of my Mini Kossel delta printers. I added a heated print bed that I wanted to mount as low as possible. This left too little room to put the RAMPS under the build plate, and with the added heat so close, it would have proven not to be a wise decision, and could have proven fatal (to the electronics) during long print jobs. I am certain the RAMPS or some component therein would have failed due to the heat. I could not have added a fan because it would have cooled the heated print bed too. Figure 8-14 shows my solution.

---

[13]Or accidentally dropping a tool, or worse, a small bolt or nut into the powered-on electronics.

Figure 8-14. *Electronics enclosure for Mini Kossel*

Thus, my solution was to put an external electronics enclosure on the lower frame and mount a fan on it. I searched Thingiverse and found one I liked, except there wasn't an easy way to mount it to the Mini Kossel frame. I downloaded it and remixed it to include a mount for the Mini Kossel.

You can find this enclosure on Thingiverse (`thingiverse.com/thing:705874`). The thing contains only the new base with integrated mounts. You also need to print the lid from `thingiverse.com/thing:567088`. You will need the following vitamins to complete the installation. While the fan is optional, I highly recommend it.

- 40×40mm low velocity fan[14]

- (4) M3×20 bolts

- (4) M3 nuts

- (4) #4 wood screws for case

- (4) M3 bolts (length dependent on the depth of your fan)Assembly is easy. Just mount your fan to the lid, route it to your 12V power source, and then mount the base to the frame using four M3×20 bolts.

■ **Caution**   Adding an electronics case to a completed printer may require partially removing all the wiring from the electronics. Be sure to label everything and make a map of the connections and their orientation so that you can get everything back in place. Take your time and take ample notes.

The challenge you may encounter is adding the required M3 nuts to your frame. If your printer is already assembled, you may need to partially disassemble it by loosening one side of each top and bottom mount, and then gently (ever so gently) prying the frame open enough to get the nuts into place. Once inserted, close the frame and retighten everything. You should plan on checking your configuration once you reassemble your printer.

---

[14]High velocity fans will be very noisy. A low-flow fan is best.

■ **Tip** I discuss many more upgrades and enhancements in my book, *Maintaining and Troubleshooting Your 3D Printer* (Apress, 2014). You may want to look at Chapter 11 in that text for more ideas and for printer-specific upgrades for popular Cartesian 3D printers.

Other Considerations

There are a number of other upgrades and enhancements that you may want to consider. I provide an overview here in case you are thinking about one or more of these. However, I should also note that some of these might be more experimental rather than proven. One reason for this is the relatively low adoption that is evident in the lack of examples and variants. I've found the more interesting and proven an upgrade or enhancement is, the more you will see it talked about and even modified for different printers.

Printer Enclosure

Unlike most Cartesian printers, delta printers don't have a profile that is conducive to adding panels or mounting doors. That doesn't mean it is impossible. In fact, you can add clear panels to delta printers that use vertical frame members that can accept mounting screws or brackets. The trick is the vertical frame is normally oriented 60 degrees away from the plane that forms the side. That is, when viewed from the top, delta printers form an equilateral triangle. There is also the possibility that the axes mechanisms and extruder will be mounted to the outside of the vertical frame rails. This also presents a small issue if you are trying to build an enclosure with no openings. However, it can still be done, as shown for a Mini Kossel at thingiverse.com/thing:711243.

If you are considering an enclosure for the purpose of eliminating stray drafts or cooling air currents, you may want to consider shorter panels mounted to the base of the printer. They need not be any taller than your maximum Z axis travel, but even panels half that size have been known to reduce issues from stray drafts. I have experimented with this myself and found panels of about 3 to 4 inches tall help a lot and do not interfere with axis movement.

Top Dust Panel

One enhancement that I've found works well is a panel for the top of the printer. Although it is a bit of a farkle, I need something like this. It blocks a lot of dust and provides a handy place to mount things like electronics, spool holders, or even a tool tray. Some printers do not need this; for example, both the Orion and Rostock Max from SeeMeCNC have a top frame that is closed. Figure 8-15 shows a nifty fiberglass panel I found on a popular online auction site. If you're interested, you can make one from thin plywood or even acrylic. Just be sure to leave room to service your axis mechanism (e.g., belt adjustors).

Figure 8-15. *Top panel for Mini Kossel*

Frame Risers and Caps

Another less popular enhancement includes adding frame risers, adjustable feet with soft rubber or silicone bumpers,[15] and end caps for your delta printer frame. Again, these enhancements are more likely something you would consider for a RepRap delta printer as most professional- and consumer-grade printers have lower assemblies with feet or are designed such that they do not need feet or endcaps.

Adding frame risers is something you might want to consider if you want to install components below the print bed, especially if you want to lower the print bed as much as possible. I did this for my Mini Kossel because I wanted to mount the upgraded power supply and electronics box to the side of the printer. In this case, I made a small cylinder that I bolted to the base of the frame by taping the center portion. You can download this enhancement from Thingiverse (`thingiverse.com/thing:705780`). Figure 8-16 shows the frame risers I designed.

Figure 8-16. *Frame riser for Mini Kossel*

Realistically, there really isn't a need for adjustable feet since the triangular frame self-balances (it won't rock on uneven surfaces like a printer with a rectangular form). Despite this, I have seen a few adjustable risers that people have made.

---

[15]Bumpers can reduce the transfer of vibration to the table surface, thereby reducing noise.

Adding endcaps may be a preventative enhancement if your delta printer has exposed frame members. The example I present here is also for a Mini Kossel; I added them because the frame members had some sharp edges on which I managed to scratch myself and my cabinet more than once. Adding a simple endcap that fits snuggly allowed me to remove this hazard, and still allowed easy belt tension access. Figure 8-17 shows the endcap in place. You can find this endcap on Thingiverse (`thingiverse.com/thing:705791`).

Figure 8-17. *Endcaps for Mini Kossel*

POST-PRINT FINISHING

I cover post-print finishing in my book, *Maintaining and Troubleshooting Your 3D Printer*, but I recently discovered an amazing product I want to introduce. It is called XTC-3D High Performance 3D Print Coating. It comes in a kit that includes a two-step process in which you apply a base coat and a top coat that hides all the ridges and many imperfections of the part. Not only does it hide imperfections, it can be sanded— making painting parts much easier.

You can buy the kit from MatterHackers (`matterhackers.com/store/printer-accessories/xtc-3d-high-performance-3d-print-coating-24-oz`), Amazon, and at online auction sites. I have used the kit, and so far it lives up to its claims. While a bit more toxic than the acetone bath process, it works with many types of plastic and even nonplastic filament.

Making Your Own Enhancements

One of my favorite a 3D printer activities is making my own upgrades and accessories. I've created a number of upgrades for my printers. Table 8-1 lists some of the things I've created and uploaded to Thingiverse. I've shown you a few of these in previous sections. I have grouped them by delta printer model. You are free to download, print, modify, and use them on your own printers. If nothing else, you may be able to use them to inspire your own creations!

Table 8-1. *Example Delta Printer Enhancements*

Printer	Description	Thingiverse URL
SeeMeCNC Rostock Max v2 (may fit v1 or Orion)	Customizable side panel	thingiverse.com/thing:865931
	Idler adjuster	thingiverse.com/thing:825230
	50mm spool holder	thingiverse.com/thing:824442
Mini Kossel	MatterControl Touch mount	thingiverse.com/thing:731012
	170mm glass clamps	thingiverse.com/thing:705910
	RAMPS enclosure	thingiverse.com/thing:705874
	Part-cooling fan	thingiverse.com/thing:705864
	50mm spool holder	thingiverse.com/thing:705838
	LED lighting	thingiverse.com/thing:705814

Creating your own upgrades can be a lot of fun. I recommend going slowly and creating a prototype printed with very low quality to check fit and ensure that the part will work. In fact, I like to create the part itself a little at a time. That is, I may create several small portions of the part to ensure that each area fits correctly before designing the entire part. I do this either using masking (the difference() method in OpenSCAD) or stopping the print at a specific height.

For example, the part-cooling fan I created for one of my Mini Kossel printers required several prototypes to get the nozzle and mount correct. Despite my careful measurements, I found that the mount needed a bit more clearance to avoid touching the delta arms when the effector was at the extreme locations within the build volume.

Thus, you should not expect to be able to design and print a part and have it work the first time.[16] Rather, you should expect to print the first several prototypes in a low resolution with a low fill value (10%) so that you don't waste a lot of filament.

To check fit, I recommend printing only the first layer or two, and then stopping the print. This will help you overcome problems with scaling or sizing. For example, if you own a Rostock Max v2 and you want to print the new side panel that I designed, print the first layer and take some measurements to ensure that it will fit correctly. If it is too small or too large, you can scale it to fit.

Finally, whenever you find an upgrade or enhancement that you want to use, check the thing site carefully. Be sure to read the description and instructions so that you understand how the upgrade works and how it is assembled, and what vitamins are needed. If the upgrade has sketchy documentation, don't use it.[17]

Summary

Owning a 3D printer can be a lot of fun. Whether you print gifts, solutions for your home or auto, or just enjoy tinkering with designs, a good 3D printer won't let you down. However, if you want to take the printer a bit further or you want to save some money by adding features to your current printer, upgrading can also be a lot of fun.

---

[16]Except for trivial things, I had this happen only once.

[17]This is a pet peeve of mine. If you cannot take the time to properly document your work, why should anyone pay your design any interest? Document your work so that others can benefit. Don't expect everyone to understand your mind or intentions—state them!

This chapter covered the types of upgrades available, as well as suggestions for optimizing your upgrade experience. I also presented descriptions of several upgrades and enhancements for delta printers. Even if your printer wasn't listed, reading through the descriptions will help you see what is possible for your own printer.

I hope you have enjoyed learning about delta printers. If you do not already own one, I hope you seek to add a delta printer to your arsenal of 3D printers. You may even decide to switch to delta printers exclusively!

APPENDIX

■ ■ ■

Common Problems and Solutions

This appendix contains a quick reference guide for many of the common problems you may encounter when using delta printers. Tables A-1, A-2, A-3, and A-4 provide descriptions of problems, sources of the problems, and solutions. I have divided the categories of problems into sections for easier reference.

The best way to use these tables is to look for the problem description that best matches the problem you are experiencing, identify which of the possible sources apply, and then execute the remedy lists. Note that there can be more than one remedy per problem and source. Further, some problems may be remedied by changes to hardware or software. It is best to test each solution one at a time. Some remedies may be worded such that you can repeat the action. For example, lowering the hot-end temperature by 5 degrees can be applied repeatedly until the problem is solved.

■ **Tip**   Well, there is a limit to this. Clearly, reducing the temperature a dozen times by 5 degrees would likely be excessive. The same is true with raising the temperature. In either case, you will reach a threshold where the process is no longer applicable. Use these techniques as a guide rather than a literal instruction.

Adhesion Problems

This category of problems includes those that relate to how the object adheres to the build plate, as well as other layer adhesion problems.

Table A-1. *Adhesion Problems and Solutions*

Problem	Cause	Solution
Objects lift on one side or at corners on one side. The object is adhered well on other sides.	Towers not calibrated	If one of the towers has an endstop that has moved, especially if moved up a small amount, it can induce lift. Check and recalibrate the towers.
		Use a raft.
		You can also use G29 to initiate auto leveling.
	Draft or air currents	Use walls (blue tape, printed) to control slight air currents.
		Move printer away from vents, open windows, and other sources of air currents.
		Place printer in an enclosure or investigate the possibility of adding panels.
Object is not sticking to print surface or comes loose during printing.	Z-height too high	Check and set Z-height lower.
	Heated bed too cold	Raise temperature of heated print bed by 5 degrees.
	Print surface dirty or worn	Clean print surface. Inspect for damage and replace if worn or you have used it for more than 10 prints in the same area.
		Use a raft.
		Use a brim.
	First-layer print speed too high	Slow the first-layer speed. Slower first-layer print speeds can help first-layer adhesion. You should not lower the first-layer speed to less than 75% of the normal print speed.
	Hot end too cold	Raise the temperature of the hot end by 5 degrees. Depending on your software, you may be able to increase the temperature for the first several layers, reducing it for other layers.

(continued)

Table A-1. (*continued*)

Problem	Cause	Solution
Object lifts on several sides or in several places around the perimeter.	Heated bed too cold	Raise the temperature of the heated print bed by 5 degrees.
	Strong air currents or drafts	Turn off all fans and HVAC vents, and close windows and doors.
		Use an enclosure or add a panels to block air currents.
	Ambient temperature too cold	Increase ambient temperature. Best to keep it stable during printing.
	Object has very thin protrusions	Add helper disks to increase surface area that contacts the print surface. Some slicers have an option for this feature. You can always add them using the `.stl` mashup procedure described in the "Object Mashup" section in Chapter 12 of *Maintaining and Troubleshooting Your 3D Printer* (Apress, 2014).
Lifting occurs when objects placed near outer edge or only when placed in the center.	Convex or concave print surface	Use `DELTA_RADIUS` to adjust for convex or concave print surfaces.
Object cracks at higher layers.	Strong air currents or drafts	Turn off all fans and HVAC vents, and close windows and doors.
		Use an enclosure or add panels to block air currents.
	Ambient temperature too cold	Increase ambient temperature. Best to keep it stable during printing.

Extrusion Problems

This category of problems includes those related to the extruder, hot end, and filament.

Table A-2. *Extrusion Failures*

Problem	Cause	Solution
Filament jams in extruder, or extruder drive pulley strips filament, or filament melts in hot end	Hot end too cold	Raise hot-end temperature by 5 degrees.
	Contaminated filament	Check filament for damage or stress (filament will show lighter color) and remove damaged section.
		Check for dusty or dirty filament and clean filament with a lint-free cloth.
		Use a filament cleaner to remove dust and small debris.
		If failures continue, discard filament (or return to vendor for partial refund).
	Nozzle obstruction	Remove nozzle and clean it using the cold pull method. Remove any obstructions on the build platform.
	Wrong nozzle size	Check your slicer settings. If your slicer settings have a value that is too low, the extruder can jam by pressing more filament through the hot end than it can handle.
	Too much tension on spool	Make sure that the spool can feed with as little friction as possible. Use a spool holder with rollers or bearings for smooth movement.
	Wrong tension on extruder door or clamp	Check and adjust tension. Too much tension can cause the filament to compress. Too little tension can permit the filament to slip.
	Too much friction in Bowden tube	Ensure that the filament is within tolerance for the inner diameter of your Bowden tube. Ensure that there are no kinks in tube and the bends are not too sharp. Realign the Bowden tube to remove constrictions.
	Hot end too hot	Use a fan blowing on the top portion of the hot end. For example, a 40mm fan that is always on (when printer is on).
	Drive pulley too hot	An overheating stepper motor can heat up the drive pulley, making the filament soft. Use a fan blowing on the drive pulley or reduce current to the stepper motor so that it runs cooler.

(continued)

Table A-2. (*continued*)

Problem	Cause	Solution
Filament curls when exiting hot end	Damaged nozzle	Check the nozzle to ensure that there is no debris, burr, or other damage to the opening. Replace the nozzle if damaged.
Burning smell from extruder	Hot end too hot	Lower the hot-end temperature by 5 degrees.
Filament oozes excessively from hot end	Hot end too hot	Lower the hot-end temperature by 5 degrees. Note: Some oozing is normal, but it should not run out like the extruder is running.
Filament extrudes unevenly	Hot end too cold	Raise hot-end temperature by 5 degrees.
	Extruder stepper motor overheating	Check stepper driver current and adjust to match stepper motor.
	Extruder stepper motor current too high	
	Extruder stepper motor current set too low	
	Loose, stripped, or worn gears	Tighten loose gears and set screws. Replace worn or broken extruder gears.
	Nozzle obstruction	Check, clean, or replace nozzle.
Popping or spitting noises when printing, or steam from hot end	Contaminated filament	Filament may have too much moisture. Use a drying agent to dry the filament for at least 24 hours.

Print Quality Problems

This category includes problems that cause print quality to suffer.

Table A-3. *Print-Quality Issues*

Problem	Cause	Solution
Object layers break apart or appear thin and weak	Wrong nozzle size	Choose the correct nozzle size in software.
	Wrong filament size	Ensure that the correct size is entered in software.
	Wrong extrusion width	Extrusion width should be between 1.5 to 2.0 times the size of the filament.
Slight variances in layer alignment	Loose or worn belts on axis	Adjust belt tension and replace worn belts.
	Loose frame components	Tighten loose bolts. Use Nyloc nuts[1] (preferred), lock washers, or Loctite (blue) to keep bolts and nuts from coming loose due to vibration.
		Reduce print speed to reduce vibration.
	Loose carriages (roller)	Adjust carriages for proper tension.
	Loose or worn delta mechanism	Inspect for excess play and worn parts. Replace as needed.
	Backlash in delta arm joints	Use springs or rubber bands to apply slight pressure to reduce backlash.
Object appears squished	Heated bed too hot	Lower heated print bed by 5 degrees.
Object has thick runs of filament	Too much filament extruded	Check diameter of filament and change slicer settings to match.
Blobs and clumps	Too much filament extruded	Check diameter of filament and change slicer settings to match.
	Insufficient retraction	Increase retraction to 10mm at 150mm/s for all travel moves longer than 5mm.
Holes slightly too small	Too much filament extruded	Check diameter of filament and change slicer settings to match.
	Object not scaled properly	Use software to scale the part by +/-2%
Circular areas oblong	Loose or worn belts on axis	Adjust belt tension.

(*continued*)

---

[1]Johann C. Rocholl recommends using Nyloc for all moving parts.

Table A-3. (*continued*)

Problem	Cause	Solution
Object layers shift in one direction	Loose or worn belts on axis	Adjust belt tension.
	Stepper motor failure	Check stepper driver voltage. If correct, replace stepper motor.
	Stripped belt drive gear	Replace belt drive gear.
	Acceleration too high	Lower acceleration parameters in firmware.
	Obstruction in axis movement	Remove obstruction.
	Plastic part failure	Check all axis parts for damage and replace.
	Damaged bearings	Check all bearings for proper lubrication and replace loose or worn bearings.
	Drive pulley loose	Use Loctite blue threadlocker to keep the grub screw(s) tight. If the motor shaft doesn't already have a flat side, it can be flattened slightly with a file to make an indentation for the grub screw.

Mechanical or Electrical Problems

This category includes a host of mechanical and electrical failures that can cause any number of print failures. Some are severe. Always use caution when working with electronic components and especially mains power.

Table A-4. *Mechanical and Electrical Failures*

Problem	Cause	Solution
Printing pauses or halts while printing	Loss of communication with computer	If printing from computer, check USB connection.
		Make sure that the computer is not going to sleep (see power-saving settings).
		Replace USB cable.
	Corrupt SD card/file	Check SD card for corrupted files. Replace SD card or replace corrupt file.
	Overheating electronics	Mount fans to cool electronics.
		Check stepper driver for correct voltages.
Hot end or heated print bed stops heating	Heating element failed	Replace heating element.
	Electronics board failure	Replace electronics board.
	Power supply failure	Check power and replace if no power to electronics. For example, it is possible for the 12V power to fail, making motors and heaters inoperable.
	Broken wire	Check all wiring for stress fractures and loose connectors. Replace as needed.
	Blown fuse	Check and replace fuse.
Stepper motor stops working	Stepper driver failure	Replace stepper driver.
	Power supply failure	Check power and replace if no power to electronics. For example, it is possible for the 12V power to fail, making motors and heaters inoperable.
	Broken wire	Check all wiring for stress fractures and loose connectors. Replace as needed.
	Blown fuse	Check and replace fuse.
	Stepper motor failure	Replace stepper motor.
	Drive pulley slipping	Tighten drive pulley grub screw and use Loctite to keep it from loosening.
Stepper motor overheats	Wrong voltage on stepper driver	Measure voltage and set it to match stepper motor.
	Excessive friction in axis mechanism	Clean and lubricate the axis mechanism. Remove obstructions and adjust tension as needed for any roller wheels or pulleys.

(continued)

Table A-4. (*continued*)

Problem	Cause	Solution
Extruder stepper motor turns but no filament extrudes	Loose drive pulley	Tighten or replace drive pulley grub screw. Use Loctite to keep screw from backing out. You can also file the motor shaft with a metal file to create a flat spot to secure the grub screw.
	Extruder jammed	Check Table A-1 and repair extruder jam.
Squeaks, creaks, scratching, or clunking sounds when axes move	Insufficient lubrication	Perform regular maintenance to clean and lubricate axis movement.
	Loose axis mechanism	Check, replace, and tighten axis mechanism.
Axis does not stop at endstop	Broken switch	Replace endstop. Use the M119 command to verify.
	Broken or disconnected wire	Check and replace as needed.
	Endstops wired incorrectly	Ensure that the wiring is correctly set for the axis. Make sure that the X/Y/Z endstops correspond with the X/Y/Z motors.
Burning smell from electronics, sparks, clicking, or smoke from electronics	Short or electronics failure	Turn computer and printer off immediately. Check electronics for damage. Remove 12V power and connect USB cable to check low-voltage operation. Replace all damaged components.
No lights or LCD display	Power supply failure	Replace power supply.
	Power cable not plugged in	Ensure that the power cable is plugging into mains power.
	Power strip turned off	If using a power strip, UPS, or other power conditioner, ensure that the unit is powered on.
	Blown fuse	Check power supply, mains, and power strip fuse. Replace or reset as needed.
Unexplained noises when axes move—not related to axis mechanism	Loose frame components	Check all frame components and tighten as needed.
Axis runs into max stop	Improper homing	Make sure that you home all axes before printing.
Printer vibrates excessively so that it moves across table	Loose frame components	Check all frame components and tighten as needed.
	Acceleration too high	Check acceleration settings in firmware. Reduce by 10%.
	Print speed too high	Lower infill print speed.

Index

■ H

■ I

■ J

Get the eBook for only $5!

Why limit yourself?

Now you can take the weightless companion with you wherever you go and access your content on your PC, phone, tablet, or reader.

Since you've purchased this print book, we're happy to offer you the eBook in all 3 formats for just $5.

Convenient and fully searchable, the PDF version enables you to easily find and copy code—or perform examples by quickly toggling between instructions and applications. The MOBI format is ideal for your Kindle, while the ePUB can be utilized on a variety of mobile devices.

To learn more, go to www.apress.com/companion or contact support@apress.com.

All Apress eBooks are subject to copyright. All rights are reserved by the Publisher, whether the whole or part of the material is concerned, specifically the rights of translation, reprinting, reuse of illustrations, recitation, broadcasting, reproduction on microfilms or in any other physical way, and transmission or information storage and retrieval, electronic adaptation, computer software, or by similar or dissimilar methodology now known or hereafter developed. Exempted from this legal reservation are brief excerpts in connection with reviews or scholarly analysis or material supplied specifically for the purpose of being entered and executed on a computer system, for exclusive use by the purchaser of the work. Duplication of this publication or parts thereof is permitted only under the provisions of the Copyright Law of the Publisher's location, in its current version, and permission for use must always be obtained from Springer. Permissions for use may be obtained through RightsLink at the Copyright Clearance Center. Violations are liable to prosecution under the respective Copyright Law.

Printed in the United States
By Bookmasters

Printed in the United States
By Bookmasters